MÔN MAM CYMRU
The Guide to Anglesey

Philip Steele *&* Robert Williams

Anglesey, anciently called MONA,
is an Island seated in a temperate
Air, enliven'd by a benign Sun, and
enrich'd with good and beautiful Soil.

HENRY ROWLANDS, *Mona Antiqua Restaurata* (1723)

MAGMA
Ynys Môn

Philip Steele, who has contributed to the Gazetteer section of the 2006 edition, lives in Llangoed. He is a leading writer of children's information books for the international market. His clients include National Geographic, Walker Books and Dorling Kindersley.

Robert Williams lives in Llansadwrn and his family has a long history in Ynys Môn and Gwynedd. He has an abiding interest in life on islands throughout the world. Work in Wales includes editorial compilations at Anglesey's Heritage Gallery – *Oriel Ynys Môn* – since its inception in 1992.

To have no errors is a Privilege above the Condition of Humanity …
Happiest is he who has fewest of them.

from *Mona Antiqua Restaurata*, Henry Rowlands 1723

Few of the historic houses in Anglesey are open to the public and mention in this guide does not imply that they are. Some may be viewed on written application to their owners; this also applies to monuments on private land.

THIRD EDITION
Cyhoeddwyd gan / Published by
LLYFRAU MAGMA
Llansadwrn, Ynys Môn LL59 5SR
Cymru ✆ (+44) 01248 810833
magmawales@hotmail.com

ISBN 1 872773 77 X

Contents

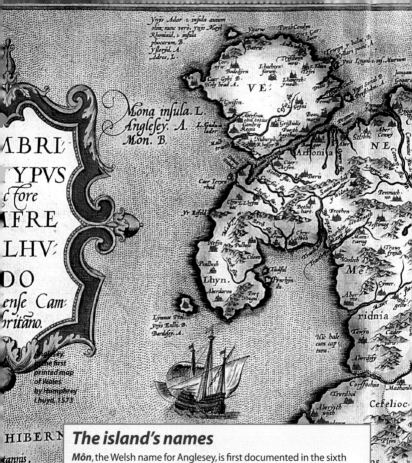

The island's names

Môn, the Welsh name for Anglesey, is first documented in the sixth century, but it has far more ancient roots, perhaps prehistoric. In general usage today the island is referred to as **Sir Fôn** (*'Sheer Vorn'* – 'County of Anglesey') or **Ynys Môn** (*'Uh-nus Morn'* – 'Isle of Anglesey').

Mona. This Latin name for the island was derived from the Celtic form, *Môn*. It was used by the Romans even before the conquest, and by monks and scholars in the Middle Ages. It still crops up in shop and business names. Confusingly the same name was sometimes used for the Isle of Man.

Anglesey. The name traditionally used for the island by the English has nothing to do with their Germanic ancestors, the Angles. The -*ey* ending means 'island' and is of Viking origin. 'Angle' is derived from a Viking personal name, Ongull. Ongull must have been a chieftain or seafarer of the early Middle Ages, when Vikings controlled Dublin and the Isle of Man.

Môn Mam Cymru. The island's motto is an epithet meaning 'Anglesey, Mother of Wales', and it is displayed at the two bridges across the Menai Strait. The phrase was used by Gerald of Wales in 1191 and characterises the island as a provider of produce for the rest of Wales, fertile flatlands in a mountainous nation.

Gwlad y Medra. This Welsh phrase means 'can-do country' and is a longstanding nickname for Anglesey. When labourers were hired for work at the mainland quarries, Anglesey men were said to push themselves forward and say "I can do that!" … "medra!"

The illustration is a detail of the first printed map of Wales, by Humphrey Lhuyd, 1573

Môn Mam Cymru

TWO high bridges over the Menai Strait lead to the island of Anglesey (in Welsh, *Ynys Môn*), the most northerly part of Wales. From car or train, the bridges offer a fleeting glimpse of glassy waters far below, of small towns, green fields and woods.

Porth Wen, on the northern coast

Anglesey is Britain's fifth largest offshore island. Much of it is rolling farmland, dotted with working villages and small towns. Traffic hurries west along the A55 to Holyhead, the port for Ireland. In the distance you may see reed-fringed lakes and rivers as well as rocky outcrops and gorse, blazing yellow in spring. Turn off the expressway and take your time. The island has more to offer.

Look back at the mountains of Snowdonia on the mainland, looming through a summer heat haze, sprinkled with snow in winter or spring, sometimes dark and sullen under a grey, rainy sky. The Menai Strait swirls between wooded banks, overlooked by the city of Bangor and Caernarfon castle on the south side, by Beaumaris castle and Menai Bridge town on the north.

Walk the coast and discover long expanses of rippled sand, high dunes tufted with marram grass, sheer cliffs, small pebble coves, offshore islands, wind-whipped reefs and lighthouses, saltmarsh and estuaries. Almost the entire coastline has been designated an Area of Outstanding Natural Beauty.

If one does run into traffic jams on the bridges, staring at coaches and caravans, or has to queue at the chip shop on a bank holiday weekend, remember that just a short distance away are peaceful meadows and hedgerows bursting with wildflowers, bluebell woods by a blue sea, perhaps, even a prehistoric burial chamber as old as the pyramids. *Môn Mam Cymru* has certainly played an important part in Welsh history, from the epic confrontation between the ancient druids and the Romans, to the coming of the railway and the industrial age. Not everywhere on the island is idyllic, but people are beginning to realise that industrial ruins or Victorian housing terraces can be every bit as fascinating as ancient standing stones or views of the mountains.

Of course the Anglesey of a hundred or even fifty years ago, with its isolated farms and chapels and the closeness of its people to land and sea, is fading fast. Even so, the island of today is rooted in that old way of life, and is sustained by it as it grows new shoots. The Welsh language is spoken as a matter of course alongside English, whether in garage, supermarket, school or council offices.

Once only Anglesey's seafarers travelled the world. Today the world comes to Anglesey, and many of the islanders themselves jet off here and there. Despite this new mobility, a strong sense of community remains. This guide explores these landscapes and these communities.

Inland Anglesey's patchwork of fields

A profile of the island

Land and sea

The island is surrounded by the shallow waters of the Irish Sea. These may lack the deep swell of the open ocean, but can nevertheless brew up furious storms, as shipwrecks in each generation bear witness.

Anglesey's western part forms a separate island, called Holy Island or *Ynys Gybi*. The most easterly part of Anglesey forms a broad headland at Penmon, culminating in another offshore island, Puffin Island or *Ynys Seiriol*.

Anglesey is separated from the Welsh mainland by the Menai Strait, *Afon Menai*, which runs diagonally along the island's southeastern flank. This narrow stretch of water experiences powerful currents and tidal surges. Sand banks have built up around both approaches to the Strait.

Anglesey has an area of 276 square miles (714 sq km), being slightly larger than the Isle of Man. Its highest point is Holyhead Mountain at 722 feet (220 metres).

Anglesey's emblem

The official county flower of Anglesey is the rare **Spotted Rock-rose / *Cor-rosyn Rhuddfannog*** (Tuberaria guttata, subspecies *breweri*).

It is a small annual, which soon drops its petals after blooming. The plant is found in scattered colonies on rocky heaths near the island's western coasts.

Population

At the time of the 2001 census, Anglesey had a population of around 68,000.

Holyhead, with 11,200 inhabitants, is the island's largest town. Other residential areas include Llangefni (4,500), Amlwch (3,700), and the eastern section of the Menai Strait (Llanfair Pwllgwyngyll through to Menai Bridge town, Llandegfan and Beaumaris).

Seaside resorts include Benllech, Cemaes, Rhosneigr and Trearddur Bay.

Climate

Anglesey has a climate typical of western coasts, Wales being moister than Britain's eastern regions. The seas around its shores, warmed by the currents of the North Atlantic Drift, keep the climate mild. Growth can be lush in sheltered spots away from sea breezes and salt spray.

Temperatures generally vary between extremes of -3° and 27°C (27° and 81°F). Mean temperatures for January are 5°C (41°F), for July 15°C (59°F). High annual rainfall, averaging 44 inches (1107mm) per year, keeps the island green. Prevailing winds are southwesterly. The island enjoys more sunshine than the mountains of Snowdonia, immediately to the south. The sunniest month is generally May.

Recommended times to visit Anglesey are in spring and early summer, or perhaps during a fine spell in early autumn. An Indian summer is known in Welsh as *haf bach Mihangel*, 'a small summer at Michaelmas'. Visitors come to the island throughout the year, but the most popular period for sandcastles and paddling remains the school summer holidays in August.

The economy

Tourism is a major service industry, although most of its employment opportunities are seasonal. It is estimated that over a million tourists visit the island each year. Seventy five per cent have been here before, and 80% travel by car. About 60% take accommodation on the island, and 40% are day visitors. Together they spend about £110 million.

Other service jobs include commerce, transport (such as the ferry services from Holyhead), council administration, education and healthcare. The chief hospital of the region, Ysbyty Gwynedd, is located just across the Menai Strait in Bangor. The University of Wales is also a major presence in Bangor, while its world-famous School of Ocean Sciences is based on the island in the town of Menai Bridge.

Manufacturing industries are chiefly based around Holyhead, Amlwch, Gaerwen and Llangefni. These include engineering, food processing and aluminium smelting. There is a nuclear power station on the north coast at Wylfa, scheduled for decommissioning in 2010.

Anglesey's farmland is mixed. Much of it is given over to the rearing of sheep and cattle, although the days when the busy weekly cattle market at Llangefni was a focus of island life have now passed. There is some cultivation of cereals, root crops and soft fruits. Farms are generally small, although several may nowadays be combined to operate as a single business unit. Some local milk production supplies a factory in Llan-gefni that uses cows' milk to make shredded mozzarella cheese for pizzas. Other milk goes to a creamery on the mainland. Niche marketing, organic farming and local farmers' markets offer some hope for farmers faced with poor prices from supermarket chains.

Politics

Anglesey was a county in its own right from 1284 until 1974, when it was amalgamated with Caernarfonshire and Merioneth into a new county called Gwynedd. In 1996 the administration of the island was separated from Gwynedd and, as a unitary authority, many of Anglesey's powers as a county council were restored. The headquarters of local government are at Llangefni, near the geographical centre of the island.

The island is represented politically at the National Assembly of Wales in Cardiff, as part of Wales at the European Parliament in Strasbourg, and also at the United Kingdom Parliament at Westminster.

The parliamentary constituency, officially known as Ynys Môn since 1983, rarely offers a safe seat for any political party, having over the years sent Liberal, Labour, Conservative and Plaid Cymru members to Westminster.

Anglesey's Member of the National Assembly for Wales (AM)

Ieuan Wyn Jones, *Plaid Cymru*   1999—
(Ieuan Wyn Jones is leader of Plaid Cymru: the Party of Wales group in the Assembly)

Anglesey's Members of the United Kingdom Parliament since 1929 (MPs)

Albert Owen, *Labour*	2001—
Ieuan Wyn Jones, *Plaid Cymru*	1987-2001
Keith Best, *Conservative*	1979-1987
Cledwyn Hughes, *Labour*	1951-1979
Megan Lloyd George, *Liberal*	1929-1951

Members of the European Parliament

Five MEPs represent Wales as one electoral region under a system designed to ensure proportional representation between the parties.

Cledwyn Hughes (1916-2001) was born in Holyhead and served at Westminster as a Labour Member of Parliament for the Anglesey constituency from 1951 until standing down in 1979, becoming Secretary of State for Wales in 1966. In 1980 he became a Life Peer and as Lord Cledwyn of Penrhos he headed the Opposition in the House of Lords for ten years during Margaret Thatcher's premiership. Cledwyn Hughes had a loyal following on the island and he never lost his love for his place of birth.

Cledwyn (right) as Commonwealth Minister in 1965 during negotiations following Ian Smith's illegal, white-led, declaration of Rhodesian independence.

Council talk

County administration was removed from unelected magistrates at the quarter sessions in 1888-89 with the formation of Anglesey County Council. From then and into the inter-war period local politics was coloured by party affiliations, especially by the domination of Liberals. Gradually, however, this was replaced by the adoption of non-party independent labels, especially in the most rural parts.

The county, as a unitary authority, sustained a good reputation as a generally well run council up to 1974 when it was absorbed into the larger Gwynedd County Council, where the interests of the other component counties often overrode Anglesey's. Before then, Anglesey had been a successful innovator in secondary education and in health and welfare matters and was active in rural regeneration.

The restoration of Anglesey as a unitary authority, following a further reorganisation of local government in the mid-1990s, has been less successful. Smaller authorities have generally struggled to maintain services as central government support has waned. In addition, the decline in interest among electors has led to the unopposed return of a majority of members and to the growth of competing cliques, independents lacking the restraints of firm party discipline.

One cannot ignore the embarrassing episodes which have seen both councillors and senior administrative members of staff run foul of regulations about propriety and procedures and which have led to interventions by district auditors, by the Welsh Office and by the Welsh Assembly. In theory, the latter could assume control of the county's affairs but then other Welsh counties have shown themselves to be equally deficient !

William Griffith

International links

Anglesey has international 'twinning' agreements with Dun Laoghaire in the Irish Republic and Mafekeng in Lesotho, southern Africa. *Dolen Cymru*, the Lesotho/Wales national link, was launched in 1985 to foster a spirit of friendship and co-operation. The two countries have many similarities and have collaborated on matters of health and education, and in other ways. Today the Lesotho Consulate in Wales, *Is-Genhadaeth Lesotho yng Nghymru*, is based on Anglesey in the Consul's house at Rhoscefnhir.

In 2006 Amlwch became twinned with Sankwia, a village with around 2,000 inhabitants in the Gambia, west Africa.

Anglesey has its own international sporting representation as an island. Twenty-four competing islands take part in the biennial *International Island Games*, including even the remote mid-Atlantic island of St Helena. The first meeting was in 1985 in the Isle of Man. Other venues for the Games, past and future, include Guernsey, Jersey, the Faeroe Islands, Åland, the Isle of Wight, Gotland, Shetland and Rhodes.

Rethabile Thamae with the family calf, Semonkong, Lesotho

Religion

The island's churches mostly belong to the disestablished Church in Wales, which is part of the Anglican communion. Some belong to the Roman Catholic Church, and a few to other Christian Churches.

The strongest Christian representation on the island is that of the Nonconformist chapels, such as those of Calvinistic Methodists and Baptists. Old rivalries between the various churches and chapels are largely a thing of the past.

Society has become increasingly secular, although perhaps less so in Anglesey than in urban England. Attendance is falling at both church and chapel: some churches and many chapels have closed.

*Above: **Capel Ebeneser (built in 1785), Newborough.***

*Below: **The Calvinistic Methodist John Elias (1774-1841) preached at Llangefni and is buried at Llan-faes.***

The Church of Saint Rhwydrus *stands on the western side of Trwyn Cemlyn (SH322932). Cemlyn was Anglesey's first lifeboat station, founded by the rector of Llanfair-yng-Nghornwy, James Williams, and his wife Frances.* ▶120 *The drawing of the church –* ***below*** *– is by the couple's great-grandson, the artist Kyffin Williams.* **'Llanrhwydrus'** *is one of a signed edition of prints produced to help fund new a Sir Kyffin Williams Gallery within Oriel Ynys Môn near Llangefni.*

Architecture

The vernacular architecture of the island includes long, low, whitewashed cottages, originally thatched (as is *Swtan* at Church Bay) but later capped with slate or rendered roofs. In recent decades many of these have been demolished or converted into modern bungalows. Ruined windmills dot the island; the restored Llynnon mill near Llanddeusant represents one in current working order. Some fine, large stone farmhouses of the sixteenth- or seventeenth-century survive. Plas Newydd the family seat of the Marquesses of Anglesey, is in the care of the National Trust and is open to the public.

Anglesey has some interesting and some-times eccentric church architecture. Some parish churches were founded very early in the Middle Ages, but many were heavily restored in the Victorian era. Every town, village and hamlet has its Nonconformist chapels, most commonly dating from the eighteenth to the late-nineteeth centuries.

The chief town of architectural interest is Beaumaris with a range of impressive domestic and public buildings dating from the thirteenth to the twenty-first centuries.

Island crafts

Until the beginning of the twentieth century, small-scale rural industries on the island thrived on the supply of goods and services to working farmers and their families. The bootmakers of Llannerch-y-medd had a high reputation, and the speciality of Llaneilian and Penysarn was clogs. Marram grass, which binds the sand-dunes of Newborough and Aberffraw, was the raw material for poorly-paid women who made mats, grass ropes and brushes for whitewashing. In the island's cottages (and later in fulling mills and small-scale woollen mills) yarn was spun, and tweed and flannel woven and finished, for clothing and blankets.

Although, like many other regions of Britain, there has not been an unbroken tradition of production in any particular medium, craftspeople are today working again on the island. Many are members of a local Craftworkers' Guild and some are firmly established and produce work to a high standard. Craft fairs and retail outlets feature the work of the island's potters, textile workers, glass makers, woodworkers and metalworkers.

Eisteddfod Genedlaethol Cymru, the annual National Eisteddfod of Wales, last visited Anglesey in 1999. Trumpeters herald the announcement of the name of each year's Chaired Bard

Arts and *eisteddfodau*

The arts on the island have traditionally been chiefly associated with poetry and music, which are also the traditional fare at the *eisteddfodau*. These festivals, at school, community, national and international level, have their orgins in bardic contests of the Middle Ages. *Eisteddfod Môn* (the Anglesey eisteddfod) is held annually in various districts of the island, its centenary celebrated at Bodffordd in 2007.

Eisteddfod Genedlaethol (the National Eisteddfod) alternates each year between locations in north and south Wales; it is a Welsh-language festival but welcomes English-speaking visitors. It came to Anglesey in 1999, and before that in 1983. Other annual arts festivals are held in Beaumaris and Holyhead.

Traditional harp music, choirs, brass bands, classical music, jazz, folk and pop music in both Welsh and English, Welsh folk dancing, amateur dramatics, ballet and modern dance all thrive on Anglesey.

Recent years have seen a rise in the profile of the visual arts. Studios open their doors to visitors during the 'Easter Arts Weeks'.

Regular venues for the arts include Oriel Ynys Môn in Llangefni and the Ucheldre Centre in Holyhead.

Kyffin Williams

One of the most celebrated of Welsh artists, Sir Kyffin Williams OBE RA, was born in Llangefni in 1918. He came from an old Anglesey family, associated with Treffos in Llansadwrn and Llanfair-yng-Nghornwy. Kyffin studied at the Slade School of Fine Art in London (1941-44) and then became Senior Art Master at Highgate School.

Returning to Anglesey in 1974, Kyffin Williams devoted himself to recording the island he loved, with a studio and home beside the Menai Strait near Llanfairpwll. In his later years Kyffin achieved public recognition, his work being widely exhibited and published.

Kyffin Williams is a master of many media. His landscapes, often palette-knifed, capture precisely the light, colours and textures of land and sea. Human figures often feature as an integral part of the landscapes, such as farmers battling with the elements or calling their dogs to order. Kyffin's portraits reveal character and features shaped by life on the island.

He has also followed the Welsh to their old colony of Patagonia, the *Gwladfa*. In South America his work took on a more vibrant colouring. Autobiographical books – *Across the Straits* (1973) and *A Wider Sky* (1991) – reveal much about Anglesey as well as himself. Sir Kyffin has inspired new generations of artists. A new **Kyffin Williams Gallery / *Oriel Kyffin Williams*** is planned at Oriel Ynys Môn, Llangefni.

"*M*OST *landscape painters react to their own country more strongly than to any other, and I am happy to remain in Wales and paint my own particular part of it.*

In Anglesey the white farms and cottages welcome me, while across the straits I can see those wonderful mountains and am able to take advantage of them whenever I wish to do so."

—KYFFIN WILLIAMS, *Across the Straits* (1973)

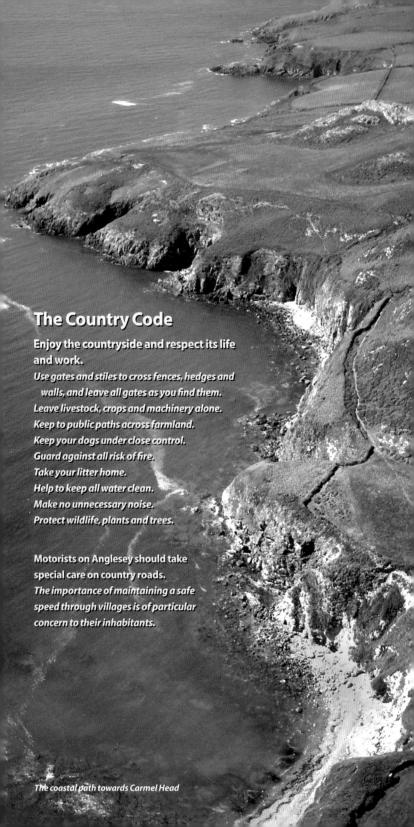

The Country Code

Enjoy the countryside and respect its life and work.

Use gates and stiles to cross fences, hedges and walls, and leave all gates as you find them.

Leave livestock, crops and machinery alone.

Keep to public paths across farmland.

Keep your dogs under close control.

Guard against all risk of fire.

Take your litter home.

Help to keep all water clean.

Make no unnecessary noise.

Protect wildlife, plants and trees.

Motorists on Anglesey should take special care on country roads. *The importance of maintaining a safe speed through villages is of particular concern to their inhabitants.*

The coastal path towards Carmel Head

Natural habitats

ANGLESEY is of great interest to geologists and naturalists, especially for the age and variety of its rocks and for its coastal environment.

Rare birds are often blown on to the island's shores and many migrant species are seasonal visitors. Anglesey marks the northern limit of some southern species, and the southern limit of some northern species.

Conservation schemes have had their successes, but the environment still comes under pressure from developments, from people who come to beaches for racing quad-bikes and jet-skis, from intensive farming methods and chemicals and from global factors such as air pollution and climate change.

Geology

Anglesey's diverse geology has been likened to 'the world on a pocket handkerchief'.

The island is a designated *Regionally Important Geological Site*. Presently under consideration is its recognition as a *European Geopark* – a status only awarded to places of international significance.

The island's Precambrian rocks, some of them 660 million years old, are amongst the world's most ancient. Known as the 'Mona Complex', they comprise two series, one bedded, the other metamorphic. Their structures are deformed by folds, thrusts and intrusions. Occasionally, minor earth tremors do still occur along the North Wales coast, reflecting its geological history.

The Mona Complex is overlain by rocks of other periods, from the Ordovician to the Carboniferous. Across the island you will find limestone and sandstone, as well as granite and gneiss. Evidence of the last ice age includes clays and large isolated boulders ('erratics') left behind by retreating glaciers.

Many rock groups have been given local names: hence the Church Bay Tuffs, the Skerries Group and the Baron Hill Volcanics. One mineral takes the English name of the island itself: *Anglesite* (lead sulphate) occurs on Parys Mountain. It is crystalline, usually pale yellow or white, and is formed from the oxidation of galena (lead sulphide).

VISIT: Ynys Llanddwyn (pillow lava), Parys Mountain (richly mineralised), Penmon Point (limestone), South Stack (intensely folded Pre-Cambrian strata).

Cliffs and stacks

The island's geology is best exposed in the cliffs (with the exception of the Menai shore) of its coastline. The highest and sheerest rockfaces are on Holy Island, opposite South Stack. Amidst the springy turf on clifftops, look for tiny blue spring squills and wiry cushions of pink-flowered thrift. Guillemots, razorbills and puffins gather on the vertiginous ledges in the breeding season. Choughs (rare maritime crows with scarlet legs and beaks), perform comical displays of acrobatics and freefall.

By way of contrast watch the streamlined peregrine falcon hurtle after a pigeon in a deadly, high-speed dive. Peregrines have even nested on the central piers of the Britannia Bridge.

VISIT: South Stack, Ynys y Fydlyn, Rhoscolyn, Llanlleiana, Point Lynas – or take a boat trip to see the limestone cliffs of Puffin Island (below).

Marine habitats

Herring gulls squabble down at shore level, on sand or pebbles or promenades, fixing tourists' sandwiches with an implacable eye. Great black-backed gulls, black-headed gulls and common gulls may also be seen.

Beach-combing may reveal dog whelks, razor shells, cowries, hermit crabs or washed up starfish and jellyfish. A boat trip to offshore islands and reefs may acquaint you with grey seals and their pups, basking on their slabs of rock or heads bobbing in the sea. Offshore, look for black cormorants and shags, beating low over the waves or perched on a rock with their wings stretched out to dry. Black-and-white oystercatchers pipe on the shore, and ringed plovers dance along the waterline or fly off in tight formation. In summer, you may spot Arctic and Common terns (known as 'sea-swallows', môr-wenoliaid, in Welsh) as they plummet into the waves, or even a school of porpoises out to sea.

Above: **Handle sea creatures for a very short time and with great care. Replace them where they were found.** *Below:* **Nesting Cormorants.**

The strand line offers just a tiny sample of the riches of Anglesey's seas. Visit at a low spring tide to explore rockpools for sea anemones, shrimps and crabs. The wave-sheltered races of the Menai Strait bring food to filter-feeders such as sponges. Remember to replace any boulder that you move – it is somebody's home. On beaches of limestone pebbles look for finger-sized holes, bored by bivalved piddocks.

VISIT: Church Island *(Menai Bridge)****, Trearddur Bay, Rhoscolyn, Rhosneigr, Fedw Fawr*** *(White Beach, Llangoed)****, Penmon, Newborough Beach, Red Wharf Bay, Fryars Bay, Cemlyn***

Whales (such as this, in the 1960s) and leather-backed turtles are sometimes washed ashore

Dunes and slacks

Sand dunes are characteristic of Anglesey's west coast, and are especially impressive at Newborough and Aberffraw. Their seaward margins shift in the wind, but they are anchored by colonies of plants: coarse spikes of marram grass, sand sedge, sea rocket, seaside pansy. Common blue butterflies fly from flower to flower amongst the vetches. Wetland hollows called slacks sprout creeping willow. Rabbits burrow in the dunes and many other sandy shores around the island. The harmless grass snake is not uncommon, but has been seen on the dunes at Newborough and Aberffraw.

VISIT: Newborough Warren *(below)****, Aberffraw, Rhosneigr***

Saltmarsh and mudflats

The tidal estuaries of the Dulas and the Cefni rivers expose rich expanses of soft mud for probing bills. Below Malltraeth Cob are saltmarshes and brackish pools, flooded by incoming tides. Plants thriving in this constantly changing world include the edible glasswort or marsh samphire, sea arrowgrass, sea lavender and cord grass. Shore crabs scuttle and grey herons stand stock-still and beady-eyed in the shallows. Other long-legged wading birds are common: redshanks, greenshanks, curlews. Geese and shelduck visit the mudflats, and sometimes a marsh harrier flies low, its legs trailing like an undercarriage.

VISIT: Malltraeth, Dulas, Four Mile Bridge (for the 'Inland Sea')

Marshes

Despite the efforts of generations of farmers to drain the shallow valleys of Anglesey, many small wetlands remain. Where these are irrigated by waters from the limestone of eastern Anglesey, a succession of reeds, sedges and orchid-rich fens develop. Dragonflies dart amongst pools in former peat diggings and grasshopper warblers herald the warmth of summer. In the north and west of the island, acidic marshes are filled with sphagnum bog mosses, cotton grasses and cross-leaved heath.

VISIT: Cors Goch, Cors Bodeilio

Freshwater sites

Anglesey is dotted with many natural lakes, both large and small, as well as lakes created as reservoirs or for fishing, such as Llyn Alaw – the largest on the island at 777 acres (314ha). The lakes attract a wide range of wildfowl, and you may see mallard, tufted ducks, moorhens and coots, swans and great crested grebes. Greylag and Canada geese are found on Anglesey. Small numbers of whooper swans arrive in the winter on Llyn Alaw and at Capel Coch.

Sea trout, grey mullet and eels swim upstream along the islands' rivers. After the dramatic decline in their population in the '50s and '60s (mainly due to the use of agricultural pesticides), otters were seen again on Anglesey in 1995 and are now increasing in numbers along some of the rivers, in particular Afon Braint.

Marginal plants along streams and ditches include the yellow flag (a common wild iris) and the rare water violet of the Cefni marshes. Seventeen species of damselflies and dragonflies occur in Anglesey. The common frog, common toad and palmate newt are the island's most numerous amphibians with the great crested newt – a tiny Welsh dragon – in a few locations.

VISIT: Llyn Alaw, Cors Goch, Llyn Cefni, Llyn Maelog, Llyn Penrhyn

Above: Yellow Flag   Above right: Ponds at Llansadwrn
Right: Yellow-winged darter dragonfly

Woodland and forest

Estates of large houses were often planted
with impressive stands of beech or sometimes exotic introductions. Pheasants raised
for shooting populate many woods. Small
areas of ancient oak woods do survive, often
shrouded in lichens and mosses.

Large conifer plantations such as Newborough Forest stand in dark, serried ranks
amidst beds of pine needles. They attract
sparrowhawks, coal tits, goldcrests and
crossbills as well as a wide range of butterflies and moths.

Grey squirrels invaded the island in the
1960s, but the smaller, native red squirrels
survived in a few locations and have been
encouraged to re-establish themselves in
areas of mature conifer woodland, such as
Mynydd Llwydiarth. To assist this
repopulation, efforts have been made to
eradicate Anglesey's grey squirrels.

*VISIT: Newborough Forest, Plas Newydd,
Mynydd Llwydiarth, Llangefni's Dingle*

*Below: **Marsh orchid on Newborough Forest's 'Hendy Trail***

Fields and heath

Hedgerows are a fine sight across the island,
with blackthorn blossom and sloes, old
man's beard, blackberry brambles, foxgloves,
primroses and violets and the red berries of
lords-and-ladies. Ivy and red or white
valerian root in old walls.

Meadows may be yellow with buttercups
or fringed with the creamy, pungent tufts of
meadowsweet. Intensive modern
agriculture has greatly reduced the
opportunities for wildlife, but field margins
still abound with birds and small rodents.
Hares are a common sight, powering their
way down rural lanes or raiding outlying
gardens.

There are records of foxes being killed in
Amlwch in 1787, but they were rare on the
island until the 1970s when the population
was said to be showing 'an alarming increase'.
During the last forty years they have become
well established. Airborne predators or
scavengers include kestrels, buzzards
(present in ever-increasing numbers), ravens
and, by night, tawny owls and barn owls.
Five species of bats certainly live on the
island, most commonly the pipistrelle.
Three other species may also be present.

Anglesey's heath and rocky uplands, with
their barricades of prickly gorse, offer
another habitat. Gorse flowers throughout
the year – it is said on Anglesey that 'the
kissing stops when the gorse is not in bloom'.
Adders are widespread on heaths, railway
embankments and disused quarries. They
have been persecuted over the centuries
because of the dangers they pose, but in
reality they are timid snakes. Warm days may
bring out common lizards and the harmless
legless lizards known as slow-worms.

*VISIT: **Cors Goch** (south of Brynteg), **Llaniestyn
Common, Bodafon Mountain***

A Shorelands view

"THERE is always something new to be discovered about birds. Also we must not forget their beauty – a difficult quality to define but one which is made up of form and colour, balance and movement – a quality to which all sensitive and alert people respond, and which birds have in abundance. But alas! modern man's activities are, on the whole, against their survival. Towns increase in size, land is drained, harmful chemicals are used in the cultivation of the soil, more and more people shoot birds, and so the destruction goes on. Will many of our birds be but a memory in a few years to come? Some are already just that."

— C F TUNNICLIFFE, Brooke Bond Picture Cards (1965)

Charles Tunnicliffe (1901-79) was born in Cheshire. He studied art in Macclesfield and Manchester and won a scholarship to the Royal College of Art. C F Tunnicliffe soon made his name as a prolific and highly talented commercial artist and engraver whose subject was the countryside and wildlife. In 1932 he illustrated Henry Williamson's *Tarka the Otter* and in 1935 *Salar the Salmon*. He was elected a member of the Royal Academy in 1954. His popular children's book illustrations in the 1950s inspired a new generation to become interested in natural history.

In 1947 Charles came to live on Anglesey. He and his wife Winifred lived in a house called 'Shorelands' which looked directly over the Cefni estuary at Malltraeth. The bird paintings produced here have an entirely natural feel, the result of painstaking study, scientific measurement and mastery of technique. He shows an innate understanding of living creatures.

Shorelands Summer Diary (1952) and *Shorelands Winter Diary* (published posthumously in 1992) do not just show birds, but unrivalled portraits of Anglesey life, often in the medium of scraperboard. We see horse shows, mussel gathering on the Menai Strait, details of thatched hayricks, Malltraeth battered by winter storms and sweltering in a long, hot summer. His pictures are a precious record of a world that has now vanished.

C F Tunnicliffe's scraperboard illustration of a male Stonechat (in Welsh, Clochdar y Cerrig). The species is frequent on Anglesey, especially around the coasts.

After Charles Tunnicliffe's death, many of his measured drawings and sketchbooks were purchased by the local authority. They are kept at Oriel Ynys Môn near Llangefni.

A chronicle of the past

Some of the main events in Anglesey's history, together with those of Wales, the rest of the British Isles, and the rest of the world, are included in the history timeline ▶250

The rising sea

From about 30,000 to 15,000 years ago, during the Palaeolithic or Old Stone Age, ice-bound North Wales was a hostile environment for human hunters. Anglesey was still joined to the mainland. It did not become an island until well after the final ending of the last ice age, about 10,000 years ago.

As glaciers lost their grip on the mountains, melting ice filled the oceans, and higher temperatures made the sea water expand. Rising levels flooded the Menai Strait and almost succeeded in creating a second channel between what is now the Cefni estuary and Red Wharf Bay.

Hunting bands

During the Mesolithic or Middle Stone Age, nomadic bands gathered roots and berries in the forests, hunted deer and caught fish. They were skilled at making fine, precise weapons and tools from flint, wood, bone and antler. Traces of a hearth and flints, and several camps dating from about 10,000 years ago, have been discovered on the banks of Afon Ffraw. No Mesolithic burials have been found here. The distribution of worked flints suggests that coastal areas, such as Aberffraw or Penmon, were favoured over the densely vegetated interior, but the sea level then was much lower than it is now.

Hunters once roamed the densely forested interior of the island

Farmers and burials

About 5,500 years ago the warming climate encouraged the growing of crops. The first farmers began the long process that eventually transformed a forested island into the patchwork of fields, separated by walls and hedges, that we know today.

Assured food supplies allowed for permanent farming settlements, long-distance trade and more complex social organisation. This was the Neolithic or New Stone Age and is marked by the introduction of pottery vessels and carefully made polished stone axes.

We know that Neolithic people had strong traditional beliefs, because for more than a thousand years their dead were buried together inside stone tombs covered by mounds of earth. Twenty impressive megalithic burial chambers, of different styles, survive on the island.

Barclodiad y Gawres, set into the headland above Cable Bay has decorated stones in the Irish style. Bryn Celli Ddu, near Llanddaniel-fab, has a similar feature. At this site and at Castell Bryn Gwyn there are remains of ritual stone rings and ditches, known as henges. Neolithic settlements are much scarcer than burial or ritual sites, perhaps because they have a slighter archaeological record. The rectangular wooden houses the farmers built have not survived, but archaeologists sometimes discover the holes in the ground where house posts were set.

VISIT: Bryn Celli Ddu, Barclodiad y Gawres, Castell Bryn Gwyn

An artist's impression of how the capstone may have been dragged over the Lligwy burial chamber — seen today in the lower photograph

Jane Durrant

Above: **Bronze Age pottery from Bedd Branwen**

although the purpose of these sites remains a mystery. During the second millennium BC the climate deteriorated, and this seems to have resulted in the abandonment of the Early Bronze Age ritual and burial sites. Emphasis was subsequently placed more on weapons and on defensive enclosures, perhaps as cultivable land became increasingly scarce.

*VISIT: Bryn Gwyn standing stones; **Llanfechell** standing stones, **Gwynedd Museum** (Bangor), **Great Orme Mines***

Beakers and bronze

The Bronze Age came to the British Isles about 4,200 years ago. At about this time copper was excavated at Parys Mountain and the Great Orme to produce new tools and, later, weapons. New burial rites tended to place more emphasis on individuals than on groups. Round barrows and cairns were built over inhumations in stone-lined graves, and later over cremations placed in urns that were often inverted at burial. Standing stones and stone circles reflect new rituals,

Above: **Bronze Age people buried their dead individually, lying crouched as if asleep.**
Below: **Bryn Celli Ddu. A reconstruction, showing a burial ceremony during the later Neolithic period.**

Jane Durrant

Din Lligwy, a reconstruction of the workshop in use during the Romano-British period

brian byron

*Right: **Celtic stone head, found at Holyhead***

Ancient Celts

The 'Celtic' way of life originated in mainland Europe and from about 2,600 years ago came to dominate all regions of Britain and Ireland. Over the centuries there were specific incursions and settlements by bands of Celts around coasts of the British Isles, but the spread of the culture was mostly due to its assimilation by the original inhabitants of the islands.

The British Celts (or 'ancient Britons') were master workers of iron as well as bronze and were famed for their gold and jewellery, their chariots and their bravado in battle. In the British Isles the Celts lived in round houses with thatched, conical roofs. These were often gathered within a hill or promontory fort, surrounded by stockades and defensive walls.

An aristocratic elite provided each tribe with its kings and queens and with its priests and lawmakers, known as druids.

The Celts, like their predecessors, worshipped the Earth Mother, as well as a 'horned god' called Cernunnos and tribal deities. Woods, springs, mountains and animals were held to be sacred, as was the Isle of Anglesey, a major centre of druidism.

The Ordovices were the dominant tribe in northwest Wales. Celtic Iron Age settlements can still be seen on the island, on the slopes of Holyhead Mountain.

The most remarkable archaeological discovery from this age is the treasure hoard retrieved from Llyn Cerrig Bach, near Valley.

VISIT: Din Lligwy, Caer y Twr *(Holyhead Mountain),* **Din Sylwy** *(Llanddona),* **Dinas Gynfor** *(Llanlleiana)*

*Below: **The archaeologist of the Llyn Cerrig Bach hoard, Cyril Fox, used the pieces of chariot he found to draw this reconstruction***

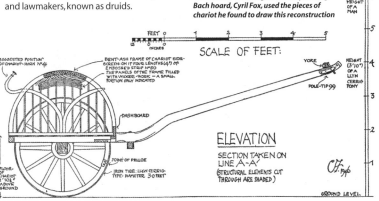

Mona Antiqua

Henry Rowlands (1655-1723) was born in Llanedwen and became rector of Llanidan Old Church. He wrote about farming practice in *Idea Agriculturae* and in 1710 produced *Antiquitates Parochiales* about the ancient monuments of the locality. His best known work was *Mona Antiqua Restaurata* (1723) – literally 'Ancient Anglesey restored' – in which he mistakenly linked the island's Bronze Age sites with the Druids, the priests and lawgivers of the ancient Celts. This fanciful anachronism, compounded by the English antiquarian William Stukeley, was seized upon in Victorian times and still persists today. However Rowlands does deserve credit for focussing attention on the island's ancient sites.

This fanciful representation of a druid is from 'Mona Antiqua Restaurata' by Henry Rowlands.

"*YET one thing there was that struck a general Terror, with which* [the Druids] *might awe and over-rule … appointing what Persons or Things they pleas'd, for the cruel Victims and Immolations of their Altars.*"

Below: A 'druid' at the Bronze Age site of Stonehenge is depicted in a membership certificate for the 'Order of Druids', 1889.

The Druids

Humanity is curious about the past, apprehensive of the future, uncertain about the gods and fearful of the dead. So from the beginning people have needed a priesthood to protect them from these anxieties.

The druids were such a priesthood. But religion and politics are intertwined from the outset and so the priesthood became inexorably involved in secular matters – for are not the affairs of men subject to the will of the gods, and kings anointed in their name? So the druids were powerful in the councils of Celtic kings in the same way as was, for example, Cardinal Wolsey in the court of King Henry VIII.

The Romans were no less superstitious than the Celts, in fact there seems to have always been doubt in the Roman mind as to who were the true gods. Thus they viewed the druids with a mixture of disgust (they followed barbarian gods) and doubt (they might be right). Classical authors report the druids practising human sacrifice (there is an element of sacrifice in every public execution) and their use of sacred groves for the worship of their gods. In this they were not so different from the Greeks, or the Romans' own ancestors for that matter.

The druids were a powerful priesthood, with much secular authority, and as such presented a distinct threat to Roman ambitions. Tacitus, a Roman historian writing in the first century AD, describes the Roman attack on Anglesey and the subsequent destruction of the sacred places of the inhabitants. This led antiquarians to speculate that the chambered tombs (which we know to be the work of the first farmers 3,000 years before the Romans), were sacrifical altars ('grooves for the blood' etc!) and that Stonehenge was a druidical temple. All this harmless nonsense has left us with make-believe druids who are much better known than the historical druids that the Romans so mistrusted.

Richard White was Director of the Gwynedd Archaeological Trust when he contributed this piece to the first edition in 1976

"THE DRUIDS preside over matters of religion, have the care of public and private sacrifices, and interpret the will of the gods. They direct and educate the young, by whom they are held in great honour. In most controversies, public or private, the decision is left to them; if any crime is committed, any murder perpetrated, if any dispute arises about an inheritance or the boundaries of adjoining estates; in all such cases they are the supreme judges. They mete out rewards and punishments; and if any one, whether magistrate or private man, refuses to submit to their sentence they forbid him to attend the sacrifices.

… The Druids are all under one chief who possesses extreme authority in that body. On his death, if any one noticeably surpasses all the others, he succeeds; but if there are several candidates of equal merit, the matter is decided by vote.

… The Druids never go to war, are exempt from taxes and military service, and enjoy many other privileges. These great immunities lead many to follow that profession from their own choice, and many are sent to it by their parents and families. They are taught to repeat a great number of verses by heart, and often spend twenty years at this work, for it is considered unlawful to commit their statutes to writing.

… One of their principal beliefs is that the soul never dies, but after death passes from one body to another, which, they think, helps greatly to exalt men's courage, by robbing death of its terrors. They also teach many things relating to the stars and their motions, the magnitude of the world, the nature of things, and the power and prerogatives of the immortal gods."

— GAIUS JULIUS CAESAR, *The Gallic War* (51BC)

Roman conquest

The Romans first invaded southern Britain in 55BC, but full-scale conquest did not begin until AD43. In AD60 they reached Anglesey, a stronghold of the druids and of warriors intent on resisting the Roman advance.

On the Menai Strait (perhaps at Tal y Foel) the Roman governor of Britain, Gaius Suetonius Paulinus, was confronted by an awesome gathering on the far shore, a host of cursing druids, screaming women and taunting warriors. Even hardened legionaries and auxiliaries needed urging on to the assault. As ever, they succeeded ruthlessly, and destroyed the sacred groves of the island. The Romans then had to withdraw hurriedly to southeastern Britain, where a savage uprising was being led by Boudicca, queen of the Iceni.

It was AD78 before the Romans returned to take full control of Anglesey. They governed from Segontium (at present-day Caernarfon) but later established a coastal fort and lookout at Holyhead, where Roman masonry is still visible. The remains at Lligwy, near Moelfre, of a wealthy farmstead in the Celtic style, shows how local chieftains managed to prosper under Roman rule.

VISIT: Holyhead churchyard wall, Din Lligwy, Caer Lêb, Segontium (at Caernarfon)

"AGRICOLA decided to reduce the island of Anglesey, from the occupation of which Paulinus had been recalled by the revolt of all Britain. As the plan was hastily conceived, there was no fleet at hand; but Agricola's resource and resolution found means of getting troops across. He carefully picked out from his auxiliaries men who had experience of shallow waters and had been trained at home to swim carrying their arms and keeping their horses under control, and made them discard all their equipment. He then launched them on a surprise attack; and the enemy, who had been thinking in terms of a fleet of ships and naval operations, were completely nonplussed. What could embarrass or defeat a foe who attacked like that? So they sued for peace and surrendered the island."

— GAIUS CORNELIUS TACITUS (cAD55-120), *Agricola*, translated by H Mattingly

Above: A Celtic bronze ox-head of the second century AD, found at Llanbedr-goch (shown here a little larger than actual size).
Below: Caer Lêb during the Romano-British period.

Brian Byron

The making of Wales

The power of the vast Roman empire began to wane in the fourth century AD. Even before legions were withdrawn at the start of the fifth century, raiders from Ireland had begun to attack western coasts.

Britain was soon left to its own devices, a patchwork of petty kingdoms. These reflected the old tribal divisions, but saw themselves as inheritors of the Roman tradition. At some point the Venedoti, a northern British tribe, came to defend and govern North Wales. They founded the royal dynasty of 'Gwynedd'. A memorial stone from Llangadwaladr records in Latin the death of King Cadfan of Gwynedd in AD625.

Germanic peoples such as the Angles and Saxons, ancestors of the English, invaded the Celtic lands to the east. They cut off the West Britons at the Battle of Chester in AD607. To this day the Welsh name for the English is *Saeson* – 'Saxons'. The Saxons called the West Britons 'Welsh' (meaning 'strangers') while the Britons began to call themselves *Cymry* ('fellow countrymen'). The seventh century marks the emergence of the Welsh language from Brythonic, and a flowering of Welsh poetry which is a milestone of European cultural development.

From AD784 the eastern border of 'Wales' was marked by the earthworks of Offa's Dyke. Modern Wales was beginning to take shape. ***VISIT: Llangadwaladr Church***

Saints and holy places

Christianity had become accepted within the Roman empire in the fourth century AD, and it rapidly took root and flourished in the western British Isles. In the fifth and sixth centuries, influences from Gaul, Spain and later Ireland, spread by hermits, monks and preachers, led to the foundation of monasteries and churches. Some of these, for example Holyhead, Penmon and Llaneilian, were considered to be of particular importance, and were referred to as 'mother churches', staffed by canons and ruled by an abbot. A number of lesser churches may also date from this period, for example Llangaffo, where there is a collection of important stone crosses, or Llangadwaladr and Llansadwrn, where there are early inscribed stones. However many churches were later foundations, some as recent as the twelfth century.

Most churches are dedicated to the local Welsh saint who traditionally founded the church, for example Saint Cwyllog at Llangwyllog. However today it is difficult to prove when these sites were first settled, and few have produced evidence from the earliest period. Some saints, for example Cybi and Beuno, were considered of particular importance and had a wide sphere of influence throughout North Wales, but others only have a single dedication.

VISIT: *Churches at* ***Llanbadrig, Llangaffo*** *and* ***Penmon*** *(medieval stone crosses);* ***Saint Seiriol's well*** *(at Penmon) and* ***Saint Gwenfaen's well*** *(Rhoscolyn)*

Left: ***King Cadfan's memorial window, Llangadwaladr.***

Below: ***A Latin inscription cast into the sides of a lead coffin found at Rhuddgaer, near Dwyran, indicate an early Christian burial, probably of the fifth century.*** *It reads, in reverse,* **CAMVLORIS H O I** *('Camvloris Hic Ossa Iacent') meaning 'Here lie the bones of Camuloris'. The coffin pieces, and other early Christian memorials such as inscribed stones from Llanbabo and Llantrisant, are on display at the Gwynedd Museum & Art Gallery in Bangor.*

Gwynedd attacked

Gwynedd thrived and under Rhodri Mawr (d877) its rule was extended to Powys, Ceredigion and parts of South Wales.

In the ninth century Vikings from Norway raided or settled many of the lands around the Irish Sea. They plundered churches and they took cattle and grain, ships and slaves. A few Scandinavian names still exist as root words in some of the island's English place-names (such as *Anglesey* itself, the *Skerries* and the word 'stack' in *South Stack*). Vikings attacked Anglesey many times, and settled on the island too. Later the Gwynedd royal dynasty intermarried with Dublin Vikings.

Half-Viking Gruffudd ap Cynan (c1055-1137) had to battle with the Normans, who launched savage incursions into North Wales after their conquest of England. A Norman motte-and-bailey fort still stands above Afon Lleiniog.

In 1170 the Norman invasion of Ireland meant that they now controlled much of the Irish sea around Anglesey.

VISIT: Aberlleiniog Castle

The Welsh Princes

The most successful ruler of the Middle Ages was Llywelyn ab Iorwerth ('the Great', 1173-1240) who was master not just of Gwynedd but of all Wales. Royal courts were convened on Anglesey, most notably at Llys Aberffraw and at Llys Rhosyr (whose ruins have recently been excavated at Newborough).

Conflict with the English had been a constant feature of Welsh life for centuries. By the Treaty of Montgomery (1267) Henry III of England recognised Llywelyn ap Gruffudd (c1225-82) as ruler of all Wales, in return for Welsh recognition of the English king as feudal overlord. After the death of Henry III, however, the agreement foundered and Edward I attacked Wales in 1276. In 1282 Llywelyn's brother Dafydd attacked English forces at Hawarden. In the conflict that followed, Llywelyn ap Gruffudd ('the Last Prince') was killed in a skirmish with the English and his severed head was taken to London. Independent Welsh rule was ended.

VISIT: Llys Rhosyr *(Newborough),* ***Penmon Priory****,* ***Siwan's coffin*** *(Beaumaris parish church)*

Coats of arms of the Welsh princes:
1 **Gruffudd ap Cynan**
2 **Owain Gwynedd**
(Gruffudd's son)
3 **Llywelyn ab Iorwerth**
(Owain's grandson)

Right: ***A stone carving, perhaps representing Llywelyn ab Iorwerth, found at Deganwy near Conwy.***

Below: **Harrowing the ploughsoil.**
This English manuscript (the Luttrell Psalter) depicts ways of life that would have been familar to tenants of the Welsh Courts

Castles and conquest

King Edward I of England subdued North Wales with a chain of castles. Beaumaris castle (1295-98) guarded the eastern approaches to the Strait. Local inhabitants were evicted to Rhosyr (later given its own town charter as 'Newborough'). The new colony of Beaumaris was settled by English and Gascons.

The peace remained uneasy however and in 1400 Owain Glyn Dŵr engaged the English in a war of independence. From 1403-05 the Welsh rebels held Beaumaris castle, but in 1406 the English king, Henry IV, regained control of Anglesey. By 1412 Owain's uprising was defeated.

VISIT: Beaumaris Castle (below), Caernarfon Castle, Conwy Castle and town walls.

Plas Penmynydd

Ships once moored at the dock of Beaumaris Castle. The land that now separates the castle from the sea, the 'Green', was reclaimed in Victorian times.

The Tudors

In the fifteenth century a family from the Penmynydd district of Anglesey came to prominence. Their name was Tudor or Tudur. Owain Tudor (c1400-61) became a squire at the court of Henry V, and on Henry's death secretly married the king's French widow, Catherine de Valois. It was their grandson who claimed the throne as Henry VII – *right* — in 1485, following his success at the Battle of Bosworth. Under his son Henry VIII, Wales was effectively annexed by England in the Acts of Union (1536-43) and detached from the Roman Church by the Reformation. This was a period of religious tumult – a William Davies, who became a Catholic priest in 1585, was imprisoned in Beaumaris castle and was executed in 1593 on account of his faith.

Anglesey prospered in the reign of Elizabeth I. Some impressive, large houses were built along the Menai shore at this time.

VISIT: Penmynydd Church, Plas Mawr (Conwy)

Squires and scholars

Fishing, farming, cattle droving, coastal shipping and smuggling became the island's sources of income. A local boy made good in England, David Hughes, founded a free grammar school at Beaumaris in 1603. The island submitted to Parliamentarian forces during the first Civil War in 1646, and during the second, in 1648, Beaumaris castle was besieged and surrendered.

The 1700s saw a growing interest in the island and its history by native-born writers and scholars, and country squires kept alive some aspects of Welsh culture through their patronage of education, music and poetry.

VISIT: Beaumaris Courthouse

The industrial age

The period between the late eighteenth and the early twentieth centuries saw the surge of Nonconformist zeal which populated the island's landscape with chapels. With the English language being enforced as the medium of instruction in the new schools, it was the chapels' Sunday schools which helped to keep the Welsh language alive.

As the industrial age came to the island along with the railway and the construction of a port at Holyhead, spiritual revival often coexisted with material hardship. There was copper mining at Parys Mountain and quarrying on the island and mainland. This was the great age of Anglesey seafaring, with ships built at Amlwch, and further afield, not just plying the coasts of the British Isles, but braving the storms of Cape Horn on the voyage to San Francisco.

Political power in the Victorian and Edwardian eras was held by the island's large landowners, such as the Bulkeleys of Beaumaris, the Pagets of Plas Newydd and the Stanleys of Penrhos near Holyhead. Princess Victoria attended an *eisteddfod* in Beaumaris in 1832 and the first tourists began to arrive, by steamboat and train.

VISIT: Menai Suspension Bridge, Parys Mountain & Porth Amlwch

Above: County Hall and Court, Beaumaris, built 1614

Right: Built in Liverpool in 1875 for local shipowners, the 'Anglesey' sailed to the Americas and the Far East

Below: Norman Wilkinson's LMS railway poster, showing the Britannia Bridge before its reconstruction following the 1970 fire

The twentieth century

The world wars took the island's young men away to fight, many never to return. Almost one thousand Anglesey men lost their lives in the First World War, more than three hundred during the Second. On Anglesey, home guards practised drill in village halls, 'land girls' toiled in the fields. Bombs were dropped on Holyhead. The Saunders-Roe factory at Llan-faes fitted out Catalina flying boats and launched them on Fryars Bay.

Comprehensive education was pioneered on the island, starting at Holyhead in 1949. Anglesey's education authority became the first in Britain to abandon the 11+ examination and adopt a comprehensive system for entry to all its secondary schools.

Mechanisation drastically reduced the agricultural labour force in the 1950s. Living conditions were improving, with even remote farms receiving mains water and electricity and council houses being built in the villages and towns.

The 1960s saw new campaigns to safeguard and revive the Welsh language. This was a decade during which the island's population increased by 15 per cent.

Major constitutional changes which affected Anglesey and Wales included accession to the EEC (later the European Union, 1973), devolution of power to a National Assembly of Wales (1997) and local government reorganisation (1974 and 1996).

*Above: **The A55 dual carriageway and the railway line serve Holyhead's modern port and ferry terminal***

*Left: **The memorial to Holyhead's losses during two World Wars and the Falklands War***

*Below: **On an excursion in the 1980s, a 'North Wales Coast Express', LMS No.5407, sets off from Holyhead***

32

Yr iaith Gymraeg
THE WELSH LANGUAGE

WELSH is spoken by about sixty percent of the island population and a further ten percent have some knowledge of the language. All speak English. Many slip back and forth between the two languages, without a second thought. Welsh is a medium of commerce, education and broadcasting. It is a Celtic language, closely related to Cornish and Breton, and more distantly to Irish, Manx and Scots Gaelic. It developed from the earlier Brythonic language in the mid-sixth century AD and the language includes borrowings from Latin and English.

 Welsh is a comparative success story amongst the modern Celtic languages, but what does the future hold for it and other minority languages in a globalised world? The 2001 Census was encouraging, in that it showed that the long decline in Welsh had been halted in Wales as a whole. However the message for Anglesey was a mixed one. While the island remained a linguistic stronghold, the use of Welsh here had declined by 2.8 percent since the previous census. The language was now spoken by five times as many people in the interior of the island as around the coast.

Factors affecting Welsh as a minority language include the current global supremacy of the English language, the legal status of Welsh and of course economic factors. The chief Welsh-speaking areas of the island are the poorest, with significant emigration from the island. House prices are out of the reach of local first-time buyers, yet offer an attractive investment to wealthy outsiders. Such problems are common in many parts of the British Isles and across Europe. Possible ways of countering the decline include economic regeneration, provision of genuinely affordable housing, legal safeguards, adult and child education. Already campaigning on behalf of the language are a wide range of public bodies, councils, educational authorities and activist organisations.

Why does it matter? There is surely a universal right for any citizen to speak his or her native language and to use it in the public domain. What is more, research suggests that bilingualism or mutli-lingualism, which is accepted as normal in very many parts of the world, is a desirable educational goal for the individual. It is also desirable for societies as a whole. Any living language contains its own view of the world, its own outlook and patterns of thought, its own culture. Just as a healthy global environment relies on biodiversity, all our cultures are enriched by linguistic diversity. As Welsh learners will testify, knowledge and use of the language helps them towards a much deeper understanding of Anglesey, its people and its history.

Some Welsh words are long, but they are not all as hard to pronounce as *Llanfairpwllgwyngyllgogerychwyrndrobwll-llantysiliogogogoch* !

How do I pronounce that word?

The Welsh language uses the Roman alphabet, but omits various letters used in the English alphabet and includes various 'double' letters. (Remember this when trying a Welsh crossword puzzle!)

The Welsh letters are ordered as follows:
a, b, c, ch, d, dd, e, f, ff, g, ng, h, i, l, ll, m, n, o, p, ph, r, rh, s, t, th, u, w, y

Consonants

b d h l m n p t are pronounced as in English.

c   is hard, as English *k*.

ch as in Scottish *'loch'* or German *'nach'*.

dd similar to English *th* as in *'this'*.

f   as English *v*.

ff as English *f*.

g   is hard, as English *'gate'*.

ng as in English *'longing'*.

ll a difficult sound. Try putting the tip of your tongue behind the teeth, in the same position as for an *L*. Raise the tongue and expel air.

ph as in English *'telephone'*.

r   is rolled, as in Scots.

rh is the same sound followed by an aspirate.

s   hard, as in English *'sea'* (never soft as in *'those'*).
        (The combination **si** may be pronounced *'sh'*)

th as in *'thing'*.

Vowels

Vowels are drawn out in some words by the use of a circumflex accent, as in *Môn*.

a   a short sound as in northern English *'man'* or longer sound as in *'part'*.

e   a short sound as in English *'men'*, or a more open sound as in English *'sane'*.

i   a short sound as in English *'king'* or a longer sound as in *'tea'*.

o   a short sound as in English *'not'* or a lengthened, guttural sound similar to English *'pawn'*.

u   in its Anglesey pronunciation this is rather like the first *'y'* in English *'mystery'*, only more attenuated.

w   no relation to the English letter: it is a short vowel, as in southern English *'cook'*; or a long one as in *'moon'*.

y   no relation to the English letter: it represents a variety of sounds including *u* as in English *'gun'*, *i* as in *'tin'* or *e* as in *'tea'*.

The stress in Welsh is normally on the last syllable but one, eg Bod**ed**ern, Llan**gef**ni.

Some initial consonants may change in certain situations.
This process, called mutation, scares learners no end: however they soon find that they are doing it automatically by themselves!

Why not try out a few words? ...

good morning bore da

good afternoon
   prynhawn da

good night nos da

I love you! rwy'n dy garu di!

thank you very much
   diolch yn fawr

please os gwelwch yn dda

supermarket archfarchnad

shop siop

car park maes parcio

hotel gwesty

single / double bed
   gwely sengl / dwbl

bed & breakfast
   gwely a brecwast

farmhouse ffermdy

campsite gwersyllfa

restaurant bwyty

cup of tea panad o de

cup of coffee panad o goffi

orange juice sudd oren

ice cream hufen iâ

milk llefrith

eggs wyau

pub tafarn

pint of beer peint o gwrw

good health! iechyd da!

it's your round
   dy dro di ydy hi

fish and chips
   pysgod a sglodion

swimming nofio

walking cerdded

fishing pysgota

football pêl-droed

sailing hwylio

sunbathing torheulo

internet rhyngrwyd

website gwêfan

computer cyfrifiadur

e-mail e-bost

1	un	5	pump
2	dau (*m*)	6	chwech
	dwy (*f*)	7	saith
3	tri (*m*) tair (*f*)	8	wyth
4	pedwar (*m*)	9	naw
	pedair (*f*)	10	deg

Maldwyn Peris

GAZETTEER

Descriptions of Anglesey in this guidebook are grouped into five regional sections …

Most of the island's towns and villages are known only by their Welsh names – for example Llangefni. Some additionally have an English name – for example *Caergybi* is known also as Holyhead.
In this English-language guidebook the English place-name is usually given precedence, and the Welsh name follows in italics – for example Holyhead/*Caergybi*.

The Gazetter entries follow the order of the English alphabet.
(The Welsh language has its own alphabet with combinations such as *ff*, *ng* and *ll* representing single letters).

Some of Anglesey's geographical features are described using the Welsh term only – for example, the River Alaw is *Afon Alaw*.
The list on page 260 contains most of these place-name elements.

A map of the island folds out from the back cover. Its grid references are used to locate the towns and villages listed in the Gazetteer: for example, Beaumaris **10D**.

More precise locations are indicated in the text using standard Ordnance Survey map references. Anglesey OS locations are prefixed with the letters SH; references are printed in brackets, eg: (SH373931). Explorer Maps 262 (Anglesey West) and 263 (Anglesey East), or Landranger map 114, cover the island.

Cross references to other pages of the guide are indicated as follows:
Wild Wales **▶47**

The Menai Suspension Bridge, seen from the Anglesey shore of the Strait

BEAUMARIS
and eastern Anglesey

THE MAP of Anglesey's east coast has three main features: the eastern Menai Strait, the broad peninsula of Penmon (meaning literally 'head' or 'end' of Anglesey) and the sweep of Red Wharf Bay. The principal towns are Beaumaris and Menai Bridge. This is an area of limestone ridges and cliffs, often rich in fossils, of long sandy beaches, woods and farmland. Almost everywhere the mountains of Snowdonia fill the southern horizon.

As in other parts of the island there are fascinating prehistoric sites, but here too are marvels from the medieval period through to the Industrial Revolution and its two great bridges across the Menai Strait.

Very few of Anglesey's old cottages have survived into the twenty-first century. This Llanddona cottage – since rebuilt – was photographed in the early 1980s.

Aberlleiniog — *see* **Llangoed** >68

Beaumaris / *Biwmares*

10D
*4ml (6.5km)
NE of Menai
Bridge on
A545*

It is hard to believe that reaching Beaumaris was once a perilous undertaking. In the 1600s, travellers bound for Ireland used to cross to Beaumaris from the mainland, walking over treacherous sandbanks to a waiting ferry. By 1718 the crossing had moved westwards, to the comparative safety of Glyn Garth.

Today, Beaumaris is approached from Menai Bridge by the A545, a winding coastal road completed in 1805. Glimpses of the Menai Strait are framed by oak woods. On the outskirts of town is **Gallows Point / *Penrhyn Safnas*** (known by the Vikings as *Osmund's Eyre*). This part of the Menai Strait is being developed as a yachting marina.

The eastward view from the point's shingle beach is unforgettable. The town houses of Beaumaris overlook the curve of the bay, where yachts and dinghies tug at their moorings. Beyond the constantly changing, luminous patterns of waves and sandbanks, the mainland coast stretches to the great rockface of Penmaenmawr, with the mountains of Snowdonia as a backdrop.

Beaumaris is not large, but it was formerly the county town and chief port of Anglesey. It has had an eventful history and this is reflected in some of the most interesting architecture on the island. However the white and greys which predominated in the town thirty years ago have been replaced by shades of violet, yellow, orange, blue and green. It has to be said that such colours look better in the brighter light of Italy. Beaumaris has the reputation of being more genteel than other towns on the island. However the underlying nature is rather more robust and the town does know how to enjoy itself. There are plenty of attractions for tourists.

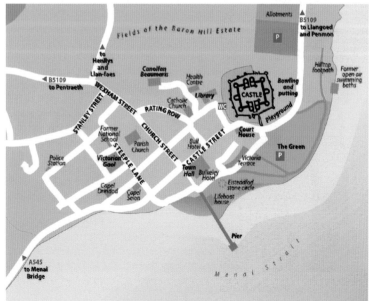

Beaumaris takes its name from the *beau marais*, the 'beautiful marsh' where in 1295 Edward I built the last of his formidable chain of castles. Local pronunciation varies from 'bow-marris' to 'bew-marress'. The latter form, which is reflected in the Welsh spelling, *Biwmares*, is perhaps closer to the Norman French dialect that would have been used by the English court in the thirteenth century. It is echoed in the pronunciation of Beaulieu in England ('Bewlay') and in the word 'beauty'.

The Welsh had been defeated by the English in 1282, but in 1294 had risen up under Madog ap Llywelyn. The Sheriff of Anglesey, Sir Roger de Pulesdon, had been hanged. The borough of Beaumaris, chartered in 1296 and colonised by English and Gascons, was the king's revenge. The Welsh population was evicted from their settlement at Llan-faes to a 'new borough' (the township of Newborough or *Niwbwrch*) in the southwest of the island. The castle walls of Beaumaris soon rose at the head of the Menai Strait, a formidable challenge to the Welsh and their potential allies, the French and the Scots. Today swans paddle peacefully past the horse chestnut trees beside the moat.

Around Castle Street

The town centre is entered along **Castle Street** / ***Stryd y Castell***, with the castle walls rising from the far end. The street is dominated by the pillars and balcony of the **Bulkeley Hotel**, from which hot pennies were once thrown to scrambling children on the first day of the Hunt, and more recently on Boxing Day. Originally named the Williams Bulkeley Arms Hotel, it was built by the partnership of Joseph Hansom (1803-82) and Edward Welch in 1835. It was Hansom who, the year before, had patented the famous horsedrawn cab which bore his name: he was also first editor of *The Builder*. The hotel was extended by the architect R G Thomas in 1873. Its gardens overlook the Strait.

Other hotels include the **Liverpool Arms** (c1700) and the **Old Bull's Head**, a posting inn founded in the 1470s and rebuilt during the seventeenth century. (The bull's head is the crest of the Bulkeley family of nearby Baron Hill.) The antique polished wood and roaring fires contrast with the bright and modern brasserie at the rear. The yard gate, set in an arch off **Rating Row** (formerly Bull's Head Street) is a record-breaking 11ft (3.4m) wide and 13ft (4m) high – the largest simple-hinged door in Britain.

An inn sign on Castle Street

Former notable buildings in Beaumaris included two town houses once occupied by the Bulkeley family. At the Castle Street end of Rating Row, opposite the Old Bull's Head, stood 'Cwrt Mawr'. Around 1480, the Bulkeleys moved to 'Hen Blas', on a site that includes the present Market Square. In 1618 they occupied the newly built house of Baron Hill, on open land to the north

'Tudor Rose'

of the town. In the eighteenth century Hen Blas served as a girls' school and was demolished in 1869 to make way for the English Presbyterian Church (1876), which is now converted as apartments. Still standing on Castle Street is the **Tudor Rose**, a town house (restored in the 1940s and '50s by Hendrik Lek), dating from about 1400. The **Town Hall** / ***Neuadd y Dref*** (1563, rebuilt 1808) on the south side of the street includes a stage for amateur dramatics and public events. Tourist literature is available from the entrance hall, where a plaque commemorates Lewes (or 'Lewis') Roberts (1596-1641). He was a successful Beaumaris merchant who traded all over Europe and the Near East, and became a director of the East India Company. In 1638 he published his major work, *The Merchants Mappe of Commerce*, the first known business manual.

Opposite the castle and in front of the **White Lion** (the site of an inn since 1612), is a small square. On Sunday afternoons in summer, this may be the scene of performances by the town's band, Welsh folk dancing, folk music or other entertainments. At one corner of the square is the **Museum of Child-hood**. Mementoes of the Victorian and Edwardian eras have been displayed here, but the museum's future is uncertain.

One side of the square is taken up by the white **Courthouse** / *Llys* of 1614, open to the public as a museum Easter to September ✆ 01248 811691. The hammer-beam roof of the court room is original. Many of the fittings were reconstructed in the early nineteenth century: the polished wood, railings and flagstones of the interior remain much as they looked at that time. The last Assize Court was held in Beaumaris in 1971. Visitors to the Courthouse should then make their way – as did many a condemned prisoner – to the town's Victorian Gaol, which is now a museum. ▶44

Beaumaris Castle / *Castell Biwmares*

The castles built by Edward I in North Wales are listed by UNESCO as World Heritage Sites. Beaumaris Castle (all year ✆ 01248 810361) may lack the massiveness of Caernarfon or the dramatic siting of Conwy, but its concentric design, by Savoyard siege engineer Master James of St George, is little short of brilliant. Walls within walls and towers for covering fire from archers made attack extremely difficult.

Beaumaris Castle

The full size of the castle is best appreciated from the walkways of the interior. The eastern tower had its own chapel and the inner ward has walls 16 feet (5m) thick. The moat was originally linked to the sea, providing a berth for ships within the defences. At full strength the garrison comprised about 20 archers, 10 men-at-arms and up to 100 footsoldiers, but much smaller numbers were common and could have withstood a siege.

Work began on the most effective and expensive military fortification of its day in April 1295, guarded by an English naval force. Stone was quarried from Penmon and other parts of the island, for a levied workforce of more than 2,000 labourers, carpenters and masons. The castle was mostly completed by 1298, but was never entirely finished. Its first Constable was a knight of Gascon descent, Sir William Pickmore.

> "*AS TO HOW things are in the land of Wales, we still cannot be any too sure. But, as you well know, Welshmen are Welshmen, and you need to understand them properly; if, which God forbid, there is war with France and Scotland, we shall need to watch them all the more closely … p.s. And, Sirs, for God's sake be quick with the money for the works … otherwise everything done up to now will have been of no avail.*"
>
> — James of St George and Walter of Winchester, to the Exchequer, February 1296

The castle was captured by Welsh rebels from 1403 to 1405, during Owain Glyn Dŵr's war of independence. There was fighting between English colonists and native Welsh again in 1440, an incident which became known as the 'Black Affray' of Beaumaris. The Constable brought in to restore order was William Bulkeley of Cheadle, whose descendants still have title to the castle.

Beaumaris Castle last saw action during the Civil War. It was garrisoned by the Royalists in 1642 but captured from its Constable, Richard Bulkeley, in June 1646. A subsequent revolt during the second Civil War two years later was again suppressed. The 1,500 strong Parliamentarian force was led by Major-General Thomas Mytton, who was quartered in the Bull's Head Inn.

The castle was abandoned in 1705 and became an ivy-clad ruin. In 1832 the thirteen year-old Princess Victoria attended an *eisteddfod,* one of the cultural festivals and competitions which still play such an important part in the life of Wales. On this occasion the winning poem was inspired by the shipwreck of the paddle-steamer *Rothsay Castle*, with the loss of over 100 lives, on the Lavan Sands / *Traeth Lafan*, off Beaumaris in 1831.

Today Beaumaris Castle is in the care of Cadw, the body responsible for ancient monuments in Wales. It includes an exhibition on castle architecture and history in the chapel tower. Annual entertainments may include New Year firework displays, or 'medieval' fairs and pageants in the summer.

The former David Hughes Grammar School

West of the castle, adjoining the **library / llyfrgell**, is the former 'free schole' or **Grammar School / Ysgol Ramadeg** founded on the site of a tannery in 1603. Its benefactor was David Hughes, an Anglesey man who had done well for himself in Norfolk. His purchase of farms on the island provided funding for free education. This became the leading school on Anglesey in the eighteenth century and in the nineteenth began to evolve into a prestigious private school. However in 1895 its status was confirmed as an Intermediate County School. Its more modern outbuildings were demolished when the school moved to Menai Bridge town in 1962. There it became the secondary school serving the south and east of the island.

Victorian water pumps

The original school building in Beaumaris now serves as a community centre and exhibition space. Note the former **town water pumps** displayed on the lawn. Alongside the old school is a **health centre / *canolfan iechyd*** and **Canolfan Beaumaris** (1990), a small sports hall which can be transformed into a 350-seat theatre. A separate gallery mounts a programme of exhibitions. An all-weather sports surface is a new development behind Canolfan Beaumaris, on land belonging to the Baron Hill Estate.

East of the castle walls, children swing or see-saw while adults play bowls. There is a putting green. Here too is a car park, beside the town's allotments.

Beaumaris seafront

The Beaumaris seafront was once the site of busy maritime trade. It was also the site of a ferry across the Strait from 1302 until 1690, when the crossing moved to Gallows Point. Whilst fishing and maritime trade declined in Beaumaris during the eighteenth century, Beaumaris did remain important as the port of registration for many island-built ocean-going sailing vessels. By the 1820s paddle-steamers too were bringing tourists from Merseyside and docking at the pier. From the 1830s sailing regattas became all the rage for the smart set. The **Royal Anglesey Yacht Club** still has its headquarters here, and the annual regatta with its booming starter gun and fluttering flags still occupies the seafront in early August.

The seafront may be reached by an archway under the Town Hall. It is fringed by the terrace of the Bulkeley Hotel, the houses of **Green Edge** (John Hall of Bangor, 1824-25) and the imposing **Victoria Terrace**, completed by the firm of Hansom and Welch in 1830-35. The shores of Beaumaris are not really suitable for bathing, but there is a **paddling pool** for toddlers and the small **beach** is ideal for picnicking.

Beaumaris with the Great Orme on the horizon

Beaumaris Pier, a truncated version of the 1846/1873 original, is popular with anglers and in summer with children catching crabs. Bait, lines and tackle are available from the kiosk. Sailing times for boat trips to Puffin Island are displayed nearby. The **RNLI station** (2000) houses an inshore lifeboat, the Atlantic-75 Class *Blue Peter II*, one of the seven lifeboats purchased with funds raised by the children's television programme. A history of the Beaumaris station, today one of the busiest in Wales, is mounted on the wall, and reports of the season's call-outs are displayed in the window.

The Green / *y Lawnt* is the place to fly kites, play football or walk along the sea's edge. A modern circle of standing stones commemorates the proclamation of the 1996 Anglesey *Eisteddfod*. Walk up the grassy hill on the eastern edge of the town, very popular with rabbits, for fine views across the town and castle. Back in 1327 this was topped by the town's first windmill, built by one Einion ab Ieuan. An open-air sea swimming pool (1912) used to occupy the base of the sandy cliff.

Chimney Corner at the opposite (western) end of the seafront, was formerly the site of brine baths (1805).

Paddle steamer 'La Marguerite' at Beaumaris pier, 1910

*"**THIS PLACE, like many others on the Welsh coast, has lately become a fashionable resort for bathing visitors of the higher grade, for which it is admirably adapted, the ground being firm, and the water clear. In 1805, hot baths were erected here, and accommodations of the first class abound. A fine spacious piece of ground, standing between the town and the water, called the Green, forms a delightful promenade, and affords a beautiful scene of vessels passing to and fro, when the tide is in, and a vast variety of company, horses and carriages scouring the beach, when it is out; while the opposite coast presents to the beholder the gigantic front of Penmaen Mawr, and the elevated turrets of Penrhyn Castle."*

— J HEMINGWAY, *Panorama … of North Wales* (1834)

Beaumaris town

Turning into **Church Street** / **Stryd yr Eglwys** one passes the **Bold Arms** and the **George & Dragon** inn. The latter dates from 1595, but the discovery of earlier wall paintings in the building suggests parts of the structure may date from about 1410. Nearby is the small, cobbled **Market Square** / **Sgwar y Farchnad**, surrounded by shops, and the post office (1908).

The parish church from Henllys lane

The fine Church in Wales foundation of **St Mary and St Nicholas** / **Santes Fair a Sant Nicolas** (one of Anglesey's *Grade 1* protected churches) stands on high ground behind the **War Memorial**, in a leafy churchyard. Saint Nicholas is the patron saint of seafarers. The church must have been started in about 1314 but the chancel was rebuilt in about 1500. The spacious interior includes items taken from the monastery at Llan-faes after the Dissolution. These include fine carved oak 'misericords' (seating supports) in the choir stalls. In the south porch is the coffin of Joan (known in Wales as Siwan, (d.1237) who was the wife of Llywelyn the Great and daughter of King John of England. See *Princess Siwan*. ▶61 A fifteenth century alabaster tomb inside the church commemorates William Bulkeley and his wife Elen Gruffudd of Penrhyn. The organ dates from 1806 and the church was restored in 1902.

The Victorian period is often over-sentimentalised. Its grimmer side may be evoked by a moving visit to **Beaumaris Gaol / *Carchar Biwmares*** in School Street, off Steeple Lane. (Easter to September © 01248 810921). Built by Joseph Hansom and Edmund Welch in 1828-29, a new wing was added in 1868. This was designed as a model prison. However the documents on display and a treadwheel in its yard, used for raising water, remind us of the hardship and harsh treatment of the poor in the nineteenth century. The last

execution was of Richard Rowlands ('Dic Rolant') in 1862, found guilty of murdering his father-in-law. Protesting his innocence from the scaffold, high on the gaol's outer wall above Steeple Lane, Dic is said to have cursed the church clock (1810) opposite. For years it certainly never worked too well – but then it was always exposed to winter gales.

Beaumaris Gaol – upper floor corridor

Wander through the backstreets of Beaumaris and you may find sections of the old town walls, dating back to 1414, rooted with pink and white valerian. Seagulls squawk from roofs and chimneys. Here too are small cottages, Georgian facades and Victorian and Edwardian terraces. Steeple Lane's **National School** dates from 1816, and **Canolfan Iorwerth Rowlands**, housed in the former parish church room, offers activities, talks and courses.

There are several notable Nonconformist chapels. The earliest is **Capel Seion**, built by Congregationalists in 1784. **Capel Drindod** (1794), which became the place of worship for Calvinistic Methodists, was followed by the chapels of the Wesleyans, Baptists and English Presbyterians. The Catholic **Church of Our Lady Queen of Martyrs**, off Rating Row, dates from 1908. A bronze plaque in the church commemorates William Davies of Llandrillo-yn-Rhos, a missionary priest who was imprisoned for his faith in Beaumaris, despite considerable local Catholic sympathies. He wrote a carol before being executed in 1593, the only priest martyred in Wales during the reign of Elizabeth I.

Just off **Wexham Street**, note the workers' cottages in **Stanley Street**, designed in brick, on a French model, for the Bulkeley estate. This leads through monumental gates to the award winning post-war **council estate** of Maes Hyfryd, designed by the architect Sidney Colwyn Foulkes. Here too is a large **primary school** (1951).

Stanley Street

The wooded valley to the east of the school, beyond a Day Care Centre, is **Coed Nant Meigan**, part of the Bulkeley estate. A footpath leads into the woods, which can also be approached by road from western sea front. Pass Porth Hir on your right, Stable Mews on your left, and park near the house of Briton's Hill. Panels describe a half-hour walk. Some of the route follows the course of mill leats – water courses – which were fed by Afon Meigan and once served two watermills. The mills were first recorded in 1528. In the nineteenth century the valley was dammed to regulate the flow of water. The footpath leads upstream, past the ruined mills to the mossy wall of the dam.

For more information about the history of Beaumaris, see the book **Beaumaris: the town's story / *hanes y dref***, which also describes a walking tour of the key sites.

Annual events in Beaumaris

✦ **The Beaumaris Festival** / *Gŵyl Biwmares* takes place over the Whit week at the end of May. Classical music concerts, art exhibitions, craft fairs and talks.

✦ **Beaumaris Lifeboat Day** on a Saturday each August (the date depends on the state of the tides). Events have included air-sea rescue displays.

✦ **Sunday entertainment** during the summer in the Castle square.

✦ **A circus** – usually focussing more on human skills than those of animals – often sets up its Big Top on the Green for a week or two each summer.

✦ **5th November** (or sometimes the nearest Saturday, check each year) sees a Guy Fawkes bonfire on the beach and a spectacular fireworks display.

✦ **Victorian Evening**: held from about 6.30pm, usually on the first Wednesday in December. Mince pies and bellringing, charity stalls. Beaumaris Band and the Parish Church Choir. Victorian costume parade in Castle Square.

✦ **Boxing Day**: around midday, hot pennies are thrown down into the street from the balcony of the Bulkeley Hotel – to be picked up by eager spectators.

✦ **New Year's Eve Firework Display**, from the castle walls.

✦ **Beating the Bounds**. The borders of the old borough of Beaumaris are ceremonially 'beaten' every seven years: 2007, 2014 etc. The route is followed so exactly that it involves scaling the roof of the old farmhouse at Cefn!

The celebrated **Beaumaris Band** is in attendance at many of these events.

Leaving Beaumaris to the west

The B5109 leaves town under the bridge on **Red Hill** / *Allt Goch Fawr*, climbing steeply through the woods of the **Baron Hill** estate of the Bulkeley family. The Bulkeleys, originally from Cheshire, owned most of Beaumaris and the surrounding countryside from the fifteenth century onwards. Some members of the family put down roots in other parts of the island – see *The Squire of Brynddu* ▶122

The large mansion of Baron Hill was begun for Sir Richard Bulkeley in 1618 and rebuilt by Samuel Wyatt in 1776. Its parkland was designed by William Emes (1729-1803). He designed other Welsh parks at Erddig and Powis Castle, properties that today are owned by the National Trust. In 1822 the Bulkeley peerage died out and the estate passed to the Williams Bulkeleys.

In Baron Hill's heyday in the nineteenth century there was entertainment on a grand scale and the house was surrounded by exotic gardens and tennis courts. At this time the family owned 16,516 acres (6,690ha) on the island. In 1907 Baron Hill was visited by Edward VII. The Bulkeleys employed huge numbers of maids and estate workers. Baron Hill was billeted with troops during the Second World War and became a regrouping centre for Polish soldiers. Some Poles settled in the area, and today a number of local families have Polish surnames. After the war Baron Hill fell into complete disrepair. Damaged by fire, and with the lead stolen from its roofs, it is now derelict.

The Bulkeley Memorial

There is no public access. A right turn at the top of the hill takes one to the **Bulkeley Memorial** (1876), a tall obelisk visible from miles around and accessible by a short path – a good spot for flying kites. Opposite the memorial another public footpath crosses a couple of fields to **Llyn Bodgylched**. Keep dogs on a lead, as sheep graze here. The shallow lake, populated by flocks of honking geese, is fringed by beds of reed and yellow flag. Just past the junction, on the B5109, one sees the **Almshouses** / *Elusendai* built in 1613 with the bequest of philanthropist David Hughes. A stone arch leads through to a central courtyard.

Benllech

8E

*7ml (11km)
north of
Menai Bridge
on A5025*

The word *Penllech* may refer to the capstone of a prehistoric burial chamber. This was the name adopted by a small farm near such a site, which was later given to the village as a whole. The area became popular with Edwardian visitors, with the completion of a (now defunct) rail link to Red Wharf Bay in 1909. The English novelist Arnold Bennett and the French composer Claude Debussy are said to have stayed at the **Glanrafon Hotel** at this time.

Benllech is one of Anglesey's most popular seaside resorts, served by a number of small hotels and guesthouses, as well as camping and caravan sites. It is also a popular destination for retirement. Streets of bungalows stretch down to the bay from the main road and its shops. The **Church of St Andrew**, in the centre of Benllech, dates from the 1960s. Benllech also has a Presbyterian church and the Libanus chapel of the Independents.

The centre of any holiday or family day out is the long, sandy **beach**, buttressed by rocky headlands. This is a pleasant, sheltered spot, safe for swimming and ideal for beach games. It is served by a car park and toilets, by beach shops and cafés.

Benllech beach – with Red Wharf Bay in the distance

The B5108 leads westwards past a primary school, a fire station and the **Goronwy Owen Memorial Hall**, through **Tynygongl** and **Brynteg**. The open farmland here has rocky outcrops, gorse and stone-walled fields, caravan parks and working quarries. Storws Wen is a 9-hole **golf course** ✆ 01248 852673. Brynteg's **California Inn** was built in the 1850s by J H Thomas, a local farmer's lad who had taken a passage to America during the California gold rush of 1849 and who returned home a wealthy man.

The area has a wealth of ancient remains, most notably the 5,000 year old limestone burial chamber of **Pant y Saer** (SH510824). The remains of 54 people have been discovered here, along with fine pottery. **Hut circles** in the bracken date from the Iron Age and the early medieval period. A tinned bronze brooch of this period is now to be seen in Oriel Ynys Môn near Llangefni. Three nature reserves lie just to the south of Brynteg and are listed under Llanbedr-goch ▶53

The parish church of **Llanfair Mathafarn Eithaf**, or 'Llanfair ME' (SH507829) can be reached from Benllech or Marian-glas. There is room to park by the church, but the access lanes are very narrow indeed. It stands in a dip, surrounded by trees, behind a trim stone wall with a lantern. The church is partly medieval, with an eleventh-century cross in the churchyard. The pulpit was installed in 1969, on the bi-centenary of the death of the poet Goronwy Owen (1723-69) who, for a short time, was a curate here.

Wild Wales

George Borrow (1803-81) was an English writer from Norfolk, the son of a recruiting sergeant. He was largely educated in Edinburgh. Borrow was a down-to-earth character with an insatiable love of travel and foreign languages. He championed the cause of the Roma or Gypsy people. In his youth Borrow also developed a great interest in Wales and learned to read and speak Welsh. In *Wild Wales* (1862) George Borrow tells of his travels on the Isle of Anglesey. He takes directions from the toll-keeper on the **Menai Bridge** and travels first to '**Pentraeth** Coch', where he visits the church and **Mynydd Llwydiarth**. He stays at an inn called the 'White Horse' and engages in conversation with the landlord, Hugh Pritchard, and an irritating drover called Bos. He makes an excursion to the parish of **Llanfair Mathafarn Eithaf**, the birth-place of Goronwy Owen whose poetry he greatly admires. He describes a rocky landscape, impoverished cottages, pigs and lime kilns. Borrow visits **Penmynydd** ('a few white houses and a mill') to see its church and its tomb ▶90 , which the villagers take to be that of Owain Tudur rather than his ancestor. He then proceeds to 'Dyffryn Gaint' (**Ceint**) and drinks with a poet who repeatedly tells him, 'A baronet is a baronet, but a bard is a bard'.

George Borrow finishes his visit at **Holyhead**, visiting the port, the market and **South Stack**.

> "*Mr PRITCHARD … took the pipe out of his mouth, and with some hesitation said that he believed the gentleman neither went to Llanfair* [Mathafarn Eithaf] *for pigs nor black cattle but upon some particular business. 'Well,' said Mr Bos, 'It may be so, but I can't conceive how any person, either gentle or simple, could have any business in Anglesey save that business was pigs or cattle.' 'The truth is', said I, 'I went to Llanfair to see the birth-place of a great man – the cleverest Anglesey ever produced.'*"
>
> — GEORGE BORROW, *Wild Wales* (1862)

A Welsh Virginian

The primary school in Benllech is named after George Borrow's 'great man', **Goronwy Owen** (1723-69), the poet known as *Gronwy Ddu o Fôn*. He was born on New Year's Day in the parish of Llanfair ME and educated at Friars' School in Bangor. As a young man he was encouraged to write poetry by Anglesey's Morris brothers and he mastered the traditional verse forms of the *cywydd* and the *awdl*. Owen was briefly curate of his native parish before moving to England.

In 1757 he left for North America. His wife and one of his children died on the voyage. Owen became a teacher at the grammar school associated with the College of William & Mary in Williamsburg, Virginia. He took to drink, re-married twice, and worked as a priest and a tobacco planter. He constantly longed to return to his birthplace, but died in far-off Virginia.

Goronwy Owen's poetry greatly influenced generations of poets. His best-remembered lines are in praise of his beloved Anglesey:

*… **Henffych well, Fôn, dirion dir,**
Hyfrydwch pob rhyw frodir.
Goludog, ac ail Eden
Dy sut, neu Baradwys hen …*

*… All hail to Anglesey, gentle land,
The delight of all regions.
Bountiful as a second Eden
Or an ancient paradise …*

Bodafon Mountain — *see* **Mynydd Bodafon** ▶84

Changes on the farm

Anglesey's farmers changed a forested island into a patchwork of fields separated by walls and hedges. This was a long process. Archaeologists can trace some existing field patterns back to the Neolithic period.

Until the twentieth century, many Anglesey people were self-sufficient tenant farmers. They ate what they grew and they made the things they needed. If they had surplus grain or livestock it was taken to market to make money. But a hundred years ago the average size of farm here was only forty acres, so there was little to sell.

Meadows were mowed by scythe, cows were milked by hand and ploughing an acre with a pair of horses was seen as a good day's work. Cottages needed repairing and thatching. At night, gathered around the hearth, there was rug-making, spinning, knitting and conversation.

The Second World War changed forever the way people lived in the countryside. Good prices were guaranteed for all the food farmers could produce. Now they could afford tractors and modern implements.

At the same time many young men left their farms to join the armed forces.

When the war ended returning soldiers discovered that the farms could get by without their labour. Some families left Anglesey to work elsewhere, and others found new ways of making a living here. The profound knowledge that so many people once had about the ways of the countryside began to fade.

The beginning of the twenty-first century has seen further changes. Now the island's milk goes to a cheese factory at Llangefni and to a creamery on the mainland. Some farmers have learned that 'niche marketing' – producing crops and rearing livestock in ways that are different from their competitors, for example earlier in the season – gives them an advantage. Other farmers have returned to the ideas of their forebears: organic production has adopted some of the older techniques of pest control and fertilisation, along with some modern innovations, and Farmers' Markets are once again being held.

Haymaking
Beaumaris castle meadow, c1905

"*Mr HUGH WILLIAMS spoke as to **Llanfair Mathafarn Eithaf** and the adjoining parishes of the Anglesey Union, to the effect that some of the farmers there live 'on bread-and-milk' for breakfast, on 'potatoes with buttermilk, and potatoes with butter' for dinner, adding that some get salt meat, but very seldom any meat except salt meat, that is to say, bacon and beef. He went on to say that they have bread-and-butter and tea in the afternoon, and porridge and buttermilk for supper. Lastly, he said that 'there are many farmers who cannot afford to get a piece of fresh meat once a year'.*"

— *Minutes of Evidence*, Royal Commission on Land in Wales & Monmouthshire (1894)

Britannia Bridge / *Pont Britannia*

8C
*2ml (3km)
west of
Bangor
on A55*

This is the most common route of entry to Anglesey, and generally the quickest. The modern Britannia Bridge is a double-decker road and rail system. However the original Britannia Tubular Bridge was for rail only, and it made engineering history. A magnificent prototype of box-girder design, it was designed by William Fairbairn (1789-1874) and Robert Stephenson (1803-59), the son of locomotive pioneer George Stephenson. Building it was no easy task. A memorial to the labourers killed during construction stands in the churchyard at Llanfair Pwllgwyngyll.

Robert Stephenson and his builders

Britannia Bridge as it is today

Work on the site began in 1846. The bridge's twin wrought-iron tubes were jacked up between the piers, and then secured by stonework. They were 1,475ft (461m) long and contained some two million rivets. As tall sailing vessels needed to pass beneath, the bridge towered 102ft (32m) above the waters of the Menai Strait, supported by piers of Anglesey limestone – one of them built on the 'Britannia' rock that gave the bridge its name. The German composer Felix Mendelssohn (1809-47), a regular visitor to the British Isles, was so impressed when he viewed the partially built bridge that he made a sketch. The Britannia Bridge was finally opened to great acclaim in 1850, and a symphony orchestra played a concert in the new tunnel. The new rail link between London and Holyhead (for Ireland) would have great political and economic significance.

The masonry towers were designed by architect Francis Thompson (1808-95) in the Egyptian style, emphasised by the 80-ton stone lions at either end of the bridge. These were carved in 1848 by the architectural sculptor John Thomas (1813-62), who worked for seventeen years on the decoration of the Houses of Parliament in London. His supercilious-looking lions caused some local amusement at the time. Take the footpath that leads from a kissing-gate at the first lay-by east of the bridge on the A4080. The path takes you down to the shore and along the water's edge (with wooden benches giving a perfect view of both bridges) towards the Britannia Bridge. The road deck forms a canopy above the narrower railway track, which is flanked by the lions. Retrace your route back to the lay-by, or, for a circular walk, make your way up the path through the National Trust's dark woodland of Coed Môr to emerge on the pavement of the A4080. Turn right to return to the lay-by.

Rail and road

The Llanfairpwll to Holyhead section of railway track was completed in 1848 and immediately began to carry passengers and goods. Until the opening of the Britannia Tubular Bridge two years later, a coach and horses service connected Bangor Station to Llanfairpwll by bringing the Chester & Holyhead Railway passengers across the Menai Suspension Bridge.

When the Britannia Bridge opened in 1850 the linking of Anglesey to the national network gave an immediate boost to the growth of the port of Holyhead. In 1876 the line became part of the London & North-Western Railway.

Over the next sixty years a local rail network was also built. The Anglesey Central Railway ran from Gaerwen to serve Pentre-berw, Llangefni, Llan-gwyllog, Llannerch-y-medd, Rhos-goch and Amlwch. From Pentre-berw another branch ran to Red Wharf Bay (for Benllech) via Ceint, Rhyd-y-saint, Pentraeth and Llanbedrgoch.

This Red Wharf Bay branch saw the first ever use of a 'Push & Pull' train.

The Holyhead road began to be tarred in 1896, and with the rise of the motor car at the beginning of the twentieth century new roads were laid and old tracks were improved all over the island. Bus services connected small villages with the towns. People living in the country-side began to have more contact with others living outside their home districts. Local crafts declined and factory-made goods were brought in and paid for by the sale of agricultural products. The material standard of living rose steadily as a result of the whole process, but values had altered and the self-sufficient character of the island's rural communities had vanished forever.

The line to Holyhead from Bangor remains open, but the branch lines did not survive the twentieth century. Classic steam locomotives occasion-ally visit the island, and there have been proposals to re-open the Central Railway.

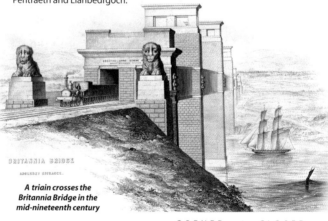

A triain crosses the Britannia Bridge in the mid-nineteenth century

Anglesey's rail network

	OPENED		CLOSED	
	Goods	Passengers	Passengers	Goods
Llanfair Pwllgwyngyll > Holyhead	1848	1848		
Bangor > Llanfair Pwllgwynygyll	1850	1850		
Gaerwen > Llangefni	1864	1865	1964	1993
Llangefni > Llannerch-y-medd	1866	1866	1964	1993
Llannerch-y-medd > Amlwch	1866	1867	1964	1993
Pentre-berw (Holland Arms) > Pentraeth	1908	1908	1930	1950
Pentraeth > Red Wharf Bay (for Benllech)	1909	1909	1930	1950

The tubular spans of the old bridge were largely destroyed by a fierce fire in 1970. The bridge was restyled under the direction of the civil engineer Sir Charles Husband (1908-83) and reopened to rail traffic in 1972. With a new road level above the railway track, it opened to vehicles in 1980. The insertion of arches in the reconstruction altered the famous profile of the old bridge forever. A section of the bridge's original tube is displayed on a plinth (SH543708), near one of the stone lions, beside the mainland end of the Britannia Bridge. It can be approached by footpath that starts from near the vetinerary clinic (SH542704) at the end of Ffordd Bronwydd – leave the A55 at junction 9, and take the first turning left off the A487 Menai Bridge road.

Peregrine falcons have been known to nest on the bridge's tall stone piers, swooping on pigeons flying from Treborth botanical gardens on the mainland.

The Cockleshell Poet

John Evans ('Y Bardd Cocos', 1827-88) was a cockle-seller of Menai Bridge town. He was a figure of fun who became famous for his rhymes and humorous doggerel. He was a familiar character at *eisteddfodau*, wearing a hat crowned with beads.

Pedwar llew tew,	*Four fat lions,*
Heb ddim blew,	*Without any hair,*
Dau 'r ochor yma	*Two over this side*
A dau 'r ochor drew	*And two over there*

Sometimes his lines reflected current radical opinion:

> **Mae'r Prince of Wales wedi priodi,**
> **A miloedd yn byw mewn tlodi.**

The Prince of Wales got married,
And thousands are living in poverty.

It is hardly surprising that Queen Victoria did not accept John Evans's marriage proposal!

His most famous lines were penned about the stone lions on the new Britannia Bridge. It is pleasing to think that his lines are often better remembered today than the more earnest poetry of some of his contemporaries.

Brynrefail — *see* **Mynydd Bodafon** ▶84

Brynteg — *see* **Benllech** ▶46

Four Crosses

8C
on A5025
1ml (1.5km)
north of
Menai Bridge
or A55
junction 8

Leaving Menai Bridge northwards, **Ffordd Pentraeth** climbs past the Ysgol David Hughes secondary school to a roundabout by the **Four Crosses** public house and a cluster of business premises. These include S Webb & Son (a book and gift wholesaler) and William Roberts & Company (a timber merchants relocated from the Menai Bridge waterfront, where, in the 1860s, they had taken over the business from the Davies family of Treborth).

Southwest on the A5025, in a field by the approaches to the Britannia Bridge, the jumble of stones which can be seen from the road is the collapsed **Tŷ Mawr** burial chamber (SH539721), dating from perhaps six thousand years ago.

Pili Palas Nature World © 01248 712474 (closed early in the year) is close to Menai Bridge town on the B5420 Penmynydd road. It has an indoor garden full of free-flying exotic butterflies, and displays of insects, reptiles and spiders. Its exhibits are popular with local schoolchildren as well as tourists, and there is a café, nature trail and outdoor adventure playground.

Gaerwen

7C

4ml (6.5km) west of Britannia Bridge, A55 junction 7; or follow A5 from Llanfair Pwllgwyngyll

Gaerwen is set amongst fields, rocks and gorse. It extends southwards from the straggling ribbon development along the old A5, which is now effectively by-passed by the A55. The name Gaerwen means 'white fort'. Irish gold dating from the seventh century BC was found near here, but there are few visible reminders of history other than two ruined windmills (Melin Maengwyn and Melin Sguthan) and the abandoned, roofless, medieval parish church of **Llanfihangel Ysgeifiog**, dedicated to St Michael, to the northwest of the village (SH478734). A bell and furniture from the old church was moved to the 'new' Victorian **Church of St Mihangel** (Saint Michael, 1847 and 1897), which borders the A5, as does a modern **Mormon church** (1985). There is also a **Baptist chapel** building dating from 1855. In front of a small Millennium Garden is the **war memorial** (1922), which commemorates thirteen men from the village who were killed during the First World War.

Chapel Street leads southwards to Llanddaniel-fab. A **business park** occupies the southwest of the village. Livestock, agricultural equipment, household goods, art and antique auctions are held at the Morgan Evans & Co *Gaerwen Auction Centre* (once known as the Smithfield – *see 'The Cattle Ring'* ▶175). The large chapel on this road is **Disgwylfa**, of the Welsh Presbyterians.

To the east of Gaerwen, along the A5, is the small village of **Star**. This comprises a cluster of retail outlets around the main road and a residential district, aross the road bridge (over the A55) at the bottom of the lane to Penmynydd. Its public house is the **Gaerwen Arms**.

Glanrafon — *see* Llangoed ▶65

Glyn Garth — *see* Llandegfan ▶58

Llanallgo

7F

1ml (1.5km) SW of Moelfre on A5025

This small village borders the main road to Amlwch, to the south of Lligwy. By the central roundabout is the Welsh Presbyterian chapel of **Paradwys**. To the southwest is the parish **Church of St Gallgo** (SH502851), approached by a walled path through the tree-lined churchyard. This has been an ecclesiastical site for more than 1,400 years.

Today's church has a thirteenth-century bell; the building dates from the fifteenth century, but was extensively restructured in 1892. An obelisk by the churchyard's rear wall commemorates the victims of the *Royal Charter* shipwreck in 1859: look too for gravestone inscriptions that mention the wreck. 140 victims are buried here. See *The Royal Charter.* ▶83 Richard ('Dic') Evans, twice an RLNI Gold Medal Winner, see *The Coxswain* ▶81, also lies here.

An ancient well to the southwest of the church, once valued for the healing properties of its waters (casting a bent pin into the well was said to bring good luck) may date back to the pagan Celtic period. A carved sandstone head of this era was found nearby.

The grave of one of the Royal Charter's victims

Llanbedr-goch *also known as* Llanbedrgoch

7E

1¾ml (3km) north of Pentraeth off A5025

This scattered village (meaning 'Red Saint Peter's') centres on a terrrace of stone houses and a small post office. Quiet lanes, fringed with tall cow parsley in the summer, lead north to Brynteg past the **Glasinfryn** chapel (1752), and southwest to Talwrn.

Excavations carried out by Mark Redknap of the National Museum of Wales between 1994 and 2001, at Glyn between Llanbedr-goch and Benllech, discovered traces of a Welsh farmstead of about AD600 which later became a defensive settlement at the time of incursions by Vikings from Dublin. It would seem that parts of the island were not just being raided by Vikings in search of wealth, but settled, for here remains have been found of a rectangular house in the Viking style, dated to between AD890 and 970. Five human skeletons, including one of a 10 year-old child, were discovered in a ditch outside the defensive wall of the settlement. Radiocarbon dating of the bones shows that they probably died during the second half of the tenth century, at a time when Vikings from the Isle of Man may have had bases on Anglesey. The positions of the bodies, carelessly thrown down, suggests that they met with violent deaths. It seems also that two of the men had bound wrists. Was this an Anglesey family who became victims of the Vikings?

Stone head set into the masonry of St Peter's church

The little parish **Church of St Peter** *(Pedr)* stands on a steep hillock not far from the main Pentraeth road (SH509799). Follow the church sign southwards down the narrow lane which leads also to Plas-y-Brain farm. Enter the gate in the ivy-covered stone wall: the graveyard, with its tombs and headstones of carved slate, looks across to Mynydd Llwydiarth. The church building dates from the fifteenth and seventeenth centuries. Patterns are carved in stone above the door. There are stone heads on either side, one of whom appears to have a pointed head or cap, perhaps a mitre. These may be medieval carvings, but equally they may date back to the Celtic Iron Age and have been reset in the wall of the church. An earlier building was sacked and desecrated by English naval forces in 1157.

About 1¼ mile (2km) northwest of the centre of the village of Llanbedr-goch is the **Cors Goch** nature reserve, managed by the North Wales Wildlife Trust. A little less than a mile (1.5km) from the centre of Llanbedr-goch, northwards along the lane that leads to the B5108 (linking Benllech to Bryneg), is an unmarked layby where cars should be left (SH505817, opposite the conifer belt between a quarry and Ynys Isaf). A gravelled track leads west into Cors Goch: at its end, by the house of Mynydd Cors Goch, is the reserve's entrance with an information panel. The reserve covers more than 114 acres (46ha), much of it fenland and heath around **Llyn Cadarn**, and supports sixteen nationally scarce aquatic species. Plants include sedges, rushes, reeds and orchids. Wetland birds, frogs, lizards and adders inhabit the reserve. Boardwalks provide access over the wet areas. Plans to extend the Rhuddlan Bach limestone quarry have raised concern, amongst conservationists, about the possible disruption to the water courses of Cors Goch wetlands.

A short walk south, following the footpath beyond Cors Goch, is a second reserve of 16 acres (6ha), **Craig Wen** (SH493803). This damp, acid heath is home to the rare, blue flowers of the marsh gentian. Additional land, at **Castell**, has recently been added to the protected reserves in this area.

Up to date information about access is provided by the North Wales Wildlife Trust – www.wildlifetrust.org.uk/northwales

Two miles (3km) due west of Llanbedr-goch, beside the B5110, is another belt of wetland. Here, another reserve, **Cors Erddreiniog** (SH477805), is managed by the Countryside Council for Wales and includes important areas of fen, as well as heathland and woodland. Public access is restricted.

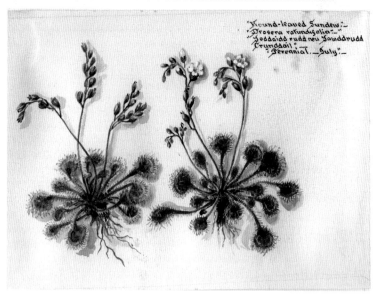

Sundew occurs in the Llanbedr-goch wetlands. (Butterwort, another insectivorous plant, is more common.) The illustration was painted in the early twentieth century, part of the collection of the Massey sisters of Llangoed ▶54

Llanddaniel-fab

7C
1½ml
(2.5km) SE
of Gaerwen
or turn off
A4080 from
Llanedwen

This attractive village is sited amidst peaceful countryside on the back lane to Newborough, separated from its larger neighbour, Gaerwen, by the railway line to Holyhead. The railway cuts across the main road through the village over a level crossing close to the **Dinam Arms** public house.

Llanddaniel- fab may mean the 'Church of Deiniol the patron saint'. There may have been a religious foundation here as early as the seventh century. The **Church of St Deiniol**, located near the crossroads by the war memorial, is the former parish church. Now deconsecrated, it was offered for sale in 2005. In 1747 the village was visited by John Wesley (1703-91), the founder of Methodism, in the company of William Williams 'Pantycelyn' (1717-91), South Wales's most famous hymn writer. The first preached in English, the second in Welsh. The village's **Cana Chapel** dates from 1906. The primary school, **Ysgol Parc y Bont**, originally the Victorian building (1874) opposite Bryn Celli Ddu, is now on a modern site at the northeastern end of the village on the road to Star. A **golf course**, the 12-hole Penrhyn Complex, is signposted from the village centre ✆ 01248 421150.

On the lane south to Llanedwen, **Bryn Celli Ddu** (SH507702) is one of the most interesting ancient monuments on the island, and may be linked in its origins to that of Barclodiad y Gawres, near Cable Bay / Porth Trecastell. This site is clearly signposted from the southern edge of the village and a car park is provided off the lane. Bring a torch. A fenced path leads to the site through farmland, a walk of about ten minutes.

Jane Durrant

A ceremony takes place within the henge during the Neolithic period

This Stone Age burial site probably belongs to the late third millennium BC. Nearby is a standing stone erected in the Bronze Age. The mound is set against a southern backdrop of the woodland around Plas Llwyn Onn and, in the distance, the mountains of the mainland.

Bryn Celli Ddu was excavated and restored in the years 1927-1931. It is believed to represent two separate dates and functions. Initially it was probably a henge, a ritual site with an outer bank (no longer visible), an inner ditch and a stone circle. Later it seems, a passage grave was constructed over the henge. This may have been a deliberate challenge to old religious practice. A burial chamber about 8ft (2.4m) across was prepared, capped with two big stones and then covered with a mound of soil (much bigger than that of the modern reconstruction).

Bryn Celli Ddu's decorated stone

The chamber can be entered through a passage which has an open and a roofed section. The latter has a ledge running along one wall. A spiral is carved on an internal stone, but it may not be original. Most unusual is an upright pillar erected in the chamber, a characteristic of some Irish sites. Ritual sites surrounded the mound: an ox-burial, a hearth, a fire-pit. The site has also revealed human remains, arrowheads, a flint scraper, a stone bead and mussel and limpet shells. Near the mound is a stone with an elaborate incised pattern of wavy lines, a design normally associated with Brittany. This is a replica, the actual stone being in the National Museum of Wales in Cardiff.

Llanddona

9E
*3½ml
(5.5km) NW
of Beaumaris*

This scattered village, lying between a tall television mast in the northeast and a radio mast in the west, includes isolated cottages and farmhouses in the traditional Anglesey style as well as modern bungalows. The **upper village** is on rocky ground high above Red Wharf Bay. It is a jigsaw puzzle of private dwellings and patches of common land. At its centre is a public house, the **Owain Glyn Dŵr** (a venue for local singers), and a village hall.

Llanddona Common / *Comin Llanddona*, comprises rocky outcrops, dry heathland with purple heather, scrub made up of willow, blackthorn, gorse and bracken and some marshy areas with sedge. Wildlife includes slow worms and common lizards.

A precipitous lane with dizzying views across the bay forks halfway down the hill. The western fork leads directly to the beach; the eastern leads to the beach via the pretty **lower village**, where the small **Church of St Dona** (largely rebuilt in 1873 under the supervision of its rector) is tucked into the hillside (SH574809). Local people once lived by fishing (remains of a fish weir may be seen at the eastern end of the beach) and by quarrying; today they do so principally by farming, tourism or commuting to Bangor.

*The eastern
end of Red
Wharf Bay,
from the
hillside of
Bwrdd Arthur*

Llanddona Beach / *Traeth Llanddona*, is reached via the small lane beside the churchyard. This is the eastern end of Red Wharf Bay / *Traeth Coch*. It offers five miles (8km) of perfect sand fringed by reeds and grasses, beneath green hills and white farmhouses. The water is shallow, more suited to paddling than serious swimming. The tide goes out seemingly to the horizon, but rolls back in at a disconcerting speed. This beach is ideal for beach games, horse-riding, bird-watching, shell collecting, or kite-flying. A shop, toilet and car park are provided on the lane that runs along the shore.

Another very steep lane from Llanddona church leads back to the tall mast of the main transmitting station for radio and television broadcasters in northwest Wales. (Relay stations for areas of the island shielded from its signal are located on Holyhead Mountain and at Aberffraw and Cemaes.)

At the curve of the lane to the north is **Bwrdd Arthur**, 'Arthur's table' (SH586815), a windy limestone plateau where sheep graze amongst brambles and blackthorn. There is now open access to this area under 2005 countryside legislation. On the clearest days there are views of the Isle of Man (a series of peaks on the horizon) and the fells of the Lake District, as well as to the mountains of the Welsh mainland. Bwrdd Arthur is the site of **Din Sylwy**, a hillfort of more than 17 acres (7ha), covering an area similar to that of Caer y Twr hillfort on Holyhead Mountain. Din Sylwy was probably first occupied in about 300BC and was probably still in use during the Roman occupation. Only the outer wall remains, with no surviving traces of settlement. A signed footpath winds around the western base of the plateau and then doubles back through National Trust land to cross fields down

*A hoard
discovered
at Din Sylwy
included
Roman coins
of Vespasian
– emperor at
the time of
the invasion
of Anglesey
in AD78*

to Traeth Llanddona. The tiny church of **Llanfihangel Dinsylwy** (SH588815) is sheltered by the eastern rim, secluded among hedges of dogrose and hawthorn. It is reached by a lane which skirts the fort. Walk across the fields to the buttercup-filled churchyard, which looks across the sea to Puffin Island. The church is fourteenth century and was partly rebuilt in 1855. It is lit by oil lamps. Fine amulets of Viking silver were discovered here.

The witches of Llanddona

People who come from Llanddona are often nicknamed in Welsh *Gwrachod Llanddona*, 'Llanddona witches'.

Behind the sarcasm lies a very old local tale. It is said that a boat full of witches was once driven ashore by storms in Red Wharf Bay. The three strange, red-haired women spoke no Welsh, and came from some foreign land. Settling in Llanddona they became known as Lisa Blac, Bela Fawr and Siani Bwt; the latter was a dwarf with two thumbs on her left hand.

They became famous for spells and curses, and were much feared.

Their husbands, who were smugglers, were said to blind people with magic, buzzing flies. Several buildings here are associated with the legend. Could it be that some foreign shipwreck victims settled here, and that their strange ways made people afraid of them?

Due east of Llanddona, rough heath gives way to hilly farmland, descending towards Llan-faes. ▶60 Follow the signs to the partly fourteenth-century – perhaps twelfth-century – parish church of **Llaniestyn** (SH585796). This contains a fourteenth-century sandstone relief of Saint Iestyn, bearded and cloaked, carved by the same hand as the Pabo stone in Llanbabo church. ▶178

Llaniestyn Common / *Comin Llaniestyn* is designated a Local Nature Reserve. This is a landscape of heather, gorse, moor-grass and varieties of wild orchid. Reptiles include slow worms, adders and lizards; bird life includes curlews, linnets, stonechats and meadow pipits. Grazing of the Common has been abandoned in recent years, but there are plans to restore this area to its previous state.

A lane from Llanddona's southern end winds westwards through gorse and rocks to **Wern y Wylan**. There are dramatic views to Mynydd Llwydiarth and across the bay. Built by the Verney family during the first half of the twentieth century, the architecture and trim lawns of the Wern y Wylan homes contrast with the wild countryside surrounding them. Walk down the small right-hand junction where a signed footpath to the right leads into magical bluebell woods.

Llanddona has played its part in both aviation and automobile history. The story of the *Bamboo Bird* monoplane, which flew from Llanddona beach just before the outbreak of the First World War, is told in *Aviation pioneers* ▶111. In 1946, immediately after the Second World War, Maurice Wilks (1904-63), the Rover Company's technical director, was staying at Wern y Wylan. Needing a replacement for the Jeep used on his farm near Newborough, he sketched designs for a new all-purpose vehicle. The prototypes that followed were tested in the countryside around Llanddona and Newborough, and the first production Landrover was unveiled at the Amsterdam Motor Show of 1948. It is said that one prototype was abandoned in the Newborough dunes after becoming engulfed by sand and remains there, buried forever.

Another lane, long and straight with fine mountain views, leads southwest (from the top of the lane to Wern y Wylan) in the direction of Llansadwrn.

Llandegfan

9D

1½ml (2.5km)
NE of Menai
Bridge, turn
off A545 or
A5025

The parish of Llandegfan is bordered by that of Llansadwrn to the north, and by the Menai Strait to the south. It is traversed by **Afon Cadnant**, which flows from peaceful sheep pastures through steep wooded gorges to the Menai Strait. The river is crossed by a small stone bridge at the western end of the village, and by an old bridge and a concrete flyover at its mouth on the outskirts of Menai Bridge town, below Plas Cadnant (1803). Llandegfan has several small artificial lakes, including Llyn Jane, Llyn y Gors and Llyn Pen-y-Parc. A lane leaves the western end of the village for the A5025 Pentraeth road, passing a tall **standing stone** (SH554739).

Llandegfan parish churchyard

Hen Bentref Llandegfan ('Llandegfan old village') lies on a lane which runs eastwards from the medieval parish **Church of St Tegfan** (SH564744). This low building with its stone tower, shielded by yews and hollies, was restored and extensively rebuilt, on medieval foundations, in the nineteenth and early twentieth century. A fourteenth-century sandstone font, uncovered during restoration in 1902, is mounted outside the church behind a railing. The tower dates from 1811, its bell from 1666. Behind the altar, and to the right, is the effigy of Thomas Davies (1649), Messenger to King Charles I. The church also contains the tomb of the family of Thomas Williams (1737-1802), the developer of the Parys Mountain copper industry – see *The Copper King* ▶124 The remains of 'Twm Chwarae Teg' himself were brought here in 1812 after first being interred at Llanidan. The burial ground is extensive, and contains many impressive examples of eighteenth- and nineteenth-century slate headstone calligraphy. These inscriptions give an insight into the economic and social conditions, in former times, of this part of Anglesey. Along the 'top' road to Beaumaris, east of the church, is **Capel Barachia** (Welsh Presbyterian) with some equally fine headstone carvings. Further east, **Cytir Mawr** Local Nature Reserve (SH578750), of birch woodland and heathland, can be accessed from this road.

A parallel lane to the south links the **newer** parts of Llandegfan. This is a dormitory area for Bangor, with modern housing estates and a primary school set amongst the older buildings. The views south to Bangor and the mountains are among the best on the island.

The two lanes meet at the crossroads at the eastern end of the village, where the journey may continue to the top of Red Hill *(Allt Goch Fawr)*, via the 'Mile Road', or down another lane passing the 9-hole Baron Hill **golf club** ℭ 01248 810231, and through woods in a steep descent down **Allt Goch Fach** past the cemetery for the Parish of Beaumaris, with its chapel, to the residential estate of Cae Mair, Beaumaris. This is a vantage point for views over the town of Beaumaris to the Great Orme at Llandudno, and across the Strait to the mountains of Snowdonia.

The southern lane links with the A545 coast road to Beaumaris. This runs alongside the shore of the Menai Strait. Large houses, amongst the most expensive on Anglesey, border the Strait amidst palm trees and rhododendrons. There are splendid Victorian houses, some hidden from view in private grounds. A private road off the A545, its access now closed by tall, white-painted, cast iron gates, once led to Baron Hill, behind Beaumaris.

When Watkin Herbert Williams became Bishop of Bangor in 1899, he crossed the Strait to live in the old mansion of **Glyn Garth**. The building was demolished in 1964 to make way for a block of flats: the 'sixties architecture, designed by Percy Thomas & Partners, seems out of keeping with its surroundings when viewed from the Arfon shore. Glyn Garth harbour, the site of an eighteenth-century ferry landing, may be reached by a steep, narrow lane.

Bangor Pier at Garth

Alternatively leave your car in the **Gazelle Hotel** car park off the main road (patrons only) and walk down to the jetty through gardens. From the Gazelle there are views across the Strait to Bangor Pier (1896) at Garth, to the peaks of Snowdonia beyond Bangor, and along the Strait to the Menai Suspension Bridge. In the summertime this is a favourite haunt of yachting enthusiasts; the sailing club for university students at Bangor is based here.

Plas Rhianfa was built in 1849/51 for Sir John Hay Williams, whose main residence was Bodelwyddan on the mainland, to the design of a Liverpool architect, Charles Verelst (the architect of the former St Seiriol's Church in Holyhead; 1854, demolished 1992). Its fine slate roofs and its many turrets give the appearance of a small French château. After the marriage in 1868 of Margaret Maria (1844-1930), Sir John's eldest daughter, it became a residence of the

Plas Rhianfa Verney family who also owned Anglesey property at Wern y Wylan (Llanddona) and Rhoscolyn, together with English estates in Buckinghamshire and Derbyshire. Plas Rhianfa is now holiday accommodation.

Walking in the Air

Aled Jones (b1970) was brought up in Llandegfan, attending the local primary school and Ysgol David Hughes in Menai Bridge. He joined Bangor Cathedral Choir when he was nine, and in the 1980s became one of the world's best known boy sopranos.

His first album was *Diolch â Chân*, and between the ages of twelve and sixteen he recorded many others.

Walking in the Air, from the film adaptation of *The Snowman* by Raymond Briggs, reached number 3 in the pop charts (although his was not the version used on the soundtrack). Aled later studied at the Royal Academy of Music in London and the Bristol Old Vic Theatre School.

Today he is established as a

broadcaster, regularly presenting *Songs of Praise* on BBC television and radio programmes on Classic FM and Radio Wales.

As an adult his albums have included *Aled, The Christmas Prayer* and *New Horizons*. An autobiography was published in 2005.

Llan-faes *also known as* **Llanfaes**

10D
1½ml
(2.5km)
north of
Beaumaris
off B5109

A *llan* is a religious settlement of the early church in Wales, while a *maes* is any large open space or field: hence, Llan-faes. Before the English invasion, the site of today's tiny village and church was the principal settlement of southeast Anglesey, with a thriving port on Fryars Bay.

Llan-faes was one of the small royal courts *(llysoedd)* of medieval Gwynedd, similar to those at Aberffraw or Rhosyr, or at Abergwyngregyn on the mainland across the Strait from Llan-faes. The court was probably located at the site later known as Henllys ('old court'). Llywelyn Fawr (1173-1240), Prince of Wales, founded a famous Franciscan friary here. Franciscans played an important intellectual role in many of the power centres of medieval Europe.

In 1295 the victorious English king Edward I ordered the removal of all Welsh citizens from Llan-faes, so that work could begin on his new castle at Beaumaris without fear of insurgency or economic competition. They were evicted to Newborough. The Llan-faes friars were keen supporters of Owain Glyn Dŵr in the 1400s, and were attacked in retaliation when the English regained control of the island. The friary was finally closed down by Henry VIII in 1538, during his dissolution of the monasteries.

Nothing of medieval Llan-faes remains above ground. A house was built on the friary site by one of Henry VIII's courtiers. This was demolished and replaced by a large Victorian house in 1866.

In 1902 the **Kingsbridge / *Pont y Brenin*** army training camp was set up between Llan-faes and Llangoed by the Royal Engineers. At the beginning of the First World War, in 1914, its tents were replaced by huts which could accommodate up to 800 soldiers. The camp was closed in 1920. Part of the land of the former training camp now serves as a caravan and camping site.

During the Second World War, Saunders-Roe (the 'Saro' company) set up a factory on the old site of the friary for assembling and arming Catalina flying boats, and after the war for fitting out high-speed inshore craft, motor coaches and buses. Between 1948–51 about 300 of London Transport's double-decker buses were built here. Taken over by Cammell Laird, and later by Faun, the site eventually produced dustcarts and other public service vehicles. The factory is now abandoned (Faun having been relocated to Llangefni) and residential development is being considered.

A Catalina is launched at Fryars Bay, 1943

A former offshore lifeboat slipway (1911) on the eastern shore of Fryars Bay was taken out of service in 1991 and later dismantled.

The B5109 at Llan-faes offers superb panoramic views of the North Wales coast across to the Great Orme. At low tide the mud and shingle flats of Fryars Bay are of great interest to marine biologists, as they are to hungry grey herons, curlews, plovers and shelduck.

The turn-off to the village passes council housing, a community centre and a shop. In the old hamlet a whitewashed smithy and a group of old cottages cluster around the spired **Church of St Catherine** (SH605778). The preacher John Elias (1774-1841) is buried in the churchyard. A plaque in the church commemorates the Hampton family, owners of nearby **Henllys** from the middle of the fifteenth century, when William Hampton of Lancashire was appointed Deputy Constable of Beaumaris Castle.

Henllys, c1854

The old mansion was demolished to make way for the present building, which was completed in 1853.

After the Second World War Henllys was sold, and in 1951 Franciscan friars took over the house: having been evicted four centuries earlier from their old friary in Llan-faes, when the monasteries were dissolved by Henry VIII, the Order had returned to live once again in Llan-faes. In 1971 the building became a hotel, **Henllys Hall**, and since its futher renovation is now a self-catering tourist complex (for Holiday Property Bond members). The Hall is set in 120 acres (48ha) of parkland and woodland, including the 18-hole **Henllys golf course** ✆ 01248 811717. Back lanes filled with wildflowers in summer continue from the village to Llangoed, Llaniestyn and Llanddona.

Princess Siwan

Joan, known in Wales as *Siwan*, was the daughter of King John of England. In 1204 Llywelyn ap Iorwerth (Llywelyn Fawr, 'the Great') recognised John as his feudal overlord, in return for John accepting Llywelyn's conquests. It was agreed that Llywelyn would marry Siwan to seal the agreement. The marriage was made in 1205, and their son, Dafydd, was born two or three years later. Siwan gained widespread respect for her cool head and political skills. However she was rash enough to have an adulterous affair in 1230 with a lord from the Welsh Marches, William de Briouze. He was hanged and she was imprisoned.

Llywelyn and Siwan did make their peace and when Siwan died – in 1237, on the mainland at Abergwyngregyn – the Franciscan friary at Llan-faes was founded in her memory, for the monks to pray for her soul. Llywelyn himself died three years later at Aberconwy abbey. Siwan's coffin and its coverstone eventually ended up in the south porch of Beaumaris Church, where it may still be seen today. The coverstone is a splendidly carved slab, showing her crowned and wimpled with a coverlet of knotwork in the form of flowers and foliage.

Siwan was the subject of a play of the same name, one of the best known dramas in modern Welsh, written by Saunders Lewis in 1955.

Llanfair Mathafarn Eithaf — *see* **Benllech ▶46**

Llanfair Pwllgwyngyll *also known as* Llanfairpwll *and* Llanfair P G
Llanfairpwllgwyngyllgogerychwyrndrobwll-llantysiliogogogoch

8C

Turn off A55 at north end of Britannia Bridge junction 8A

The local name for this village is Llanfairpwll, which is certainly easier to pro-nounce than its complete name! The translation may be rendered as

***St Mary's Church in the hollow of white hazel near a rapid
whirlpool and the Church of Saint Tysilio near the red cave***

The longest name in Britain is really a nineteenth-century hoax which has been pulling in the tourists ever since it was coined.

The spired parish **Church of St Mary**, *Mair* (SH537712) may be found near the Britannia Bridge turn-off: turn south by the **Carreg Brân** hotel. The small church has a setting almost as romantic as its long appellation, despite the traffic thundering over the Britannia Bridge nearby. To the south lies a shin-ing bend of the Menai Strait. The present building dates from 1852, but medieval material from the site was re-used in its construction. Workers and their families lived close to the site of the bridge during its erection, and the churchyard contains a memorial (1847), surmounted by an obelisk, to eight-een members of this community who lost their lives, including Emma Greave, aged five. A further three men died during the reconstruction of the bridge in the 1970s, and they are remembered here too.

On the shoreline below the churchyard stands a statue of naval hero **Lord Horatio Nelson** (1758-1805). The monument was erected in 1873 above a slate plaque – *'England expects that every man will do his duty'* – as an aid to navigation by Lord Clarence Paget, himself an admiral and son of the first Marquess of Anglesey. His home was **Plas Llanfair**, which later passsed to other owners. A regular visitor to Plas Llanfair in the early twentieth century was Vivien Haigh-Wood, who later married the poet TS Eliot. In 1944 the building became a school for merchant navy cadets, the *Indefatigable*. This closed in 1995 and now is a Joint Services Mountain Training Centre, operated by the Ministry of Defence. To the west of Plas Llanfair is **Pwll Fanogl**, a former centre of local industry, the site of a jetty and an old flour mill. Writing slates for schools were made here from slate that was shipped across the Strait from Y Felinheli, milled flat and framed.

Horatio Nelson's statue

The first Marquess of Anglesey has his own memorial to the north of the church. The 112ft-high (34m) **Anglesey Column** (open every day © 01248 714393), made of Moelfre limestone, was erected in 1816-17 as a tribute to the hero of Waterloo. Its architect was Thomas Harrison of Chester (1740-1829), who also designed Holyhead's Admiralty Arch. The bronze figure of the Marquess in hussar uniform (by Matthew Noble, designer of Man-chester's Wellington memorial), was hoisted on top in 1860. The column's wooden central support is made from two masts, salvaged from sailing ships and mounted end to end. The Column's inscription reads:

The inhabitants of the counties of Anglesey and Caernarvon have erected this column in grateful commemoration of the distinguished military achievements of their countryman Henry William Marquess of Anglesey the leader of the British cavalry in Spain throughout the arduous campaign of 1807 and the second-in-command of the armies confederated against France at the memorable Battle of Waterloo on 18th of June 1815.

Climb 115 steps to view the mountains of Snowdonia: closer to your vantage point, look out for the Nelson statue on the shore of the Menai Strait.

Tolls to be taken at
LLANFAIR GATE
                                                s. d.
For every Horse, Mule, or other Cattle drawing any
Coach or other Carriage with springs the sum of.........4
For every Horse, mule or other Beast or Cattle drawing any
Waggon, Cart, or other such Carriage, not employed solely in
carrying or going empty to fetch Lime for manure the sum of......3
For every Horse, Mule, or other Beast or Cattle drawing
any Waggon, Cart, or other such Carriage, employed
solely in carrying or going empty to fetch Lime
for manure the sum of...........................1½
For every Horse, Mule, or Ass, laden or unladen,
and not drawing, the sum of.....................1
For every Drove of Oxen, Cows, or other neat Cattle
per score, the sum of...........................10
For every Drove of Calves, Sheep, Lambs or Pigs per
score, the sum of...............................5
For every Horse, Mule, or other Beast drawing any
Waggon, or Cart the Wheels being less than 3 inches in
breadth, or having Wheels with Tires fastened with
Nails projecting and not countersunk to pay double Toll.
A Ticket taken here clears Carnedd Du Bar.

The rock on which the Anglesey column stands, surrounded by bluebell woods, was used in ancient times as a hillfort: its name is **Craig y Ddinas**. This upper end of the village (Pentre Uchaf) is the original centre of settlement, as it existed before the coming of the railway.

Continuing eastward into the modern village centre, note the old A5 **Tollhouse** (c1823) at the A4080 junction. The A55 now by-passes the village – its buildings line the original route of the A5.

Thomas Telford's road across Anglesey

Thomas Telford (1757-1834) designed and built five octagonal tollhouses in Anglesey along the course of his A5 road – at Llanfair Pwllgwyngyll, Nant Gate, Gwalchmai, Caergeiliog and by the Stanley Embankment near Holyhead. The Holyhead road was the last surviving turnpike in Britain. A plaque remaining on the wall of the Llanfair Pwllgwyngyll tollhouse displays its charges. In 1895 – fifty years after the Rebecca Rioters, disguised as women, had won their victory over the turnpikes of south-west Wales – Telford's road was freed from toll. The increase in railway traffic had made it no longer worthwhile to tax road users and upkeep of the road was transferred from the Turnpike Commissioners to the county council.

Iron gates, patterned like the rays of the sun, can be seen at the mainland end of the Menai Suspension Bridge, and elsewhere along the A5. They were designed by the attentive Telford as part of his overall scheme.

Milestones along the A5 were made from stone quarried at Red Wharf Bay. Recessed cast iron plates show the distance from Holyhead and two other key locations: the plates were painted black, with white text.

Telford's milestones are 'listed' structures and a conservation and restoration project has replaced, with replicas, milestones that had become damaged or lost during two hundred years of the road's life.

The Gwalchmai tollhouse

Jam and 'Jerusalem'

Llanfair Pwllgwyngyll saw the first ever meeting of the **Women's Institute** in Britain, in 1915.

This movement had begun in the Canadian town of Stoney Creek, Ontario, in 1897. In the First World War, with so many farm labourers away fighting, it was realised that women could play a more important part in the rural economy, especially by learning how to produce and preserve foods. The Agricultural Organisation Society invited Canadian WI member Margaret Watt (1868-1948) to recruit members in Britain, and the Llanfairpwll branch was her first success. The local WI received the enthusiastic support of Colonel Henry Stapleton-Cotton of Llanedwen, who was a passionate local campaigner for rural self-sufficency. The President was Mrs Stapleton-Cotton. During the Institute's early years in Llanfair Pwllgwyngyll, meetings were held in the summerhouse of Graig (off Lôn Graig), belonging to Mrs W E Jones, the Vice-President and Treasurer. After 1921 the branch met in a corrugated iron hut, which still stands next to the old Tollhouse on the main road.

Today the WI, anxious to move forward from its tradition of making jam and singing the hymn *Jerusalem*, has about 200,000 members in England, Wales, Man and the Channel Islands, and an all-Wales office in Cardiff. It also has links with over eight million women in sixty countries around the world. *Merched y Wawr*, a Welsh-speaking breakaway movement, was started near Bala in 1967.

There are still WI branches throughout Anglesey. Two have their own premises: the Llaneilian branch meets in its hall, and the 1920s metal hut at Llanfair Pwllgwyngyll continues to serve its members.

*The story of the founding of the Women's Institute in Anglesey is told in the book **A Grain of Mustard Seed** by Constance Davies (1954)*

Thirty-eight members of Britain's first Women's Institute at the 'Graig' summerhouse

> *"*T*HE FIRST MEETING to launch the Women's Institute was held on September 25th. ... Mrs Watt spoke on Fruit and Vegetable preserving. There were numerous exhibits. Miss A Thomas gave a few selections on the harp. Three wounded soldiers were the guests of the afternoon. 'Land of my Fathers' and 'God Save the King' were sung. Mrs Cotton and Mrs W E Jones gave the tea."*
>
> F W Wilson, Hon. Sec.

— Minutes of the meeting, 25th September 1915

The **railway station** (1848), on the main line to Holyhead, is at the centre of the modern village. Giant platform tickets with the long name make popular souvenirs. A **Tourist Information Centre** is sited at the entrance to the **James Pringle Weavers** store, part of the Edinburgh Woollen Mills group. The store is designed in the style of a railway station and stocks knitwear, blankets, clothes and Welsh crafts. It also has a coffee-shop. Two 15" gauge Atlantic Class steam locomotives, built in Wales in the 1920s, are on display here: *Railway Queen*

The entrance to James Pringle Weavers

and *Michael* are on loan from the Rhyl Steam Preservation Society. Many coachloads of tourists stop off at Llanfair Pwllgwyngyll, despite the fact that the village itself offers little in the way of standard tourist attractions.

A passion for Welsh

John Morris-Jones was born at Trefor on Anglesey in 1864, but was brought up at Llanfair Pwllgwyngyll and lived there as an adult. His home was Tŷ Coch (opposite the War Memorial clock). Educated at Christ's College, Brecon, John went on to Jesus College, Oxford, where he studied mathematics. However his true interest lay in Welsh language and literature, and he became Professor of

Welsh at the University of Wales in Bangor. He published major works on Welsh grammar and spelling throughout his life; indeed, he helped to shape Welsh as a modern language. John Morris-Jones was an inspired interpreter of medieval Welsh verse and its traditional forms and metres. He was a poet himself, in the romantic mould, and translated the poetry of Heinrich Heine and Omar Khayaam into Welsh.

Sir John died in 1929.

Llangoed

10E
2⅓ml (4km) north of Beaumaris on B5109

Llangoed is the largest village to the east of Beaumaris. In the south of the village is a housing estate and modern **primary school**. Here too are playing fields. Each June Llangoed hosts a **Rugby 'sevens'** tournament with teams from all over Britain and some from overseas. Lining the main street are the **Jerusalem Baptist Chapel** (1862), a general store, a post office and terraced cottages. The street descends steeply to a low stone bridge over a brook, **Afon Lleiniog**. This skirts a public house, **Tafarn y Rhyd**, and the large **Village Hall**. The car park at the bottom of the hill is the starting point for several signed walks and a path to the coast – see *Aberlleiniog* ▶68

Llangoed Common / *Comin Llangoed* borders Afon Lleiniog between Tafarn y Rhyd and Glanrafon and is crossed by a footpath. An ancient hut circle suggests that this was the earliest part of the village to be settled. The area has become increasingly wooded since the reduction of grazing in the last fifty years and has ponds, scrub and damp meadow. Along with the lower reaches of the Lleiniog, this is designated a Local Nature Reserve and is being managed for wildlife conservation.

A northerly lane leads past the former primary school (1896) to the small stone-built parish **Church of St Cawrdaf**; the north transept dates from c1612, whilst the remainder was rebuilt in 1881. A baptismal font is designed for total immersion. Small cottages make up Park Terrace, the steep hill which climbs the limestone ridge behind the church. Here are fine views south to the mountains and also **Capel Mawr Tŷ Rhys**, a Calvinistic Methodist Chapel (founded in 1794, later rebuilt and renovated). Three lanes provide routes from Llangoed eastwards to Penmon. ▶86 The top lane along the ridge offers glorious views to the north, east and south as the coastlines converge. In the summer this route is the haunt of swallows and bats.

The Massey sisters

Edith (1863-1946) and **Gwenddolen Massey** (1864-1960) were sisters, members of a family which owned Moston Hall in Cheshire and built a mansion called Cornelyn on the site of Llangoed's old tithe barn in 1861.

Throughout their lives the sisters enjoyed riding and hunting and exploring the countryside. They were especially interested in gathering and painting flowers. Wild orchids, snowdrops, wild cherry blossom and bluebells are all lovingly recorded and labelled in English, Latin and Welsh. Fortunately more than five hundred of their fine botanical paintings have survived, to be purchased by the local authority in 1982. The paintings are now at Oriel Ynys Môn near Llangefni.

Neither sister married and they were buried in the churchyard at Penmon.

Bramble / Mwyaren ddu

"Variety of the
"Common Bramble".—
"Rubus fruticosus".—

Llangoed is surrounded by productive farmland, amidst which stand several large houses. **Haulfre** was built in the 1850s by a retired Indian Army doctor, Robert Briscoe Owen. Later owners, the Chadwicks, had been made wealthy through cotton weaving in Lancashire. Haulfre is now a residential home for the elderly, its outbuildings used as workshops and a plant nursery.

Haulfre Stables / *Stablau Haulfre* (open by appointment ✆ 01248 724444) were renovated in 1987 to house an equestrian collection. It affords some idea of how the Chadwicks and the hunting, shooting and landowning class lived a hundred years ago, before the coming of the motor car. Signs also lead to **Plas Bodfa** (all year ✆ 01248 490100), the *Elizabeth Bradley* tapestries centre. Finished work is on display throughout the Plas, and tea and cakes are served in the gardens. There are animals for children to feed and admire.

Turn northwest from Llangoed main street before the bridge to reach the settlement of **Glanrafon** (or Glan-yr-afon). This lies below the limestone ridge of **Mariandyrys** (SH604809), where gorse and heather grow by a disused quarry, the haunt of jackdaws. Grassland flowers include fragrant orchid and columbine. This is a 15-acre (6ha) nature reserve of the North Wales Wildlife Trust. At the centre of Glanrafon small houses cluster around grassy common land. The lane climbs past the small cottages of Marian Terrace and continues westwards towards Llanddona; stop by a tiny chapel-schoolroom, **Ysgoldy Llanfihangel** (1887) for a view through the pines to Puffin Island and the Great Orme.

Fedw Fawr
White Beach

To the northeast of Glanrafon, beneath the converted windmill at Tros y Marian, a narrow lane leads northwards to National Trust land around **Fedw Fawr**, which is grazed by ponies. Take an exhilarating walk along clifftops, looking either for seabirds below or birds of the heathland behind you, or climb down steep steps through ramsons (wood garlic) to the white pebble cove, known in English as **White Beach**. Swimming is best at high tide. The water is generally cold but clear, although algal blooms have been known in warm summers.

Fedw Fawr was formerly one in a chain of limestone quarrying sites, extending from Dinmor round to Llanddona. The whole of this coast is now designated as a Site of Special Scientific Interest (SSSI).

Aberlleiniog

From Llangoed's bridge, follow the eastward course of the Afon Lleiniog by a footpath. This ends by a hazel grove and a long water-meadow which was once an arm of the sea. The woods to the left conceal **Aberlleiniog Castle / Castell Aberlleiniog** (SH616793), presently undergoing archaeological excavation, conservation and restoration. Public access is planned. This fortification is two centuries older than Beaumaris, being raised by Norman raiders during their incursions into North Wales between 1088 and 1098. The original fortification consisted of a high earthen mound (or 'motte') surmounted by a bailey or stronghold made of timber. This was the prototype of European castle design, and at this time was still used by the Normans during military campaigns of this type. For their more permanent castles the Normans were already building great keeps of stone, but the low, square stone keep visible at Aberlleiniog Castle today was erected at a later date. Aberlleiniog was last used as a fort in the 1640s, during the Civil War.

Keeping the Wolf from the door

The castle builder of **Aberlleiniog** was the detested figure of Hugh d'Avranches, Earl of Chester, a fat man known as Lupus, 'the wolf'. His fellow invader was Hugh de Montgomery, Earl of Shrewsbury. One of their chief opponents was Gruffudd ap Cynan, king of Gwynedd (1055-1137).

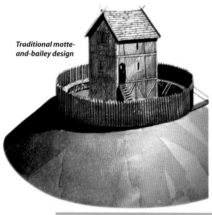

Traditional motte-and-bailey design

Gruffudd was half Viking, his mother being Ragnell or Ragnhildr, daughter of the Norse ruler of Dublin. Gruffudd spent his youth and many years of exile in Ireland. He had to fight to reestablish the authority of his line in Gwynedd and also to deal with raids by both Vikings and Normans. In 1094 he attacked and burned Aberlleiniog Castle.

In May 1098 the Normans were back at Aberlleiniog but they got more than they bargained for. The Norse king Magnus 'Barefoot' sailed in from his base on the Isle of Man, and Hugh of Shrewsbury died with an arrow, or javelin, in his right eye in a fierce battle which was described in the poetry and chronicles of the day. Magnus then left the island.

By the end of his reign, Gruffudd ap Cynan was undisputed ruler of Gwynedd. He was buried beside the altar in Bangor cathedral.

Woodland, riverine and marine habitats meet around the Lleiniog; at different times and seasons one may see waterfowl, waders, crows, barn owls, swallows and bats. The mouth of the Lleiniog was excavated and diverted in the 1980s to minimise flooding, but this remains quite common. There is a picnic site and car park beside the reed beds. Banks of boulder clay have been heavily eroded by winter storms.

The road southwest passes the mast of the BBC Penmon Transmitting Station which opened in 1937 and now transmits Radio Wales on the medium wave (882Khz). Continuing along the road returns you to the crossroads at the southern end of Llangoed village.

Llaniestyn — *see* **Llanddona** ▶56

Llansadwrn

9D
3ml (4.5km)
west of
Beaumaris
on B5109

Between Menai Bridge and Pentraeth two lanes lead eastwards to Llansadwrn. To the west of the A5025 are the Iron Age earthworks of **Bryn Eryr**. Dating back to perhaps 200BC, they mark a farming settlement which remained occupied during the Roman era. The tree-lined southern lane leads east off the A5025, passsing two large houses, **Treffos** (now a private school) and **Gadlys** (now converted into separate dwellings). The attractively glazed building opposite the gate to the parish church is a **church room**, built in 1894 by the McCorquodale family of Gadlys.

Outside the church, a tall stone cross designed by Harold Hughes, decorated with snakes writhing in a Celtic knotwork pattern, commemorates Hugh Stewart McCorquodale:

> … youngest son of George McCorquodale of Gadlys, who at the call of duty volunteered for active service in South Africa and fell gallantly fighting on Spion Kop Natal on 24 January 1900 and was buried on the field of battle.

The Saturninus stone

The patron saint of the **parish church**, Sadwrn 'the knight', was a brother of Saint Illtud; he died here in about AD520. In 1742, part of an early Christian gravestone was found under the churchyard and is now set in the wall of the chancel. Its inscription records the burial of the 'blessed Saturninus' and his 'saintly wife'.

The church was repeatedly 'restored' in the nineteenth century. One grave in the yard has an unusual headstone: a glacial boulder commemorates the Scottish geologist Sir Andrew Crombie Ramsay (1814-91), Director General of the Geological Survey and pioneer of the study of the rocks of North Wales. Some of his most important research was on glaciation, explaining how certain mountain valleys and lakes were formed by the ice that once flowed through them. Sir Andrew was a son-in-law of James and Frances Williams of Llanfair-yng-Nghornwy. ▶120 Mary Louisa (1825-1917), his wife, is also remembered on the memorial. Her grandfather was the Reverend John Williams, of nearby Treffos.

The lane continues through farmland, past an elaborately enlarged building that seems at odds with the subdued architecture of the Anglesey countryside, to the centre of the village, a housing estate. In front of the old primary school, now the **community centre**, a slate plaque commemorates Thomas Williams, the Parys Mountain industrialist, who was born in Llansadwrn in 1737– see *The Copper King* ▶124

Hendrefor burial chamber, Llansadwrn

The collapsed stones of the **Hendrefor** burial chamber (SH551773), perhaps 6,000 years old, may be seen from the B5109 near to the Llanddona turning. The two groups of fallen stones may be the remains of a single long chamber, or of two separate chambers. This site has never been excavated.

The north of the village is sheep pasture, broken by gorse and pinewoods around the road to Llanddona. Here is **Hafoty** (SH563783), a hall-house perhaps dating from the fourteenth century. This is the oldest surviving domestic building on the island, sturdy, whitewashed and with a slate roof. It appears that the walls were originally of wattle or mud, and that they were gradually infilled with stone during the fifteenth century. A two-storey west wing was added in the period 1509-53. There is a sixteenth-century fireplace with a decorated stone surround. Its ornately lettered Latin inscription reads: *Si Deus nobiscum quis contra nos* (*'If God is with us, who can be against us?'*).

Hafoty, Llansadwrn

Five hundred years ago, Hafoty belonged to the Norris family, who came from northwest England. It seems that God was not on the side of Henry Norris, Constable of Beaumaris Castle, who in 1536 was executed for involvement in the fall of Ann Boleyn. Ever since, the house has been in the possession of the Bulkeley family (then of Hen Blas, Beaumaris, and later to become the Williams-Bulkeleys of Baron Hill, Beaumaris). The dilapidated building was restored, at great expense, during 1999-2000 and is in the care of Cadw. It is hoped that Hafoty will be opened to the public, seasonally and on certain days of the week.

Lligwy (*properly known as* **Llugwy**)

7F
1mile (2km) NE of Llanallgo off A5025

The long, sandy beach of **Traeth Lligwy** is ideal for swimming and family picnics. Afon Lligwy drains the slopes of Mynydd Bodafon and the heathland of Penrhos Lligwy, entering the sea at the beach. Remains of fishing weirs may be seen here. The north end of the beach is of old red sandstone, while the south end is of limestone, which was once quarried here. There are car

parks at each end of the beach and caravan and camp sites. Access is from Moelfre, Llanallgo or Brynrefail. Coastal footpaths lead to another sandy beach, **Traeth yr Ora**, and to the peaceful **Dulas estuary**. ▶113 Look for seals offshore. The lane from Llanallgo passes some of the most fascinating of the island's archaeological sites. Lligwy **burial chamber** (SH501861) dates back to the late Neolithic period, perhaps 5,000 years ago. It has a massive, low capstone. An artist's

Traeth yr Ora

recreation of its construction appears on page 21. Archaeological excavation in 1909 revealed the remains of thirty burials, and shards of pottery.

Din Lligwy (SH496862) is a ruined first- and second-century AD settlement which fires the imagination. Walk westwards across the fields and through a wood to a small limestone plateau overlooking green fields, the breakers of the bay and (immediately to the south) Plas Lligwy. The archaeological site may have been the home of a Celtic chieftain during the Roman occupation of the island, commanding the surrounding farmland which provided crops and pasture. Perhaps the estate sold grain or hides to the Romans.

Brian Byron

Brian Byron

The well-preserved, thick outer walls are built of limestone and rubble, with a gateway to the east. The buildings within include some with circular walls about six feet (2m) high. These would have been thatched dwellings. The settlement's rectangular foundations once supported farm buildings and workshops used for smelting and working iron. Roman coins, a silver ingot, glassware and pottery were unearthed in one hut. The occupation of Din Ligwy continued into the fourth century.

Return to the road via **Hen Gapel Lligwy**, a ruined chapel within a circular enclosure. Its foundations are twelfth-century and the walls (with a bellcote on the west wall) are mostly fourteenth-century. A short flight of steps leads down to a small vault underneath the sixteenth-century south chapel. A stone slab on the floor may have once been part of a churchyard cross. The chapel stands alone in open fields. It is defined as a 'chapel of ease', which means that it was subsidiary to a larger church. However its history remains unclear.

Marian-glas — *see* **Traeth Bychan** ▶97

Menai Bridge town / *Porthaethwy*

9C

On the island, across the Menai Suspension Bridge

The English name for this small town dates from the opening of the Suspension Bridge in 1826. ▶79 Before then, it was known only as *Porthaethwy*, which remains the name for the town in Welsh. The word *Aethwy* is very ancient, deriving from a Celtic tribal name. In everyday Welsh the name of the town is often abbreviated to *y Borth* ('the port').

This was always a crossing point of the Menai Strait, with ferries taking across people, livestock, horses and even carriages. Each year thousands of cattle would be swum across the Strait from the rocky slab known as Ynys Moch ('pig island'), which now supports the Anglesey tower of the bridge.

The Menai Bridge town waterfront

Perhaps the best view of the town is from the mainland shore, where you see the port as returning sailors would once have seen it in the nineteenth century: a village rising from the waterfront, backed by the larger houses of the shipowners. Today, one may enter the town by the road leading down from the roundabout at the end of the Menai Suspension Bridge. The road due north from the first roundabout, **Ffordd Mona**, passes the **Anglesey Arms** (1830). Across the road on a grassy hillock is **St Mary's Church** (designed by Henry Kennedy, 1858). One of Thomas Telford's A5 milestones ('Holyhead 22 miles') stands by the church gate. The stone building just below the church is the former **National School** which opened in 1854. Until the completion of St Mary's four years later, English-language services were conducted here on Sunday afternoons, morning worship in Welsh continuing at the small island church of St Tysilio. Exhibitions about the Menai and Britannia bridges have been held in the old school. The site of the former smithfield, where livestock sales were once held weekly, with special sales of Welsh black cattle in April and October, is now occupied by a Co-op supermarket.

Northwards from the second roundabout, off **Ffordd Pentraeth**, lie extensive housing estates, **Ysgol y Borth** primary school, and a large secondary school, **Ysgol David Hughes**, which draws its pupils from the south and east of the island. The school is named after a local man, whose bequest in 1603 funded the school's foundation in Beaumaris, where the original schoolhouse still stands. David Hughes became steward of the Woodrising estate in Norfolk and with his savings purchased a number of farms on his native island. The income from these paid for the school and almshouses in Beaumaris. The school, by now a comprehensive, moved to its present site in 1962. **Menai Bridge Cricket Club**'s beautifully set playing field, overlooking Snowdonia, is reached along the Tyn-y-caeau lane immediately to the left of the entrance to David Hughes School.

An eastern turn from the first roundabout over the bridge takes one past the **Bridge Inn / Tafarn y Bont** and the **English Presbyterian** Church (built by Menai Bridge architect R G Thomas in 1888) whose spire looks rather like the minaret of a Turkish mosque. The **Victoria Hotel** (the 'Vic', 1852, with a recently built wing in matching stone) has gardens at the rear which look towards the Strait. In addition to hosting wedding receptions, every now and then the hotel provides a venue for visiting musicians from Wales and around the world, playing anything from delta blues to Congolese soukous.

Roads converge at a busy junction called **Uxbridge Square** / *y Sgwar*, in front of the **Bulkeley Arms**. From here **Dale Street** / *Lôn Cilbedlam* returns to Ffordd Mona, passing a ruined Baptist chapel on the left (Moreia, 1884), and, across the road, a row of fake shop facades, a location set for the Welsh television series *Rownd a Rownd*. Here too is the Catholic church and hall of **St Anne** *(Santes Ann)*, completed in 1956. The bus stands and **library** are on **Wood Street** / *Ffordd y Ffair*.

Ffair y Borth – The Menai Bridge Fair

In 1691 a pony fair, later a general livestock fair, was moved to the town from the mainland shore near the present-day Antelope Inn, so that Anglesey farmers did not have to risk their profits by swimming their beasts across the Strait before the sale. *Ffair y Borth*, held at the time of the annual sale, became famous in Victorian times for its merrymaking, wrestling matches and freak shows. Cattle and horses are no longer sold, but a street market and funfair, complete with fortune-tellers, roundabouts and stomach-wrenching rides still takes over the town at the end of October each year and is as popular as ever.

The fair occupies the two main car parks for several days, but on 24th October the streets are closed for the main day of the fair. *(If 24th October is a Sunday, the event is moved to the day before – Saturday.)*

The centre of Menai Bridge contains cafés, small shops and offices, banks and Victorian houses. Several antique or bric-a-brac shops and a delicatessen have set up in recent years and there are also butchers and bakers and a proper hardware store, Evans Bros, of the sort which is increasingly rare. Large car parks are sited on either side of the main thoroughfare, but street parking often causes congestion.

Water Street / *Stryd y Paced* runs south from Uxbridge Square towards the Menai Strait. Passing the **War Memorial Community Centre** / *Canolfan Goffa Gymdeithasol*, and the **Auckland Arms** one comes to the ever popular **Liverpool Arms**. A promenade leads from the inlet of **Porth Daniel** through the **pier gatehouse** (a millennium restoration project by the Menai Bridge Civic Society) to the waterfront. The promenade continues eastwards beneath public gardens to **St George's Pier**. In the Victorian period, paddle-steamers from Llandudno and Liverpool, bringing the first day-trippers, moored at this pier. The voyage from Liverpool to Menai Bridge in the early nineteenth century took five to six hours. The pier was rebuilt in 1904 and was declared open by David Lloyd George, Liberal MP for Caernarfon and later Britain's Prime Minister during the First World War. A modern sloping walkway leads down from the end of the shortened pier to the berth of a marine research vessel, the *Prince Madog* (named after the Welsh prince Madog ab Owain Gwynedd, who is claimed in Wales as the discoverer of America in about 1169). This ship is a business-like trawler operated by the University's **School of Ocean Sciences**, which is based around **Askew Street** / *Ffordd y Coleg*. The school is one of the leading marine study centres in

Europe. St George's Pier can also be approached along **St George's Road / Ffordd Cynan**, passing the pier gardens and the **Mostyn Arms**.

Until the Menai Suspension Bridge was completed in 1826 the quayside in front of the Liverpool Arms had been the landing point of a ferry. From 1828 to 2005 a busy timber yard dominated this part of Water Street. It was originally owned by the Davies family of Treborth, whose ships exported slates and carried emigrants far away from the poverty of Wales; timber provided ballast for the return voyages. In the mid-1860s it changed ownership and traded as William Roberts & Company. The land vacated by the yard's relocation at Four Crosses is being developed as a residential area.

The wharf built by the Davies family to the east of the slipway at **Porth y Wrach** is known as the **Prince's Pier / Pier y Dywysog**. In addition to timber, the Davies fleet regularly carried coal from South Wales to San Francisco, with grain from North America or guano from South America as the return cargo. Current plans are for the former warehouse on this pier to be turned into a permanent heritage and educational centre, where visitors can learn about the town and the bridges. To the west of Porth y Wrach is the oldest part of town,

Capel Mawr

a fascinating mixture of working and residential buildings of many different periods. Here is the impressive **Capel Mawr** (1838) of the Presbyterians.

Roads lead back past the **Tabernacl** chapel to the eastern end of town and **Ffordd Cadnant**.

William Mathias

The composer, pianist and teacher **William Mathias** (1934-92) was born at Whitland / *Hendy-gwyn* in South Wales and studied music at the University of Wales, Aberystwyth. From 1959 he was a lecturer at the University of Wales, Bangor, and from 1969 until his retirement in 1987 was head of its School of Music / *Ysgol Cerddoriaeth*. Professor Mathias lived in Menai Bridge.

Early works such as the *First String Quartet* (1967), later choral works such as *World's Fire* (1989, based on the poems of Gerard Manley Hopkins) and an anthem for the royal wedding of 1981 (*Let the people praise thee, O God*), brought the composer widespread acclaim.

The Grove Dictionary of Music (in an entry by Geraint Lewis) records that:

"Mathias is regarded as one of the most significant Welsh composers of the twentieth century and one of the few to establish an international reputation. He enjoyed early success with instrumental and orchestral music, but eventually composed in virtually all musical genres. His later popularity in the fields of choral and particularly church music gave him a high profile. He often stressed that he did not regard his church music as peripheral in any way to his main output, observing no distinction between the sacred and the secular and viewing his vocation very much in line with the medieval Welsh 'praise' poets."

Walk westwards underneath the Suspension Bridge for a stunning view of stonework, towering perspectives and swirling water. Continue up the lane past the small wood, in which a modern stone circle commemorates the Anglesey Eisteddfod of 1965. Then turn off down the path to the shore, a popular bathing spot in Victorian times, and follow the curving **promenade**, built in 1914-16 by Belgian refugees (and re-built in 1965). The steep landward bank was originally known as **Craig y Borth**. In 1814 it was planted with trees by the Earl of Uxbridge – who became the first Marquess of Anglesey, see *Cool in the face of fire* ▶215 – but it is now known as **Coed Cyrnol** ('Colonel's Wood') after a Colonel Sandys who lived nearby. It was opened to public access in 1951 by Lady Megan Lloyd George, who, having represented the island at Westminster for 22 years, lost her parliamentary seat as a Liberal MP in the general election held that year. Today it is a Local Nature Reserve, a lovely place for a stroll amidst Scots pine and oak. A hoard of Roman coins was discovered here in 1978. Coed Cyrnol can also be reached from the car park off Ffordd Mona, between the two roundabouts.

Ynys Tysilio,
Church
Island

The promenade and the footpath which leads down through Coed Cyrnol meet at a causeway across to **Church Island / Ynys Tysilio**. This rocky isle lies below the town's rugby grounds, past the tidal reach of Llyn y Felin: the pool's name indicates that it was once the site of a tidal mill. The island offers fine views of both bridges. Swans, ducks, herons and smaller wading birds may be seen on the mud flats and the whirling currents of the Strait often seem bright and glassy. The tiny, peaceful **Church of St Tysilio** (SH552717) dates from the fourteenth century. The saint settled here in the seventh century, the son of a prince of Powys. It was probably on Church Island that English Archbishop Baldwin preached the Crusade in 1188. His companion, Gerald of Wales, records an early example of conscientious objection. None of the Welsh knights present would volunteer to fight in the Holy Land. They were duly afflicted and punished by God – or so Gerald assures the reader.

One path circles the churchyard through yew trees and Victorian statuary, while another climbs to a war memorial cross. The gravestones, in Welsh or English, tell their own story of Menai Bridge town: here lie seafarers, young men killed in wars, daughters and wives, a litany of house and street names and dates. Among them is the grave of Albert Evans-Jones (1895-1970), a Welsh-language poet whose bardic name was Cynan, and a leading figure in the modern history of the national *eisteddfod*. His best known verse, written in Salonika during the First World War, imagines a goldfinch flying back across southern Anglesey: *Anfon y Nico* ▶202

On **Ffordd Cadnant**, the Beaumaris road leading eastwards from Menai Bridge town, there is the long-established **Tegfryn Gallery / Oriel Tegfryn** which exhibits and sells the work of local artists. On the eastern edge of town the river Cadnant meets the Menai Strait. Its waters run through a steep, wooded valley over a series of weirs. They pass beneath the old stone bridge and a modern concrete flyover. A woollen mill was established here in the 1840s, powered by a water-driven wheel. A steam engine was used when there was insufficient water. An ancient ferry route, the 'Bishop's Crossing', used the Cadnant creek as its Anglesey landing point for six hundred years.

The nearby shore of the Menai Strait is dotted with small, wooded islands: **Ynys Faelog**, **Ynys Gaint**, **Ynys Castell** and **Ynys y Big**. The stretch of water around Menai Bridge town is a popular mooring for yachts and is also a centre for angling.

Menai Strait / *Afon Menai*

19ml (30km) from Puffin Island (Ynys Seiriol) to Abermenai — *also known as in English as* **The Straits** *and in Welsh as* **Y Fenai**

The Menai Strait features in both the eastern and southern sections of this guide. It may look like a large river, with its wooded banks and meanders (the Welsh name means the 'River Menai'), but this is of course a strip of the Irish Sea, which experiences a turbulent exchange of currents as the tides affect it from both east and west. It reaches a depth of more than 65ft (20m) at its westernmost point off Abermenai. Most of the Strait is about half as deep, but another deep stretch lies between Britannia Bridge and Plas Newydd, off **Pwll Fanogl** (possibly the 'fennel pool', although 'frog infested pool' – from *Pwll Llyffanog* – has also been suggested). Here there is a fourteenth or fifteenth century wreck of a clinker-built vessel that had been carrying roofing slates quarried at Llanberis. The timbers of the vessel survive beneath its heavy cargo, and the archaeological site is officially protected.

The rapid tidal currents, sheltered from ocean waves, create a very unusual marine environment. Coupled with the variety of rocks (hard schists, limestone boulder fields, mud, gravel and sand) it supports a diversity of marine life virtually unrivalled in Britain. The Menai Strait provides a saltwater habitat for perhaps over 1,000 species of marine life. It is home to bass, whiting, tope, eels and plaice as well as rare forms of sea anemone and sponge, to hermit crabs, velvet swimming crabs, sea slugs, scorpion fish and gobies. The Strait is designated a special area of conservation. Peaceful enough on a mild summer's day, the waters of the Strait can be stormy in winter, and have many treacherous sections, such as the whirling **Swellies** / *Pwll Ceris* – a 'tidal gate', through which large vessels only pass safely at slack tide.

The end of HMS Conway, 1953

During the Second World War the magnificent old sail-training vessel *HMS Conway* (formerly the 92-gun battleship *HMS Nile*) was moved to the safety of the Strait to escape the bombing of Liverpool Docks. From 1941 she occupied the Glyn Garth moorings opposite Bangor Pier, the former location of another training vessel, the *Clio. HMS Conway* was later taken to moorings off Plas Newydd, and the Merchant Navy training school, to whom she had been the flagship since 1876, set up a shore base in its grounds ▶216. In April 1953, whilst being towed by tugs to Birkenhead for a re-fit, *HMS Conway* came to grief on rocks known as the Platters, close to the mainland end of the suspension bridge. Her back was broken by the falling tide and in 1956 the hulk burned to the waterline whilst being dismantled.

The crossing of the Strait in the days before the bridges was often hazardous, involving the traverse of sandbanks on foot and the use of small ferry boats at various points along the shore. In 1664, 79 passengers died when the Abermenai ferry capsized off Newborough. She had drifted away from the dock into deep water whilst the ferryman argued with a passenger about the penny fare. Ferries continued to be used until the 1950s.

"*IN COMMON with other straits which separate any island from the continent, or from a larger island, this area of the sea exhibits peculiarities in its tide, which, twice in every twelve hours, runs in different directions, and frequently with great velocity. The rise at ordinary spring-tides is about twenty-two feet, sometimes as much as thirty feet; and being in the vicinity of the Snowdon range of mountains, it is subject to violent gusts of wind, from which liability, and from the ferry passage being frequently made in the night, this part of the journey was rendered a disagreeable object of anticipation, and was sometimes really dangerous.*"

— THOMAS TELFORD, *The Life of Thomas Telford* (1838)

Larger vessels may still be seen in the Strait. In Victorian times this was a major thoroughfare for shipping. The bridges built over the Menai Strait – the suspension bridge ▶79 and the Britannia tubular bridge ▶49 – had to be high enough to allow tall-masted ships to sail beneath. By the 1870s over 700 vessels were registered at Menai ports.

Ynys Gorad Goch in the Menai Strait

There are a number of small islands in the Strait. The most prominent, lying between the two bridges, is **Ynys Gorad Goch** ('island of the red weir'), with its private residence. In Victorian times the family living here was operating the island as a commercial fishery. Great quantities of herrings were trapped in its stone-built weirs. A 'smoke tower' on the island's highest ground was used to cure the fish.

The Menai shore between the two bridges is bordered by a National Trust footpath, offering fine views of the Strait and Ynys Gorad Goch. It may be accessed from the layby to the east of Britannia Bridge.

Beaumaris ▶38 and **Menai Bridge** ▶72 are the chief towns on the Anglesey shore. Over the ages, the natural barrier of the Strait resulted in the **main-land shore** being more populated. At its western end is **Caernarfon**, with its great castle. **Plas Menai**, opposite the Anglesey parish of Llanidan, is a national centre for watersports. **Y Felinheli** (once known as Port Dinorwic) is a former slate port for the quarries of Llanberis. East of the bridges lies the university and cathedral city of **Bangor**, with its restored Victorian pier at **Garth**. Bangor's **Port Penrhyn**, originally another slate harbour serving Bethesda, is today the largest working port on the Strait.

Regattas are held each year at the end of July and the beginnning of August. They are based at Beaumaris, Bangor, Glyn Garth, Menai Bridge, Y Felinheli and Caernarfon, and include races through the Strait and around the island. Participants include the Royal Anglesey Yacht Club, the Royal Welsh, the Royal Dee, and sailing clubs from Y Felinheli, Caernarfon, Conwy and Red Wharf Bay.

A charity **raft race** is also held on the Whit Bank Holiday at the end of May, between Felinheli and Menai Bridge: all kinds of outlandish, home-made craft compete.

Yachts of the West Kirby Star class take part in a regatta

Menai Suspension Bridge / *Pont Grog Menai*

9C
*Crosses the
Menai Strait
1ml (2km)
west of
Bangor*

The Menai Suspension Bridge was the world's first large iron suspension bridge. At its mainland end, plaques proclaim its status as an 'International Civil Engineering Landmark'. The classic design was submitted in 1818 by Scottish engineering genius Thomas Telford (1757-1834). His contractor, John Wilson, began work the following year. The deck was to be suspended from sixteen wrought iron chains, forged across the border in Ironbridge, birthplace of the Industrial Revolution. These chains, each weighing 23 tons, were hauled into position by ropes and pulleys, operated from the tower on the island side. The lifting power was provided by a capstan turned by 150 labourers. The piers were faced with Penmon limestone.

*The Menai
Suspension
Bridge*

The new bridge carried the road Telford had created, the A5, over the Menai Strait, thereby linking London with Holyhead, the port for Dublin. Construction work cost £120,000, and the bridge was opened amidst public rejoicing in January 1826. The first vehicle to go across was the London to Holyhead mail coach.

The total length of the bridge is 1,007ft (305m), with a central span of 584ft (177m). Tolls were originally collected at the building on the mainland end (beside the turn off to Treborth Botanical Gardens) and later, until the bridge was freed from toll at the beginning of 1941, from a central booth. The roadway and footpaths passed over 100ft (30m) above the waterline – this height being set, at the insistence of the Admiralty, to allow the passage of tall ships. The supporting chains were treated against rust with linseed oil – not wine, as Lewis Carroll's White Knight claims in *Through The Looking Glass*. The wrought-iron chains were replaced by steel links when the bridge was strengthened in the 1930s and '40s. (Telford's suspension bridge at Conwy has retained its original ironwork.) During 2005 the bridge underwent its first complete repainting for 65 years: the one-way system imposed over a period of ten months caused considerable disruption to the island's traffic.

The best views of the bridge may be obtained from Church Island or from the lay-bys on the road from Menai Bridge town to Llanfair Pwllgwyngyll. For a closer view of the base, walk underneath from Menai Bridge town. At the foot of the bridge is a grassy, waterside picnic area, occupying the site of the former quayside.

Moelfre

8F

*On A5108,
7¹/₂ml (12km)
SE of Amlwch*

Shore & Village, Moelfre.

Moelfre's small harbour is a shingle cove backed by a high stone wall. At the end of the nineteenth century this was one of the busiest fishing villages on Anglesey, with a fleet of thirty boats landing herrings during a winter season lasting from November to February. It is typical that few structural improvements were carried out to the harbour: boats were simply hauled high up on the beach, as they still are today. The narrow main street winds past the **Old Ship's Bell** restaurant and the **Kinmel Arms**, and skirts the harbour walls. Well-marked coastal footpaths lead along the cliffs, with views towards **Ynys Moelfre**; the hills of Llanddona lie low on the southwestern horizon beneath Snowdonia's more distant peaks.

Guided walks are organised along the coastal paths from a visitor centre run by the local authority, **Seawatch / *Gwylfan*** (Easter to September, closed Mondays except bank holidays © 01248 410277), opposite the Post Office. Small-scale displays give an insight into life above and below the ocean's surface, the world of ships and shipwrecks. Climb aboard a former lifeboat, the *Birds Eye* which served between 1970–90 in New Quay / *Cei Newydd* (south of Aberystwyth, on the mainland), saving 42 lives.

Outside Seawatch is a section of steel plating recovered from the wreck of the sailing clipper *Royal Charter* (1859). ▶83 A pillar (1935) commemorating its many victims, stands directly above the site of the wreck, on the cliffs to the northwest of Moelfre, at Porth Helaeth.

The 'Birds Eye' lifeboat is the centrepiece of Moelfre's Seawatch

Nuggets of gold, coins and jewellery are amongst the items recovered from the wreck of the 'Royal Charter'

The road continues out of town past the **Carmel** congregational chapel and the modern community school, towards Lligwy. The outskirts of town are occupied by seaside bunglows.

As Coxswain Evans drove his lifeboat against the Hindlea's side, to hold her there, he remembered seeing the stricken ship's bow "coming in like a concertina"

The Coxswain

A lifeboat station was established at Moelfre in 1830: one of the most famous in Britain. Its crews have saved hundreds of lives and won many awards for bravery.

A bronze statue by sculptor Sam Holland, unveiled in 2004 outside **Seawatch / *Gwylfan*** in Moelfre, commemorates the gallantry of *all* lifeboat crews – but it is in the image of the best known of Moelfre's lifeboatmen: **Richard Evans** (1905-2001). 'Dic' Evans twice won the Gold Medal of the Royal National Lifeboat Institution, its highest award.

Dic was awarded his first Gold Medal in 1959, five years after succeeding his uncle as coxswain of the Moelfre lifeboat. During a hurricane one hundred years, almost to the day, after the wreck of the *Royal Charter*, the *Hindlea* (a 506 ton Cardiff coaster) was in distress in rough seas to the north of Ynys Moelfre. Damaged telephone lines prevented the mustering of a full crew of lifeboatmen – Dic was joined by only two regular members and a shore helper who had never before been to sea in a lifeboat. Nevertheless, all eight members of the *Hindlea*'s crew were saved before she struck the rocks. A bench and a plaque set on the clifftop commemorates the event, and the anchor of the *Hindlea* can be seen, propped up against a wall, near the car park by Moelfre's shingle cove.

Seven years later a second Gold Medal was awarded after Richard Evans had gone to the aid of a Greek motor vessel, *Nafsiporos*, which was disabled and drifting dangerously off Point Lynas. During this rescue Coxswain Evans remained at the wheel throughout the whole twelve hours.

Moelfre's present-day offshore lifeboat is the *Robert and Violet*. Its Lifeboat Day is held on a Saturday each August, usually during the Bank Holiday weekend.

LIVERPOOL & AUSTRALIAN NAVIGATION COMPANY

Steam from Liverpool to Australia,

UNDER 60 DAYS.

THE MAGNIFICENT STEAM CLIPPER

"ROYAL CHARTER,"

2719 Tons Register and 200 Horse Power, with Fire-proof and Water-tight Compartments,

F. BOYCE, Commander,

IS APPOINTED TO LEAVE THE RIVER MERSEY FOR

MELBOURNE, PORT PHILIP,

ON THURSDAY, 2nd OCTOBER.

THIS noble Steam Clipper, built expressly for the Company, one of the finest models yet constructed, combines all the advantages of a Steam with those of a Clipper Sailing Ship, and offers the only opportunity yet presented to the Public of certainty in the time required for the voyage. She has just made the extraordinary passage of **59 days to Melbourne**—a performance never before accomplished. On this voyage she ran one day 358 knots, during which she attained the astonishing speed of 18 nautical miles in the hour. Her daily average for the whole distance to Melbourne was 223¾ knots, or 10½ miles per hour. Her accommodations for all classes of Passengers are unrivalled.

FARES TO MELBOURNE.

AFTER SALOON...60, 65, and 75 Guineas. | **SECOND CLASS**......25 and 30 Guineas.
THIRD CLASS, ... 16, 18, and 20 Guineas.

Including Stewards' Fees, the attendance of an experienced Surgeon, and all Provisions of the best quality, except Wines, Spirits, and Malt Liquors, which will be supplied at fixed moderate prices on board.

Children from One to Twelve Years, Half Price. Infants Free.

Passengers booked to be forwarded by the First Opportunity after arrival to SYDNEY, ADELAIDE, HOBART-TOWN, &c., at an extra charge of 7 and 8 Guineas 1st Class; 4 and 5 Guineas 2nd Class; 3 and 4 Guineas 3rd Class.

In the AFTER SALOON every requisite will be provided, including Beds, Berths, Bedding, Plate, Table Linen, Crockery, Glass, &c., supplied with the best articles of Food, and an abundant Dietary Scale. Live Stock, Poultry, &c.

The AFTER SALOON is fitted with Ladies' Boudoir, Baths, &c., &c., &c.

DECK.—The Poop aft is appropriated to the After Saloon Passengers alone. The Deck amidships to the First and Second Class Passengers, and forward to the Third Class Passengers.

No Passenger can be accommodated in a State-room by himself, so long as he can be placed with other passengers, unless the State-room is specially arranged for; Berths may be changed, if necessary, unless a whole State-room is secured.

DEPOSITS.

One-half of the passage-money must be paid before a Berth can be secured. The Berths are appropriated in rotation as the Deposits are paid. Passengers in the country can have Berths secured by enclosing a Bank or Post-office order to the undersigned for half the amount of passage, and they are requested to give their Christian names, ages, and trade, and if married, names and ages of each member of the family.

LUGGAGE.

THE REGULATIONS BELOW WILL BE STRICTLY ADHERED TO.

Forty Cubic Feet allowed each Adult Passenger in After Saloon
Thirty   do.   „   „   „   „   Second Class
Twenty   do.   „   „   „   „   Third do.
Children in proportion.

{ *All packages to be marked with the name of the Passenger, and labelled "Wanted on the Voyage," or "Not Wanted on the Voyage," with the Cabin and State-room to which they belong, and must be at the Ship's side at least two days before the time appointed for mustering the passengers as per Contract Ticket. Each package should have a bag to contain sufficient linen for a month's use. Packages wanted on the Voyage must not be larger than 2 feet 3 inches in length, 1 foot 5 inches in breadth, and 1 foot 4 inches deep, so that as many as possible may be placed below the berths, and it is also recommended that packages for the hold should not exceed above size.* }

Freight on any excess, not exceeding 10 feet, will be charged at 3s. per foot. If, however, the excess be more than 10 cubic feet, it must be previously engaged as cargo. Such overplus must be along side the vessel six days prior to sailing, *or it cannot be taken on board;* and all less specially engaged previously, cannot be taken if the ship is full.

PASSENGERS MUST TAKE CHARGE OF THEIR LUGGAGE UNTIL ON BOARD SHIP.

Before Luggage can go on board all Passage-money must be paid. The Luggage to be distinctly marked with Paint, two inches long, with the owners name and destination, *(and cannot be delivered elsewhere,)* State-rooms, Berths, and Cabins to which it belongs.

The owner's not responsible for loss or damage to Luggage. Merchandise cannot be carried as Luggage. All Bullion, Specie, Watches, Jewellery, or Treasure, above the value of £150, must be declared, and pay the Freight.

DOGS are charged £5 each.

SERVANTS.—Females are charged one-half After Saloon Fare. Men Servants are charged Third Class Fare, and are berthed and provided accordingly.

All Extra Luggage must be alongside by Saturday, the 27th September. All other Luggage (Hat Boxes and Carpet Bags excepted) on Monday, the 29th Sept. She will proceed into the river on Tuesday, the 30th. A Steamer will leave the Prince's Pier-head at 9 o'clock in the morning of the 1st October, when all (except Saloon) Passengers must be on board. Saloon Passengers embark on Thursday, the 2nd October, at 9 A.M.

'The Royal Charter'

During the night of 26th and 27th October 1859, the 2700-ton sailing clipper with an auxiliary engine was homeward bound for the port of Liverpool from the goldfields of Australia, when she ran into a terrible storm. Huge seas prevented the launch of the lifeboat, and the ship foundered on the rocks offshore. A fortune in gold was scattered in the waves and over 459 passengers and crew were drowned. Not one woman or child was among the survivors. That night, 133 ships were sunk off the coasts of Britain, during what became known as the 'Royal Charter Storm'. The event led, in 1860, to the first publication of daily weather reports.

Wreckage of the 'Royal Charter'
painted by J J Dodd

Charles Dickens, already famous as a novelist, came to Moelfre to find out the individual human stories that lay behind the grim statistics. He stayed nearby with the rector of Llanallgo where 140 victims are buried in the churchyard.

"*A MAN, living on the nearest hill-top overlooking the sea, being blown out of bed at about daybreak by the wind that had begun to strip his roof off, and getting upon a ladder with his nearest neighbour to construct some temporary device for keeping his house over his head, saw from the ladder's elevation as he looked down by chance towards the shore, some dark troubled object close in with the land. And he and the other, descending to the beach, and finding the sea mercilessly beating over a great broken ship, had clambered up the stony ways, like staircases without stairs, on which the wild village hangs in little clusters, as fruit hangs on boughs, and had given the alarm.*

… And as they stood in the leaden morning, stricken with pity, leaning hard against the wind, their breath and vision often failing as the sleet and spray rushed at them from the ever forming and dissolving mountains of sea, and as the wool which was a part of the vessel's cargo blew in with the salt foam and remained upon the land when the foam melted, they saw the ship's life-boat put off from one of the heaps of wreck; and first there were three men in her, and in a moment she capsized, and there were but two; and again she was struck by a vast mass of water, and there was but one; and again she was thrown bottom upward, and that one, with his arm struck through the broken planks and waving as if for the help that could never reach him, went down into the deep."

— CHARLES DICKENS, *The Shipwreck*, in *The Uncommercial Traveller* (1860)
Published in the booklet *Shipwreck!* (Magma, Llansadwrn 1997, reprinted 2007)

Mynydd Bodafon / **Bodafon Mountain**

7F

*4ml (6.5km)
west of
Moelfre; turn
off A5025 at
Brynrefail*

Brynrefail is in the parish of **Penrhos Lligwy**, on the A5025. It is a hamlet around a chapel (1896) and a craft shop. A lane leads eastwards to Traeth Lligwy, another westwards to the church of **Sant Mihangel** in the parish of Penrhos Lligwy. Sheep scatter as one crosses the small field to the circular medieval churchyard – keep to the footpath here. A sixth-century grave-stone set in the chancel features the Irish name Maccudecceti. This church was built in the late fourteenth century (the date of its stone cross). Its pred-ecessor may have been used by royal princes of Gwynedd, for Penrhos Lligwy was the site of a *llys* or court. The church includes a plaque in memory of Margaret, mother of the Morris brothers ▶114 who died at the age of 81 years. Next to the plaque is a memorial to her youngest son, John ('Siôn', 1713-40). The church was heavily restored in 1865, six years after the ship-wreck of the *Royal Charter*; 45 victims are buried in the churchyard.

Bodafon

The lane continues past Plas Bodafon, skirting the abrupt rocky outcrops of **Yr Arwydd**, **Pen y Castell** and **Mynydd Bodafon**, which rise to 587ft (178m) and offer panoramic views over the island. The area has been called 'a kind of Lake District sur-prise among the lowlands'. In 2005 it was opened to general public access under new countryside legislation. The slopes, a pleasant spot for a picnic, are covered in bracken and heather and flanked to the south by conifers. The lane passes a small glacial tarn, named Llyn Bodafon or Archaeddon. It is surrounded by scattered houses amidst a natural amphitheatre of eroded rocks. Mynydd Bodafon was the site of ancient hut circles and a medieval homestead.

The pi man and the linguist

π In 1706 **William Jones** (c1675-1749) became the first mathematician to use the Greek letter π *(pi)* to signify the ratio of a circle's circumference to its diameter.

He was born at Y Merddyn, at the foot of Mynydd Bodafon, the son of a farmer called Siôn Siors, of Llanbabo, and was schooled at Llanfechell. He travelled to London to be apprenticed to a merchant, and sailed to the Caribbean. Jones wrote a treatise on navigation, published in 1702, and in 1706 what became a standard work on mathematics. William Jones found a wealthy patron in the person of Lord Macclesfield and became tutor to his son. He knew the great Sir Isaac Newton and the astronomer Edmond Halley, and was a friend of Richard Morris, one of the famous Anglesey brothers. He eventually became a vice-president of the Royal Society.

William Jones's youngest son, **Sir William Jones** (1746-94), was equally accomplished. An orientalist and brilliant linguist, he published a book on Persian grammar in 1771, and is said to have been the first British person to have mastered Sanskrit. In 1786 he became the first person to draw attention to the close affinities between many Asian and European languages, so that scholars began to talk of an 'Indo-European' language family. Welsh, English, German and French are indeed related to languages such as Persian, Punjabi, Urdu and Hindi.

Welsh	*English*	*Sanskrit*
ieuanc	young	yuvan
dant	tooth	danta
tenau	thin	tanas
gweddw	widow	mi vidhava
tri	three	trayas

To the southwest of Mynydd Bodafon, green fields, dotted with Welsh black cattle, stretch towards **Maenaddwyn** and **Hebron**, clusters of dwellings on the long lane from Brynteg to Llannerch-y-medd.

The lane south from Maenaddwyn passes the small church of **Llan-fihangel Tre'r-beirdd**, 'St Michael's at the Town of the Poets', a medieval name (SH459837). The church, behind a stone wall, is approached through its gate head-on, passing yew trees and some rather grand gravestones and memorials. This is another church associated with the Morris family of Pentre-eiriannell. ▶114 It is the burial place of the Morris brothers' father, the cooper and farmer Morys ap Rhisiart ('Morris Prichard', c1674-1763), who had been born in the parish. Parts of the structure date back to the fourteenth century. The octaganol gritstone font is medieval, but most of the church is Victorian, being reconstructed in 1811 and again in 1888.

A short distance to the south is the **Tŷ-mawr** primary school and a tall standing stone, now called **Maen Addwyn** (SH460833). The original stone of that name stood a half-mile (800m) to the north and gave its name to the village. Both stones are thought to be of the Bronze Age, though their purpose is not fully understood.

Cacennau cri, *a recipe for Welshcakes*

Welshcakes may have suffered from the decline of afternoon tea served in the home, but they are still the staple of tea rooms all over Wales and of school fêtes or Womens' Institute meetings – warm from the griddle and deliciously simple. There are many different recipes, each claimed as the definitive one.

Ingredients

½ tsp salt.
1 lb (500g) plain flour.
1 teaspoon baking powder.
1 teaspoon mixed spice.
8oz (250g) butter.
3oz (90g) sugar.
4oz (125g) currants.
2 medium eggs.
2 or 3 tablespoons of milk, to mix.

Method

Sift the flour, baking powder, salt and mixed spice. Rub in the butter. Add sugar and currants, and then beaten egg and milk to make a stiff dough. Roll out ¼" (0.5cm) thick. Cut into 2" (5cm) rounds. Bake on a hot griddle or in a frying pan until brown, about four minutes each side. The cakes should have a sandy texture.

Penmon

10E

*4ml (6km)
NE of
Beaumaris;
turn off
B5109*

The eastern corner of Anglesey is approached on the road from Llangoed past Aberlleiniog. Turn north at the bus shelter and at the hilltop follow the narrow lane to the right through **Penmon Village / *Pentref Penmon***. Before Dinmor, stone steps lead through a high wall to a footpath which follows the limestone ridge eastwards to the Priory. There are fine views southwards to Penmaenmawr and the Great Orme.

This lane continues to the hamlet of **Caim**. Footpaths lead from the edge of Caim across green pasture to cliffs and rocky slabs, a favourite spot for local anglers. To the east lies Dinmor Quarry, last used during the construction of the A55 coastal expressway in the 1980s, but now the site of a fish farm. This is a high-intensity operation in which turbot are raised in concrete tanks, the saltwater being purified by ozone and recirculated. It is intended that reedbed purification of the effluent will replace the present method of discharge into the sea. A footpath skirting the old quarry to the west leads through farmland to Penmon Priory.

To drive to the Priory directly, follow the Aberlleiniog road eastwards alongside the sea wall, battered by winter gales. High walls on your left protect grassy meadows and pools, the haunt of curlew, shelduck, teal and wigeon. The road follows the long sweep of a shingle beach; oystercatchers roost on the shoreline. Look for seals offshore, and cormorants and shags flying low over the waves. The rounded 'island' visible at low water is the upturned hull of the sand dredger *Hoveringham*, which sprang a leak and capsized in 1971.

From the eastern end of the bay, limestone used to be shipped out from the Penmon quarries. Note the building (on private land) where the stone was once cut and dressed, the chimney and pier. The abandoned workings of Flagstaff Quarry *(Chwarel y Becyn)* follow the coast round to Trwyn Du, providing a clamorous nesting ground for gulls. There is no public access and the buildings and workings are unsafe. The quarry still visible on farmland to the landward side was known as Park *(Chwarel Parc)*.

*Saint Seiriol's
church and
priory*

High, ivy-covered walls lead to **Penmon Priory** lying amidst peaceful fields in the lee of two sweet-chestnut trees. Tradition dates its foundation to the reign of Maelgwn Gwynedd, who died in AD547. The founder may have been Cynlas, who was succeeded by his brother, or, perhaps, cousin Seiriol. Seiriol was a monk, related to the royal family of Gwynedd. The original church was probably destroyed by Vikings in 971; its replacement was built between 1120 and 1170 and endowed by the Welsh rulers of Gwynedd.

The monasteries of the Celtic Church submitted to a more 'Roman' discipline during the thirteenth century and Penmon's monks were incorporated into the Augustinian order. The Augustinians practised a less formal monasticism than some other orders. This provided the opportunity to continue to follow the individual rhythms of life and worship to which, as part of the Celtic Church, the monks had become accustomed. It had also become necessary to seek the protection that a powerful order would provide. The Augustinians offered the best chance of continuing to follow a contemplative life in uncertain and changing times, and the existing priory building dates from this period of incorporation. These circumstances were similar to those on the island of Bardsey, *Ynys Enlli*, off the tip of the Llŷn peninsula – a place that has many similarities to Penmon.

Penmon Priory as it may have been in the early sixteenth century

Brian Byron

The large room next to the mounting block was the monks' refectory and kitchen; below it were the cellars, and a dormitory formed an upper storey. The small room to the east was a warming house. The monastery was dissolved in about 1537 and passed to the Bulkeley estates.

One of Penmon's stone crosses

The sixteenth-century prior's house, modernised in 1923 and now private, links the priory to the **Church of St Seiriol**, one of Anglesey's *Grade 1* protected churches. Enter the nave, and you are transported to the world of the Middle Ages. Dim light filters in to reveal massive Romanesque arches and masonry. Note the thousand year-old font and the two stone crosses, originally standing in nearby fields, one as old as the tenth century. Their elaborate knotwork patterns suggest a Norse cultural influence. Amongst the church's collection of carved stones found in the vicinity is a (much weathered) figure of a woman with her legs spread apart, probably dating from the twelfth century. Such fertility symbols are generally known by the Irish term *sheila-na-gig* and curiously are quite often found alongside churches of this period. The thirteenth-century chancel was partly rebuilt in 1855, a trim Victorian place of worship still used for services. In the little churchyard, carved slate slabs amongst the snowdrops commemorate victims of shipwreck.

A path leads past the monks' fish pond to **Ffynnon Seiriol** (St Seiriol's Well). This still, clear spring is housed in a brick shelter probably dating from the eighteenth century. Springs were sacred to the ancient Celts, and were used by the early Christians for baptism. The foundations of Saint Seiriol's cell, dating back to cAD540, may be seen next to the well.

Penmon dovecote, c1600

Penmon Dovecote is a vaulted stone building, probably erected for Sir Richard Bulkeley of Baron Hill in about 1600. Inside is a stone pillar, which once supported ladders to nearly 1,000 pigeon holes. The birds provided eggs and meat. In the eighteenth century the Bulkeleys made Penmon into a deer park. Over 2½ miles (4km) of high stone walls still stand, stretching over the fields towards Caim.

From the dovecote a toll road leads eastwards to **Trwyn Du** ('Black Point'). The fee is payable to the Baron Hill estate, as is the Priory car park charge. If you prefer to walk, leave your car by the Priory. The road descends through a broad sweep of bramble, blackthorn, bracken, meadow-sweet and honeysuckle. Look for wild orchids on the verge, but do leave them well alone. The long mounds of earth to your right are not prehistoric barrows, but the reverses of the old Flagstaff quarry workings. There are panoramic views across the bay to Conwy and the Great Orme. At the foot of the road is a beach of white pebbles, banked high by storms. The pebble beach is a relatively recent phenomenon, the result of quarrying activity. The original nature of the rocky shore may be seen behind the ridge. In the late summer the waves can be silver with sprats, chased ashore by predatory shoals of mackerel. Keep an eye open for seals. Currents are strong and bathing is dangerous, but there are plenty of rockpools to explore. Across the sound lies Puffin Island.

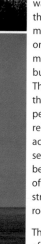

Trwyn Du lighthouse, 1838

The Trwyn Du **lighthouse**, built in 1836-38 to the design of James Walker, guards submerged rocks on this shore; ships pass through the sound between the light and a marker buoy. Its beam, 15,000 candela strong, can be seen 13½ miles (21km) away; a fog bell chimes mournfully every half minute. The houses at the point were built by Trinity House, the body responsible for lighthouses, and its crest is set over the front doors. The houses were constructed of Penmon limestone in 1839. Behind them is an unmanned coastguard station. A café is open in summer months in a typical old Anglesey cottage.

Puffin Island / *Ynys Seiriol*

This uninhabited island lies about half a mile (800m) off Anglesey's eastern tip, beyond the Trwyn Du lighthouse. It covers an area of 78 acres (32ha). Access is restricted to naturalists with permits, but it may be viewed from the sea; trips leave Beaumaris pier during the summer. This is the best way to see the island's Atlantic Grey seals, though there are small breeding groups in other places around Anglesey too. The island is also the home of gulls, guillemots, razorbills, kittiwakes and shags, and is one of Wales's most important cormorant breeding sites. Look out too for black guillemots, which have taken up residence: there are other smaller colonies at Fedw Fawr and at Point Lynas, but 3,000 have colonised Puffin Island.

Puffins do still breed here, but numbers have dwindled, and puffin watchers should visit South Stack, near Holyhead, instead. The island's population of rats, which are said to have first come to the island from a wrecked ship, are amongst the factors blamed for the decline – they invade the puffins' nesting burrows. However it should also be pointed out that puffins were once caught, filleted, pickled in brine or vinegar, and eaten as a delicacy! The wholesale price at the end of the eighteenth century was four shillings for sixty birds: *'Puffins which pickled bring profit'*, went the Anglesey saying.

In recent years, efforts to rid the island of rats have begun to take effect.

> *"THE YOUNG PUFFINS before they are quite feathered, are fledged and opened and strew'd with pepper and salt and Broiled and Eat pleasant enough. But the nice way of managing them is to Pickle them, and these are sent as rarities for ye Tables of the Great."*
>
> — LEWIS MORRIS

Penmon lifeboat house and Puffin Island

Puffin Island, an inclined plateau of limestone, has been given many names over the ages, including *Ynys Lannog* and *Ynys Glannauc*. Another name, *Priestholm*, refers to the island's ecclesiastical history. It derives from the Norse *Prestr Holmr*, 'Priest Island'. Its most common Welsh name, *Ynys Seiriol*, derives from Saint Seiriol, the sixth-century hermit who founded a settlement here. Remains of monastic buildings on the island date from the seventh to the thirteenth century. Gerald of Wales visiting Anglesey in 1188, told of a community of monks living and working on this island. He said that whenever they quarrelled with each other, God sent a plague of mice to consume their provisions. Other ruins on the island include those of a nineteenth-century telegraph station.

Penmynydd

8D
3½ml
(5.5km)
NW of
Menai Bridge
on B5420

The B5420 road from Four Crosses to Llangefni enters an avenue bordered by trees and takes a sharp turn at the entrance to this scattered farming village. Follow one of two northern lanes to the parish **Church of St Gredifael** (SH517749). Pines and yews mark this sixth-century site. Today's church is medieval. If you look carefully at the south wall you can see stones, decorated with Romanesque carved chevrons, that were reused during the restoration of 1848. Heraldic devices link the church to the *Tudur* or 'Tudor' family of Penmynydd. They are found on a finely carved alabaster tomb of about 1385, which features effigies of Gronw Fychan and his wife Myfanwy, ancestors of the Tudors. The tomb was originally in the friary at Llan-faes ▶60

*"T*RAVELLERS *were not so much interested in Penmynydd being the historical place whence sprang the Tudors... as in getting over the ground without broken bones. And the horsemen who preceded coach-travelling looked dismayed in each others' faces at such a wild spot... reassured, however, on descending the rough and stony hill by a sight of gallows... cheered by this evidence of law and order extending to the uttermost verges of the land, they removed their hands from their pistol holsters and spurred onwards with renewed vigour."*

— GEORGE HARPER, *The Holyhead Road* (1902)

**Plas
Penmynydd**

The road to Llangefni continues past whitewashed **almshouses** (1627), chapels, a schoolhouse (1877, now used by nursery playgroups) and isolated farms. The northwestern limits of the village are defined by the river valley of **Afon Ceint**.

The Tudors of Penmynydd

The Tudur or Tudor family was descended from Ednyfed Fychan, a courtier of Llywelyn I 'the Great'. Family members were patrons of poetry. After the conquest of Wales, family member Tudur ap Goronwy made a name for himself at the English court, as did his son Goronwy (Gronw Fychan), who fought in France during the Hundred Years' War.

However, many family members, such as Maredudd ap Tudur, (fl.1388-1404) supported Owain Glyn Dŵr in the uprising of 1400-1415. His son Owain Tudur (c1400-1461) returned to favour with the English and joined the court of Henry V in London. After the king's death, his widow Catherine de Valois (Shakespeare's 'dear Kate' in *Henry V*) secretly married Owain, her

impoverished but lusty Welsh squire.

It was their grandson who claimed the English throne in 1485, as Henry VII. He sailed from exile in Brittany and landed at Milford Haven (*Aberdaugleddau*) in South Wales. He went on to defeat Richard III at Bosworth Field.

The dynasty of Tudors he founded – Henry VII, Henry VIII, Edward VI, Mary I and Elizabeth I – was to rule both England and Wales until 1603.

The home of the Anglesey Tudurs was **Plas Penmynydd**, near Ceint. In 1576, by which time the local branch of the family was heading for comparative obscurity, eclipsed by their royal relations in England, this was replaced by the house which still stands today. The extensively restored building is in private ownership.

Masonry surrounding the doorway of Plas Penmynydd is decorated with heraldic symbols, including a Saracen's head.

In the parish church, effigies of Gronw Fychan and Myfanwy, his wife, lie beneath a Tudor rose stained-glass window

Penrhos Lligwy — *see* **Mynydd Bodafon** ▸84

Pentraeth

8E

5ml (8km)
north of
Menai Bridge
on A5025

The name Pentraeth means 'head of the beach', but the centre of today's village lies inland from **Red Wharf Bay / Traeth Coch**. It is grouped around the crossroads of the B5109 and the A5025, with terraced cottages, a housing estate and a cluster of shops.

Pentraeth originally developed as a stop on the old post road from Beaumaris to Holyhead and became a small but thriving market town. During the first half of the twentieth century Pentraeth was a halt on the branch railway line to Red Wharf Bay, now closed.

Plas Gwyn

As early as the seventeenth century, the village of Pentraeth had benefited from charitable schools founded by Dr John Jones of **Plas Gwyn**, who became Dean of Bangor in 1689. He also set up schools at Llanfihangel Ysgeifiog, Beaumaris, Llandegfan and Llanfechell. The name Plas Gwyn ('white manor') refers to the original whitewashed building. Plas Gwyn in its present form is a large, pink, brick-built country house in the Georgian style, constructed for lawyer William Jones (1688-1755) in 1754, with parts dating from the nineteenth century. Thomas Pennant wrote that the house *'may be reckoned among the best on the island'.* Its best-known inhabitant was Paul Panton (1727-97), who came from Bagillt in Flintshire, but married a great-niece of Dr John Jones. Panton was a lawyer and agriculturalist, as well as an antiquarian and collector of old Welsh manuscripts. The house, just south of the Beaumaris road, remains in private ownership.

Pentraeth Parish Church, 1785

Just by the crossroads is the parish **Church of St Mary** *(Santes Fair)*, dating back to the twelfth century, although most of the building was reconstructed in 1882. Opposite is the **Panton Arms** public house, where Charles Dickens stayed on his way to report on the wreck of the *Royal Charter* off Moelfre in 1859.

A visitor to a former inn in the village was the always entertaining travel writer George Borrow ▸47, who in *Wild Wales* (1862) described an overnight stay:

"*P*UTTING out the light I got into bed, but instantly found that the bed was not long enough by at least a foot. 'I shall pass an uncomfortable night,' said I, 'for I never yet could sleep in a bed too short. However, as I am on my travels, I must endeavour to accommodate myself to circumstances.' So I endeavoured to compose myself to sleep: before, however, I could succeed, I heard the sound of stumping steps coming upstairs, and perceived a beam of light through the crevices of the door, and in a moment more the door opened and in came two loutish farming lads whom I had observed below, one of them bearing a rushlight stuck in an old blacking bottle. Without saying a word they flung off part of their clothes, and one of them having blown out the rushlight, they both tumbled into bed, and in a moment were snoring most sonorously.*"

— GEORGE BORROW, *Wild Wales* (1862)

The leaping bard

In a private field on the outskirts of Pentraeth (by the speed restriction sign on the Beaumaris road) is a group of ancient stones, the 'Three Leaps', *Tair Naid*. Legend claims that they mark the course of a prodigious hop, step and jump by a poet, **Einion ap Gwalchmai** (fl.1203-23), who won the hand of his lady, Angharad, by demonstrating his athletic prowess. Another story tells how Einion went on pilgrimage and was away so long that his wife did not recognise the aged, bearded traveller who returned – until he played his harp. He then presented her with one half of his wedding ring, she having retained the other half when he departed so many years previously. The historical Einion was the third in a line of great poets. His work praised drinking and feasting, but also the love of God.

To reach the actual *pentraeth*, the 'head of the beach', turn north off the Beaumaris road just to the east of the village, down a wooded lane. **Afon Nodwydd** flows north-east to the beach, emerging beneath a low stone bridge to a stretch of saltmarsh, a rich feeding ground for wading birds. This is the central sector of Red Wharf Bay, with beach walks towards Llanddona ▶56 or the *Ship Inn*. ▶94 Enjoy magnificent wide open spaces and the sea breeze.

A **memorial stone** by the Nodwydd river tells of the **Battle of Pentraeth** in 1170. This saw the death of Hywel ab Owain Gwynedd, natural son of the ruler Owain ap Gruffudd and an Irish mother named Pyfog. Hywel battled with his half-brothers, Dafydd and Rhodri, for the succession. Although he was a tireless fighter, Hywel left behind some remarkable poetry of love and landscape, influenced by French poetic convention as much as the Welsh.

To the east of the beach rise the dark slopes of **Mynydd Llwydiarth**, partly managed by the Forestry Commission. Conifer plantations (known as Pentraeth Forest / *Coedwig Pentraeth*) cover this rocky ridge, frequented by ravens and buzzards. It has also been the site in recent years of efforts to re-establish the red squirrel. There is a small lake, **Llyn Llwydiarth**. Access on foot is permitted through the gated entrance off the Beaumaris road to the east of the village (SH534784), but this is not a site (such as Newborough Forest) for which public facilities are provided. Opportunities to park cars near the gate are very limited: if you do so, take care not to leave valuables on view.

At the northern end of the village, off the A5025, there are plant nurseries and a small industrial estate. Past the **Bull Inn**, Lôn Clai offers access to the beach halfway between the Nodwydd bridge and the Ship Inn. There is no car park at this point.

Puffin Island — *see* **Penmon** ▶86

Red Wharf Bay / *Traeth Coch*

8E

2¹⁄₂ml (4km) north of Pentraeth; turn off A5025

The small village of Red Wharf Bay or Traeth Coch takes its name from the great sweep of sand stretching five miles (8km) eastwards to Llanddona. Over ten square miles (25 sq km) of the bay are uncovered at low tide. The beach offers safe paddling and shallow swimming, walking, birdwatching and beachcombing. However, beware of the speed of the incoming tide, which rapidly floods the maze of channels in the sand.

The western shores of Traeth Coch, Red Wharf Bay

The lane through the upper village descends past a general stores and a caravan park to a quayside by a café/restaurant, the **Old Boathouse**, and the **Ship Inn**, an ideal spot for lunch. There was once a small shipbuilding industry here. Now children play on the sandbanks and there are moorings for yachts. (Red Wharf Bay Sailing Club is based to the north, at Traeth Bychan.) There are spectacular views from the shore across to the conifer forests of Mynydd Llwydiarth ▶93 and Snowdonia beyond. The spot may be crowded on summer bank holidays, but inspiring on a weekday out of season.

Follow the paths through the woods around the inner shore, or walk seawards beside the tidal channel, alongside the headland of **Trwyn Dwlban**. Its great limestone cliff, set amongst wooded hollows and caves, is appropriately named **Castell Mawr** ('big castle'). It is a nesting site for gulls. Castell Mawr is the remnant of quarrying. On the lower rocks by the shore, look for strange, circular sandstone blocks, which infilled earlier water-worn holes in the carboniferous limestone. The rocks here are overlaid with gravel and clay from the last glaciation. Scratch marks (striae) of the moving ice sheet are still visible in the smoothed limestone where it emerges from the overlying soil. Red Wharf Bay was a busy place in the 1800s; at one time about two hundred men worked the old limestone quarry.

A second lane accesses the beach from the A5025, just to the south of the village.

Rhoscefnhir

8D

1¹⁄₂mi (2.5km) off A5025 south of Pentraeth

This small residential village occupies peaceful farmland along two lanes off the busy Pentraeth road. Little remains of Melin Orsedd, the windmill that dominated the village in the nineteenth century. At **Pen y Garnedd**, beside the main road and opposite the former site of a tithe barn, is a Calvinist chapel built in 1876.

Talwrn
7D

2½ml (4km) west of Pentraeth on B5109

Talwrn took its name from a local farm called y Talwrn Mawr. The Welsh word *talwrn* can mean 'cock-pit', 'threshing floor' or 'clearing', and any of these meanings is possible in this context.

Approaching Talwrn on the B5109 westwards from Pentraeth, look for an ancient standing stone and the small parish **Church of St Dyfnan** (SH503 787) with its carved doorway. The round stone head may be medieval, or it may possibly belong to the Celtic Iron Age, and have been incorporated into the church's masonry in the Middle Ages. The nave dates back to the fourteenth century, the chancel to the fifteenth.

A huge brachiopod – Gigantoproductus giganteus, 20cm across – from the Carboniferous limestone of Benllech, is part of the Stone Science display

Across the road from the church, an annexe to Llanddyfnan's former rectory (c1870) houses **Stone Science Gwyddor Carreg**, offering geological and archaeological exhibits and sales (✆ 01248 450310, open daily Easter to the end of October, also winter weekends & school holidays). On a lawn in front of the the rectory, amongst ducks and rare breed chickens, is a reconstruction of a rush-thatched Iron Age round house.

Some of Talwrn's other country houses, all in private ownership, belong to the seventeenth century; they include **Marian**, **Plas Llanddyfnan** and **Bodeilio**.

To the east and southeast of the village is the National Nature Reserve of **Cors Bodeilio**, a large area of tawny fenland with reedbeds and clumps of green vegetation. It is seen from a back lane leading southwest from Pentraeth. Enter the reserve through a gateway where the road makes a sharp left turn (SH507773, by the no through road to Penrhyn Farm). Although the gated entrance has no sign, by the side of the reserve's footpath a panel displays a map and nature notes. Visitors must keep to the boardwalk. The margins of the fen – watered by calcium-rich springs – provide a habitat for a variety of orchids. The fen was formed as peat slowly filled a lake left here after the last Ice Age.

Cors Bodeilio boardwalk

The old centre of Talwrn surrounds the crossroads and was formerly known as Rhyd Dymai ('ha'penny ford'). To the left of the war memorial, a plinth commemorates the thirteenth-century poet Gruffudd ab yr Ynad Coch (fl.1280) – see *The poet of grief.* ▶96 These memorials lie opposite **Cors y Farl**, another long strip of fen. The road south passes through the lower village, which includes a small, partly pebble-dashed church dedicated to **Saint Deiniol** (1891), an Independent chapel, **Capel Siloam** (1841, reconstructed 1880), and a shop. This tree-lined road leads towards the hamlet of **Ceint**. On the way, turn through an open gate (marked 'Eglwys Llanffinan') and along a gravel-surfaced track. Ample parking at the end of the track gives access to the **Church of St Ffinan** (SH496755), rebuilt by John Welch of St Asaph (1841) in, unusually for Anglesey, a neo-Romanesque style. **Llanffinan** stands above Afon Ceint opposite Plas Penmynydd, from where it can also be accessed by public footpath.

Back to Talwrn cross-roads: the main road continues southwest through the modern, residential part of the village towards Llangefni. The other lane leads from the crossroads to Llanbedr-goch. The village primary school is located on a back-lane to the northwest.

The poet of grief

A memorial stone at the crossroads in Talwrn commemorates the poet **Gruffudd ab yr Ynad Coch** (fl.1280).
   Little is known of his life, other than his connection with this parish. However his work survives, in the form of a moving elegy written for Llywelyn ap Gruffudd, the 'Last Prince', killed in a skirmish with the English in 1282. This is one of the great poems of the Welsh language, a passionate outpouring of grief expressed in alliterative verse, suited to the pivotal moment when Wales lost its independence. Its most famous lines sound a note of doom:

Poni welwch-chwi hynt y gwynt a'r glaw?

See you not the way of the wind and rain?

Poni welwch-chwi'r deri'n ymdaraw?

See you not oaktrees buffet together?

Poni welwch-chwi'r môr yn merwinaw 'r tir?

See you not the sea stinging the land?

Poni welwch-chwi'r gwir yn ymgyweiriaw?

See you not truth in travail?

Poni welwch-chwi 'r haul yn hwylaw 'r awyr?

See you not the sun hurtling through the sky?

Poni welwch-chwi'r sŷr wedi r'syrthiaw?

And that the stars are fallen?

Poni chredwch-chwi i Dduw, ddyniadion ynfyd?

Do you not believe God, demented mortals?

Poni welwch-chwi'r byd wedi r' bydiaw.

Do you not see the whole world's danger?

Och hyd atat-ti, Dduw, na ddaw – môr dros dir!

Why, O my God, does the sea not cover the land?

Pa beth y'n gedir i ohiriaw?

Why are we left to linger?

*English translation by **Tony Conran***

Traeth Bychan

8F
*2ml (3km)
north of
Benllech; turn
off A5025*

Traeth Bychan means 'little beach'. The car park at its northern end is approached along a lane, passing caravan sites and a beach café. The shoreline is sandy, backed by rocks. There is a public slipway, making the beach popular with boating enthusiasts. Red Wharf Bay Sailing Club is based here. Follow signs to cliff walks offering views south towards Llanddona. The coastline southwards to Red Wharf Bay is rich in fossils.

Dibunophyllum, a fossil coral from Traeth Bychan. The presence of this genus helps to date the limestone in which it was found as the youngest rock of the Carboniferous period.

Traeth Bychan was formerly quarried for fine limestone. This building stone was sometimes known as 'Mona Marble' (as was ornamental, coloured stone found elsewhere on Anglesey). Outcrops of conglomerate were also worked: the stone was exported and 'dressed' to make millstones of a high quality. The limestone blocks and the roughly hewn millstones were shipped out on coastal vessels from a little harbour. At the northern end of the beach is a small cluster of holiday cottages and the harbourmaster's house.

The bay was also the salvage site for the submarine *HMS Thetis,* which sank with terrible loss of life during sea trials off the Great Orme / *Pen y Gogarth,* in 1939. After being recovered and refitted as *HMS Thunderbolt,* the submarine was later lost at sea during wartime action off Sicily in 1943.

The small village of **Marian-glas** (meaning 'a green, stony place') clusters around a broad green and a memorial cross on high ground to the west of the A5025. Marian-glas was the birthplace of the actor Hugh Griffith (1912-80) who attended school in Llangefni and went on to the Royal Academy of Dramatic Art in London. He became a star of the West End and an award-winning interpreter of Shakespeare, famous for his 1946 role in *King Lear.* He also made a name for himself in the cinema, taking leading parts in the 1959 epic, *Ben-Hur* (for which he was awarded an American Academy 'Oscar') and in *Tom Jones* (1963). His sister, Elen Roger Jones, remained in Wales; here she achieved prominence in Welsh-language radio, television and theatre.

*Parciau
dovecote*

The village has a caravan park, past the **Parciau Arms**.

The village and the **Parciau** district to its west are rich in ancient remains, with a hut circle and a hill fort. The parish **Church of St Eugrad** (SH495842), reached by a lane from the B5110 Brynteg road, is built amidst fourth-century fortifications. The chancel and nave date from the twelfth century, the stone crucifix in the nave from the thirteenth. The north chapel dates from the sixteenth century. Some victims of the *Royal Charter* wreck are buried here.

Southeast of the church, standing on private land but visible from a gateway on the lane to the church (SH499840), is a tall gritstone **dovecote / *colomendy*** of the early seventeenth century, with gables and a cupola. It was designed for 150 nests.

Tynygongl — *see* **Benllech** ▶46

Sioe Môn
The Anglesey Agricultural Show

The author writes of his love for his native island.

MÔN, MÔN I MI

Bedwyr Lewis Jones

PUMP oed oeddwn-i yn dod i Fôn i fyw. Byth oddi ar hynny rwyf wedi bod yn crwydro'r ynys, ar droed, ar feic, ac mewn cerbyd. Rwy'n dal i daro ar ryw gongol newydd arni byth a hefyd.

Clwt o dir gwastad, isel, meddai'r gwerslyfrau daearyddiaeth amdani, gan awgrymu ei bod hi braidd yn undonog. 'Fu 'rioed y fath gamsyml-eiddio. Amrywiaeth cartrefol diderfyn sydd yma. I'w flasu mae gofyn ichi droi oddi ar briffyrdd y twristiaid a chrwydro'r cefnffyrdd a'r mân draethau, ac mae hynny'n golygu gadael y car bob hyn a hyn a cherdded.

Cerddwch i lawr i Ynys Lawd neu at drwyn Pwynt Leinws (*Trwyn Eilian*) a sylwi ar y plygion ar wyneb y creigiau, ac ystyriwch fod y creigiau Cyngambrian hyn yma cyn i fynydd-oedd Eryri ymffurfio. Ewch i Farclodiad y Gawres neu i Fryn Celli Ddu a sefyll a gwrando ar donfeddi distawrwydd hen wareiddiad. Cerddwch dros y tywod i Ynys Llanddwyn. Ewch i chwilio am Lyn Llywenan (heb fod ymhell o Fodedern). Rhowch dro i Langefni. Ie, dilynwch eich trwyn a chrwydro.

Ond y mae yna un daith yr hoffwn-i ei hargymell arnoch yn arbennig. Ym Mhentre Berw y mae honno'n cychwyn. Trowch oddi ar yr A5 yno a dilyn lôn B4419 nes dod at feindwr eglwys Llangaffo – y tŵr y parodd Cynan i'r nico beidio â loetran wrtho. Stopio a wnawn-ni a mynd i mewn i'r eglwys ac i'r festri, ar yr ochr chwith ym mhen yr allor. Yno yn y gongol fe welwch garreg a'r enwau 'CUURIS' a 'CINI' wedi eu torri arni. Creffwch ar y llythrennau. Yr ydych yn edrych ar yr enwau Cymraeg ysgrifenedig cynharaf a gadwyd inni. Fe'u cerfiwyd, meddir, rywdro tua 625. Os oedd y Gymraeg yn ddigon parchus i gael ei defnyddio'n 'swyddogol' ar garreg goffa yr adeg honno, fe ellwch fentro bod yr iaith yn cael ei siarad yn yr ardal ers dwy genhedlaeth a rhagor cyn hynny. Ers rhywdro tua 550, felly. Mae hynny bedwar cant ar ddeg o flynyddoedd yn ôl. Yn festri Llangaffo mae dyfnder daear ein treftadaeth yn ddychryn ac yn ysbrydoliaeth.

O ddilyn y lôn yn ei blaen dyna chi ar eich pen ym mhentre Niwbwrch. Dyma'r fwrdeisdref newydd a sefydlwyd gan Edward y Cyntaf yn 1303 ar gyfer y Cymry a symudwyd o Lan-faes er mwyn gwneud lle i Fiwmares. Trowyd y *'new borough'* yn Niwbwrch a'i gwareiddio. Hanner canrif ar ôl ei sefydlu daeth Dafydd ap Gwilym heibio a hithau'n wylmabsant. Gwelodd ferch yn dringo i lofft. Fe'i hoffodd. Heb golli dim amser gyrrodd ei was â dau alwyn o win yn rhodd iddi. Cymerodd y ferch y gwin ac yn dalog ddiseremoni ei dywallt am ben y gwas. Roedd cyrch caru

Dafydd wedi methu, ond fe gafodd-o destun cywydd hwyliog, cywydd wedi'i lunio i beri llonder a chwerthin.

Yn Niwbwrch trowch ar y dde am Falltraeth a chroesi'r twyni i'r Berffro. Aros yno, croesi'r hen bont ar droed a cherdded trwy'r pentre. Yma gynt yr oedd prif lys Gruffudd ap Cynan a Llywelyn Fawr a Llywelyn y Llyw Olaf. Byddaf fi yn synnu bob tro wrth ddarllen y frawddeg honno yn y llyfrau cyfraith sy'n dweud yn syml na thelir aur am sarhad 'namyn i frenin Aberffraw'. Does dim carreg o'r llys brenhinol yn aros bellach. Gofalodd gwŷr Edward am lwyr ddinistrio'r sumbol hwnnw o gadernid Gwynedd. Aed â choed ohono a'u hailddefnyddio yng nghastell Caernarfon, sumbol y drefn newydd. Beth amser yn ôl yng ngardd gefn un o dai y Berffro fe ddoed o hyd i gerflun trawiadol o ben carreg. Fe awn ar fy llw mai o lys Aberffraw y daeth hwnnw, gweddillyn briw o'r hen wychder pan oedd beirdd fel Meilyr a Gwalchmai yn llunio'u hawdlau yma a chyfarwyddiaid llys yn adrodd eu chwedlau.

Ifan Gruffydd (1896-1971)

Mae adrodd straeon a chreu chwerthin a dyfnder Cymraeg wedi para yma. Yn Bangor Street, 'y stryd ddiri-dani' sy'n mynd i lawr at yr afon, y mae stori gyntaf *Teisennau Berffro* Tom Parry Jones yn dechrau; ar y codiad uwchben Malltraeth y mae cartref yr awdur. Yn y Berffro y cafodd W J Gruffydd ei ysbrydoli; mae'r Henllys Fawr, ei gartref yntau, filltir y tu ucha i'r pentre, ar y dde oddi ar lôn Rhosneigr. Yn yr un darn daear y mae gwreiddiau Ifan Gruffydd. Ewch yn eich hôl o'r Berffro i Langadwaladr – 'Abaty Westminster' llys Aberffraw – a chadw ar y chwith yno. Ymhen rhyw bedair milltir fe fyddwch yn mynd heibio i gartref *Y Gŵr o Baradwys* – y clasur diymhongar hyfryd hwnnw. Mae bedd yr awdur ym mynwent Cerrigceinwen. Mae'n werth troi ar y chwith a phicio draw yno.

Mae yna daith arall yr hoffwn-i eich tywys arni, taith i Fodafon a bro'r Morrisiaid. Dilyn lôn Amlwch, yr A5025, sydd ei eisiau nes eich bod chi wrth y *Pilot Boat Inn* – y Refail Fawr ar lafar pan oeddwn i'n blentyn. Tu cefn i'r dafarn, uwchben Traeth Dulas, mae Pentre-eiriannell, cartref Lewis a Richard a William Morris yn hogiau. Trowch yn ôl oddi yno i bentre bach Brynrefail a chadw ar y dde, heibio eglwys Penrhosllugwy – lle claddwyd mam y brodyr, a thros Fynydd Bodafon a'r llyn Tylwyth Teg ar fin y ffordd ar ei ben, ac ymlaen i Faenaddwyn. Yno ar y dde mae eglwys Llanfihangel Tre'r Beirdd lle claddwyd tad y Morrisiaid. Bron gyferbyn mae'r Tyddyn Melys lle ganwyd Lewis Morris, yr athrylith fawr amlddoniog hwnnw.

Mae llefydd eraill yn galw. Penmon, er enghraifft. Cofiwch adael y car a throedio'r hanner milltir olaf gyda'r traeth at y fynachlog. Cerdded y darn yma un Sul yng nghwmni W J Gruffydd a barodd i T Gwynn Jones lunio'i gywydd godidog,

> Onid hoff yw cofio'n taith
> Mewn hoen i Benmon unwaith.

Mae'r harddwch a'r heddwch yn aros.

Bedd Branwen, eto, er nad yw hi mor hawdd dod o hyd i fan'no. Dilyn yr hen lôn bost o Langefni, y B5109, sydd orau, trwy Fodffordd ac ymlaen i Drefor – yn y siop ar y gongl yno y ganwyd Syr John Morris-Jones. Ar ôl gadael Trefor i gyfeiriad Bodedern, cymryd y tro cyntaf ar y dde a chanlyn yn eich blaen i'r bedwaredd croeslon, yna dal ar y dde fymryn a thros Afon Alaw heibio i glwstwr o dai.

Ychydig wedyn mae lôn ddidarmac ar y dde at fferm Glanalaw. Does dim olion trawiadol yma, dim ond carnedd wyrddlas ar dafod o dir ar lan yr afon. Ond dyma Fedd Branwen, hen gladdfa o tua 1,400 Cyn Crist. Y fangre hon a ysgogodd ryw awdur anhysbys o Gymro i lunio un o'r paragraffau trasig mwyaf cofiadwy yn holl lenyddiaeth Ewrop. Ewch i chwilio am y lle. Gorau oll os ewch yn niwedd Mai neu Fehefin pan fydd wyneb yr afon fach yn llathru'n wyn o flodau alaw'r dŵr. Os methwch daro ar y llecyn, pa wahaniaeth. Fe fyddwch wedi cael golwg ar ganol Môn ac ar amrywiaeth cyfoethog ei thirwedd.

Hwyl fawr i chi.

Ganed **Bedwyr Lewis Jones** (1933-92) yn Wrecsam tra oedd ei dad, Percy Ogwen Jones o Laneilian (gweler 'In the newsroom' ▶118), yn sefydlu papur newydd Y Cymro yno.

Symudodd y teulu yn ôl i Sir Fôn yn 1938. Addysgwyd Bedwyr Lewis Jones ym Mhen-y-sarn, Amlwch a Llangefni, ac yn ddiweddarch ym Mhrifysgol Cymru, Bangor, a Choleg yr Iesu, Rhydychen. Daeth yn bennaeth Adran y Gymraeg ym Mangor yn 1974.

Roedd Bedwyr yn ysgolhaig a beirniad llenyddol, yn frwd dros bob iaith Geltaidd ac yn arbenigwr ar dafodiaith ac enwau Sir Fôn. Ni fu erioed yn athro sych, ac roedd yn nodedig am rychwant helaeth ei ddiddordebau a hefyd yn ddarlledwr tan gamp.

Y geiriad ar y lechen sy'n ei goffáu ar fur ysgol Pen-y-sarn yw:
Athro a Chymwynaswr ein Hiaith.

Bedwyr Lewis Jones (1933-92) was born in Wrexham whilst his father, Percy Ogwen Jones of Llaneilian (see In the newsroom ▶118), was setting up Y Cymro newspaper there.

The family moved back to Anglesey in 1938. Bedwyr Lewis Jones was educated at Pen-y-sarn, and later at Amlwch and Llangefni, the University of Wales in Bangor and Jesus College, Oxford. In 1974 he became head of the Department of Welsh in Bangor.

Bedwyr was a literary scholar and critic, an enthusiast for all Celtic languages and an expert on the dialect and names of Anglesey. He was never the dry professor, always maintaining a wide range of interests and excelling as a broadcaster.

His commemorative plaque by the door of Pen-y-sarn school reads: **Athro a Chymwynaswr ein Hiaith**, … 'teacher and benefactor of our language'.

Parys Mountain

AMLWCH
and northern Anglesey

TWO LIGHTHOUSES signal the northern approaches to the island. One stands in the northwest, on the wicked offshore reefs known as the Skerries. The other tops the high, broad headland of Point Lynas in the northeast. Northern shores are mostly rugged and rocky, interspersed with small coves and bays. The northernmost point of all Wales is at Llanlleiana.

This part of the island is crossed by a loop of the A5025. Narrow lanes lead from this to some of the island's more out-of-the-way places. There are exhilarating coastal walks from Mynachdy and around Carmel Head. Amlwch is the chief town. Copper, mined from Parys Mountain, was once shipped from its port. The village of Cemaes is an ideal base for exploring the north of the island.

The sparkling stained glass and the blue tiles in the Church of St Padrig, at Llanbadrig near Cemaes, were the gift of Henry, third Lord Stanley of Alderley (1869-1903) who had converted to Islam after spending time in the Middle East

Amlwch

6H
20ml (32km)
NE of
Holyhead
on A5025,
or 17ml
(27km) north
of Menai
Bridge
on A5025

Amlwch is located on the rocky coast of northern Anglesey, to the west of Point Lynas / *Trwyn Eilian* ▶119. It overlooks the main shipping lanes for the port of Liverpool. A small uninhabited island called **East Mouse / Ynys Amlwch** lies offshore. On 9th May 1877 this was the scene of a major shipwreck when the liner *Dakota*, bound for New York from Liverpool, ran aground in dense fog with 530 passengers on board. Thanks to the prompt action of the Bull Bay lifeboat crew, no lives were lost.

Amlwch town

The ground rises at Pentrefelin in the southwest of the town. This district takes its name from a former windmill now converted into a residence, Melin Adda (1790s). Beside it is the **Leisure Centre** (1975), with a five-lane indoor pool and sports facilities. In the same elevated position is a large, modern secondary school, **Ysgol Syr Thomas Jones**. The school is named after a local doctor who, during the first decades of the twentieth century, had been an influential member (and chairman) of Anglesey's Education Committee. Dr Jones proposed that 'multilateral' education should be made available to all pupils, irrespective of social background and differing abilities. The school opened in 1953 as Britain's first purpose-built comprehensive school.

Amlwch has a modern library and a 1930s snooker hall. The town centre is the area around **Dinorben Square** and **Queen Street / Stryd y Frenhines**. Shopping opportunities may be limited, but there is a 'Country and Western' outfitters, a tribute to one of the island's more enduring sub-cultures.

Opposite the **Dinorben Arms Hotel** is the imposing tower of **St Eleth's Church** (1800). Its clock, chiming the hours by day but silent at night, is wound each week by a local butcher. The church was endowed by the Parys Mine Company at the height of the copper boom, and it replaced a previous church on the same site. The architect was a 'Mr Wyatt' – but which one? Might it have been James Wyatt (1746-1813), one of the most fashionable British architects of the day who had at that time been rebuilding Plas Newydd ▶214 in the south of the island? Such was his zeal for demolition – and reconstruction – that he was nicknamed 'the Destroyer'. Or was it perhaps one Samuel Wyatt, or indeed his brother Benjamin – both in the employ of the Penrhyn estates near Bangor? At any rate, by 1866 the congregation was complaining that the interior was 'utterly at variance with church architecture', and St Eleth's underwent a Gothic 'makeover'. Today's classical facade gives no clue to the contemporary interior, the result of further alterations completed in 1999 by the architect Adam Voelcker. Enter through the base

Amlwch's Catholic Church

of the tower: the font has been placed in the middle of the passageway in a dark, warm, womb-like space, with light filtering down through a canopy of copper. The nave has been made smaller, with pews on three sides.

What must be the most unusual church building on the island is the modernist Roman Catholic Church, dedicated to **Our Lady, Star of the Sea, and St Winefride**. Legend tells that during the seventh century Gwenfrewi, or 'Winefride', met a violent death before being raised again to life by her uncle, Saint Beuno of Clynnog-fawr, south of Caernarfon. The architect of the church was Giuseppe Rinvolucri, who was Italian by birth but lived at Conwy. He designed the building to resemble the upturned hull of a boat, complete with circular windows representing portholes. The church was consecrated in 1937. Serious problems with the reinforced concrete structure, and difficult access for infirm members of the congregation, have made the future of this Grade 2 protected building uncertain.

Amlwch has a number of disused chapels such as that of **Salem** (Baptist, 1827, reconstructed 1861). Open chapels include the **Wesleyan** chapel on Wesley Street and **Capel Mawr** on Bethesda Street.

In recent years Amlwch has attracted funding for the development of its social amenities through the Welsh Assembly Government's 'Communities First' scheme. With its help, the **Memorial Hall** in Wesley Street has been developed as a well-equipped community centre with space for performances. The Hall was built in the 1930s and had accommodated a county secondary school in the 1940s. The **Town Hall** has also been renovated. The old **National School** (1824) now houses a nursery.

Porth Amlwch

The most interesting part of town is the little cove and harbour of **Porth Amlwch**, to the northeast of the town centre, below the **Liverpool Arms** and **Adelphi Vaults** public house. In the nineteenth century, Amlwch had no fewer than 70 pubs and three breweries. The most popular waterside taverns in those days were the *Waterman's Arms* and the *Royal Oak*.

Porth Amlwch's impressive Presbyterian chapel, **Peniel**, was built in 1900 in the 'High Classic' style. The Independent Capel Carmel (1826, enlarged 1861) on Lôn Llaneilian was closed and sold at auction in 2006 for £140,000.

The port is formed by a narrow fissure in the rocky coast. Trawlers, yachts and small boats are still moored alongside deep quays and sea walls. The harbour structures – including dock walls built with vertically-placed stones – have a Cornish appearance, and Cornish miners and shipbuilders played their part in the port's history. The port is industrial, not picturesque – and it is fascinating.

Porth Amlwch by the painter and engraver William Daniell (1769-1837)

The name Amlwch means 'by the pool' or perhaps 'by the inlet'. In the sixteenth century Amlwch was little more than a few fishermen's cottages by the cove. Its rapid growth was due to Parys Mountain, the great expanse of copper-bearing rock to the south. ▶123 This saw a boom in mining between

Porth Amlwch

1768 and 1815, during which period it became the world's largest copper mine. In 1793 the tiny Porth Amlwch harbour was enlarged and new sea defences constructed. By the time the copper industry was at its peak in at the beginning of the nineteenth century, the population of Amlwch had risen to about 5,000 and Porth Amlwch had become the most important port in Wales. In 1816 moorings were extended further with a pier. It was said that up to forty vessels could find shelter here, but it must have been a squeeze. There is barely room for two vessels to pass. Copper ore, sometimes partly smelted, was the outward cargo, bound very often for Liverpool, Swansea or Cardiff. It was kept in stores known as 'bins', still to be seen on the harbour's eastern wharf. The ships' holds were sometimes filled with tobacco leaf for the return voyage, and this was processed as snuff and pipe tobacco in Amlwch factories.

Mining agents engaged in general shipping and became prosperous, and a thriving shipbuilding industry grew up, based on two shipyards – **Iard Newydd** (New Yard) at the eastern harbour entrance and **Iard Ochr Draw** (Other Side Yard), naturally on the western side, further from the harbour entrance. Big names in Amlwch shipping were William Thomas & Sons and James & Nicholas Treweek. Schooners and other vessels built in these yards towered over the small harbour. Shipbuilding outlasted the copper boom and Amlwch ships sailed the seven seas throughout the nineteenth century.

For the best view of the harbour's long, narrow layout, drive along the lane above the east side to the car park. Walk down to the harbour **Watchhouse** and light (1817, rebuilt 1853). Note the ruined **kiln** on the southeast side of the harbour, formerly used to produce lime for agriculture and construction. High on the western ridge are the remains of what was once the island's tallest windmill, known as **Melin y Borth** or Mona Mill (1816).

The **Heritage Centre** and café (Easter to September ✆ 01407 832255), in an old sail loft (c1870) off the harbour road, has the Amlwch Industrial Heritage Trust's small but interesting exhibition about both Parys Mountain and the port. Here is a protective plate from the bottom of *HMS Victory* (completed 1778, later Horatio Nelson's flagship at the Battle of Trafalgar), made of course out of Parys Mountain copper. Three ratings who served on the *Victory* during the battle in 1805 were Amlwch men: Edward Lewis (aged 22), William Pritchard (25) and William Jones (28). Here too are rock samples from the mines, and also some shipwreck items recently recovered by divers. Who would have thought that the captain of the *Galermo* (wrecked in 1860) could have had such a fancy toilet bowl installed? Today, Amlwch is promoted as the ancient copper town and is part of a European route of industrial heritage. A conservation and interpretation project, the 'Copper Kingdom', links Amlwch with the source of its prosperity in former times, Parys Mountain.

A later chapter in Amlwch's industrial history lasted from 1973 to 1987, when Rhos-goch, to the east, was the land base of an offshore terminal where tankers of over 500,000 tonnes could discharge crude oil – see *Rhos-goch* ▶126. Shell UK pumped the oil through an underground pipeline across the island to higher land on the mainland near Llanfairfechan, from where it flowed, mainly under gravity, to Stanlow in Cheshire – a total distance of 78 miles (125km). Since 1987, to keep the pipe in good condition, it has been filled with a weak alkaline solution to neutralise corrosive acids formed by bacterial action on the remaining traces of oil. Proposals for the future have included its use as a gas pipeline.

From the early 1950s bromine was extracted from seawater by the Amlwch factory of the Associated Octel Company (later part of the Great Lakes group). At the height of production, 150 people were employed here. Amongst its other applications, bromine is an ingredient of the anti-knock additive in petrol. The change to unleaded petrol was a significant factor in reducing the demand for bromine and led to the closure of the plant in 2004. Plans to use the site to process liquid natural gas have been considered. Although a factory producing polymer components employs 100 local people, the economy of Amlwch is in urgent need of new investment.

Bodewryd — *see* **Rhos-goch** ▶126

Bull Bay / *Porth Llechog*

6H
*1½ml
(2.5km)
NW of
Amlwch
on A5025*

Bull Bay is a sweep of coastline just to the west of Amlwch, with rugged rocks and caves. Entering this small resort from the east you pass the links of the Bull Bay **golf club** (18-holes © 01407 830960), with views north over the Irish Sea. A viewing point set up in a roadside lay-by offers views to **East Mouse**.

The **Trecastell Hotel** stands alongside holiday homes and bungalows. Turn from the main road to the small, rocky cove at the western end, below the **Bull Bay Hotel**. Once a pilot station, lifeboat station (1868-1926), fishing port and a shipyard, Bull Bay today relies on tourism. Walks lead westwards from the village to beautiful countryside and cliffs.

Burwen is a small village with a chapel, to the south and west of Bull Bay.

Carmel Head / *Trwyn y Gadair* *also known as* Trwyn y Gader

3G
*6½ml
(10.5km) west
of Cemaes*

The cornerstone of the island's northwest coast is a broad headland to the northwest of **Mynydd y Garn**. It is approached by narrow lanes from Church Bay ▶112 and Llanfair-yng-Nghornwy ▶120. There are clear views northwest to the Skerries rocks and their lighthouse ▶128 and the offshore island of **West Mouse / *Maen y Bugail***. Carmel Head offers some of Anglesey's finest landscapes. Cliff birds may include choughs and peregrine falcons, and wildflowers include coarse tufts of thrift (known also as sea pink) which flowers from March to September, and the yellow flowers of tormentil.

Parts of Carmel Head are owned by the National Trust. The north may be accessed from a small car park sited at a right-angled bend of the road from Llanfair-yng-Nghornwy to Cemlyn. From here, one path leads eastwards to **Trwyn Cemlyn**. The other leads westwards over broad, open sheep pastures; it passes through the large farmyard of **Mynachdy** on its way to the National Trust land. This name (meaning monastery) recalls the fact that in the Middle Ages this land was part of the estates of Aberconwy abbey. There were copper workings on Carmel Head in the eighteenth and nineteenth centuries, and there are also two aerial navigation beacons from the Second World War (known as 'the White Ladies'); there is a third on West Mouse. This is a landscape absolutely typical of Anglesey: wide expanses of close-cropped grass, interrupted by rocks ablaze with yellow gorse. Bullocks with muddy flanks gather by small, still pools.

Walking the coastal path

NORTHERN ANGLESEY

Ynys y Fydlyn

A southern National Trust site is divided from the northern by a long valley planted with conifers, in which pheasants are reared for shooting. From the western lane to Church Bay, follow the grassy path down to the seashore. A broad bar of pebbles protects a long inlet surrounded by rocks and pine trees. Offshore lies the great hump of **Ynys y Fydlyn**, its northern side eroded into a dramatic natural arch. This island is thought to have been the site of an Iron Age promontory fort before becoming isolated. The National Trust also owns several sections of the coast to the south. A coastal path leads over steep bluffs, weathered and yellowed by lichen, to the northern National Trust land. (A section of the route is barred for the shooting season, between October and February 13th, during which time other paths and a minor road can be followed around the closed land.) The path south from Mynachdy leads you back to the lane to Church Bay.

The bonesetters

It is said that two boys were the only survivors of a shipwreck off Carmel Head in the 1740s, but the language they spoke was unintelligible. One of the companions in misfortune was adopted by a Llanfair-yng-Nghornwy family and given the name Evan. He learned to speak Welsh.

Whatever the truth of the story, **Evan Thomas** did achieve fame as a naturally gifted healer and maker of splints for broken limbs – a 'bonesetter'. He died in 1814; a memorial tablet in Llanfair-yng-Nghornwy's Church of St Mary reads, in Welsh and in English:

> To the memory of Evan Thomas of Maes in this Parish who, in humble life, without the aid of education or any other advantage, by an extraordinary gift of Nature acquired such a knowledge of the human frame as to become a most skilful Bonesetter, whereby he rendered himself pre-eminently useful to his fellow creatures.

Evan Thomas's third son, Richard (1772-1851), farmed near Llanfaethlu, but was also called upon to set broken bones.

Other descendants of Evan Thomas and their relatives shared his gifts, practising in Liverpool and elsewhere. His grandson, **Hugh Owen Thomas** (1834-91), is regarded as a great pioneer of orthopaedic surgery. Hugh Owen developed the 'Thomas splint' which, during the First World War, was used to great effect by his nephew, the distinguished surgeon **Sir Robert Jones** (1857-1933). Sir Robert brought his skills to the Agnes Hunt Home at Gobowen, across the English border in Shropshire, and made it a famous centre of orthopaedic treatment.

Sir Robert Jones

Carreglefn — see **Mynydd Mechell** ▶122

Cemaes

4H

5ml (8km) west of Amlwch off A5025

The proper spelling of the place-name, *Cemais*, means 'bend'. Cemaes, the northernmost village in Wales, has remained attractive, grouped around a small harbour beyond the **Olde Vigour** and **Stag** inns. A stone breakwater, built to the design of Ishmael Jones between 1828 and 1835, after a severe storm damaged the existing pier, shields fishing and pleasure boats at their moorings. The breakwater was rebuilt after futher storm damage in 1889, and improved in 1900.

Traeth Mawr, Cemaes

In the medieval period Cemaes was the centre of one of the island's administrative units (a *cantref* or 'hundred') and the location of one of the small royal courts of Gwynedd. Originally called Porth Wygyr, after its little river, this was the main port on Anglesey's north coast, a centre for fishing, shipbuilding and smuggling (from the Isle of Man). In the eighteenth and nineteenth centuries Cemaes exported ochre, lime and salted herrings. Ships were built here too, but by this time the centre of industry and economic activity was already moving eastwards to Amlwch, especially once Cemaes was bypassed by the railway. A lifeboat station was set up in 1872. The last lifeboat in service here, until closure in 1932, was the *Charles Henry Ashley*, brought to Cemaes in 1907. Efforts are being made by the RNLI to renovate this rare example of a 38ft rowing and sailing lifeboat.

The abandoned industrial site of the **Cemaes brickworks** lies on the inland side of the A5025 (SH373931). Its tall chimney and kiln were built in 1907 where a medieval water mill once stood. Production ceased in 1914. A fifteen-minute riverside walk leads to the works from the site of an old quayside at the mouth of Afon Wygyr – now the Beach car park. The signposted footpath, along ***Nant y Dyfrgi*** ('otter valley'), follows the route of a narrow-gauge railway that once carried the bricks down to the sea. Some lengths of rail still survive.

On the High Street is the **Bethel Congregational Chapel** (1827, rebuilt 1910), and next to it a **heritage centre** with a small display and a café (open all year © 01407 710004). The **Village Hall** (1899) across the road, with an elaborate clock tower, was presented to the inhabitants of Cemaes by David Hughes of Wylfa. The Victorian church of **St Patrick** *(Padrig)* was built in 1865, in the 'Early English' style. It stands just to the west of the roundabout on the A5025. The Catholic Church, dedicated to **Saint David**, was opened on St David's Day 1965. The sturdy building was erected by workers engaged in the construction of the Wylfa nuclear power station. The **Bethesda** chapel (1894) is on the western edge of the village.

At the southern limits of Cemaes, on the road to Llanfechell, is a tall windmill, **Melin Cemaes (**1828). It is converted into a private dwelling.

At the eastern end of the village is a sandy beach, **Traeth Mawr**, overlooked by a small coastguard station; its car park may be reached via a lane from Llanbadrig ▶115. The road through the village passes housing estates and small shops. The headland to the west of the village is the site of the Wylfa nuclear power station ▶129, the chief employer in northern Anglesey.

Cemaes Bay is set in beautiful countryside and is a council-designated conservation area. The village is a good starting point for cliff walking.

Cemlyn

4H

2½ml (4km) west of Cemaes, turn off A5025 at Tregele

Tregele is a residential village just to the south of Wylfa nuclear power station, at the northwestern corner of the A5025 circuit. The **Douglas Inn** provides refreshment. Take the northwest lane to visit a stretch of unspoiled, rural northern Anglesey, with large stone farmhouses and farmyards. The power station looms incongruously on the skyline.

A lane leads to **Cemlyn Bay** from Tregele. Off the lane, towards the coast, is **Cestyll**. The house is now demolished, but its rock gardens in the Cafnan valley include a watermill, **Melin Cafnan**, c1840. (Cestyll is occasionally open to the public: further information is provided in the *Directory* section.)

At the beginning of the nineteenth century, many wealthy landowners bought property at Cemlyn because its bay, which offered safe deepwater moorings, was considered for development as the main packet port for Ireland. In the event, a parliamentary Select Committee chose Holyhead. Some of the buildings at Cemlyn – those with doors and window frames painted cornflower blue – are a reminder of the speculative rush for land: the colour scheme is that of the Meyrick Estate of Bodorgan. The National Trust retained the colour when it acquired these properties for use as workshops.

The Cemlyn shingle bar

Below the grassy headland of **Trwyn Cemlyn**, northerly gales have formed a crescent-shaped shingle bar which encloses a brackish lagoon. The bar and lagoon are a nature reserve, leased at a nominal rate by the National Trust to the North Wales Wildlife Trust. The reserve supports the major nesting colony of sandwich terns in Wales. Other birds nesting here include common and Arctic terns, black-headed gulls, ringed plovers, oystercatchers and redshanks, as well as waterfowl such as shelduck, mallard and red-breasted mergansers. In winter one may see teal and wigeon. Car parks are located at both the eastern and western ends of the bar, though the western car park can become submerged during high tides, at which time crossing the outfall stream at the western end of the bar may not be possible either. Please do not walk on the crest of the bar during the birds' breeding season (from April to July) – use only the seaward-side footpath at this time. Dogs should always be kept on a lead. A footpath from the western car park leads to Trwyn Cemlyn, with views westwards along the rocky coast to the Skerries. A plaque commemorates the launching of Anglesey's first lifeboat at Cemlyn in 1828 – see *James & Frances Williams* ▶120.

The brick house on the bay's western shore is Bryn Aber, once owned by the remarkable, and wealthy, Captain Vivian Hewitt (1888-1965). The story of his pioneering aeroplane flights is told in *Aviation pioneers (opposite)*. Amongst many other interests, Vivian Hewitt was a racing car driver and a collector of butterflies, stamps, gold coins and guns. He also collected birds' eggs and taxidermy specimens. It is said that he was:

> … *celebrated, in particular, as a serial collector of the Great Auk and its eggs, at one time owning nine eggs and four stuffed specimens.*

(The Great Auk had become extinct in 1844.)

Wanting to attract and study living birds, in 1939 the reclusive Captain built the high walls that surround his house. A sheltered garden was created in which trees could flourish and cats could be excluded. Sections of the walls include concealed walkways equipped with spy-holes for bird watching. Captain Hewitt managed Cemlyn Bay as a 272-acre (110ha) private nature reserve, building a weir that is still used to maintain the lagoon's water level. After his death, many of Vivian Hewitt's extensive collections were purchased by museums in the United States and in Great Britain. His Cemlyn estate was acquired by the National Trust through funds raised by 'Enterprise Neptune'. Bryn Aber is not open to public view.

Arctic tern   The abandoned sheds just northeast of Bryn Aber were used to store the coal shipped here during the Second World War to heat the area's homes.

Aviation pioneers

The first years of the twentieth century were exciting times in aviation. In 1903 the Wright brothers made that first flight, at Kitty Hawk in the United States.

Seven years later, some towns in North Wales were witnessing their first ever aeroplane landings. **Vivian Hewitt** (1888-1965), then living in Rhyl, had inherited a fortune made in the brewing industry and was already an experienced pilot when be bought his first Blériot monoplane in 1910 – just six months after Louis Blériot had made the first flight across the English Channel. On 26th April 1912, Captain Hewitt, in a Gnome-Blériot, made a pioneering flight of his own – 60 miles (96km) across the Irish Sea from Holyhead to Dublin.

At that time **William Ellis Williams** (1881-1962) of Bethesda, near Bangor, was already building his own plane, the so-called *Bamboo Bird*. The son of a quarryman, William had always

been fascinated by flight and aerodynamics. He had studied at the university in Bangor and had also carried out research in Scotland and Germany. In 1906 he became a physics lecturer in Bangor and began work on a powered monoplane with a wooden fuselage. Landowner Sir Harry Verney allowed him to build a hangar by the beach at **Llanddona**. It was there in September 1913 that the *Bamboo Bird* at last took off, reaching an altitude of 7 feet (2m) and a breakneck speed of 37mph (59kph).

Williams worked for Vickers during the First World War and later became the first professor of electrical engineering at Bangor.

In the 1930s Vivian Hewitt settled at Cemlyn, where he established a private nature reserve on the lagoon. This land is now National Trust property.

*A biography, **The Modest Millionaire** by William Hywel – from which the photograph, below, is taken – was published in 1973 (Gwasg Gee, Denbigh).*

On the western side of Trwyn Cemlyn, accessed by footpaths from the lane, is **Llanrhwydrys**. The **Church of St Rhwydrys** (SH322932) is a small stone building amidst green fields beside the blue sea. Rhwydrys was of royal Irish descent. The church's font and nave date from the twelfth century, the chancel from the thirteenth, and it has a minstrels' gallery (with a beam dated 1776). Cruck timbers, forming the roof, are of particular interest. Amongst the graves in the churchyard is that of a Norwegian captain whose vessel was wrecked off Cemlyn in 1869.

Church Bay / *Porth Swtan*

3G

2¾ml
(4.5km)
NW of
Llanfaethlu,
off A5025

Porth Swtan means 'whiting port' in Welsh, and fishing and farming were the livelihoods here before the arrival of motor traffic and tourism. This remains a peaceful and timeless part of Anglesey, especially out of season. The lanes are narrow and winding and bordered with clumps of montbretia. Heathland here, grazed by ponies, is one of the few localities where Anglesey's floral emblem, the Spotted Rock-rose, grows. Stone farm buildings lie amidst green hills, rising to **Pen y Foel**. The tower of a former windmill still stands. This is Melin Drylliau, also known locally as Melin Caerau (the private Caerau estate, with a house dating from the seventeenth century, lies to the northeast). The mill burned down in 1914, a few years after the death of one of the miller's children from being struck on the head by the whirling sails – a not uncommon occurrence. The bay is approached by a lane which leads down past the **Lobster Pot** restaurant.

From the Church Bay car park (with toilets) a path leads to **Swtan** (SH301 891). This is a fine example of a traditional whitewashed Anglesey cottage, thatched with wheat straw over gorse laid on hazel laths and bordered by a herb garden. The living quarters are flanked by animal and store sheds, all restored and furnished to their appearance in the years around 1900. Swtan is owned by the National Trust and operated by volunteers. During the summer it opens on Fridays, Saturdays and Sundays © 01407 730501.

*Swtan, and
Church Bay*

Church Bay has a fine sandy beach; its broad reefs are ideal for rockpooling at low tide. The bay is backed by high cliffs of red sandstone, a nesting site for gulls, fulmars and choughs. Holyhead Mountain rises from the southern horizon. Follow the signposted coastal walk from the head of the beach southwards to **Porth Crugmor**, also known as Cable Bay after its (abandoned) communications cable which, it is said, is still visible at the lowest tides.

Another path leads north for views of the lighthouse on the rocks of the Skerries.

The village of **Rhyd-wyn** lies one mile (1.5km) inland. On the way there, climbing steeply from the beach, note the slender-spired parish **Church of St Rhuddlad**, built to replace an older foundation in 1858. This landmark gives Church Bay its English name. It is reached through an ivy-clad stone arch. Its rector from 1859 until his death was Morris Williams (1809-74), a cleric and hymn writer, with the bardic name 'Nicander'. Rhyd-wyn itself is a small resi-

The parish church (left) and Capel Bethel at Llanrhuddlad

dential village clustered around a **Baptist chapel** (1914). Northwest of Rhydwyn is **Craig y Gwynt**, the site of an 1841 **telegraph station**, one of a chain set up across the island to report the sighting of inward-bound ships heading for the port of Liverpool – see *Pen-y-sarn* ▶126.

The village of **Llanrhuddlad** borders the A5025, 1½ miles (2.5km) to the west of its parish church. A war memorial stands at the centre of the village. The salt-cellar spire of the **Bethel** chapel (1771, rebuilt 1905, Calvinistic Methodist) rises at the village's northern end. It has been written that 'its spire was consciously built as a jibe to the local Anglican church'. The chapel faces a wide panorama of the mountains of Snowdonia, which rise in the distance over the lowlands of central Anglesey.

Dulas
7G
4½ml (7km) SW of Amlwch, turn off A5025

Afon Goch was called the 'red river' because its headwaters were once stained by the polluted drainage from Parys Mountain. (It has been estimated that about 40 per cent of the Irish Sea's heavy metal content is derived from Parys Mountain run-off!). The river drains the northern slopes of Yr Arwydd as it flows northeastwards, crossing beneath the A5025 at **City Dulas**, to the north of **Brynrefail** ▶84 and the **Pilot Boat** public house.

The river enters a long and beautiful estuary, **Traeth Dulas**, whose mudflats are exposed at low tide. Gulls and wading birds wheel over reeds and bladderwrack washed up to the high water line. This was once a busy waterfront, with lime kilns and brickworks. Today boats lie moored peacefully on the flats. Across the rolling breakers is **Ynys Dulas**, the haunt of grey seals. The small island has a tall tower, built in 1824 as a beacon and refuge for shipwrecked mariners.

The Afon Goch estuary and the Dulas estate

There is a car park at the head of the estuary on the north shore. The north bank of the estuary is occupied by the **Llys Dulas** district of scattered farms and woodland. Llys Dulas takes its name from a sixteenth- to seventeenth-century mansion, which was lavishly rebuilt in the eighteenth and nineteenth centuries. The rebuilding of 1856 was to the design of Benjamin Woodward, architect of the Oxford Museum. Its estate was greatly improved by Gertrude, Dowager Lady Dinorben, widow of William Lewis Hughes, first Baron Dinorben, who had inherited a fortune made during the Parys Mountain copper boom. In 1871 their daughter, Gwen, married Sir Thomas Arundell Neave. The Neave family, of Dagnam Park in Essex, were merchants and financiers. They made Llys Dulas their chief residence during the Second World War. After the war, bomb-damaged Dagnam Park became derelict, and Llys Dulas itself was demolished in 1976. The old garden of the Llys is under restoration, and its estate is being redeveloped.

The medieval parish **Church of St Gwenllwyfo**, which lies in ruins seawards from the old Llys, was replaced by a Victorian church of the same name in 1856 (SH477893), built near the Llys Dulas main lodge. Its benefactor was Gertrude, Lady Dinorben. Designed by the Bangor architect Henry Kennedy to accommodate the family, guests and servants of the Llys, it is large for the island, with a narrow spire. In 1877 the church was fitted with precious fifteenth- and sixteenth-century Flemish stained glass from the Neave family collection, illustrating scenes from the New Testament. Much of the glass was purchased from the Carthusian Monastery of Louvain (or Leuven) in Belgium. The rest of the collection today is in London's Victoria and Albert Museum, in Glasgow's Burrell Collection and in New York's Metropolitan Museum of Art.

Flemish stained glass, Church of St Gwenllwyfo

On the southern side of the estuary, a footpath skirts the private land of Pentre-eiriannell and links with the lane from the northern end of Traeth Lligwy. From the lane, a turning descends to the southern shore through ancient beech trees. There is no car park at the bottom. A well-marked coastal footpath leads from the top lane to a secluded sandy beach, **Traeth yr Ora**, and on southwards over low, grassy cliffs to **Traeth Lligwy** ▶70

The Morris Brothers

Near the *Pilot Boat Inn*, by the A5025 just northwest of Brynrefail, look out for an inscribed slate commemorating *Morrisiaid Môn* – the remarkable Morris brothers of Anglesey. Climb the public footpath to a grassy knoll overlooking the Traeth Dulas estuary (SH478873), where a modern cross (designed by the Bangor architect Harold Hughes) is also erected to their memory. It stands on the land of Pentre-eiriannell, the brothers' family home. In the eighteenth century their multi-faceted talents made an important contribution to the Age of Enlightenment in Wales.

• **Lewis Morris** (1701-65) was a surveyor, mining engineer, writer, cartographer and publisher. He was also a poet, with the bardic name *Llywelyn Ddu o Fôn*. In 1724 he surveyed the Bodorgan estate and in 1729 worked as a customs official at Holyhead and Beaumaris. Lewis continued in various employments around Wales, and interested himself in lead-mining around Aberystwyth. He was always a passionate promoter of Welsh literature, printing and publishing an influential anthology *Tlysau yr Hen Oesoedd* ('Gems of Past Ages') in 1735. He studied the poetry of Dafydd ap Gwilym, antiquities and natural history. In 1737 he began a famous hydrographical survey of

the Welsh coast, producing two fine publications of charts in 1748, a real boon to navigation.

Lewis Morris (artist unknown) 1748

• **Richard Morris** (1703-79) collected folk tales and songs of Anglesey. In 1746, whilst working in London as chief clerk of foreign accounts in the Navy Office, he published a revised edition of the Welsh Bible and in 1751 founded the *Honourable Society of Cymmrodorion* ('earliest inhabitants') to encourage Welsh literature, science and culture.

• **William Morris** (1705-63) lived at Holyhead, where he was Comptroller of Customs. He was a collector of manuscripts, a church choir master and a dedicated gardener. His botanical work laid the foundations for the work of Hugh Davies – see *The Botanology* ▶187

• **John Morris** (1706-40) served in the navy and shared many of his brothers' interests. As a mate on the *Torbay* man-of-war he perished of the 'bloody flux' – dysentery – on the island of Dominica in the Caribbean.

All four of the Morris brothers were avid writers of letters, and much of their correspondence survives.

" A CORRESPONDENT of mine is about publishing the natural history of the birds of Britain, and wants the Welsh names of birds. If you will take the trouble of writing down the Welsh names of birds in your neighbourhood, I shall be obliged to you; I may possibly meet with an uncommon name among them." — LEWIS MORRIS, *in a letter to Edward Richard*, 11th March 1761

NORTHERN ANGLESEY

Llanbadrig

5H
4ml (6km) west of Amlwch, turn off A5025 east of Cemaes

Llanbadrig Point

To the east of Cemaes a lane loops to the north of the A5025; it crosses some of the most beautiful scenery of Anglesey's north coast. From this one can turn west to a large car park at the eastern end of Cemaes Bay, or continue northwards to the **Church of St Padrig** (SH376947). There is a car park next to the rounded stone arch of the churchyard.

This is one of the oldest ecclesiastical sites in Wales, possibly dating back to about AD440. Local tradition maintains that the Romano-British Saint Patrick *(Padrig)*, who played an important part in the conversion of Ireland to Christianity, was saved from shipwreck here.

Today's church dates from the fourteenth century, but contains earlier material: a ninth-century gravestone inscribed with a Celtic cross, a stone pillar from the same period featuring early symbols of Christianity including the *Ichtheus* (fish), and a twelfth-century font. Its restoration in 1884 included decorative details in the Islamic style, including blue tiles and sparkling stained glass windows. ▶103 The project was endowed by Henry, third Lord Stanley of Alderley (1869-1903, an uncle of the philosopher Bertrand Russell), who spent his youth in the Middle East and became a Moslem. Llanbadrig church has suffered two disastrous attacks by vandals in recent years. A sacred well, **Ffynnon Badrig** lies to the north.

In recent years, hardy varieties of grapevines have been planted on land near St Patrick's church, and a small **vineyard** – bottling red, white and sparkling wines – is becoming established. Unlike the rows of vines in southern Europe, here they have been planted in a number of small plots, sheltered from the wind and from frosts in May. The problems of viniculture in this part of the island have little to do with a lack of sunshine: Llanbadrig water is drawn from wells, and drought has proved to be the real difficulty.

Llanbadrig church is surrounded by National Trust land: follow precipitous cliff paths eastwards from the churchyard to Porth Llanlleiana. There are views westwards to the Skerries lighthouse.

Porth Llanlleiana

Llanlleiana may also be reached by the lane which runs parallel with the coast. A half-mile (800m) east of Llanbadrig's church car park, another footpath leads to **Llanlleiana Head**, the most northerly point in Wales – unless you count the little offshore island of **Middle Mouse / Ynys Badrig** ('Patrick's Island', said to be the site of St Patrick's shipwreck). Crossing hilly sheep pasture, the path divides at a long valley of sedge. The western path leads to the stony cove of **Porth Llanlleiana** (SH388951) where ruined buildings are all that survive of a nineteenth-century china clay industry. Waves pound the stony beach. The mouth of the cove frames the bare, rocky Middle Mouse. In 2005 the two-acre (1ha) uninhabited island was offered for sale as part of a 160-acre (64ha) coastal estate. The price was £895,000. No sale being agreed, it was taken off the market. The headland with its sheer cliffs is the site of an ancient (probably Iron Age) promontory fort, **Dinas Gynfor**, with an area of about 24 acres (10ha). The limestone walls on the southern side are the remains of its defences. Part of this headland became the National Trust's first property on Anglesey. A derelict tower of 1901 (SH389952) commemorates Edward VII's coronation.

The eastern path skirts the bracken-covered slopes of the headland to steep National Trust land above **Hell's Mouth / Porth Cynfor** and **Porth Adfan**. Follow the path through a blaze of gorse to the western edge of the bay at **Porth Wen**, one of the most beautiful bays on Anglesey and an ideal place for a summer picnic.

Porthwen brickworks

The beehive-like kilns and towers are the ruins of the Porthwen **brickworks** (SH402945), which operated from 1889 until about 1924, and was finally abandoned in the 1930s. Porthwen produced bricks for building, and also fire-bricks for furnaces, using quartzite from the cliffs. An experienced tile-maker came from Japan to teach the Anglesey workers the techniques of his craft. The demise of the works was due to technical problems as well as poor access from the sea. Today the brickworks are in a dangerously dilapidated condition and should only be viewed from the clifftop. Paths continue to the Llanbadrig lane and east to Trwyn Bychan and Bull Bay.

Llaneilian

7G

3ml (4.5km)
east of
Amlwch

Llaneilian occupies the northeast corner of Anglesey; the grassy slopes of Mynydd Eilian rise to the south – see *Pen-y-sarn* **▶126** The fascinating **Church of St Eilian** (SH469928), one of Anglesey's *Grade 1* protected churches, is approached via lanes leading from Amlwch (past a **Women's Institute Hall** with its millennium garden) and from the A5025. It is said that a hermitage was established on the site of the present church in the fifth century. **Ffynnon Eilian**, a sacred well to the north, attracted medieval pilgrims.

The Church of St Eilian

The tower of St Eilian's Church dates from the twelfth century, but the nave and chancel were built between 1480-81, as indicated by dated stones on the outside of the church. Dendrochronological dating of the roof timbers has confirmed construction around 1480. An unusual pyramidal spire surmounts a broad tower. The church is a striking example of what medieval churches on the island looked like before they were 'improved' by the Victorians. Sensitive repairs were undertaken in 1929 by the Bangor diocesan architects William Griffith Williams and Harold Hughes. A major but non-intrusive restoration took place in 2002, during which, amongst other work, the tower was lime-washed. The ochre pigment used in the mix was identical to that once produced locally (and used previously to decorate the church) by the St Eilian Colour Works as a by-product of the copper precipitation process. The nave's crenellated parapet is much weathered, as is the stepped stone arch and cross at the southern gate. The corner structure on the south side was added in 1614 as a passageway to **St Eilian's Chapel**, projecting to the southwest. The chapel is thought to overlie the grave of the saint. This type of chapel is known at other churches, and is called *capel y bedd*, or 'chapel of the grave'. A marked difference in the alignments of chapel and church suggests that the chapel pre-dates the twelfth-century church.

The interior of the church is noted for its wooden carvings, which include angels playing on flutes and bagpipes. The late fifteenth-century rood screen features a seventeenth- or eighteenth-century painting of a skeleton with a scythe, bearing the stern text *COLYN ANGAU YW PECHOD* ('the sting of death is sin'). During refurbishment, some faint traces of medieval paintings were also revealed, one of a bearded man.

In past centuries Llaneilian, like many other villages in Anglesey, celebrated the day of their patron saint with a *mabsant* festival. The festivities included markets and fairs, high jinks and sporting contests. At Llaneilian, in order to ensure a long life, the custom was to try to lie in the oak chest *(Cyff Eilian)* used to collect offerings from medieval pilgrims. Not to be outdone, and to bring them good luck too, youngsters would try to squeeze through a narrow gap in the chapel shrine – but if they touched the sides the penalty would be misfortune.

Slate slabs in the churchyard mark the graves of many a Victorian seafarer. The days of the tall ships are recorded in the letters of a second mate from Llaneilian, John Roberts (1858-82). He served on the *Countess of Kintore*, a ship built in the William Thomas yard at Porth Amlwch. Letters were sent back to Wales from exotic ports such as Rio de Janeiro and Rangoon; however his ship, last sighted on 15th September 1882, was never seen again.

NORTHERN ANGLESEY

In the news room

Percy Ogwen Jones (1894-1982) was a Llaneilian boy who became interested in the ideas of socialism and pacifism at a very early age.

When he was twenty, the outbreak of the First World War led to his imprisonment as a conscientious objector: he spent over three years in a number of prisons, including Dartmoor. The contacts he made during this period with like-minded people were to shape his future life. After the war he became a journalist, gaining experience on English-language newspapers including the *Daily Herald*. Back in Wales, and based in Wrexham / *Wrecsam*, he worked alongside another journalist from Llaneilian, John Tudor Jones, known as **John Eilian** (1904-85).

Their political views were opposed – John Eilian was later to stand in Anglesey as the Conservative candidate in a parliamentary election – but together in 1932 they established the weekly newspaper *Y Cymro* ('The Welshman'), to 'unite Wales and create a Welsh view and opinion on all things pertaining to Wales and the Welsh'. John Eilian was its first editor. He was also a poet, winning the Chair (1941) and Crown (1949) at National *Eisteddfodau*.

Percy Ogwen Jones played an important part in two other influential Welsh-language publications: *Y Dinesydd* (the Welsh Labour newspaper) and *Y Faner* (a weekly journal). After 1938, now settled back in Llaneilian, he became an energetic Anglesey county councillor and worked in education and promotion of the Welsh language.

*Bedwyr Lewis Jones, one of Percy Ogwen Jones's sons, became Professor of Welsh at the University of Wales, Bangor. When the first edition of this guidebook was published in 1976, he contributed the Welsh-language essay **Môn, Môn i Mi** (which is reproduced again on page 99).*

Percy Ogwen Jones (on the left) and John Eilian

The running of the deer

An old legend states that in the mid-fifth century AD, Saint Eilian was sent to Anglesey by the Pope, to treat with the then ruler of the island, Cadwallon Lawhir. The ruler's men stole the cattle off Eilian's ship, so the monk made him blind as a punishment. A bargain was struck. In return for getting his sight back, Cadwallon would grant Eilian as much land as a deer could cover before being brought down by the royal pack of hounds. The deer finally succumbed on the brow of Mynydd Eilian. It was agreed that this tract of land would become the saint's domain.

Porth Eilian

Continue downhill from the church gates and visit **Porth Eilian**. This pretty cove, of pebbles, sand and rock, is sheltered by a curved wall of lichen-covered cliffs. Signs indicate coastal walks, with views southwards to the distant mountains. To the west of Porth Eilian a plaque commemorates Edward Greenly (1861-1951), the first geologist to attempt a detailed interpretation of the complex structure of the island's rocks. The task took 24 years and his survey, the two-volume *Geology of Anglesey,* was published in 1919. The plaque marks a famous glacial 'erratic' block, brought here from the north of England by the ice sheets.

Point Lynas
Trwyn Eilian

This corner of the island is formed by a rocky headland, **Point Lynas / *Trwyn Eilian***, also known as *Trwyn y Balog* or *Penrhyn Gwybedog*, which extends due north into the Irish Sea. This is one of the best places on the island to spot porpoises and dolphins. It was agreed to base a pilot station on Point Lynas in 1766; as the port of Liverpool grew in importance, so did the work of the pilots. Six-oared gigs would meet incoming vessels. It should be remembered that at the height of the British empire, a staggering proportion of global trade passed through Liverpool, so the pilots' work was crucial. Today, Merseyside has undergone decline; however there are generally still many large vessels to be seen riding in the lee of the headland and down Anglesey's east coast.

An oil-fired lighthouse was erected by the Liverpool Pilotage Service in 1779 as a warning beacon. The present day castle-like **lighthouse** was commissioned by the Trustees of the Liverpool Docks in 1835, designed by the civil engineer Jesse Hartley. The light was modernised in the 1960s and today is automated under the control of Trinity House in Liverpool. It stands 95 feet (29m) above high tide level and has a range of twenty miles (32km). It flashes every ten seconds. When visibility is poor a foghorn blasts, also every ten seconds. Buildings at the foot of the lighthouse are privately owned.

The tower standing on higher land above the lighthouse was used as a semaphore station – one of a series set up along the North Wales coast from Holyhead to signal to Liverpool shipowners the safe return of their ships. The semaphore was replaced from 1860 by morse code messages transmitted by an electrical system, although the old tower still stands.

Llanfair-yng-Nghornwy *also known as* **Llanfairynghornwy**

3G

4½ml (7km) SW of Cemaes, turn off A5025

The tiny village of Llanfair-yng-Nghornwy is scattered amongst peaceful farmland in the northwest of the island, beneath **Mynydd y Garn**. A maze of narrow lanes leads south to Llanrhuddlad and Church Bay, northeast to the nature reserve at Cemlyn and northwest to the walks around Carmel Head. The parish **Church of St Mary**, *Santes Fair* (SH327908), next to the rectory (1824), is reached by a wooded lane in the southeastern part of the parish. Cawing rooks nest in trees nearby. The church dates back to the eleventh or twelfth century, with much of it from later centuries. Nineteenth-century restoration was carried out by its rector, the Reverend James Williams and others. This is one of Anglesey's *Grade 1* protected churches.

'The Preservation of Life from Shipwrecks'

James Williams was born at Treffos, Llansadwrn, in 1790. He was educated at Jesus College, Oxford, and became rector of Llanfair-yng-Nghornwy in 1821. James married a remarkable woman called **Frances Lloyd** (b1798), who was a friend of the Darwin family and a painter of watercolours.

Shortly after their wedding in 1823 James and Frances witnessed the terrible shipwreck of the Irish packet *Alert*. 143 people drowned when she was becalmed and drifted onto offshore rocks at West Mouse. The couple decided to devote themselves to saving lives at sea. They raised funds tirelessly and by 1828 had founded 'The Anglesey Association for the Preservation of Life from Shipwrecks'. They based the Association's first lifeboat at Cemlyn. James was himself coxswain of the boat and took part in many heroic rescues, as did his son Owen Lloyd Williams after him. James was awarded the first RNLI Gold Medal in Wales after two wrecks in 1835: five

sailors having been saved from the *Active* (wrecked in Cemaes Bay) and fourteen from the *Sarah* (wrecked near Porth Trecastell).

Frances was equally used to stormy seas, tending to the lighthouse keeper on the Skerries when he was taken ill. Together they saved hundreds of lives. After the death of Frances, the Anglesey Association became part of the Royal National Lifeboat Institution and James continued his work for lifeboats until his own death in 1872. He was also a magistrate who supported the National Eisteddfod, and argued for educational reform. His many interests contributed to the efforts being made to improve the conditions of Anglesey life in the middle of the nineteenth century .

The fascinating story of James and Frances Williams, who are buried in Llanfair-yng-Nghornwy, is told by their great-grandson, the painter Kyffin Williams, in **Across the Straits** *(1973), the first volume of his autobiography.*

Today, four Royal National Lifeboat Institution stations are based on Anglesey. The stations at Holyhead and Moelfre operate both offshore and inshore craft. Trearddur has two inshore craft, Beaumaris has one.

Anglesey's **offshore craft** each carry crews of six. On station at Holyhead is the *Christopher Pearce*. This is a **Severn class** boat and at 17 metres it is presently the largest class of the RNLI fleet. They carry an inflatable boat and the top speed is 26 knots. Moelfre's offshore boat is the 14.3-metre **Tyne class** *Robert & Violet*, with a low-profile wheelhouse, a separate cabin behind the steering position and a speed of nearly 18 knots. She will be replaced by

a 16-metre boat of the new **Taymar class**.

Anglesey's **inshore craft** are either **D Class** (such as *Angel of Holyhead*) with a speed of 25 knots and GPS navigation, or the 32-knot **Atlantic 75** boats (such as the Beaumaris *Blue Peter II*). Intended to work in sight of land, or within sight of another offshore lifeboat, they cannot, in general, operate in winds of more than force 7, moderate gales. (The *Royal Charter* storm, Britain's most severe of the nineteenth century, was force 12 on the Beaufort scale – a hurricane.) Trearddur's Atlantic-75, the *Dorothy Selina*, will eventually be replaced by an **Atlantic 85**, the newest class of the RNLI fleet.

www.rnli.org.uk

Llanfechell

4G

*1½ml
(2.5km)
south of
Cemaes, turn
off A5025*

A group of three tall stones, standing in a unique triangular arrangement on high ground to the northwest of the village (SH364916), suggests that this may have been an important ritual site during the Bronze Age.

In early Christian times a saint named Mechell, possibly from Ireland, established a *llan* here. The limewashed parish **Church of St Mechell**, dating in part from the twelfth century, stands amongst yews in a broad, walled churchyard. The stout, crenellated tower is crowned by a beehive-like

corbelled cupola. (William Bulkeley of nearby Brynddu ▶122 blamed the vibration of the church bells for spoiling the brewing of his ale.) The oldest surviving parts of the church are the nave and the western section of the chancel, which belong to the twelfth century. Although the recent limewashing of the church aroused local controversy (as it did when this was also proposed for the island church of St Cwyfan ▶198 near Aberffraw), it

*The Church of
St Mechell*

was stated in a medieval manuscript that *'Gwynedd* [north-west Wales] *sparkled with limewashed churches like the firmament of stars'.*

Local industries once included quarrying of decorative stone, 'green marble', and fulling (treating cloth): Anglesey's first recorded fulling mill, or *pandy*, was built here in 1430. Until around 1920, when agricultural wages became fixed, the centre of the village used to be the site of hiring-fairs. Here, labourers would come in search of employment by local farmers – see *Y Ffair Gyflogi gyntaf* ('My First Hiring Fair') ▶185

*A memorial
plaque on
Llanfechell's
clocktower*

The village centre is marked by a **clocktower** raised to commemorate the dead of the First World War, 1914-1918. It was unveiled by Margaret Lloyd George in 1921. She was the wife of David Lloyd George (1863-1945), who had become Britain's Prime Minister in 1916 during the war in which nearly one thousand Anglesey men lost their lives. Lloyd George remained in office until 1922. The Llanfechell war memorial tells a poignant story: it records the names of the three Thomas brothers, formerly of Brynddu: Trevor (who died in 1916, in France), Robert (d1917, Palestine) and Owen (d1918, in a military accident, whilst flying over England).

Opposite the church is the **Libanus Chapel** of the Calvinistic Methodists (1832, rebuilt 1903). To its left is a schoolroom (1914), bearing the inscription *Er cof am ein rhieni* – 'In remembrance of our parents'.

In the 1830s, Nonconformist ministers in Wales began to see the benefits that moderation in the consumption of alcoholic drink might bring to the piety of their congregations. In 1832 the Holyhead *Cymdeithas Ddirwestol*, 'Temperance Society', was the first to be founded in Wales. In Llanfechell the idea was taken a step further: the country's first teetotal society began here in 1835, with the encouragement of the preacher John Elias. During their meetings, signatories of the 'pledge' would wear a distinctive tunic. Today a non-teetotal public house, **Y Cefn Glas**, stands close to the chapel.

Leaving Llanfechell on the lane to Mynydd Mechell, one passes a primary school, and the startling sky blue frontage of the **Ebenezer** chapel (1862, Independent), with its steeply-pitched roof.

The squire of Brynddu

The diarist **William Bulkeley** or 'Bwcle' (1691-1760) was squire of Brynddu, to the east of the village of Llanfechell. He came from a branch of the same Bulkeley family that lived at Baron Hill, Beaumaris. His diaries are full of interest to the social historian and describe every aspect of everyday Anglesey life in the eighteenth century, from food and entertainments, to agricultural labour and smuggling. Bulkeley reveals an engaging character with a sardonic wit. Bulkeley married Jane Lewis of Cemlyn, but she died in childbirth in 1713. Their daughter, Mary, married a certain brewer called Fortunatus Wright, of Liverpool, who became the most famous privateer commander of his time. Based in Italy he became engaged in acts of piracy in the Mediterranean. He disappeared in 1748 and it was left to William to bring up his elder grandchildren, Ann (known as Nancy) and Grace. They were educated in Beaumaris and Chester.

An interesting feature of eighteenth-century life amongst the squires of Anglesey is their close links with Ireland ... the sea voyage to Dublin was easier and faster than the land journey to London.

The diarist's story is told in the book **Mr Bulkeley and the Pirate**, *B Dew Roberts (1936, reissued 1941)*

"*THERE fell such heavy cold rains two or three hours before Day that it killed all my young Turkies that were three months old, killed the young Hawks in the Nest that were ready to fly, and filled all the highways with Water.*" — July 1736

"*The foot ball contest between Llanfechell and its allies and Llanbadrig and its allies was won by the former, they carrying all before them with such irresistible force that in 2 hours time the play was over, having drove the football over the precipice beyond Borth Badrick ...*" — March 1743

The two surviving volumes of William Bulkeley's diaries, 1734 to 1743 and 1747 to 1760, are held by the Department of Manuscripts at the University of Wales, Bangor and are being made available for internet access: **www**.bangor.ac.uk *(link to the Department)*

Llanlleiana — *see* **Llanbadrig** ▶115
Llanrhuddlad — *see* **Church Bay** ▶112
Llanrhwydrys — *see* **Cemlyn** ▶110

Mynydd Mechell

4G
2½ml (4km) south of Cemaes via Llanfechell

Mynydd Mechell is a cattle-farming village to the southwest of Llanfechell, set amidst a green and hilly landscape criss-crossed by winding lanes. The village takes its name from a tract of rocky upland which lies between two lakes, **Llyn Llygeirian** and little **Llyn Bwch**. **Melin Mechell** is a nineteenth-century windmill tower, partly restored and converted to a private home. The village is served by two chapels, **Calfaria** Baptist chapel (1897) and, at its centre, **Jerwsalem** Calvinistic Methodist chapel. To the west of the *Mynydd*, the 'Mountain', is the small church of **Llanfflewin** (SH350891), on a site dating back to AD630. The direction of the church is signposted along a farm track. To the southeast of Llanfechell, on the lane northwards from Llyn Alaw, is **Carreglefn**, a residential village with a primary school.

Nebo — *see* **Pen-y-sarn** ▶126

Parys Mountain / *Mynydd Parys*

6G
*1½ml (2.5km)
south of
Amlwch,
between
B5111 and
A5025*

Parys Mountain may be accessed from a network of footpaths which leave the car park at Pen-y-sarn ▶126 or most easily from another car park by the B5111 on top of the Mountain between Amlwch and Rhos-y-bol (SH438906).

The desolate landscape of the mountain dominates the skyline of northeast Anglesey. Close to, the rocks display marvellous colours: reds, purples, browns, umbers and ochres. The long, rocky hill has been devastated by centuries of mining. The scarring has left little vegetation but heather and coarse grasses. It is surrounded by **pools** and lakes into which mineral-rich water drains. This water was once used for the extraction of copper: scrap iron was thrown into it, and over time, electrolytic action replaced the iron with copper oxide. The copper oxide was removed and the remaining water – rich in iron sulphate – was evaporated to leave hydrated iron oxide, 'yellow ochre'. The ochre was crushed in a windmill to be used as a pigment for paint.

Mynydd Parys

The high ground is surmounted by a ruined **windmill** (1878). When turning, the power generated by its five sails was used to assist the work of a steam engine in pumping water out of the Cairn's Engine Shaft, raising ore, and transporting workers. The **beam engine-house** (1819) at Pearl Shaft, in the Cornish style, has been restored.

An early Bronze Age spoil heap on the north slope of the mountain shows that its ores were being worked 4,000 years ago. It is likely that metals were also extracted during the Roman occupation of the island. The mountain eventually yielded a variety of riches, from copper (in the mineral chalcopyrite), zinc (in sphalerite), and lead (in galena), to silver and sulphur.

During the fifteenth century an official of the English government, one Robert Parys, had been given the Mountain (then known as *Mynydd Trysglwyn*) as a reward for collecting fines from Welsh people involved in Owain Glyn Dŵr's unsuccessful rebellion. Although the Mountain's copper had ceased to be extracted when the Romans withdrew from Wales, during the eighteenth century the practice of protecting the hulls of naval vessels by cladding them with copper plate – providing a 'copper-bottomed' guarantee that marine worms would be unable to bore through the timbers – led to a sudden rise in the value of the metal. The then owners, including the grandfather of the first Marquess of Anglesey, recognised that the riches of Parys Mountain should be exploited.

Anglesey's great copper boom began in 1768, when the Macclesfield mining firm Messrs. Roe & Co. engaged Jonathan Roose, a mineral agent from Derbyshire, to prospect Parys Mountain for the best places to sink shafts. Close to the surface, one of his miners, Roland Puw, struck a rich vein. Roose's tombstone at St Eleth's Church commemorates not only the achievement, but also the course his life would then follow:

> *'He heard the miner's first exulting shout,*
> *Then toil'd near 50 years to guide its treasures out.'*

In 1778 the Parys Mine Company was formed by the lawyer Thomas Williams, the son of a farmer and landowner, in partnership with other shareholders. The higher wages offered to workers lured many farm labourers away from their fields to work in the mines. Under Williams, the Parys workings were to become the greatest copper mine in the world.

NORTHERN ANGLESEY

The Copper King

Copper Mountain by John Rowlands (1966, reprinted 2002) is a history of Anglesey's copper industry

Thomas Williams (1737-1802), born in Llansadwrn (where a memorial plaque stands in front of the old village school), was a lawyer who became a prominent figure of the Industrial Revolution and a millionaire. He reopened copper workings on Parys Mountain and made Anglesey, briefly, the leading producer in the world. By the end of his life Thomas Williams controlled half of all copper production in the British Isles. He was buried in the churchyard of Llanidan (where he had an estate), only to be re-interred ten years later in the tomb of his son, Owen, at the Church of St Tegfan, Llandegfan. Unusually for a successful capitalist in that age, Williams was reckoned to be a straight dealer and fair employer, and was known locally as *Twm Chwarae Teg* ('Tom Fair Play').

The mineral Chalcopyrite.
The source of Thomas Williams's wealth glistens like gold on a base of white quartz.

Mining was initially carried out in deep opencast pits with scant regard for safety; lowered over the edge on ropes, the miners hacked and blasted out the rock as best they could. Later, the Mona Mine Co., also owned by Thomas Williams, took over other existing workings and sank shafts and excavated twelve miles (19km) of tunnels at depths of up to 1,050 feet (320m). This work was carried out by Cornish miners. The entire workforce of up to 1,200 included men, women and children. Wages were about fourpence a day.

Chalcopyrite, Parys Mountain's copper mineral, is a mixed copper/iron sulphide: $CuFeS_2$. This is often concentrated in veins through quartz. Women workers – known as *Copar Ladis* ('copper ladies') – prepared the ore for smelting, hammering it into small pieces and gathering together the chalcopyrite-rich fragments.

The *Ladis* were praised in an anonymous Welsh song from about 1800:

Yn gweithio'n llon a diwyd	*They are so happy in their work*
A chyson maent bob dydd,	*Rarely counting each day*
Er ennill eu bywoliaeth	*Earning their living*
(Mae hynny yn ddi-gudd);	*(It's a well known fact);*
Mae yno fechgyn ifainc	*There are young lads too*
A dynion yn eu man,	*And older men as well,*
Ond y merched ydy'r gorau	*But the women are the best*
A'r hardda' ym mhob man.	*And most beautiful anywhere.*
I ferched Mynydd Parys	*May the women of Parys Mountain*
Sy'n curo'r mwyn yn fân,	*Who break up the ore,*
Boed dwy oes i bob dynes	*Live twice as long*
Ar bwys ei bwthyn glân.	*In their little cottages.*

A rather too cheerful view, no doubt, of the backbreaking, monotonous work involved – their labour was the most poorly paid of all Parys Mountain's work.

The conclusion of the Napoleonic Wars in 1815 reduced the demand for copper, and prices began to be undercut by competition from the Americas and Africa. The mines finally closed in the 1880s.

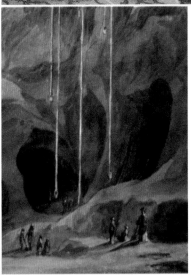

*"O*N THE EDGE of the chasms are wooden platforms which project far: on them are windlasses by which the workmen are lowered to transact their business on the face of the precipice.

There suspended, they work in mid air, pick a small space for a footing, cut out the ore in vast masses, and tumble it to the bottom with great noise. ... Much of the ore is blasted with gunpowder, eight tons of which, I am informed, is annually used for the purpose.'

— THOMAS PENNANT
Tours in Wales (1778-1781)

Parys Mountain.
In 1800 (top) by Edward Pugh, and in 1785, by John 'Warwick' Smith

The smile on the Druid's face

Between 1787 and 1793, when national copper coinage was in short supply, the Parys Mine Company of Amlwch issued its own currency, known as **Anglesey pennies**. Halfpennies were also struck. The coins were copper tokens, decorated with a druid's head in a wreath of oak leaves and acorns.

Indented into the edge are the words *ON DEMAND IN LONDON, LIVERPOOL OR ANGLESEY*.

More than ten million coins in over two hundred varieties are thought to have been minted. Die differences range from the number of acorns in a wreath and type styles, to the smile on the druid's face.

Does Parys Mountain have a future? With modern mining methods the Mountain's reserves could once again be viable, this time in different zones. All depends on world supplies and prices of zinc, lead and copper. Anglesey Mining plc *(Cwmni Mwyngloddio Môn)* is the site's modern operator. It has been estimated that 6.4 million tonnes of ore can be mined, containing more than 10% metal: 5.4% zinc, 2.6% lead and 2.3% copper. If the company's forecasts are correct, this could amount to around fifteen years of mining activity, employing more than 100 people. New test drillings were started in 2005.

The **Heritage Centre** at Porth Amlwch ▶105 has a small exhibition about Parys Mountain. It includes samples of rock as well as illustrations and descriptions of the miners' work .

Pen-y-sarn *also known as* **Pensarn**

6G

2ml (3km) SE of Amlwch on A5025

This residential village (commonly pronounced 'Pen-sarn') is by-passed by the main Amlwch road near **Tafarn y Bedol**, a public house. The history of Pen-y-sarn is closely linked to that of Amlwch ▶104 and Parys Mountain. Copper miners lived here, together with the suppliers of the clothes and clogs worn in those days by working people. Today the view to the west includes an extensive wind farm.

Pen-y-sarn has two Victorian chapels, **Carmel** (1900) and **Bozrah** (Calvinistic Methodist,1864). Bozrah was built on a square plot of land, to a square plan with a pyramidal roof. Its courtyard is flanked by the minister's house on the left and a substantial schoolroom and storehouse to the right. The **Memorial Hall** / *Neuadd Goffa* (1926) displays a commemorative plaque in honour of miner's son Lewis Williams Lewis ('Llew Llwyfo', 1831-1901) who became a poet and leading Welsh-language journalist, both here and amongst the Welsh community in the USA.

Passing the Carmel chapel turn east to **Nebo**. This is a small village with fine views out to sea, and, on a clear day, down the east coast to Snowdonia. Lanes lead south to Dulas. Northeast Anglesey's rocky coastline rises to the green hill of **Mynydd Eilian**, whose radio masts (originally ship-to-shore, now for telecommunications) provide a landmark. The summit provides spectacular views. Mynydd Eilian is best accessed by footpaths from the car park in Pen-y-sarn. To the north of the 'mountain' is an old **telegraph station** (1841), part of a chain stretching across the island – see *Church Bay* ▶112 – which were used to signal the approach of vessels to the port of Liverpool. The first signals made use of a mechanical semaphore system. Later, an electric telegraph system was installed.

On the northern slopes of Mynydd Eilian is the village of **Pengorffwysfa**; another small village, **Cerrig Mân**, lies between Pen-y-sarn and Amlwch.

Porth Wen — *see* **Llanbadrig** ▶116

Rhos-goch *also known as* **Rhosgoch**

5G

3ml (5km) SE of Amlwch

Rhos-goch is a residential hamlet lying amidst the maze of small lanes to the north of Llyn Alaw. To its north is the site of the former Shell terminal which piped oil onwards from the offshore facility at Amlwch from 1973 to 1987 – see *Amlwch* ▶126. In recent years this has been considered as a possible location for a new gas-fired power station, for a biomass energy plant and for another wind farm. The future of the site remains uncertain.

Take the northwestern turn from the Four Crosses junction and continue to **Bodewryd**. The parish **Church of St Mary** *(Santes Fair)* stands on an eleventh-century religious site (SH400906). Some medieval masonry remains and one sixteenth-century window. Most of the church is Victorian, extensive reconstruction having become necessary after a lightning strike.

Just to the north of the church is Plas Bodewryd (sixteenth to eighteenth centuries). Near to the lane, one cannot miss a most unusual tall, gabled brick building. This is an eighteenth-century dovecote, **Colomendy Bodewryd** (SH399908). It could accommodate about 400 nesting birds.

Power of the wind

The Anglesey windmill tradition (see *Anglesey's Windmills* ▶160) takes on a modern spin to the northeast of Rhos-y-bol village. **Trysglwyn Fawr**, below the southern slopes of Parys Mountain, is the site of a wind farm, opened in 1996. The turbines are mounted on 82ft (25m) -high steel towers and are driven by rotors which activate at windspeeds of 6 to 56mph (10 to 90kph). The blades are made of fibreglass-reinforced polyester and whirl at 20 to 30rpm. Together they feed 5.6 megawatts into the grid via substations at Amlwch and Llanfair Pwllgwyngyll. Wind farms like this are now an established feature of the landscape of northern Anglesey, stretching from **Parys Mountain** to **Rhyd y Groes** and southwards to **Llyn Alaw**. To some people, wind farms are an eyesore, but to others they have their own beauty, if located judiciously. They are certainly more attractive than electricity pylons, and future designs may be more discreet or aesthetically pleasing. Many more towers may yet be placed offshore, as has already happened further east along the coast of North Wales.

Wind power makes sense in the age of global warming, for it does not emit damaging 'greenhouse' gases or deplete reserves of fossil fuels. Unlike nuclear power it is not a potential security or health risk and it avoids the associated problems of radioactive waste. However the contribution of wind to total energy generation is necessarily small-scale, and on Anglesey tidal power and energy conservation may prove to be the most important considerations for the future.

A website of the operator of the Llyn Alaw and Trysglwyn wind farms provides information about renewable energy:
www.npower-renewables.com

Rhos-y-bol *also known as* **Rhosybol**

6F
3ml (5km) SW of Amlwch on B5111

This village lies amongst the rolling green fields of northeast Anglesey, to the south of Parys Mountain. It was developed in the eighteenth century, on former farmland, to provide mineworkers' housing. Cottages and houses stretch along two parallel, interconnected, roads – the B5111 and a narrower lane to its west. At the centre of Rhos-y-bol is the small stone **Christ Church** (disused) and the **Marquis** public house. In the south of the village, **Capel Gorslwyd** (Calvinistic Methodist, 1867) lies behind railings next to its school room, an early twentieth-century addition. To the north, a **war memorial** and the village's present school, **Ysgol Gymuned Rhos-y-bol**, stand opposite another open chapel, **Bethania** (Independent, 1883).

To the west, electricity pylons march across farmland to the north of Llyn Alaw ▶187. The modern pithead of Parys Mountain rises to the north of the village.

Rhyd-wyn — *see* **Church Bay** ▶112

The Skerries / *Ynysoedd y Moelrhoniaid*

2H

2ml (3km) off Carmel Head

A long, semi-submerged platform of treacherous rocks lies off Anglesey's northwestern coast. It covers an area of 38 acres (15ha). The name Skerries derives from a Scandinavian source, meaning 'rocks'. The Welsh name means 'seal islands'. The Skerries may best be viewed from Carmel Head ▶107

The Skerries lighthouse, built in 1804

The Skerries threaten the shipping lanes to Liverpool and have claimed many shipwrecks over the years. These include the sloop *Mary*. She had been built by the Dutch East India Company for presentation to Charles II on the restoration of the monarchy in 1660. As the Royal Yacht she was used for official journeys and for royal leisure trips before her loss in March 1675. The wreck, discovered by scuba-divers in 1971, contained silver, cannons and skeletons. Many of the finds, including bronze cannons and the anchor, are in the collection of the Merseyside Maritime Museum in Liverpool, where a model of the ship is also kept.

The first Skerries lighthouse by Lewis Morris, 1748

Fig. 2. A Porcupine to clear old Bars.

A coal-fired beacon was built on the Skerries by an Irishman called William Trench in about 1716. Trench hoped to collect dues from passing shipping, but he died penniless. A successor, William Morgan, was more canny when it came to business, operating what is said to have been the only private lighthouse left around Britain's coasts. When the Skerries finally came under control of Trinity House in 1841, his successors were paid a fortune in compensation – nearly £445,000. The lighthouse had been converted to oil and rebuilt in 1804; it was modernised in 1967. In 1987 it became automatic: every broadcaster's favourite Christmas story – provisions being brought out to the lighthouse keepers – became redundant overnight. Now unoccupied, the keepers' cottage (built in 1716 and said to be Britain's oldest) has recently undergone an award-winning renovation.

Today's solar-powered light, four million candela strong, has a range of 29 miles (46km). It flashes twice every ten seconds; a fog signal sounds twice every minute. There is a helicopter landing pad on the rocks.

During the summer months, the Skerries are designated as a reserve of the RSPB, when Arctic, common terns and an occasional roseate tern arrive to breed. There are also puffins, herring gulls and both lesser and great black-backed gulls. Seals frequent the islands. Visiting sailors and canoeists are asked to respect the birds' nesting areas, and should contact the RSPB research staff who spend four months on the island.

The Skerries and the surrounding sea area, experiencing such powerful winds, waves and tides, are of great interest to scientists researching renewable energy options in Wales.

Tregele — *see* Cemlyn ▶110

Wylfa
4H

*1ml (1.5km)
NW of
Cemaes*

Wylfa means 'lookout' in Welsh and this headland provides a vantage point for viewing the island's north coast. A trail of 1½ miles (2.5km), signposted from the car park (SH356938), winds around **Wylfa Head / *Trwyn yr Wylfa***, which is a Local Nature Reserve of 31 acres (12.5ha). The habitat is mixed: much of it is acid grassland. Grazed turf and scrub borders low cliffs and rocks. Look out for choughs, skylarks, peregrine falcons and oystercatchers.

*Atlantic
grey seal*

The butterfly population includes meadow browns and common blues. Out to sea one may spot Atlantic grey seals, porpoises or dolphins.

The skyline is dominated by the buildings of **Wylfa nuclear power station**. Building work on this project, which was then the largest of its kind in the world, began in 1962. It opened for operation in 1971. Powered by twin Magnox reactors, Wylfa has a capacity of 1,000,000 kw. Each hour, 55 million gallons (over 250 million litres) of seawater are used for cooling. The power station has been kept open past its planned closure date. In recent years it has suffered from many technical problems, with long, costly periods of reactor shutdown. The plant is now scheduled to close in 2010. Decommissioning, currently at planning stage, will take many years.

Plans for a new pressurised water reactor ('Wylfa B') were proposed in 1989, but eventually shelved on economic grounds. In 2005 it was reported that construction of new nuclear stations in the United Kingdom remained a possibility. Wylfa has been a major employer on the island for 35 years, so the station has had strong political support. The operators claim nuclear power is clean and safe and a pressing alternative to carbon emitting stations in the age of global warming.

However there has also been fierce opposition on the island to the existing station and to plans for new-build. Anti-nuclear pressure group PAWB (*Pobl Atal Wylfa B* / People Against Wylfa B) claims a poor safety culture at the plant, health risks to workers and local people from low-level radiation, the lack of any long-term solution to the storage and transportation of radioactive waste, also the threat posed by a terrorist attack on the plant. They propose a range of alternative solutions, from greater investment in renewable energy to improved conservation.

NORTHERN ANGLESEY

Sail training in
Holyhead Bay

THE SEAFARERS

Aled Eames

CHILDREN playing happily on the sunny beaches of Anglesey, dinghy sailors racing enthusiastically in the Menai Strait, off-shore yachtsmen beating out against lively winds, less energetic tourists simply sitting and enjoying the seafaring ethos of a village like Moelfre – all share an awareness that the sea has long played a dramatic role in the story of the Isle of Anglesey. The small boy who tows his tiny sailing craft, bobbing, into the waves at Benllech, Red Wharf or Cemaes, is the inheritor of an age-old tradition which reaches back to ships of friends and foes in those far off days of prehistoric Anglesey.

*The 714 ton barque **Lord Stanley** was built on the east coast of Canada in 1849 for the Davies family of Menai Bridge*

The Romans knew these shores well; an ancient lead anchorstock, dating back to the first century BC and belonging to a Mediterranean vessel, was discovered by a sub-aqua club off the Gwynedd coast. The naval base established by the Romans at Holyhead and the many settlements of the Celtic Saints – the sea routes they used meant that the Celtic Church was in touch with Ireland, Western Britain, Western Gaul, Spain and the Mediterranean – indicate how Anglesey's position as an off-shore island in the Irish Sea affected its history. The Vikings, the men of the North whose fine ships controlled the Irish Sea in the ninth and tenth centuries, sailed from the Norse kingdom of Dublin to sack the wealthy churches at Holyhead and Penmon, and raided the home of the Welsh princes at Aberffraw. To conquer these Welsh princes the Normans later sent powerful fleets, and the beaches of Anglesey witnessed many a bloody battle and commando raid during the days of Magnus Barefoot, Gruffudd ap Cynan and Henry II.

It was sea power that finally enabled Edward I to control the island from his mighty castles at Beaumaris and Caernarfon, strategically placed at the entrances to the Menai Strait. The western and northern shores, however, continued for centuries to suffer from occasional raiders from Scotland, France and Ireland. When Henry VIII faced the Catholic powers of Europe in the early sixteenth century, Sir Richard Bulkeley of Beaumaris, in a letter to Thomas Cromwell, expressed vividly the fears of generations of Anglesey people:

The Isle of Anglesey lies open upon all countries; it is but a day's sail from Scotland, Breton lies open on it, and the men of Conquest know it as well as we do; so also the Spaniards know every haven and creek; and Ireland and other countries lie open upon it.

There is evidence that secret agents reported to Philip II of Spain at the time of the Armada campaigns regarding the possibilities of landing invasion forces from Ireland, and a Spanish pilot who knew the coast well, optimistically suggested that there was a suitable anchorage for invasion ships off Beaumaris: 'There is room for two hundred sails' … and a potentially co-operative population ashore … They speak a language apart, there are many Catholics and they are very friendly to Ireland.' It was an invasion that never came. The Welsh, for the most part, saw that their future prosperity lay with the Tudors, their countrymen. In the days of Elizabeth 1 the merchants of Beaumaris flourished and their ships sailed with Caernarfonshire slate, mainly for Ireland and Chester, returning with Bordeaux wine, Irish linen, cloth and, particularly at the time of poor harvest, corn. On 28th April 1595, for example, the *Bartholomew* of Chester brought a typical cargo to Beaumaris. It included small quantities of iron, salt, soap, sugar, pepper, canvas, raisins, currants, prunes, nails, '2 trunks apparell … 1 pair cart wheels, 2 bundles frying pans … 1 jointed bed.'

This was the legal, and therefore recorded, trading. The younger sons of the Welsh gentry and many seamen recognized the lucrative possibilities of piracy: a Chester vessel bound from Ireland was seized off Moelfre; known pirates, it was alleged, lived openly in Beaumaris and the leading gentry had a network of contacts with the trade. Apart from petty coastal piracy, some went further afield and there was much excitement when Pyrs Griffith of Penrhyn, across the Strait from Beaumaris, brought the Spanish vessel, *Speranza*, laden with silks, olive oil and earthenware, to the mouth of the Menai Strait in 1600, a prize which he had captured during his privateering ventures 'in a certain man-of-war called the *Grace*'.

The decline of the Navy under the early Stuarts brought a new slant to piracy. It was no longer Welsh pirates who preyed upon shipping but pirates of all nations who infested the British seas, and the Vice-Admiral of North Wales reported in 1633 the great dangers to 'commerce betwixt Wales and Ireland by pirates which rove in the St George's Channel', threatening the coast and who 'strike terror into the inhabitants, not without fear that they will surprise them in their own houses'. The Navy of Blake and the campaigns of Cromwell in Ireland eventually drove away the pirates and the development of both legal and illegal trade continued apace from the small havens of Anglesey. By the eighteenth century little vessels like the *Golden Apple* of Red Wharf, the *Hopewell* of Amlwch, the *Fox* of Dulas and the *Bullshead* of Beaumaris were trading regularly to the rapidly developing port of Liverpool. High duties on tobacco, rum, brandy, gin, tea, and the proximity of the Isle of Man, a veritable storehouse for smuggled goods until 1765 when it ceased to be privately owned, meant that the Revenue cutter stationed off Anglesey had a busy time attempting to intercept smugglers' vessels from both Ireland and the Isle of Man. Her commander ruefully admitted that the smugglers had allies in Anglesey: 'the smugglers on shore make fire on the hills for a signal … so that they may avoide us'. Red Wharf, Cemaes, Moelfre, Amlwch and Beaumaris were favourite landing places for smuggled goods; the *Young Tom*, a pilot boat of Beaumaris, was described as a 'very remarkable smuggler for some years' having strong links with The Sign of the Coffee, a Beaumaris inn. On the much more exposed western shores of the Island, wrecks came as manna from heaven to the often starving population, particularly in years of bad harvests. The trial of the notorious gang who plundered wrecks at Crigyll rocks made a great impression on their contemporaries in the 1740s.

The naval wars of the eighteenth and early nineteenth centuries brought considerable wealth to some Anglesey families; their careers are recorded in the vast collection of letters of the Morris brothers whose memorial stands hard by the Pilot Boat Inn, overlooking Dulas. No one, however, made a fortune to compare with that of Thomas Williams, the Anglesey solicitor who developed the Parys Mountain copper industry so dramatically and who became, for a time, the monopolist millionaire whose copper sheathing was in demand not only by slave ships and the British Navy but also by the navies of France, Holland and Spain.

Ships were needed for transporting the copper from Amlwch to smelting works at St Helens and Swansea, and also for the slate trade, which was increasing as a consequence of the rapid growth of industrial towns in England, Europe and North America. The early nineteenth century was a period of feverish shipbuilding in North Wales. Farmers, shopkeepers, landowners, quarrymen, spinsters and mariners all invested their meagre capital in small ships, built, often enough, on open beaches, in fields and sheltered coves, as well as in small ports like Holyhead, Amlwch, Cemaes and the Menai Strait. Today's visitors will occasionally stumble across a long disused slipway or a ring bolt in the rocks, used long ago by small vessels which dried out on the beaches and unloaded cargoes of coal and general goods into horse drawn carts.

The Amlwch shipyard of William Thomas & Sons, 1879

In the 1840s, from ports in the Menai Strait, hundreds of Welsh emigrants sailed to North America in the slate ships, which returned with cargoes of timber from Quebec. Many Anglesey boys went to sea in the North American built full-rigged ships and barques, ought by the most successful shipowners: the Davies family of Menai Bridge, William Thomas of Llanrhuddlad and Liverpool, and Humphrey Owen of Rhuddgaer, near Newborough.

For the majority of the seaside villages of Anglesey the sea was a place of work, but by mid-nineteenth century increasing numbers of visitors came by paddle steamer. In 1848, for example, the

Promenade deck passengers on the paddle steamer *La Marguerite*

Cambria and the *Prince of Wales* sailed on alternate days from Menai Bridge for Liverpool, returning the next day when 'coaches for Holyhead, Carnarvon and Amlwch wait the arrival … to convey Passengers forward, and return in the Morning in time to proceed to Liverpool'. The reduced fares were advertised in the local press: 'Cabin 4*s*., Fore Cabin 2*s*., children under 12, half fare.'

Since the visit of the Princess Victoria in 1832 much publicity had been given to the Beaumaris regattas. Each year the Green attracted, as the enthusiastic reporter of the North Wales Chronicle noted, 'a splendid assemblage of the fair and the fashionable' to watch the races.The Beaumaris Book Society, which first met in the Bull's Head Inn in 1802, was the direct ancestor of the Royal Anglesey Yacht Club. Officially recognized under its new title in 1885, the RAYC has played a major role in developing yachting in the North West.

On a sparkling, sunlit, regatta day when the Menai Strait or Holyhead Harbour are filled with the gaily coloured sails of modern yachts, it is hard to realise that the sea can be cruel. Throughout the centuries, dwellers on the coasts of Anglesey have seen the sea take its toll, not only of mighty ships – like the *Royal Charter* near Moelfre with the loss of over four hundred men, women and children and its golden cargo – the fine tea clipper *Norman Court* wrecked in Cymyran Bay in 1883, when great gallantry was displayed by the crews of the Rhosneigr and Holyhead lifeboats, and many people ashore – and the *Primrose Hill*, wrecked a few days after Christmas 1900 with tragic loss of life in a fierce south-westerly gale in the bay known as Abraham's Bosom near South Stack – but also of little smacks like the *Active* of Belfast, whose crew of five were rescued in 1835 from the waves on Cemaes beach by the Reverend James Williams, vicar of Llanfair-yng-Nghornwy and the first in North Wales to be awarded the Gold Medal of the RNLI. Thanks to the efforts of James Williams and his wife, Frances, out of the first nineteen lifeboats stationed around the coasts of Britain six were in Anglesey.

The story of the Anglesey lifeboats is well exemplified in the career of Coxswain Richard Evans of Moelfre, twice awarded the Gold Medal of the RNLI for gallantry in rescues from the *Hindlea* in 1959 and the Greek motor vessel *Nafsiporos* in 1966. Anglesey has bred many such fine seamen; its havens and beaches have played a significant role in the story of man's encounter with the sea.

ALED EAMES was born in Llandudno in 1921. During the Second World War he served on North Atlantic convoy escort duties and commanded tank landing craft. After the war he studied History at the University of Wales, Bangor, and was later appointed Lecturer there. He was the author of 'Ships and Seamen of Anglesey' (1973), 'Porthmadog Ships' (1975), 'Ventures in Sail' (1987), and other books in both Welsh and English. In 1982 he presented an acclaimed BBC2 television series, 'Tradewinds', and the Welsh language series 'Halen yn y Gwaed' ('Salt in the Blood'). He was a founding editor of the Gwynedd Archives Service journal 'Maritime Wales' and Caird Research Fellow at the National Maritime Museum, Greenwich. Aled Eames died in 1996. In 2005 an inaugural 'Aled Eames Memorial Lecture' was delivered in Moelfre, where he lived for a time.

The Bronze Age standing stones at Penrhos-feilw, near Trearddur Bay

HOLYHEAD
and western Anglesey

WESTERN ANGLESEY has a ragged coastline, indented with inlets, offshore stacks and little islands. Holy Island covers an area of 28 square miles (73 sq km), pointing west towards Ireland and the setting sun. It is joined to the west coast by Four Mile Bridge and by the Stanley Embankment. Holy Island has the sheerest cliffs and highest land on Anglesey and is the location of Anglesey's biggest town, the port of Holyhead.

The west as a whole has a wide-open landscape, with patterns of fields set like green slabs beside bright expanses of ocean, and views south to the distant mountains of the Llŷn peninsula, on the mainland.

For those tourists not catching the ferry to Ireland, the chief holiday destinations are Trearddur (on Holy Island) or Rhosneigr.

Porth Tywyn Mawr

Bodedern

4E
6½ml
(10.5km) east
of Holyhead
on B5109

This small, compact farming town is centred on the parish **Church of St Edern**, which is set back from the road behind a stone wall through which a lychgate gives access. The church dates back to the fourteenth century and includes an eighteenth-century gallery. It was extensively restored in 1871, but still includes medieval timbers and masonry. In the church is a sixth-century Christian memorial stone that may have been set within a ring of small wooden posts at the focal point of an early Christian cemetery discovered ¾ mile (900m) ESE of the church at Arfryn. Cemeteries of this kind must lie close to many of Anglesey's early church sites. The inscription on the stone reads *ERCAGNI* – meaning 'the grave of Ercagnos' or 'Erchan'. The name is Irish.

Bodedern was once an important market town, with a hiring fair where labourers could seek employment on local farms. There were two woollen mills and a fulling mill or *pandy*. The town's importance declined in the nineteenth century, when the old post road, which passed through Bodedern, was superseded by the A5 to the south. Bodedern's *Gwylmabsant*, a Welsh 'patron saint festival' with folk dancing, music and traditional costume, was revived in the 1980s and is held on the first Saturday of May in evenly numbered years.

Gwylmabsant Bodedern

Four pebble-dashed chapels still serve their dwindling congregations. Baptist Street / *Stryd Batus* terminates in the yard of **Capel Tabernacl**. *Stryd Wesle* has the Wesleyan **Capel Soar** (1822), which stands next to its chapel house. **Capel Saron** of the Independents was built in 1880 on the same street. Though this building is small, its gable-end façade includes a balcony and other decorative features, emulating some of the grand chapels found in larger Welsh towns. The Calvinistic Methodist **Capel Gilgal** on London Road / *Ffordd Llundain* dates from 1911, late in the chapel-building period. Further along London Road, at the southern edge of the town, is **Ysgol Uwchradd Bodedern** (1977), the large secondary school.

Bodedern's water pump shelter

The **Crown Hotel** marks the old centre of Bodedern. Shops here include **E T Jones, Sons & Daughter**, the only butcher remaining on the island with its own abattoir. A glittering array of championship cups and shields, recently awarded, is proudly displayed in the shop window. Nearby, east of the Crown Hotel on the B5109, a neo-classical memorial stands by the roadside. It was donated by the Stanleys of Alderley – see *Penrhos Portraits* ▶150 – in 1897, to house the town's water pump.

Further east along the B5109, turn north to **Llyn Llywenan**. This is Anglesey's largest natural lake, with extensive reed banks, visited by wild geese, ducks and black-headed gulls. **Afon Llywenan** flows from the lake to Bodedern.

On the southern shore of Llyn Llywenan is the **Presaddfed burial site** (SH347809), over 5,000 years old. This is actually made up of two chambers of different periods, later brought together as a single monument. Part of it is collapsed. The burial site shares its name with the mansion in whose land it lies: **Presaddfed** (or 'Prysaeddfed') was built in 1686 and reconstructed in 1821. It played an important part in the cultural and political history of the island. In the early part of the twentieth century the gardens were redesigned by Gertrude Jekyll (1843-1932) the English landscape gardener who advocated 'natural gardens of the cottage type', with plentiful herbaceous borders. In recent years the house has offered self-catering for large groups, and shooting parties of eight guns (1st October to 1st February) are also accommodated here.

Just to the south is the historic mansion of **Treiorwerth**, which has a Bronze Age tumulus on its land. This borders the B5109 on its eastwards route to the hamlet of **Trefor**. Another famous old house is **Mynydd-y-Gof**, to the west of Bodedern on the road to the little village of **Llanynghenedl**.

From fleece to flannel

Until mechanised production was introduced, the island's needs for tweed, flannel and quilts were satisfied by home production. This cloth was known as *brethyn cartref*.

Sheep's fleece was hand 'carded' between two wire-toothed brushes to untangle the fibres and make them lie straight. The carded wool was then spun by twisting the fibres together on spinning wheels to make lengths of yarn. Carding and spinning was the work of women and children. The yarn could be dyed, using plants such as lichens, or it could be left with its natural colour. Men wove the yarn on hand looms to make cloth. Fifteenth-century records show that some men were full-time weavers, working in their own homes. Many others were farmers by day. In the evenings, before an open fire, families would work together to make their own clothing and blankets, and youngsters would be lulled to sleep by the rhythmic slap of the weaver's shuttle.

In 1832, Princess Victoria, in Beaumaris to attend an *eisteddfod*, was presented with a mantle woven by a Llanrhuddlad man, Robert Pryse ('Gweirydd ap Rhys' 1807-89), who was a talented weaver of herringbone patterns. The self-educated Pryse later became a prolific author.

To thicken and strengthen the handwoven cloth it was sent to a local mill – a *pandy* – where water-driven wooden hammers beat it in a mixture of urine, soda, fuller's earth and water.

The fine Anglesey bedspread in the picture below (folded to show both its sides), was made around 1835 at Llanfachraith, from wool shorn, spun, dyed and woven on Tŷ Croes farm. It can be seen at the Gwynedd Museum & Art Gallery in Bangor.

Weaving mills began production in Anglesey at the beginning of the nineteenth century. To begin with the mills bought in handspun yarn to weave on their looms. Later machines were installed to complete the whole process – from raw fleece to finished cloth. They could also supply wool to knitters. By 1870 nine woollen mills were working continuously, two of them in Bodedern.

The island's textile producers were never sufficiently productive to meet local demand, and the larger woollen mills of the mainland – Penmachno, Trefriw and Bryncir, and many more – supplied the markets with the cloth they called 'Anglesey tweed'.

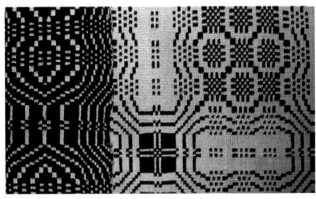

WESTERN ANGLESEY

Bryn Du

4D

1½ml (2.5km) east of Rhosneigr

Leaving the A55 at Junction 5, take the A4080 towards Rhosneigr. To the east of the road is a broad tract of land with scattered farms. Inscribed stones from the sixth century, found in this area, feature names which are Irish in origin: Cunogusi and Mailis. From the former comes 'Conysiog', which was once the name of the district. In the twelfth century this land was granted to Hwfa ap Cynddelw by the princes of Aberffraw.

Bryn Du lies just to the east of Llanfaelog ▶167. Its road passes housing estates, the 1901 **chapel**, the **Queen's Head** public house and a former 5-storey windmill tower (**Maelgwyn** mill, 1789), which is still standing. Another windmill, Melin y Bont, stands a short way to the southeast, though damaged by fire in 1973. It doubled up as a watermill, a rare combination. It was at Bryn Du that the stern preacher John Elias (1774-1841) delivered his first sermon on the island. His brother David, a kindred spirit, became a shopkeeper in this village.

The road continues to the halt of **Tŷ Croes** on the railway line to Holyhead.

Pencarnisiog derives its name from Conysiog (see above). This is a cluster of dwellings around lanes which converge off the A4080. It has a **primary school** and the old Wesleyan Methodist church of **Maelog**. To the north and northeast are the farming hamlets of **Dothan** (around a chapel built in 1902) and **Engedi**. Due east of Pencarnisiog, on a parallel lane, is the tiny **Church of St Mary** *(Santes Fair)* at **Tal-y-Llyn** (SH367728). This is one of Anglesey's *Grade 1* protected churches. It stands exposed in wide, open farmland, and is occasionally used for services. Parts of the structure may date back to the twelfth century. It was restored in 1969, and again in 1999 by the Friends of Friendless Churches after the interior was badly vandalised.

Bryngwran

4D

8ml (13km) SE of Holyhead, A55, junction 5

The prefix *Bryn-* denotes a settlement's position on higher land, or a hill, and *Gwran* is a personal name. During the construction of the A55 a settlement of the Romano-British period was found on the southern slopes of the hill. Today's small village grew around a road junction following the construction of the old A5. The village has nineteenth- and twentieth-century housing, the small **Church of the Holy Trinity** (*Y Drindod Sanctaidd*, 1841) and **Salem Chapel** (1824, rebuilt in 1900). The inn sign ouside the **Iorwerth Arms** seems more characteristic of an English village green than of Anglesey life. **Afon Crigyll** flows through marshy land to the southwest.

The **Cartio Môn go-kart track** ✆ 01407 741144, lies off the A5 north of Bryngwran. (Leave the A55 at junction 4). The A4080 leads south, from near Bryngwran's centre, to Llanfaelog and the holiday resort of Rhosneigr.

The creator of 'Madam Wen'

William David Owen (1874-1925) of Bryngwran was a lawyer who suffered from ill health and took to writing.

His best known work is *Madam Wen*, which first appeared serially in 1914-15 and finally in book form in 1925. It became a popular adventure story for Welsh readers and has attracted new audiences with television adaptation. It tells an exciting tale of smuggling on the Crigyll river, and its heroine is Einir Wyn, who secretly doubles as the mysterious Madam Wen or 'white lady', who takes from the rich to give to the poor. The character may be based on a historical figure of the eighteenth century, Margaret Wynne, who was wife of Robert Williams, squire of Chwaen Wen in the parish of Llantrisant.

Cable Bay / *Porth Trecastell*

4C
2ml (3km)
NW of
Aberffraw
adjoining
A4080

This pretty, sandy beach, backed by rocks and marram dunes, is perfect for family bathing, and is popular with canoeists and surfers. It lies amidst the open green fields of Anglesey's west coast, beneath the clustered farm buildings of **Trecastell**. Access could not be simpler: a car park adjoins the main road to Rhosneigr. Efforts are being made to regenerate the bay's eroded sand dunes: visitors should avoid the dunes, using the steps opposite the main entrance or the path from the beach car park. Camping is prohibited.

In 1902, Porth Trecastell became the eastern terminus of a GPO telegraphic cable service to Howth in Ireland (linking up with the Atlantic cable), hence the name of the beach in English. The old cabling has long been abandoned.

Cable Bay
Porth Trecastell

After exploring rockpools under the cliffs, take a short walk along the grassy headland to the burial chamber of **Barclodiad y Gawres** (SH329707) – the Welsh name suggests that the mound was carried here in the 'apron of a giantess'. This is one of the most important Neolithic (New Stone Age) sites in the British Isles, dating back some 5,000 years. The extensively restored mound (1953) encloses a series of burial chambers. These include stones carved with spirals, chevrons and zig-zags. The Newgrange tombs, across the sea in Ireland, are decorated in a similar manner. Excavations here have revealed cremated human bones: the central area was probably the scene of funeral rituals. The ingredients of a magic potion – tiny bone fragments of toad, snake and shrew were found here amongst the ashes of a fire. At sunset on a stormy

A decorated
stone at
Barclodiad
y Gawres

winter's day, few ancient burial places could be more dramatic than this promontory. To enter the burial chambers, obtain a key (a deposit is required) from 'The Wayside Stores' at Llanfaelog, 1½ miles (2km) north of Porth Trecastell on the A4080 © 01407 810153. You will need a torch.

Follow the footpath around the northern side of the headland to another sandy beach with easy access, **Porth Nobla**.

Caergeiliog

3D

5ml (8km) SE of Holyhead, A55, junction 3

Caergeiliog ('fort of the cockerel') is at a junction of the old A5 with the A55. The old **tollhouse** for the A5 still stands. This small village is a ribbon development with housing estates, a school, the **Sportsman's** public house and the Arts & Crafts styled **Church of St David** (*Dewi Sant*, 1920). The well-preserved **Calvinist chapel** (1786, rebuilt 1872) has retained its Georgian facade. It stands opposite the little post office, next to the village hall (1930). The farmland to the south borders **Llyn Dinam** and the other lakes of the west, beyond which lie the RAF Valley airfield ▶169 and the Llyn Penrhyn RSPB reserve.

Four Mile Bridge / *Pont Rhydybont*

2D

¾ml (1.5km) SW of Valley on B4545

A low stone bridge built over tidal flats provides the southern link between Holy Island and the rest of Anglesey. There is evidence that a bridge was sited here as early as the 1530s. The lagoon or 'inland sea' between here and the Stanley embankment is a popular venue for kayaking enthusiasts, as the tidal flow is 'trapped' between these two structures, creating powerful currents. Footpaths follow the eastern shore northwards from the bridge, passing the peninsula of **Ynys Leurad**, the site of an Iron Age settlement.

The English name refers to the fourth milestone from Holyhead. It is difficult to determine the original form of the Welsh name, which in its modern spelling is tautologous, meaning 'Ford-at-the-bridge Bridge'.

There are fine views of the coast to the south and of Holyhead Mountain to the northwest. Housing follows the main road westwards from Valley to the **Anchorage Hotel**. The B4545 continues westwards past housing estates to the holiday resort of Trearddur Bay. ▶168 Lanes turn southwards from the road to the beautiful southern part of Holy Island and the cliffs and bays of Rhoscolyn ▶164

Holyhead / *Caergybi*

2E

20ml (32km) NW of Britannia Bridge, A55 junction 1

Holyhead port

The A55, the old A5 London Road and the railway all converge at the **ferry terminal** for the port of Holyhead, a town which faces northwards from the centre of Holy Island's north coast.

On his way home to Dublin in 1727, the renowned Jonathan Swift (who had published *Gulliver's Travels* during the previous year) complained that his accommodation in the port was 'comfortless'. Today things are rather better: the **railway station** was refurbished in 1998, and the modern terminal building beside the **inner harbour** is modest in its size, but light and bright.

One of the high speed ferrycraft

Ferries sail from Holyhead to the twin ports of Dublin and Dun Laoghaire in the Irish Republic. 2,500,000 ferry passengers pass through the port each year, 25 per cent of them on foot. Sailing times on the fastest services to Dun Laoghaire are about one hour 40 minutes. Holyhead is also a port of call for several cruise ships each summer, their passengers disembarking on sightseeing excursions.

Royal posts were dispatched from Holyhead to the Dublin port of Howth from at least 1599, when, towards the end of the reign of Elizabeth I, this became the official route of the Royal Mail across the Irish Sea. A regular service was established in 1635 when Charles I opened the posts to use by the public. In 1784 postboys on horseback were replaced by mailcoaches with armed guards.

Traffic increased steadily, and in 1811 work started on the task of *'improving and completing of the Harbour of Holyhead in the Isle of Anglesea'*, to the design of John Rennie (1761-1821). John Rennie died in the course of his work and it was completed in 1824 under the direction of his son, another John. The harbour was linked to the city of London, 267 miles (427km) away, by the new A5 toll road designed by the great Scottish engineer Thomas Telford (1757-1834). **Admiralty Arch** marks the Holyhead end of the A5. Erected to commemorate the visit of King George IV to Holyhead in 1821, it was designed by Thomas Harrison, a Chester architect who had previously designed the Marquess of Anglesey column at Llanfair Pwllgwyngyll. ▶62 The Marble Arch in London (which was moved in 1851 to its present position at the top of Park Lane) marks the English end of the A5.

Shipwrecks were common in those days; an **obelisk** on high ground above the Turkey Shore Road at Môrawelon, overlooking the harbour, commemorates John Macgregor Skinner:

> *This monument was erected by his numerous friends to the memory of John Macgregor Skinner, R.N. for 33 years Captain of one of the Post Office packets on this station, in testimony of his virtues, and their affectionate remembrance of him in his public capacity.*
>
> *He was distinguished for zeal, intrepidity and fidelity. In private life he was a model of unvarying friendship, disinterested kindness and unbounded charity.*
> *MDCCCXXXII* [1832]

The Skinner memorial, Holyhead

John Skinner was born in America around 1760. He joined the Royal Navy in 1776 and served as an officer on *HMS Phoenix* during the War of Independence. He later lost an arm and one eye whilst on naval duties. In 1793 Skinner entered the Post Office shipping service, becoming master of the Holyhead to Dublin steam packet boats *Wizard*, *Dragon* and *Escape*. His pet raven would fly out from Holyhead to meet its returning master. Captain Skinner was drowned in 1832 when he was washed overboard, together with his ship's mate, in heavy seas off North Stack. The loss of this much-liked man caused genuine grief in the town. The circumstances of the death of the men were part of an Inquiry held in 1836. The mismanagement of the Post Office ships, revealed during the Inquiry, led to the transfer of responsibilty for the packet boats to the Board of Admiralty.

At the end of Turkey Shore Road is Holyhead's Fish Dock, a base for several fishing boats. Live lobsters and crabs are transported from here to Spain and France. Whelks are sent to Korea, where they are considered a delicacy.

The original harbour master's office and custom house occupy the southern part of **Salt Island / *Ynys Halen*** where women once packed herrings ready for dispatch by rail. A lifeboat was stationed here until 1997, when the *St Cybi II* went down its slipway for the last time. In 1966 the Holyhead lifeboat, a former *St Cybi*, joined with the Moelfre lifeboat in the rescue of five crewmen from a Greek vessel, the *Nafsiporos*. Both crews received gallantry medals. Salt Island now provides berths for ferries and is the site of the harbour-master's control centre.

With the opening of Britannia Bridge ▶49 in 1850, rail links were opened with London, and Holyhead's position as the major port for Ireland was assured. By 1860 you could leave London at 7.30 in the morning and be in Holyhead just after two in the afternoon.

Holyhead Harbour from the Mountain

A pier extending from Salt Island divides the **Old Harbour** with its **Marine Yard** from the **New Harbour**, which is sheltered on the seaward side by James Meadows Rendel's great **Holyhead Breakwater**. Designed and con-structed between 1845 and 1873, this is just short of two miles (3km) long and topped by a promenade leading from **Soldier's Point**. The breakwater culminates in a lighthouse designed by John Hawkshaw, who had taken over as Engineer in Chief following Rendel's death in 1856; the lighthouse was last manned in 1962. The castle-like mansion at Soldier's Point housed the break-water's main building contractor. The breakwater's limestone facing blocks came from Anglesey's eastern coast at Moelfre ▶80 but rock quarried on Holyhead Mountain ▶153 was used as the infill. The main growth of Holyhead came during this time, swelled at first by labourers from all over the British Isles. During a ten year period, the population of the town rose from 3,869 to 8,863, and the villages of Holyhead Mountain expanded too.

The New Harbour could shelter a hundred or more ships in a storm. Today, Holyhead's **marina** lies within the new harbour: work began in 2005 to dou-ble its 200-berth capacity and to build waterfront apartments.

Improved port facilities – a new dock, station and hotel – were opened by the Prince of Wales in 1880: the black and white clock tower at the station entrance commemorates the event. The use of the harbour increased, and by 1908, seven steamers were leaving Holyhead each day, with a further seven arriving. The Port began handling containers of goods – of smaller dimensions than modern containers – as early as the 1920s.

During the Depression of the 1930s, one-third of Anglesey's workforce was unemployed. Men and boys from Holyhead, together with others from Amlwch and Moelfre, enlisted to serve alongside Norwegian crews in the Antarctic aboard factory ships of *The Southern Whaling & Sealing Company*.

Throughout the Second World War (1939-45) the port was a naval base and was a home-from-home for exiled sailors of the Royal Netherlands Merchant Marine, stationed on the ship *Medusa*. Today, several Holyhead families have Dutch surnames – some arising from the wartime connection, others from sailors who settled in Holyhead in peacetime.

R.M.S. "LEINSTER"

A wartime tragedy

The Holyhead to Kingstown (now known as 'Dun Laoghaire') Royal Mail Steamer **Leinster** was one of four identical sister ships, all twin-screw steamers. They were built at the Birkenhead yard of Lairds for the City of Dublin Steam Packet Company, and were launched in 1896. The ships replaced four paddle steamers and took the same names: Connaught, Leinster, Munster and Ulster – the four provinces of Ireland. In 1915, during the First World War, Connaught was requisitioned by the Admiralty to ferry troops across the English Channel. After two years service she was torpedoed in March 1917. Three of her crew were lost. During the last days of the War, on 10th October 1918, Leinster left Carlisle Pier,

Kingstown, for Holyhead. On board were 77 crew, 22 postal sorters, three Naval gunners, 180 civilian passengers and 489 military passengers. An hour into her passage, a torpedo fired by the German submarine U-boat 123, struck Leinster on her port side. A further torpedo then struck the starboard side and she sank. More than 500 men, women and children were killed in the explosions or drowned in the rough seas – the greatest loss of life ever in the Irish Sea. Twenty-four of her crew came from Holyhead. Just eight days later all on board the UB-123 lost their lives after the submarine struck a mine in the North Sea.

Part of the Leinster's forward deck was raised in 2005 to become the focal point of a memorial garden in Holyhead.

On **Newry Beach / *Traeth Newry***, past the Trinity House Depot, is the **Holy-head Maritime Museum / *Amgueddfa Arforol Caergybi*** © 01407 769745, open Easter to Autumn. The town's seafaring history is celebrated here in an former lifeboat house of the mid-nineteenth century, Wales's oldest. The museum is run and staffed by enthusiastic and knowledgeable volunteers and has a pleasant café/bistro. Exhibits include a model of the ferry steamer *Connemara*, lost in 1916 when bound for Holyhead after colliding with the collier *Retriever* during a gale. Thirty-four Anglesey people were amongst the 93 drowned: only one man – a non-swimmer – survived.

A Celtic stone head ▶23 discovered in the town is one of the few items on display in the museum's main hall that does not have a nautical flavour. An air raid shelter facing the entrance (Holyhead was on the receiving end of bombing raids in the early years of the Second World War) houses the museum's collection from both world wars.

When not at sea, Holyhead's present-day lifeboat – the 7-Class *Christopher Pearce* on service since 2004 – can be seen at moorings in the expanding marina. She was joined in 2005 by a D-Class boat, the *Angel of Holyhead*, purchased with a £28,000 donation by the Lifeboat Fund. The RNLI operations centre for Holyhead is based in offices of the old **Trinity House Depot** (closed 1987), on the Prince of Wales Road. There is a shop and a display about the history of the service here since the formation of the 'Anglesey Association for the Preservation of Life from Shipwrecks' in 1828. ▶120

Holyhead town

The town of Holyhead is Anglesey's largest, a grey-stone port rising steeply from **Victoria Road**, which skirts the west side of the Inner Harbour. Holyhead is not a generally beautiful or prosperous town, but it is a lively, busy place with a character and energy all its own and a very long history. In recent years the town's facilities have been improved, and steps are being taken to improve its economic prospects too. Like many ports, it has a transient atmosphere and, due to its location, a sizeable population of Irish descent.

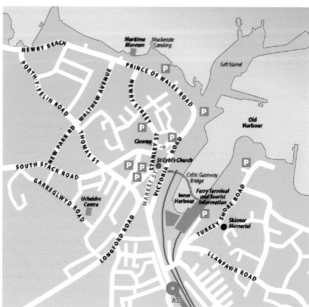

The A55 leads into town through a roundabout and on to Victoria Road. For access to the shopping centre, fork left at the *Eagle & Child* (once a coaching inn, the terminus of the London/Holyhead service) up **Market Street**. At this junction stands a cenotaph. Its bronze reliefs, sculpted by L F Roslyn in 1920, depict a First World War infantryman and a naval marine. The memorial records Captain John Fox Russell's posthumous award of the Victoria Cross in 1917, for his 'most conspicuous bravery' in Palestine, together with the names of Holyhead's fallen in both world wars. A more recent addition is the name Guardsman D R Williams, First Battalion Welsh Guards, a casualty of the 1982 Falklands War.

By-passing the shops, traffic follows a one-way system to a number of car parks. The central shops line pedestrianised sections of Market Street and **Stanley Street**. A large market hall (1855) is presently disused; commercial development is being considered. A street market takes place on Mondays. Smaller roads lead downhill (in this area is a public **library**) to the harbour. The **Celtic Gateway** foot and cycle bridge, completed with European Objective One funding in 2006, links Market Street in the town centre with the ferry terminal. Its steel arches span Victoria Road and the railway. Further investment for Holyhead's regeneration has come from a number of sources, including the Heritage Lottery Fund and Welsh Assembly Government.

The Roman naval fort at Holyhead

The walls around the **parish churchyard**, at the centre of town, include distinctive herringbone-patterned courses of late-Roman masonry. A signpost by the modern Celtic cross at Market Square leads you towards an arched gateway cut through the wall, and into the churchyard. These are some of the best preserved Roman walls in Britain, marking the perimeter of the **naval fort** they founded in the fourth century AD to defend the island from Irish raiders. The east wall, overlooking the harbour, is of a later date. This is a good vantage point to watch the movements of the ferry boats.

WESTERN ANGLESEY

Graham Sumner

Following the Roman withdrawal, a Christian settlement was founded here in the sixth century by Saint Cybi – see also *The Meeting Place* ▶186 – possibly the son of a Cornishman called Selyf. The Welsh name for Holyhead is Caergybi, 'the fortress of Cybi'. The settlement was endowed by King Maelgwn Gwynedd (d547), during whose reign the church at Penmon was probably also founded.

In the southwest of the churchyard, to the left as one passes through the churchyard gate, note the little fourteenth-century chapel of **Eglwys y Bedd**. This may mark the original site of Cybi's burial, or cell, and another tradition claims that this is the burial place of Sirigi, an Irish chieftain who established rule on Anglesey in the mid-fifth century AD, before being slain by Cadwallon Lawhir. In about 1748 this chapel became a schoolhouse for poor children of the parish. It was restored in 1980.

An archway through the Roman wall leads into the yard of St Cybi's Church

There were many raids on this rich ecclesiastical site in the early Middle Ages. Particularly determined attacks came from Irish Vikings in AD961 and 971, but still Caergybi survived. The **Church of St Cybi**, one of Anglesey's *Grade 1* protected churches, dates from the thirteenth century. In the Middle Ages this was an important centre of Christian teaching, a collegiate church or *clas* with twelve lay canons. The present structure dates mainly from the late fifteenth century. It is a low, broad stone building with a crenellated parapet. The sturdy seventeenth-century tower is surmounted by a gilded weathervane in the shape of a fish, first placed there in 1793.

The church was restored between 1877 and 1879 by Sir Gilbert Scott, who also worked on the rebuilding of Bangor Cathedral. The Stanley Chapel, to the south of the chancel, was built in 1896-97 and includes stained glass designed by Edward Burne-Jones (1833-98) and made in the workshops of his friend William Morris (1834-96). The chapel includes the massive angel-surrounded tomb, in Carrara marble, of William Owen Stanley (1802-84), son of the first Lord Stanley of Alderley and a major benefactor to the town of Holyhead. He married Ellin Williams of Bodelwyddan and was Liberal Member of Parliament for the island. He was keenly interested in Anglesey's archaeological sites and presented to the Natural History Museum in London the bones of a mammoth that had been dredged

The Stanley Chapel's pomegranate window, designed by Edward Burne-Jones

from the mud in Holyhead harbour in 1864. On loan from London, they can be seen in Holyhead at the Maritime Museum. To the west, the streets rise steeply, passing splendid Victorian and Edwardian chapels: **Tabernacl**, **Hyfrydle**, **Brynhyfryd** and **Bethel**. Contrasting strongly with the architectural style of the chapels is the modernist Catholic **Church of St Mary, Help of Christians** (1965), off the bottom of Market Street.

Holyhead's more notable citizens have included the poet R S Thomas ▶152 (born in Cardiff, but raised here), who was nominated for the Nobel Prize for Literature, and the European Parliamentary politician Glenys Kinnock (born Glenys Parry in Holyhead, 1944). The comedian Dawn French was also born here in 1957, while her father was serving with the RAF at Valley.

Situated at the highest point in town and approached from Walthew Avenue
and and Garreglwyd Road, the **Ucheldre Centre / *Canolfan Ucheldre*** (all
year ✆ 01407 763361) is a lively community arts centre. Its central hall was
formerly the chapel of a Roman Catholic convent run by a French order of
nuns, dedicated to the *Bon Sauveur* (Good Saviour). The designer of the
chapel was the eminent Dublin architect Prof. R M Butler. The convent closed
in 1982 and in 1989 local residents put together an ambitious plan to save
the chapel, whose tower had long been a feature of the Holyhead skyline.

Since opening in 1991 the centre has boosted artistic activity on the island,
with progressive art and sculpture exhibitions, poetry readings organised
by its Literary Society, dance, multimedia events and film showings. The main
hall, which seats 200, has also hosted regional public meetings of the
National Assembly of Wales. The landscaped garden at Ucheldre includes
sculptures by local artists (including Trefor Fôn Owen's pole vaulter) and an
amphitheatre for performances. There is a shop and a licensed restaurant.

Holyhead Heritage Trail. A leaflet and a series of information boards guide
visitors along a town trail past thirteen historic sites, from the railway station clock
to the Ucheldre Centre. **www**.holyheadtowncouncil.com

A large secondary school, **Ysgol Uwchradd Caergybi**, is sited in the western
part of town. Following the 1944 Education Act, Holyhead's County School
and St Cybi Secondary Modern were amalgamated to become, in 1949, the
first school in Britain to adopt a 'comprehensive' system of admission. Lanes
lead westwards to the magnificent cliffs above South Stack ▶156

Holyhead includes large housing estates as well as a variety of streets in
suburban styles of the last 100 years. Western suburbs include **Llaingoch**
and **Ponthwfa**, overlooked by the old Mountain Village that was once populated by the quarry families.

The Môrawelon district, with large shops in the expanding **Penrhos Retail
Park** (junction 2 of the A55), and industrial estates, forms the eastern part of
town between the ferry terminal and Penrhos beach / *Traeth Penrhos*. Beside
Penrhos Beach is a small community hospital, **Ysbyty Penrhos Stanley**
(1996). Specialising in care of the elderly and in community support, it
replaced former hospitals at Valley and Salt Island.

Kingsland and Penrhos

Southeast of the town is a smelting works operated by Anglesey Aluminium
Metals, which is sandwiched between the old A5 and the end of the new
A55. Alumina and cryolite are offloaded from ships at the long company pier
and conveyed to the plant by an underground conveyor belt. Here a reduction process has delivered more than four million tonnes of aluminium metal
since 1971. Current annual output is nearly 150,000 tonnes. The 400ft (122m)
high chimney can be seen from Snowdonia, over 20 miles (35km) to the
south. The future of the plant – its 588 staff make it the island's largest
employer – may depend on the future of power generation on the island. A
new business park, on a 130 acre (53ha) site at **Tŷ Mawr** that once belonged
to Anglesey Aluminium, is intended to become Anglesey's major business
estate, including hotel, restaurant and leisure facilities.

The B4545 leads from the ferry terminal to Trearddur Bay, passing the
Hebron chapel (1902) and the **Ebenezer** chapel of the Calvinistic Methodists (1850). On Kingsland Road is a well-equipped **leisure centre** (1975), with
a five-lane pool and a learner pool, and an all-weather football pitch. Nearby
is the white tower of a former windmill, Melin yr Ogof (c1825).

Tŷ Mawr Road, a left turn off the B4545, leads to the extraordinary Neolithic burial chambers of **Trefignath** (SH259805), which date to three different phases of construction between the fourth and early third millennia BC. The western chamber represents the first phase of construction, the eastern represents the last.

Telford's tollhouse, Penrhos Coastal Park

The A5 leads eastwards to **Penrhos**. This part of the former estate of the Stanleys of Alderley (see *Penrhos Portraits* below) lies between Penrhos Beach and Beddmanarch Bay, a feeding ground for geese and other wading birds. Turn off the A5 by the octagonal **tollhouse**, one of the five erected on the Anglesey stretch of Thomas Telford's London Road (1826). To allow for the laying of a water main in the late 1960s, during the preparation of the Anglesey Aluminium site, the tollhouse was taken down and rebuilt nearby. Today it opens as a tearoom. Here is the entrance to the **Penrhos Coastal Park**. From the car park set off on one of the clearly marked woodland nature trails of the 200-acre (80ha) park, the foraging grounds of nocturnal badgers.

Penrhos portraits

The headland of Penrhos, at the end of the Stanley Embankment on Holy Island, is said to have been granted to John ap Owen in 1533. During the next two hundred years the family estate was considerably enlarged by marriage. The old 'Tudor House' was replaced by a mansion in 1720. The estate became Stanley property in 1763 through the marriage of Sir John Thomas Stanley to the heiress of Penrhos, Margaret Owen (*whose portrait, **right**, was painted by Joshua Reynolds in 1761*). Their son became the first Lord Stanley of Alderley.

Stanley forebears had first come to Britain in 1066 with William the Conqueror and there had been Anglesey connections since a previous Sir John Stanley was appointed Sheriff in the fifteenth century.

Throughout the development of the port of Holyhead in the eighteenth and nineteenth centuries, the Stanley family was the most prominent on Holy Island and family associations are still to be found everywhere. They include Ellin's Tower overlooking South Stack, and in Holyhead the parish church has a Stanley Chapel; there's a Stanley Street and the

Stanley Arms Hotel, and a coaching inn, *The Eagle & Child*, was named after the family crest. In her book *The Ladies of Alderley* (1938), the novelist and biographer Nancy Mitford, a relative of the Stanleys, outlined the family's characteristics as 'vigorous health, stubbornness, delight in opinionated conversation, boundless energy and a perverse tendency to adopt outlandish beliefs and practices simply to annoy other members of the family'.

The Stanleys sold Penrhos in 1947 and the house was later demolished, but the present Lord Stanley, the eighth, returned to live and farm on Anglesey. His memoirs, **The Stanleys of Alderley, 1927-2001**, *were published in 2004.*

The stone-faced **Stanley Embankment** was one of Thomas Telford's engineering masterpieces, completed in one year by the contractors Gill and Hodges. It was opened in 1823. Telford provided a dramatic short cut on the

traditional route to Holyhead (which took travellers over Four Mile Bridge) by running a causeway across the sands at Penrhos. The embankment had a base width of 114 feet (35m), a top width of 34 feet (10m), a height of 16 feet (5m) and a length of 1,250 yards (1,143m). A railway line was laid alongside the embankment road in 1848.

Today, Telford's A5 road has been sidelined by the A55, which runs on a newly widened stretch of the Stanley Embankment alongside the railway line. High walls shield passengers from views of the sea and allow little sense of passing over water between the island of Anglesey and Holy Island.

Annual events in Holyhead

✦ **Holyhead Leisure Festival** is held annually at Newry Beach over three days – Friday to Sunday – at the end of July. Its varied events have included comedy and musical performances in a marquee, a Saturday morning parade, lumberjack displays, and majorette championships. Funfair and stalls.

✦ **Holyhead Maritime Festival** takes place on Newry Beach, over a weekend each August, the date depending on the tides. Organised in conjunction with the Maritime Museum the events are centred around safety at sea, diving and maritime history. A **Lifeboat Weekend** in August coincides with the Festival.

✦ **Llaingoch Horticultural Show** features flowers, vegetables, crafts, and other displays in a one-day event held every August.

✦ **Holyhead Arts Festival** is an eight day festival – exhibitions, performances and lectures – held annually during the schools' half-term week during the second part of October. The festival is hosted by the Ucheldre Centre.

✦ **Anglesey One-Act Drama Festival**. Many of North Wales's amateur dramatic societies participate in this springtime festival held over two or three days at Boston Centre Stage on Boston Street.

A great number of small-scale events and entertainments are held throughout the year. Community events are often aimed at families with children. Sometimes, events are organised during calls by cruise ships.
Holyhead Tourist Information Centre ℡01407 762622 has the dates and details

Carnivals and Rosebuds

Every summer, boards are erected outside Anglesey villages and housing estates advertising the local Carnival, a tradition stretching back to at least the 1920s. The damp green fields and parks of Anglesey cannot exactly compete with Rio de Janeiro or even Notting Hill, but the efforts made are intense, the rituals are arcane and the politics often Byzantine.

The focus of all is the young Carnival Queen, crowned at a fête, with her retinue of Princesses, Pages, Rosebuds and so on. Each queen visits the other fêtes and joins carnival parades in elaborate 'coaches' of plywood, built on car trailers. Ahead march the baton-twirling majorettes, behind come the floats of children and adults in all kinds of fancy dress, crammed on to tractor trailers or the backs of lorries. Finally comes the mayor's

speech, the judging, the trophies, the bouncy castles, the jumbo hotdogs with *saws coch* (ketchup) and the *bara brith* or rice-krispie cakes from the Guides' or Brownies' stall. And probably the umbrellas …

Queen Corrie, Llan-faes

WESTERN ANGLESEY

R S Thomas

Ronald Stuart Thomas (1913-2000) was born in Cardiff but moved to Anglesey as a child, being raised in Holyhead from the age of five. He is commemorated there by a plaque on the school. He studied Classics at the University of Wales in Bangor and became an Anglican priest in 1936. He served in parishes from Flintshire to the Llŷn peninsula, where he settled at Aberdaron. Some of his final years were spent back on Anglesey at Llanfair-yng-Nghornwy.

R S Thomas was an ardent pacifist and at the same time a political 'stirrer'. He deplored the dilution and destruction of rural Welsh culture by English settlement in the 1960s and 70s. He was himself an English-speaker who learned Welsh, the language of his autobiography *Neb* ('nobody', 1985). R S Thomas published his first volume of verse, *Stones of the Field,* in 1948. This introduced the character of Iago Prytherch, a Welsh 'everyman', who appears repeatedly in his work.

R S Thomas may be considered one of the foremost poets of his generation in the English-speaking world. Although Thomas was a priest, much of his verse is concerned with the apparent absence of God. His poetry is rooted deeply in the landscape and history of Wales, but avoids the exuberance and flamboyance of his contemporary Dylan Thomas. Instead it is spare and bleak, unsentimental but beautiful.

✦ *Collected Poems, 1945-1990*; Dent, London 1993
✦ *Collected Later Poems, 1988-2000*; Bloodaxe Books 2004.

A University of Wales Press *Writers of Wales* paperback, *R S Thomas* by Tony Brown, was published in 2006.

The Bush

I know that bush,
Moses; there are many of them
in Wales in the autumn, braziers
where the imagination
warms itself. I have put off
pride, and knowing the ground
holy, lingered to wonder
how it is that I do not burn
and am yet consumed.

And in this country
of failure, the rain
falling out of a black
cloud in gold pieces there
are none to gather,
I have thought often
of the fountain of my people
that played beautifully here
once in the sun's light
like a tree undressing.

Peter Hope Jones

Holyhead Mountain / *Mynydd Twr*

1E
*2ml (3km)
west of
Holyhead*

Rising above Holyhead town and the spectacular Holy Island coast is Holyhead Mountain, 719 feet (220m) high. Rough tracks lead through the gorse and heather to the summit. There are views southwards to Snowdonia and the Llŷn Peninsula and eastwards to the Great Orme. On clear days it may even be possible to look northeast to the Isle of Man and westwards to Ireland's Mourne Mountains and the Wicklow Hills.

Virtually the whole of Holyhead Mountain (and Penrhosfeilw Common) is owned by the local authority and managed by the RSPB for its breeding seabirds and its heathland. Ninety per cent of Welsh coastal heathland was lost during the twentieth century: this is the largest remaining area on Anglesey, a feeding ground for the red-billed chough. Here also is a botanical rarity, a ragwort named the South Stack, or Field, Fleawort / *Chweinllys Arfor* (*Senecio integrifolius*, subspecies *maritimus*). Holy Island is its only location in the world. On the summit is the 17-acre (7ha)

*South
Stack
Fleawort,
drawn by the
Massey sisters
of Llangoed*

hillfort of **Caer y Twr**, which dates back to the Iron Age. The fort is defended by high ramparts and natural precipices. Within its perimeters, next to the modern triangulation pillar, stand the ruins of a **Roman watchtower** or beacon, erected in the fourth century AD.

*Holyhead
Mountain
hut circles:*
*Right: The
walls of one
of the huts.*
*Below: The
settlement
during the
Romano-
British period.*

On the lower southwestern slopes (accessible from the lane to South Stack) excavations (1860s, 1970s-80s) have revealed low circular stone walls – the remains of perhaps eight ancient farmsteads, separated by terraced fields, known as the **Tŷ Mawr hut group** (SH212820). Some of the huts still have hearths and stone furniture such as benches and basins. Evidence of settlement here goes back at least 2,500 years and extends well into the Roman period. Such remains were once called *cytiau'r Gwyddelod*, 'huts of the Irish'. Many Irish people have indeed settled on the island throughout history, but no identifiably Irish items have been found on the Tŷ Mawr site.

WESTERN ANGLESEY

Brian Byron

"F*ROM THE SUMMIT of Holy Mountain on Ynys Cybi the whole world can be seen. The oceans lie in a gleaming arc around, and are speckled here and there with the distant humps of continents, rising majestically from the surface of the water, and sometimes tipped with snow. No matter that it is only the Irish Sea really, that those beckoning lands are only the mountains of Ireland, the English Lake District or the Isle of Man: on the right day it is the world and all its oceans, and its grand presence out there to the west, uncluttered, free, has summoned Welsh people always out of their narrow valleys and frustrations."*

— JAN MORRIS, *The Matter of Wales*, 1984
(Revised edition: *Wales, Epic Views of a Small Country,* Penguin Books, 2000)

A quarry on the southeastern slopes of Holyhead Mountain opened in 1847 to provide stone for the great breakwater. Millions of tons were extracted to be transported by rail to the water's edge at Soldier's Point and onwards along wooden staging built out to sea.

After the completion of the breakwater the quarry remained open as the site of a brickworks. A tall chimney marks the site. To make the silica bricks, a purer form of quartzite was needed. At first, rock from the Castell quarry, just west of the main quarry, was brought here to be ground and mixed with clay before being formed into silica bricks and fired in beehive and Scotch kilns. Later other small quarries were worked too. The yellow bricks were used to line blast furnaces throughout the United Kingdom, and some as far afield as Italy. The brickworks closed in 1973, and small-scale quarrying continued until 1985.

The site is now the setting of the **Holyhead Breakwater Country Park /
Parc Gwledig Morglawdd Caergybi** (all year ✆ 01248 752428 or ✆ 01407
760530). The lane to the park from Soldier's Point (at the end of Newry Beach
Promenade) leads to the foot of Holyhead Mountain. Next to the car park
are the walls of the brickmakers' crusher, where the quarried rock was
ground, and the remains of a beehive kiln. Nearby stands the tall chimney
of the furnaces. A little lake has dabbling ducks: the lakeside is a pleasant
place to have a picnic. Wheelchair users can also take the 550-yard (500m)
path around the lake. Model boat enthusiasts use the lake on Sundays
and Wednesdays. Learn about the history of the site at the information
centre, where you can pick up a leaflet about the mountain and coastal footpaths that lead from here. An adjoining café and shop is run by the North
Wales Wildlife Trust. A 'land train' service occasionally carries passengers to
the Breakwater Country Park from the Maritime Museum on Newry Beach.

South Stack / *Ynys Lawd*

Signposted roads from Holyhead and Trearddur Bay lead to the precipitous cliffs above
South Stack. Here is a reserve managed by the
Royal Society for the Protection of Birds (RSPB).
Walk through the heather to the cliff edge. The
best time to visit is during early summer, when
the seabirds are breeding. Then the high rock
ledges – eroded from folds in the pre-Cambrian
rock – are crowded with thousands of guillemots and razorbills. Fulmars, kittiwakes and
gulls also breed here, and puffins burrow into
the clumps of sea pink at the lower levels. Below
the clifftops, pairs of choughs nest in the sea
caves. Peregrine falcons (these are the world's
fastest living creatures!) and ravens, linnets and
rock pipits can also be seen. Manx shearwaters
and gannets often fly close to the shore.

*Gannets
spend most
of their
lives on the
open sea*

The crenellated building on the cliffs, **Ellin's Tower**, was once a summerhouse, erected in 1868 by William Owen Stanley (1802-84), Liberal MP for
Anglesey from 1837 to 1874, for his wife, Ellin Williams of Bodelwyddan
Castle. W O Stanley made many archaeological excavations on Holyhead
Mountain and some of his finds were once stored in the tower. Although he
carefully documented his collection, his methods were careless by modern
standards. Nevertheless, he was a pioneer of archaeology on the island.

Ellin's Tower RSPB Information Centre (Easter to the end of September
✆ 01407 764973). The Centre was established when the tower was restored
in the 1980s. Here are informative displays, records of sightings, and direct
video links with the breeding sites. The RSPB staff readily assist with identification and can help interpret the bird behaviour you will observe. Regular
events, including guided walks, are programmed throughout the season.

The views around South Stack are dizzying. Watch the Irish ferries come
and go across a sparkling expanse of sea. Be very careful of sheer cliff edges,
especially with children. Climbers enjoy the challenge of the cliffs around
this part of Holy Island. A longstanding agreement between the RSPB and
the British Mountaineering Council aims to prevent disturbance to breeding birds during the season.

WESTERN ANGLESEY

"*BY EARLY AFTERNOON I was on the South Stack cliffs again, and a quick look through the glasses showed the nestlings squatting in the nest. No parents were present. I was about to set up the telescope when I heard a high 'keck! keck! keck!' of a peregrine and caught a glimpse of a swiftly flying brownish bird passing the lighthouse rock. It circled round, still calling, and as it presented a side view I saw that it was carrying something. Round it came again and then, passing low under my cliff, swooped up and landed at the tip of the nest and began to tear at its burden which proved to be a puffin.*"

— C F TUNNICLIFFE, entry for 30th June 1947, *Shorelands Summer Diary* (1952)

South Stack bridge in the 1840s, by William Bartlett

The island-rock of **South Stack** lies at the foot of 197 foot (60m) cliffs. The rock is approached by 400 stone steps which give spectacular views of the contorted strata of the cliffs. In the breeding season it also gives an excellent view of the birds – bring binoculars! At the foot of the steps, a suspension bridge was built across to the rock in 1828 (it was replaced in 1964 and again in 1997); before this, the lighthouse keepers had to brave the swirling chasm in a basket hauled along a cable. In 1859, during the hurricane that wrecked the *Royal Charter* off Moelfre, one of the keepers was fatally struck on the head by a falling rock as he came on duty.

The first **lighthouse** on the stack was completed in 1809. The tower was built to the plans of the architect and engineer Daniel Alexander (1768-1846), who, from 1796 to 1831 was responsible for the early development of the London Dock Scheme at Wapping. He also designed Dartmoor Prison (1806).

Having been appointed Surveyor to Trinity House, South Stack was his first lighthouse. Together with Joseph Nelson of Leeds, he went on to build several other lighthouse towers, including those at Bardsey, Lundy and Harwich.

The South Stack tower was made taller in 1874, when the present optical system of lenses and prisms was installed. Since 1909 the optics have floated in a bath of mercury, which enables smooth rotation. The lighthouse was electrified in 1938: three keepers manned it until automation in 1984.

Today's white light is 197 feet (60m) above high water and 2,500,000 candela strong. Flashing every ten seconds it can be seen 28 miles (45km) out to sea. In fog a warning blast is sounded every thirty seconds. Control is by computer link from the Trinity House Operations Centre at Harwich in Essex.

South Stack can be visited from Easter to September ✆ 01407 763207 or ✆ 01248 724444. Entry to the tower (subject to a minimum height requirement of one metre) offers a fascinating look at the lighthouse engine room and its revolving light – for those who do not suffer from vertigo. Remember too that climbing up the cliff steps after your visit is a strenuous undertaking! Neither picnics nor dogs are permitted on the island of South Stack.

Car parking and tickets for the lighthouse. The 'South Stack Kitchen' offers car parking to its patrons. Those purchasing tickets at the café, for entry to the lighthouse, may park here. Tickets are also available on the bridge to the island. A public car park is located on the RSPB land to the south of Ellin's Tower. There is additional space for a few cars near the top of the South Stack steps, although, particularly out of season, this offers less secure parking.

Paths continue from the lane across the western slopes of Holyhead Mountain, around Gogarth Bay to views over **North Stack / Ynys Arw**. Seals may be seen offshore and gulls breed here. Once people took great risks to collect seabird eggs from these cliffs, descending on ropes fastened to stakes. The fishy eggs were considered a great delicacy. The cliffs also offered the edible plant samphire in great quantities. The *Craig Gogarth* cliffs are now the delight of rock climbers who come from far to the challenging routes – some of Europe's best sea-cliff climbs. Their exertions can be observed more easily however on the southwest-facing slopes of Holyhead Mountain.

A fog signal station stands on the headland above the Stack, together with a former wireless telephony station. A telegraph station, installed by the Trustees of Liverpool Docks, once stood midway between the Stack and the Mountain's summit. In a test in 1830 a semaphore message was sent from Liverpool to Holyhead and back again, 140 miles (225km) in all, in just 23 seconds.

Llanddeusant

4F

*9ml (14.5km)
NE of
Holyhead
between
Llanfachraith
and
Llanbabo*

This is the 'village of two saints', Marcellus and Marcellinus. Their **church**, at the eastern end of the village, was entirely reconstructed in 1868.

*Howell
Watermill
Melin Seler*

The dammed waters of Afon Alaw were used to power **Howell Mill** (SH351844) known locally as *Melin Seler*, which was grinding wheat as early as the fourteenth century. The present mill, dating from early in the nineteenth century, was enlarged in 1850 and was restored to working order in the 1960s. The privately owned building is occasionally open to public view: it has three pairs of mill-stones driven by an overshot wheel.

Another privately owned watermill, once used to grind animal feeds, has been restored at **Llynon Hall** (SH333847). Its watercourse has also been cleared: the mill pond is fed by a leat from a weir on the Alaw Fach stream (also known as Afon Llynon). The new galvanized-steel waterwheel, nine feet in diameter, matches the pattern of an earlier cast iron wheel.

Llanddeusant's glory is a working windmill, **Llynnon Mill / *Melin Llynnon*** (SH341853), sited to the west of the village and linked by a three-mile (4.5km) 'Mills Trail' from the Howell watermill, with views over the parish towards the modern wind turbines on the eastern horizon. The mill is open from Easter to September ✆ 01407 730797. Llynnon Mill was built in 1775-76 for a Herbert Jones. Like many other windmills on the island it was damaged by storms, and in 1918 fell into disrepair.

*Melin Llynnon,
Llanddeusant*

Restored by the local authority sixty years after being damaged, Llynnon Mill was opened to the public in 1984. With its three storeys and movable cap, it is an impressive sight when its great sails – spanning 69½ feet (21.2m) – are turning in a stiff breeze. The three pairs of millstones and the hoists now work once again, grinding flour. An exhibition tells the story of milling on the island. Next to the mill is a tea room and the shop of the Anglesey Craftworkers' Guild. Festival days are held occasionally at the mill, with the sails decked in bunting and crowds watching wood-cutting contests, pony rides, Welsh folk-dancing and craft activities.

Llynnon's miller in the 1980s

Close to the mill are the ruins of a **bakehouse**. This building was originally a small cottage, inhabited by the mill's carrier, who carried out the important tasks of keeping the miller supplied with sacks of grain and taking away the milled flour. It was converted into a bakehouse early in the twentieth century.

A new development on land adjoining Llynnon Mill is the recreation of an **Iron Age village**, including round huts with conically thatched roofs, a granary and shelters. Paddocks, agricultural plots and woodland are also laid out on the four-acre (1.6ha) site. This programme of reconstructional archaeology gives an idea of how a settlement, such as the Tŷ Mawr hut group on Holyhead mountain ▶153, may have looked when inhabited two thousand years ago. The emphasis at Llynnon is on the use of timber: the huts being built here will

Recreated roundhouse at 'Stone Science', Talwrn

not have the low stone walls that still survive on Holyhead mountain and at Din Lligwy. A similar roundhouse reconstruction, with a rush-thatched roof, can be seen at Stone Science, near Talwrn on the B5109.

Llantrisant Old Church lies to the southeast of **Llanddeusant**, in woods across the fields (SH349841). It trumps it neighbour in the dedication stakes, for its name in Welsh reveals that it has no fewer than three patron saints: **Afran** (whose sacred well is by the lychgate), **Ieuan** and **Sannan**. The church probably dates from the fourteenth century, although its font is 200 years or so older. The South Chapel is seventeenth-century. The church is maintained by the Society of Friends of Friendless Churches. In 1899 Llantrisant **New Church** was built about one mile (1.5km) to the southeast (SHSH364836).

The **Llantrisant stone** was found at Capel Bronwen and is now displayed at the Gwynedd Museum, Bangor. It is a large memorial or gravestone which dates from the sixth century and its inscription commemorates a Christian priest named Bivatigirnus and his wife, whose name is illegible.

Anglesey's windmills

During most of the Middle Ages, wheat was ground by watermills, but Anglesey is a flat island and there is not much force in its running water. During the fourteenth century, however, records show that windmills began to be built all over Anglesey. The raw materials – grain and wind – were abundant, and locally quarried millstones were of high quality.

The earliest windmills, such as the Beaumaris post-mill (1327) have now disappeared. They were wooden structures rotating around a post to face the wind. Most of the stone-built mill towers were built during the Agricultural and Industrial Revolutions of the eighteenth and nineteenth centuries. The largest was Melin y Borth, built at Porth Amlwch in 1816, seven storeys high with the capacity to grind 70 bushels (560 gallons / 2,500 litres) of corn per hour.

The decline in the island's windmills followed the repeal of the Corn Laws in 1846. This resulted in the import of cheap grain from overseas, which benefited the urban poor but reduced home production.

On the island, livestock farming rapidly became more important than grain crops. Although 37 windmills still stood in 1929, some with sails, nearly all were in disrepair. Today there are the remains of 31, mostly ruined. Some have been converted as dwellings. The remains of sturdy, round towers are to be seen all over the island, from Kingsland, Holyhead across to Tros y Marian, near Llangoed.

Melin Llynnon sydd yn malu,
Pant y Gwydd sy'n ateb iddi,
Cefn Coch a Melin Adda,
Llannerch-y-medd sy'n malu ora.

Llynnon Mill is grinding,
Pant y Gwydd is answering,
Cefn Coch and Adda Mill,
Llannerch-y-medd grinds best of all.

— traditional rhyme

Ieuan Williams

Windmills of Anglesey by Barry Guise and George Lees (1992, out of print but available on reference shelves of Anglesey libraries), describes the history of the island's windmills

Llanfachraith *also known as Llanfachraeth or Llanfachreth*

3E

3ml (5km) north of Valley on A5025

This sizeable farming settlement is sited to the north of **Afon Alaw**, which opens into its estuary below the village. The **Holland Hotel** / **Gwesty'r Holland**, marks the centre of the village. Near to a **primary school**, the parish **Church of St Machraith** lies to the north, fronted by a wall with a stone stile. It is Victorian, replacing an older foundation and contains earlier memorials including the head of a tenth-century cross. **Capel Abarim** of the Calvinistic Methodists (1860, rebuilt 1908) stands in a gravelled yard next to its House.

To the north of Llanfachraith is its smaller neighbour, **Llanfwrog**. By its disused parish **Church of St Mwrog** (rebuilt 1864), a small lane leads southwest over fields and marsh to **Traeth y Gribin**, the tidal flats to the east of Holy Island. Fans of Welsh pop music will recall that Llanfwrog was the title of a track by the group *Gorky's Zygotic Mynci*.

Another lane leads northwest from here and then forks. Take the left-hand lane to **Porth Penrhyn Mawr**, where old farm buildings – and modern caravans – cluster around a shingle beach. Take the right-hand lane to **Porth Tywyn Mawr** ▶137 (known also as 'Sandy Beach'), with safe swimming, beside a caravan site. Here there are dramatic views of Holyhead Mountain and of shipping approaching the harbour.

African Americans' champion

Thomas Jesse Jones (1873-1950) was born in Llanfachraith, the son of a saddler. After his father died, his mother became an inn keeper in the village, but in 1884 emigrated to Ohio in the United States. Thomas studied hard at school and gained several degrees. He was a Baptist who turned his attention to sociology, working at the Hampton Institute in Virginia.

He later moved to Washington DC and finally became education director of the Phelps-Stokes Foundation, from 1913 to 1946.

Thomas cared passionately about the welfare and education of African Americans and worked tirelessly in this field. He also concerned himself with education in colonial Africa and with Native American issues. His publications include *The Sociology of a New York Block* (1904), *The Alley Houses of Washington* and *The Navajo Indian Problem*.

In 1933 he presented a bible to the Pont yr Arw chapel in Llanfachraith, where a slate plaque commemorates his achievements.

A lane northeast from Llanfachraith leads towards Llanddeusant. At the junction by the **Ty'n y Maen** chapel (1904) turn south to **Llanfugail** (often pronounced Llanfigel or Llanfigal). The little medieval **Church of St Bugail** (mostly rebuilt in 1835) is set on a corner of the lane beside Georgian **Plas Llanfigael**, its churchyard ringed by tall trees. The church interior reflects the class structure of the old days: box pews for the well off, benches for the farm labourers and standing room for the poor.

Llanfaelog — *see* **Rhosneigr** ▶166

Llanfaethlu

3F
9ml (14.5km) north of Holyhead on A5025

To the southeast of the village, near the **Soar** Baptist Chapel (1903), there is a tall standing stone, dated to 4,000 years ago. It is about 10ft (3m) high. The main road takes a sharp turn by the **Black Lion** public house. Across rolling fields are fine views of hills and coast. The parish **Church of St Maethlu** has a fifteenth-century nave, but is mostly rebuilt, with a chancel added in 1874.

The Doctor of Llanfaethlu

Siôn Dafydd Rhys, also known as 'John Davies', was born at Llanfaethlu in 1534. He was educated at Christ Church, Oxford, and at the University of Siena, in Italy. He studied divinity and medicine and was headmaster of Friars School in Bangor from 1574,

later practising medicine in South Wales. He published books about Latin, Greek and Welsh grammar, and about Welsh literature and poetry. He became a Catholic and died in about 1619. He was one of the foremost scholars of the Renaissance in Wales.

WESTERN ANGLESEY

Carreg-lwyd

To the northwest of the church is **Carreg-lwyd**. William Griffith (1515-97), a descendant of the Griffith family of Penrhyn on the mainland, first lived here in 1544 when he was made rector of the parish. The house was rebuilt in 1634 by the rector's grandson, Dr William Griffith (1597-1648), who was Chancellor of the dioceses of Bangor and St Asaph and later became Master of the Rolls to Charles I. In 1755 the estate became joined, through marriage, with that of Plas Berw near Pentre-berw. Mary Griffith and afterwards her son, Holland Griffith (1756-1839), remodelled Carreg-lwyd. The marriage in 1880 of a successor, Maria Conway-Griffith (1840-1917), to a Deputy Lieutenant of Anglesey, Sir Chandos Stanhope Reade (1851-90), was childless and her 3,800-acre (1,540ha) Anglesey estate passed to cousins, the Carpenter family.

The house was extensively renovated in the 1980s, and together with its wooded grounds and gardens opens to the public for a few weeks each spring. Nearby is Llyn Garreg-lwyd: the silted lake is a Site of Special Scientific Interest. The Carreg-lwyd 'signal tower' is a former semaphore station, in use from 1840 to 1860, the second of the twelve relay stations linking Holyhead to Liverpool.

Llanfaethlu's coffee house

Lady Maria Reade was an early collector of textiles. One of her quilts, from Llanfachraith, can be seen in the Gwynedd Museum, Bangor – see *From fleece to flannel*. ▶139 Lady Reade's wholehearted support for philanthropic causes, in particular the Welsh temperance movement (which had first come to Anglesey in 1832), led, in 1892, to the closure of two of Llanfaethlu's public houses and the establishment of a coffee house in their place. Today the **Tŷ Coffi Griffith-Reade** is a flourishing focus of village life.

Lady Reade might not have approved, however, of the name given to the local primary school on the Llanfwrog road. **Ysgol Gynradd 'Ffrwd Wîn'** – the 'wine stream' – takes its name from a tributary of Afon Penrhyn that runs through the parish. A plaque on the school's wall remembers John Roberts (1910-84) of Llanfwrog, an expressive bard, preacher and hymn writer for whom the work of the English poet John Keats became a lasting inspiration.

A lane branching westwards from the Llanfwrog road leads to **Porth Trefadog**, a vantage point for viewing Holy Island and the shipping lanes off Holyhead. Lanes leading west from the village pass through a landscape of green fields and stone farmhouses to Church Bay, affording views of the coast around **Porth Trwyn**. Nearby **Plas y Gwynt** is the home of a Working Horses Trust, which cares for shire horses and ponies.

Llanfair-yn-neubwll

3D

1ml (1.5km) south of Caergeiliog, turn off A55 at junction 3

This is an area of dunes, bogs and lakes, opposite Holy Island. The name means 'St Mary's of the Two Pools', namely the lakes **Llyn Penrhyn** and **Llyn Dinam**. Part of the land is an RSPB reserve, the 'Valley Wetlands': this is one of the best places in Wales to see wildfowl all year round. Jets from RAF Valley ▶170 roar overhead; the runways extend from here to the southeast. The little village owes its fame to another small lake, called **Llyn Cerrig Bach** (SH306767). A monument by the reedy lake on the runway edge records the incredible discovery of a treasure hoard at this site. The simple **Church of St Mary** (*Santes Fair*, SH297778) has its origins in the fourteenth century.

A Celtic treasure hoard

In 1943, during a wartime extension of the airfield at Valley, peat was dug from the marshes and small lakes to the south of Caergeiliog in order to stabilise sand around the runways. Closer examination revealed that a chain being used as a tractor coupling during this work was in fact ancient Celtic ironwork, used to fetter the necks of a gang of five slaves or captives. Further inspection of one lake, **Llyn Cerrig Bach**, brought to light a magnificent hoard of Iron Age treasure, the best known in Britain, including iron swords, spearheads, metal parts of chariots, bridle bits and a trumpet.

It seems possible that Llyn Cerrig Bach (the 'lake of small stones') was a holy site of the druids from the third century BC through to the Roman invasion of AD 60. Warriors – perhaps from all over Britain, though it is also possible that the equipment could have been in use locally – may have hurled their weapons and finery into the lake as votive offerings to a god or goddess.

In a fascinating book called *The Druid Prince* (Century Hutchinson / Rider, 1989) a theory is put forward that the offerings mark the catastrophic arrival of the Roman invaders. The authors link the story of the lake with that of Lindow Man, a figure discovered in a peat cutting near Manchester in 1984. They believe that this body was that of a druid, and that druids on Anglesey controlled the trade in Irish gold. This may seem to be a fanciful tale, but the authors are serious scholars: Dr Anne Ross, author of the classic *Pagan Celtic Britain* (Routledge & Kegan Paul, revised 1992), and Dr Don Robins, an archaeological chemist.

Most of the Llyn Cerrig Bach finds are now far away from Anglesey in the National Museum of Wales in Cardiff, but a few minor pieces are displayed on the island at Oriel Ynys Môn near Llangefni.

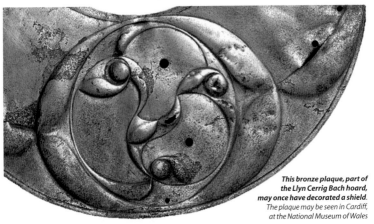

This bronze plaque, part of the Llyn Cerrig Bach hoard, may once have decorated a shield. The plaque may be seen in Cardiff, at the National Museum of Wales

"*THE MAKE-UP of the collection is predominantly masculine, a bracelet being probably the only thing which might have belonged to a woman; it is moreover overwhelmingly military in character. More than half the finds are metal fittings from chariot or pony harness; and the numerous swords and spears – which are the two weapons shown by continental burials to be carried by the warrior in his chariot – are consistent with the probability that the deposit, in its military aspect, is solely concerned with this form of warfare.*"

— SIR CYRIL FOX, from his finds report (dated 1946, published 1947)

Llanfihangel-yn-Nhywyn *also known as* **Llanfihangel yn Nhowyn**

3D
1½ml (2.5km)
SE of
Caergeiliog,
off A55
junction 4

This village lies between two large lakes surrounded by reedbeds, **Llyn Traffwll** and **Llyn Penrhyn**, attracting many waterfowl. The district is dominated by Ministry of Defence housing estates, serving RAF Valley ▶170. The stone-built **Church of Llanfihangel-yn-Nhywyn** ('St Michael's in the Dune') stands at the centre of the village. Closed by the Church in Wales, it is maintained by the Royal Air Force. The road continues to the airbase itself.

Llanfwrog — *see* **Llanfachraith** ▶161
Llantrisant — *see* **Llanddeusant** ▶158
Pencarnisiog — *see* **Bryn Du** ▶140

Rhoscolyn

2D
3ml (5km)
south of
Trearddur, on
Holy Island;
off the B4545

Southern Holy Island is a unique area of Anglesey, a landscape of rocky outcrops, gorse, reed beds and unspoiled meadows. The sleepy parish is scattered with isolated farms, linked by a maze of narrow, winding, high-banked lanes. Farming provides the main source of work, aided by tourism in the summer. There are plenty of campsites and caravan sites tucked away, excellent walks, and opportunites for sea canoeing, climbing and diving.

Formerly, the Rhoscolyn area (also referred to as *Llanwenfaen*) was known for quarrying; its 'Mona Green Marble' – a green, black and purple stone – was used to decorate many cathedrals, such as those at Bristol, Worcester and Peterborough. There was also a china clay works, extracting kaolinite used in the manufacture of porcelain, and oysters were dredged from beds around the coast, pre-

The lifeboat house on the cliffs of Borthwen

served in salt, and dispatched to the Welsh mainland and England.

The airy primary school of **Ysgol Gwenfaen** is located on the northern edge of the Rhoscolyn district. The lane continues south past the spikes and railings of **Rhoscolyn Chapel** (1906).

The parish church, dedicated to a sixth-century female saint called **Gwenfaen** (SH268757), is perched high on a rocky outcrop, approached by stone steps and a gate. The church, with its bellcote, has fifteenth-century features, but was mostly rebuilt by Gilbert Scott (the restorer of Bangor Cathedral and St Cybi's, Holyhead) in 1875; its font is of the fifteenth century, as is the south doorway. The chancel was added in 1879. The stained glass includes some by Edward Burne-Jones. The churchyard, with its old slate tombstones, offers a swallow's eye view of Holy Island, looking south to the rolling breakers of the coast and north to Holyhead Mountain. A polished granite memorial in the churchyard commemorates five of the crew of the Rhoscolyn lifeboat *Ramon Cabrera*, who lost their lives in a bid to rescue the crew of the *SS Timbo* in 1920. After capsizing twice, the remaining eight members of the crew eventually managed to get the lifeboat ashore at Llanddwyn.

The lane from the church leads past the **White Eagle** public house to the car park at **Borthwen**. Here is a broad sandy beach amidst rocks and islands. The sand dunes here are part of a conservation programme: please do not disturb. The first Rhoscolyn lifeboat station was built in 1830 and the existing building at Borthwen was the fourth. The station closed in 1929 when it became too difficult to muster a crew. A 'Neolithic' chambered tomb by the house *Tŷ Crainc* at the head of Borthwen bay is a twentieth-century creation.

East of Borthwen, vehicle access to **Silver Bay** is restricted to occupants of the local caravan site. A public footpath leads down to the beach, but there is no public car park nearby.

Silver Bay

Rhoscolyn Head is at the southwestern tip of Holy Island. It is very popular with climbers. A **coastguard lookout** is nearby, and the slate memorial set into the ground next to it commemorates the geologist Professor Dennis Wood (1934-2001), an authority on the scientific study of slate, who especially loved Rhoscolyn.

Saint Gwenfaen's holy **well** (SH259754) 450 yards (400m) north-west of the coastguard lookout at Rhoscolyn Head, has stone-built chambers and was once revered for its ability to soothe troubled minds and to heal wounds. The personal name Gwenfaen means 'white stone', and so pebbles of quartz were cast into the water as offerings. Poets too would come here to regain a lost muse. Lewis Morris – see *The Morris Brothers* ▶114 – tells of drinking Saint Gwenfaen's water for inspiration.

Sacred wells

In the book *Enwau Lleoedd Môn / The Place-names of Anglesey* by Gwilym T Jones and Tomos Roberts (Cyngor Sir Ynys Môn 1996), no fewer than 74 freshwater *ffynhonnau* ('wells' or springs) are listed for the island, and their names explained.

Many wells were of course simply providers of fresh water in the days before piped water supplies. However many too were associated with the island's early saints, such as Gallgo, Caffo, Seiriol or Gwenfaen. Many of these wells would have been sacred to the pagan Celts before them, and come the Christian era were used instead for Baptism. Wells continued to be used through the Middle Ages into modern times, for healing every complaint from arthritis to warts, for

divination, sometimes even for cursing and casting spells. **Ffynnon Oer** ('cold well') was popularly associated with the witches of Llanddona and **Ffynnon Eilian** (at Llaneilian) also became associated with sorcery. Rituals involved animal sacrifice at one time, or more commonly dropping in pebbles, bent pins or cloths, or watching the movements of small fish or eels.

Saint Gwenfaen's Well, Rhoscolyn

On a ridge overlooking Rhoscolyn Head is 'Lady Verney's Seat' – a dry stone windbreak built by Margaret Maria Verney (1844-1930). Lady Verney was an historian and a promoter of higher education in Wales. The Verney's main Anglesey residence was Rhianfa on the Menai Strait. They also owned **Plas Rhoscolyn**: this private house dates from the eighteenth century.

'White Arch', Bwa Gwyn

Footpaths turn back from Rhoscolyn Head towards the church, or continue northwards past **Porth Saint**, where water is forced upwards through a blowhole. Continue northwards along the footpath around the rocky west coast. Look out for seams of green serpentine rock and the natural arches of **Bwa Du**, the 'black arch', and **Bwa Gwyn** (SH762260) – the 'white arch', of quartz and felspar, which was once quarried and crushed for use in ceramics and as an abrasive.

Remembering loyal Tyger

Offshore rocks such as the **Ynysoedd Gwylanod** and **Maen Piscar** have long posed a threat to shipping.

In 1819 a Liverpool-bound ketch was wrecked on the latter; the captain's retriever, Tyger, was said to have saved the crew of four. He swam towards land through the dense fog, with the ship's boy clinging to his collar, and returned to guide the others ashore. Tyger died of exhaustion after his brave ordeal, and was buried on the cliffs under a simple stone. *Tyger's memorial – with a weathered inscription – faces seawards between the footpath and the cliff edge just north of Bwa Gwyn, the White Arch.*

A privately-owned country house, **Bodior**, lies between Rhoscolyn and Four Mile Bridge. It dates from 1529 but over the years has been modernised and enlarged. During the nineteenth and early part of the twentieth centuries it belonged to the Hampton Lewis family, who also owned the Henllys estate at Llan-faes.

Rhosneigr

3C

On A4080
4½ml (7km)
SW
of A55 at
junction 5

One of Anglesey's best-known resorts, Rhosneigr is set on slightly raised ground amongst dunes to the south of **Cymyran Bay / Bae Cymyran**, at the mouth of a river called **Afon Crigyll**.

The area was notorious in the eighteenth and nineteenth centuries as the haunt of gangs of wreckers, who lured ships to their doom and then plundered them. In 1715 one gang was found guilty at Beaumaris Assizes of looting the wreck of the sloop *The Charming Jenny*. In 1741 other known wreckers were captured, only to be discharged by a drunken judge. Their story is recounted by Lewis Morris, who summed up the mood of indignation felt by the people of the island in a dozen verses, *Lladron Grigyll*, that became a popular ballad:

... *Pentref yw di-dduw, di-dda,*	*It is a village without the fear of God,*
Lle'r eillia llawer ellyll,	*Where many a devil shaves,*
Môr-ysbeilwyr, trinwyr trais,	*Bandits of the waves, vicious villains*
A'u mantais dan eu mentyll;	*Hiding their lanterns under their cloaks;*
Cadwed Duw bob calon frau	*May God keep innocent voyagers*
Rhag mynd i greigiau Grigyll ...	*From wrecking on the rocks of Crigyll.*

A scattered fishing village with fine views, and centrally situated on three miles (5km) of sandy beaches, Rhosneigr first became a popular holiday resort more than a hundred years ago, when the completion of the Chester to Holyhead railway spurred development. Amongst its chapels and more traditional housing are large Edwardian family houses, alongside bungalows from the 1930s and 50s and holiday developments from the 60s and 70s.

The A4080 makes a loop westwards at Llanfaelog. It passes the dunes and sandy beach of **Traeth Llydan**. To the north, opposite the **Maelog Lake Hotel** (1863), the still waters of **Llyn Maelog** are bordered by beds of reeds. The lake and the dunes are ideal spots for birdwatching. The centre of town is marked by the stone war memorial clock, in front of a powerboat centre.

Rhosneigr looks westwards across rolling breakers. The broad sands of **Traeth Crigyll** and **Traeth Cymyran** are perfect beaches for swimming and building sandcastles. Large areas of dunes stretch back from the beach. Rhosneigr is a year-round centre for windsurfing and kitesurfing – reefs shelter the bay from the Irish Sea's winter storms. Visitors can enjoy horseriding, fishing or walking the network of footpaths. Sports facilities include **golf** (Anglesey Golf Club ℂ 01407 811202, with an 18-hole links course amongst dunes and heathland), tennis and crown green bowling. At quieter times sand yachts 'sail' the beach of Traeth Crigyll.

The northern part of the A4080 loop passes Rhosneigr railway halt and the golf links before returning to **Llanfaelog**. Opposite the small post office and a long wooded hollow rises the steep triangular roof of **St Maelog's Church** (SH337730). The church was completely rebuilt in 1848 by Henry Kennedy. The window dedicated to Saint Cecilia, the patron saint of music, is probably by Sir Edward Burne-Jones (1833-98). In 2000 a bequest from a former member of the congregation assisted a refurbishment, designed by the architect Adam Voelcker of Garndolbenmaen, that has gained the interior a Civic Trust Award. The pews were replaced by oak chairs, the altar and lectern decorated with a 'Tree of Life' motif, and the dark stain of the roof timbers was overpainted in grey. As the organ needed replacement, the old organ stops were reused as coat hooks. On the north wall is a marble memorial to:

Tŷ Newydd burial chamber

... the fifty-six unfortunate persons who lost their lives in crossing the River Menai on the Fatal fifth day of December 1785.

Many of the graves in the churchyard are of the victims of other shipwrecks. Across the road from the churchyard is the village's community hall: its garden was established by volunteers.

The back lane from Llanfaelog to Bryngwran passes **Tŷ Newydd** burial chamber (SH344 738). It is a collapsed passage grave, with the capstone propped up by a modern support. It dates from the fourth to early third millennium BC, but later Bronze Age remains were also found at this site.

Trearddur Bay / *Trearddur*

2D

*On Holy
Island, 2ml
(3km) south
of Holyhead
on B4545*

Holy Island has a narrow central section, where Trearddur Bay occupies the western shore, looking westwards across the Irish Sea. The resort is easily reached via Holyhead or Four Mile Bridge. ▶142 The bay itself is beautiful, a great sweep of low, grassy coastline indented with rocky coves and sandy beaches. Waves break over offshore reefs. Major hotels nearby include the **Trearddur Bay Hotel**, which includes a modern centre for conferences and functions.

This is a thriving holiday centre popular with watersports enthusiasts and bathers who appreciate its sheltered waters. Divers can visit a service centre on Ravenspoint Road. **Trearddur Bay Sailing Club** operates during August only: a limited number of tidal moorings can be hired. An Atlantic-75 inshore lifeboat, the *Dorothy Selina,* is presently stationed at Trearddur Bay (although funds are being raised to replace her with an Atlantic-85 boat), together with a smaller inflatable D-Class boat. Subject to operational needs, the modern **lifeboat house** (1993) may be open to visitors during summer weekends. The mounted gun displayed on the terrace here is an Admiralty pattern cannon, cast in the 1820s. It was salvaged from the sea below North Stack, having been used there as a fog signal since 1861. When sirens replaced the two North Stack cannons in 1956, they were pitched over the cliff's edge.

The **Holyhead Golf Club** ✆ 01407 763279 is a heathland 18-hole course on the outskirts of Trearddur Bay, along the B4545 towards Holyhead.

Trearddur

The resort of Trearddur stretches from the bays of **Porth Diana** (formerly Porth Dwna) in the south, to **Porth Dafarch** in the north. The North Wales Wildlife Trust **nature reserve** at Porth Diana (SH254781) is a rocky escarpment, surrounded by houses. This is one of the few sites of coastal heathland in Britain where the Spotted Rock-rose grows. It flowers in late April and during May.

In the early nineteenth century Porth Dafarch was considered as an alternative site for the berthing of the Irish packet boats, prior to the construction of the New Harbour at Holyhead. Today it remains a sandy bathing bay, visited also by divers and canoeists. Porth Dafarch has ancient hut circles. A peninsula to the southwest (SH223794) is the site of a promontory fort, known as Dinas; the southeast headland belongs to the National Trust.

A plaque at Porth Dafarch commemorates Samuel Jonathan Griffith (1850-93) of Kingsland, Holyhead. He was a hymn writer, best known for the Welsh words of *Craig yr Oesoedd ('Rock of Ages')*. The rocks of Porth Dafarch were said to be his inspiration. Liberal in his politics, S J Griffith was also a journalist, a founder of the *Holyhead Mail*. He was a keen *eisteddfodwr*, with the bardic name 'Morswyn'. A Welsh-language primary school in Holyhead – Ysgol Morswyn – was named after him when it opened in 1974.

Tywyn y Capel, a sandy mound that once stood seawards from the Trearddur post office, was the site of a Celtic Christian chapel. Its burial ground was in use between the sixth and seventeenth centuries. The old mound is now greatly reduced by erosion and in recent years a final excavation was undertaken by the Gwynedd Archaeological Trust to recover the remaining historical evidence. Bridget, in Welsh *Ffraid*, in Irish *Bhraid* – a patron saint of Ireland – is said to have landed here at the end of the fifth century. A stone from her monastery at Kildare has been brought to the site of Tywyn y Capel to commemorate the Anglesey connection and it is flanked by a modern Celtic cross with inscriptions in Welsh, Irish, Latin and English. Trearddur's small church (1932) is dedicated to **Santes Ffraid**, Saint Bridget.

Standing stones at Penrhos-feilw

At the northern end of the Bay turn left off the B4545, passing the Trearddur Bay Hotel, to follow the coastal lane toward the great cliffs above South Stack. ▶155 **Penrhos-feilw** (SH227809) is the site of two impressive standing stones, a ritual Bronze Age site from the second millennium BC. It has been proposed, although there is no evidence, that the ten-foot high (3m) stones may once have been at the centre of a stone henge. Penrhosfeilw is protected as an RSPB reserve. The area also contains ancient hut circles. Public access was extended by legislation in 2005.

Valley / *Y Fali*

3E
3½ml (5.5km) SE of Holyhead, from A55 junction 3

The name Valley is thought to derive from a cutting made by engineer Thomas Telford (1757-1834) to obtain soil for the construction of the Stanley embankment into Holyhead in 1822. Its common Welsh name is a simple transcription.

Today's large village sprawls around the crossroads by the **Valley Hotel**. The road northwest to Holyhead passes the small stone **Church of St Michael** (*Mihangel*), built in 1867 with an endowment from W O Stanley, the island's MP. A cattle market was formerly held beside the Holyhead road at Valley. A workhouse was built here too, by the Holyhead Poor Law Union, established in 1852. This was part of an island-wide organisation whose aim was to regiment the destitute and give them food in return for labour. The 'Institution' later became a cottage hospital for this part of the island. This served as a local hospital until its closure, being superseded by the Penrhos Stanley hopital in Holyhead in 1996.

The B4545 west to Four Mile Bridge leads past the **Tabor Chapel** (1881) and over a level crossing next to the **station** on the main railway line to Holyhead. Land at **Cae Mwd Fali** ('Parc Mwd', OS 292790) has recently been transformed by the planting of trees. Access is along boardwalks, with a riverside viewing platform. The B4545 continues westwards over the A55.

The airfield and meteorological station of **RAF Valley** lies two miles (3km) south of the village, by Llanfihangel-yn-Nhywyn ▶164. Access is signposted from the A55. The RAF station was established during the Second World War in 1941. It served to defend merchant shipping convoys en route for Liverpool and early units to be based there included Hurricanes flown by Czech airmen and Beaufighters in service with the Royal Australian Air Force. Sand blowing off the dunes did no good to the aircraft engines and had to be damped down with silt excavated from local lakes. From 1943 to 1945 RAF Valley was a trans-Atlantic terminal for United States military flights to Britain. Today the base is a centre for training Hawk jet fighter pilots, especially in ear-shattering low-level flying runs across the island and the mountains of Snowdonia. They are part of No.4 Flying Training School. During weekdays, spectators can view the runway's operations from a car park opposite the main entrance.

A broad area of common land lies between the airfield and Traeth Crigyll, to the northwest of Rhosneigr. It is called **Tywyn Trewan Common** / *Cytir Tywyn Trewan*.

Search and Rescue

RAF Valley has one of the busiest operational search and rescue units in Britain, being the home of C Flight, 22 Squadron. Its Sea King Mk3 helicopters are a familiar sight, often being put through their paces at Lifeboat Days and other festivals. Their more important work is of course saving lives – winching aboard crew members from ships in trouble, rescuing sailors from yachts or injured climbers from sea cliffs. The helicopters also play a vital role in mountain rescue operations in Snowdonia.

The Mountain Rescue Team was first formed in Valley in August 1943, with the aim of rescuing aircrews who had crashed in Snowdonia.

THE SPIKE ON THE CHAPEL GATE

Vernon Hughes

ANGLESEY is a secret land, unknown to all but the initiated and those born on the island. And the buildings share this experience, for in winter the island is gale-lashed with a fury that few coasts seem to know and the old buildings are crouched behind any shelter from the fierce prevailing winds. A flat land with only three hills, the surface is broken with ridges and streams, and rocks tear themselves away from the soil in every field. Golden in early summer with gorse, red and white later, with valerian, everywhere the sky dominates. The fields are separated with sod walls faced with stones, large circular gate posts, and every gate is iron.

Thatching the roof of Swtan, Church Bay

The atmosphere of mystery is enhanced by the signs of early man, as though time has stood still; burial mounds, cromlechs and standing stones are everywhere. Bryn Celli Ddu and Barclodiad y Gawres are two of the finest and most exciting burial chambers in Britain, and Din Lligwy is the most surprising and splendid early village this side of the Irish Sea.

The Romans, not to be outdone, built a fort at Holyhead, the walls of which still stand – and present a puzzle, for there was no gateway! Christianity came early to Anglesey, Celtic monasteries remaining on Ynys Seiriol (Puffin Island) and at Penmon. The first is only approachable by small boat, but the second is open to the public and consists of a splendid complex of church, monastic buildings, sacred well, crosses and later (but not to be missed by anyone interested in buildings) the dovecote. The churches generally are small, simple, isolated structures; two occupy islands, Saint Tysilio at Menai Bridge, now approachable by causeway, and Saint Cwyfan, approachable only at low tide. Exceptions are the splendid English buildings at Beaumaris and Holyhead.

Little evidence is left to show that Aberffraw was once Llywelyn the Great's capital, but at Beaumaris the evidence is for all to see that Edward I of England conquered Wales. The Castle is the great final development of medieval military building, splendidly romantic with a water-filled moat. The Castle is open to the public and it is possible to get lost in its stone corridors and towers. Unfortunately, few traces of the town walls remain. Very little medieval work is to be found elsewhere on the island; the only domestic work is at Hafoty, a house at Llansadwrn. After the English conquest Wales experienced a period of great unrest and it was only with the Tudors that prosperity enabled any building to begin.

Baron Hill, Beaumaris, after it was rebuilt in 1776 to the designs of the architect Samuel Wyatt

The Tudors were from Plas Penmynydd, where a house is still to be seen, but built a generation later to replace the earlier house. The houses of the Tudor period can only be glimpsed occasionally, hidden away, and this applies to the later large houses. Tantalising glimpses are to be had of Georgian houses with unusual features, full of furniture from Dublin, and possibly designed by Irish architects. The most important of all, Baron Hill, was the exception and can be seen from Beaumaris (when the encroaching trees are bare of leaves), set against a wooded hill – but not in all its glory, for it is now roofless and derelict. Further along the Menai Strait, Plas Newydd, built for the Marquess of Anglesey, is now a National Trust Property and open to the public. Inside is the incomparable Rex Whistler mural depicting a landscape of mountains, islands, towns and buildings, a glimpse of an ideal world where everything is beautiful. No visitor to the island should miss the experience of seeing this.

The route to Ireland opened Anglesey to the tourist. First came Telford's splendid bridge and his road with its characteristic toll-houses and then the railway with Robert Stephenson's Britannia Tubular Bridge, alas destroyed in the mad pursuit of childish pleasure, and now made commonplace with arches of steel, and to crown it, a road bridge above the rails! Still to be seen are original railway stations by Francis Thompson, the architect to the railway company, with their shelters between two end pavilions. At Holyhead the harbour of refuge is protected by a superb breakwater built in 1855. The town is typical of all cross-channel towns, rows of rendered houses being occupied by sailors and their families.

The rest of the island is characterised by single storey cottages standing singly or in rows (though few remain roofed with the cement-covered slates of former times), and large villages with no obvious economic support, for who would think of marram grass – the basis of a thriving industry in the nineteenth century!

Everywhere, dominating the scene awkwardly like a country lad in his Sunday best, are the Nonconformist chapels. Built with a vigour and a pride unmatched today, many designed by architects who had received no recognised training, these are genuine architectural primitives. Still retaining their newly varnished sticky seats, the smell of wax polish and oil lamps, gleaming with care and love, these are still the real centres of Anglesey life. Don't look at the outside – go inside and marvel at the skill of the architects, that they could seat so many people in the space and achieve the maximum effect at the minimum cost. But go inside when there is an *eisteddfod* and the atmosphere is stifling and thick with excitement; you'll sense something of the mystery of the island that scared hard-bitten Roman legionnaires or excited the crowds around Bryn Celli Ddu those many centuries ago. And when you come out look at the gate, look at the spikes and think how proud the smith was to be making gates for his own chapel. Those spikes were an act of faith and that is what architecture in Anglesey – as everywhere – is all about.

Capel Siloh, the Baptist Chapel in Caergeiliog, built in 1847

There are many other kinds of buildings on the island, such as the prison at Beaumaris designed by Hansom (of cab fame) to strike fear into the breaker of the law. Amlwch's Catholic Church is a pre-war concrete building by an Italian architect, Giuseppe Rinvolucri; there is Farmer & Dark's nuclear power station at Wylfa, and the splendid council housing at Beaumaris by Colwyn Foulkes.

VERNON HUGHES *was born in 1926 and spent his early life in Abergele. After training as an architect, he worked briefly on historic buildings for London County Council before being appointed conservation architect for Monmouthshire. With characteristic diligence he immediately applied himself to the task of getting to know every one of the listed buildings in his care. He later became an Inspector for Cadw: Welsh Historic Monuments.*

Vernon Hughes was exceptionally well informed about nineteenth century architects in Wales. He had a lifelong passion for vernacular architecture and was active in groups such as CAPEL: the Chapels Heritage Society. He died in 2004.

LLANGEFNI
and central Anglesey

CENTRAL ANGLESEY is for the most part sparsely populated. It is a landscape of rolling green pastures crossed by country lanes, of small farms and villages, of lakes and reservoirs. The south of the region is taken up by the broad river valley of the Cefni, an area of flat wetlands flanked by low ridges, extending to the southwest.

The A55 dual carriageway and the railway to Holyhead traverse the south of the region.

The small market town of Llangefni, on the Cefni river, is the administrative centre of the whole island.

'The Cattle Ring' – including many faces still familiar to Anglesey's farmers – was painted by Charles Tunnicliffe in 1973 for the auctioneers, Morgan Evans. Mr Evans wields the gavel.

Bodffordd

6D
2ml (3km) west of Llangefni on B5109

In the Middle Ages this village in the parish of Llangwyllog ▶188 was known as *Bodffordd Esgob* ('Bishop's Bodffordd'), for it was part of the estates of the Bishop of Bangor. The village is located on what was once the old post road or *lôn bost* across the island, with several fords in the vicinity.

Today's village, which borders the RAF Mona airfield, has grown up around the B5109 and its junction with the Heneglwys lane. There is a post office, a primary school and the **Sardis** chapel (Independent, 1865). Across the field behind the chapel is the roofed tower of a former windmill, **Melin Ffrogwy**.

At **Heneglwys**, just to the south of the village, is **Eglwys St Llwydian** (i.e. the church of the 'blessed saints'; the original patron here may have been *Corbre*, the Welsh form of the Irish name *Cairbre*). The peaceful, tree-ringed churchyard, amidst slate gravestones, is entered through a stone arch. The attractive windows are over 600 years old. The church was rebuilt in 1845 and has a triple bellcote. Carved Romanesque stones have been set above the door. The former east window was removed to Gwalchmai.

Bodffordd was the childhood home of the hugely popular Welsh broadcaster, actor and comedian William Charles Williams ('Charles Penffordd', 1915-90). Working as a farm labourer, he became king of the *noson lawen* (the ever popular home-spun entertainment night) and soon made a name for himself on radio and on televison, starring in Wales's longest running soap opera, *Pobl y Cwm*.

A small lake, **Llyn Frogwy**, lies on farmland to the north. To the east is a large reservoir popular with anglers, **Llyn Cefni** ▶188

Capel Coch — *see* **Llyn Cefni** ▶188

Carmel

5E
2½ml (4km) SW of Llannerch-y-medd on B5112

Carmel takes its name from an 1854 chapel, with an entrance of decorative brickwork behind a spiked gate. The surrounding settlement is a farming village due south of Llyn Alaw, on the B5112 between Trefor and Llannerch-y-medd. It is located on rising ground, with views southwards across the flatlands of Central Anglesey and northwards to the windfarm by the lake.

The B5112 leads southwest to **Llechgynfarwy**. The **parish church**, beside the lane, has a nave and chancel of an uncertain date, but the south chapel is eighteenth-century and the north porch is Victorian. The font is twelfth-century. Church and district take their names from a large standing stone (a *llech*) that once stood to the north – alongside the old post road at Trefor – perhaps a memorial to an individual named Cynfarwy or Cynfarwydd. The stone was removed in the nineteenth century.

Cerrigceinwen — *see* **Llangristiolus** ▶184
Coedana — *see* **Llyn Cefni** ▶188

Gwalchmai

5D
5½ml (8km) west of Llangefni on A5, or either junctions 5 or 6 off A55

The farming landscape around Gwalchmai is interrupted by rocky outcrops of granite and thickets of gorse. The Caer Glaw quarry lies to the northwest of the village, and the wetlands of Cors Bodwrog to the northeast. Llyn Hendref was drained in 1970 as part of an agricultural reclamation scheme – though little agricultural benefit ensued. It is now surrounded by willow.

Busy through-traffic has been relieved by the construction of the A55, which passes to the south, but the village can be approached along the A5. Travelling northwards note the **tollhouse** which collected dues when Thomas Telford opened his new road. A witch on a broomstick is its (modern) weathervane. On higher ground to the left lies the small, simple **Church of St Morhaiarn**, set in a peaceful churchyard with carved slate tombstones. The church has sections dating back to the sixteenth and seventeenth centuries but was rebuilt in 1845. One doorway, now blocked, was the entrance for the villagers of the upper village. Another doorway, still in use, was for the parishioners of **Gwalchmai Isaf** – the lower village, which borders the A5. A Catholic church, dedicated to **St Patrick and St Jude**, was consecrated in 1967. Chapel-going residents of Gwalchmai Isaf are served by the green-painted **Capel Moriah** (Independent, 1902). Gwalchmai's war memorial, nearby, was built by a Llangefni stonemason in 1926 in the form of a clock-tower – the clock, with four faces, is wound by hand each day. One of the fallen comrades remembered here is a John Jones, who was just sixteen years old when he died in 1916.

Gwalchmai Uchaf (the upper village) lies to the southwest. **Capel Jerusalem**, its large, square, Calvinistic Methodist chapel, was built in 1780 and was rebuilt and improved in 1849 and 1925. The grand interior has semi-circular seating focused on an elaborately carved pulpit. Capel Jerusalem's burial ground also serves the Moriah chapel of Gwalchmai Isaf, which has no yard of its own.

The redundant **Church of St Peulan** (SH373754), with a twelfth-century nave, stands southwest of Gwalchmai up an overgrown track.

The joyful poet

Gwalchmai ap Meilyr (fl.1130-80) was one of the great poets of medieval Wales. The modern village takes its name from his family estate, Trewalchmai, which is still the name of the parish. Gwalchmai's greatest verse took the form known as *gorhoffedd*, a 'boasting-poem' or exultation. In this he delights in the world of nature, in sea and rivers and birdsong, in the love of women and in the greatness of his patron, the ruler Owain Gwynedd. The inn sign for the **Gwalchmai Hotel** 'depicts' the poet.

Northeast of Gwalchmai, a back lane through the parish of **Bodwrog** takes a right angle bend past the house of Bodwrog. The initials above its door, *RBWB*, mark this as Bulkeley property: it was built in 1840 for the Baron Hill Estate of Beaumaris. Covering more than 450 acres (180ha), Bodwrog was one of the largest farms on the island. A group of solid agricultural buildings stands next to the house. The ruins of a former farmhouse, Bodwrog Bellaf, lie in a field to the northwest. Further along the lane, in the direction of Llynfaes,

Carving over the door of St Twrog's Church

is the small late fifteenth-century **Church of St Twrog** (SH401776). The bull's head, carved in stone above the doorway and also appearing inside, is the family crest of the Bulkeleys of Baron Hill, Beaumaris, who were patrons of the church. Inside are short, boxed pews. The roofless, stone walled building next to the churchyard once served as a storehouse for the bier and for the sexton's tools. The narrow lane, a roller-coaster ride past rocky outcrops and stone walled green fields, continues northeastwards to join the A5109 close to Llynfaes.

Llanbabo

5F
2½ml (4km)
NE of
Llanddeusant

This sparsely populated farming parish is scattered across the green fields of north central Anglesey, affording fine views of Llyn Alaw ▶187. The creation of this reservoir in 1966 flooded the marshes of Cors y Bol, on the parish's eastern boundary. The southwestern part of Cors y Bol was spared from flooding, but is now pump-drained, upwards, into Llyn Alaw.

The stone carving of legendary 'King Pabo'

The tiny **Church of St Pabo** (SH378868) is medieval, with surviving masonry from the twelfth and fourteenth centuries: chevron stones of the twelfth century are re-set around the south door. Pabo is said to have been a British Celt from the Old North who sought refuge in Wales after wars against the Picts at the beginning of the sixth century. Although there is no evidence that the north British Pabo died in Anglesey, a fourteenth-century stone low relief carving shows a bearded king with a crown and sceptre and the Latin inscription *Hic iacet Pabo,* ('here lies Pabo'). It was discovered, according to Lewis Morris, in the churchyard during the reign of Charles II and is one of a group of three, all carved in sandstone by the same hand, including memorials to Saint Iestyn in Llaniestyn church ▶57 and the 'Eva Stone' in Bangor cathedral. The circular wall of the churchyard includes a weathered stone face, said to represent the Devil. Throughout the island, circular boundaries are indicators of the earliest ecclesiastical sites.

In the nineteenth century, the name 'Llanbabs' was given to Anglesey men who went to work in the slate quarries of Dinorwig, on the mainland. Inhabitants of Deiniolen, one of the former quarrying villages serving the quarry, are still known by this nickname today.

Llandrygarn — *see* **Trefor** ▶191
Llanfrydog — *see* **Llannerch-y-medd** ▶186

Llangefni

6D
7½ml (12km)
NW of
Britannia
Bridge, A55
junction 6
or B5420
from Four
Crosses

Llangefni's central situation has made it a busy market town and the administrative centre of the island. It stands on high ground at the head of the wetlands of the Cefni valley. **Afon Cefni** is the largest of Anglesey's rivers, rising to the north of Llangwyllog and flowing six miles (10km) to the sea at Malltraeth. In ancient times the Cefni was navigable as far as the town.

The Cefni runs beneath a stone bridge at **Bridge Street / *Stryd y Bont***. From here, its course can be followed along a new walkway and cycle track, over the footbridge (which also leads to the County Council's headquarters) and then downstream as far as its estuary at Malltraeth.

On **Lôn y Felin**, where once stood a corn mill, there is an excellent **library** next to a car park, and a Church of the Welsh Presbyterians (1903). Further council departments such as the Record Office and Marriage Rooms may be found in a Victorian building, the old **Shire Hall** (1899), just across the river on **Lôn Glanhwfa**, behind the **War Memorial**. The builder of the Shire Hall (to a design by Lloyd Williams of Denbigh) was Owen Morris Roberts of Porthmadog, a ship's carpenter who became a self-taught builder and architect. Llangefni's **Magistrates Court / *Llys Ynadon*** sits in the Shire Hall: another court is located at Holyhead. The Shire Hall also accommodates the **Town Council** offices (open Tuesday, Wednesday and Thursday). In their entrance corridor is displayed one of the original wrought-iron links of the Menai Suspension Bridge, replaced during strengthening works in the 1930s and '40s.

Llangefni played an important part in the rise of Welsh Nonconformism and there are two chapels on this road. Next to the Shire Hall stands **Capel Moreia** (or 'Moriah'), a chapel with one of the most impressively designed interiors on the island – its organ looming behind a high pulpit. This is a Grade II* listed building: to view inside, make arrangements with the caretaker. Moreia was built in 1897 (by O M Roberts who was to build the Shire Hall two years later), as a memorial to the famous Calvinistic Methodist, John Elias (1774-1841). Elias was a staunch fundamentalist and the scourge of political radicals. Llangefni's Calvinistic Methodist chapel during John Elias's time was **Capel Dinas**, on Chapel Street. These days, this former chapel serves as a car showroom. Its slate roof is the only reminder that, on the Sabbath Day two hundred years ago, this was a building where resounding sermons were delivered to rapt congregations.

To the left of Capel Moreia is **Doldir**, a house swathed in Virginia creeper. This listed building – originally a doctor's surgery and residence – was completed in 1913, an example of the influence exercised by the prevailing Arts & Crafts movement on a Menai Bridge architect, Joseph Owen. Arts & Crafts houses were also built elsewhere on Anglesey by other architects, notably at Rhosneigr and Trearddur Bay.

Across the road from the Shire Hall is the **County Court / Llys Sirol**. **Capel Smyrna** (1844, rebuilt 1903) stands next to a vestry building.

Llangefni's Thursday market

Llangefni's central square, **Maes Bulkeley**, is overlooked by a former coaching inn, **Gwesty'r Bull** (the **Bull Hotel**, c1852) which has been renovated in recent years, and by the **Market Tavern** on the opposite side of the High Street. As in many other Anglesey towns and villages, the centre of Llangefni is marked by a stone **clock tower**, this one erected in 1902 as a memorial for George Pritchard-Rayner of Tre-Ysgawen (at Capel Coch, north of Llangefni), who died of typhoid at the age of 29 in 1900 whilst serving in South Africa with the Imperial Yeomanry during the Boer War. It is built of Traeth Bychan limestone. So too is the **Town Hall** (designed by R G Thomas and completed in 1884), which replaced an earlier market hall. Many stormy addresses were delivered from the Town Hall balcony when the count on general election nights still took place here.

Stalls for a bustling street **market**, established in 1785, are set up each Thursday and Saturday on the adjoining car park. The livestock market for which Llangefni was once famous, held behind **Church Street / Stryd yr Eglwys**, is now defunct and the sound of bleating and lowing no longer fills the streets each Wednesday. Llangefni's cattle market was the last of many once held on the island, although livestock auctions do still take place at Gaerwen. A road, and from autumn 2006 a new supermarket, now occupy this part of town. The **stone circle** by the Somerfield supermarket is a twentieth-century creation, erected to proclaim and commemorate *eisteddfodau* which have been held in the neighbourhood. Behind the supermarket is a modern community hospital, **Ysbyty Cefni**, built to replace the town's Druid Hospital and a former Cefni Hospital. It offers recuperative care: there is no accident and emergency service.

In the southeast of the town is a **business estate**, comprising factories, building and agricultural suppliers and offices. A **primary school** on the outskirts of the encroaching estate is likely to be relocated in more appropriate surroundings. The A5114, heading west out of town, accesses the A55 at junction 6. Close to this junction, on the left hand side of the A55 in the direction of Llanfair Pwllgwyngyll – set into the foot of the higher land that borders the Cefni valley – is a large, solid building, with two arched openings at ground level (SH457737). A similar structure lies beyond it, further up the valley. Until the end of the nineteenth century these buildings, on land at Lledwigan belonging to the Bulkeley's Baron Hill estate, were used as lime kilns. Limestone was quarried from the top of the escarpment and packed into the kilns over a firing of locally-mined coal. A siding linked to the Anglesey Central Railway branch line. **Nant yr Odyn**, the hotel opposite the kilns on the other side of the A55, bears, in Welsh, the place-name 'brook of the kiln'.

In the north of the town, the stone tower of the parish **Church of St Cyngar** rises against a backdrop of woodland. This church, with an aisleless nave, was entirely rebuilt in 1824 and added to in 1898 (and again in the 1930s). It contains a gravestone from the fifth century and a font from the twelfth. Below the churchyard, with its laurels and cypresses, is a large car park. A footpath from here, into the Dingle, is marked by a giant wooden dragonfly. Nearby is the well of St Cyngar, which provided water to baptise countless generations

Walk from the car park below the church through the **Dingle / *Nant y Pandy***. Its development as a Local Nature Reserve has received an environment award from UNESCO, and a Gold Award from the Royal Welsh Agricultural Society. A network of footpaths and boardwalks (giving wheelchair access) leads through oak and beech woods, presently extending to 25 acres (10ha) around the banks of Afon Cefni. It is intended that a further 10 acres (4ha) of woodland, behind the church, will soon be added to the Reserve.

The Reserve's motif is a kingfisher, although woodpeckers and herons are more frequent. In the spring, Nant y Pandy is carpeted with bluebells and wood anemones. A sinuous Welsh dragon, sculpted from living willow, sprouts green leaves. The Cefni broadens at *Llyn Pwmp*, the pool created to provide water to the the Anglesey Central Railway, although advances in steam locomotive engineering made it unnecessary. Water tumbles over weirs and fish ladders. The disused railway bridge and a series of new wooden bridges cross the river. Further upstream, an old pumphouse, once used to supply the town before the reservoir of Llyn Cefni was created, has been adapted as a holt (a den) to attract otters; it is hoped that bats will begin to roost in an upper level. The main footpath continues upstream, emerging from the trees below the site of the *Pandy* – a fulling mill, now demolished.

Nigel Talbot's Station Gateway Sculpture, Nant y Pandy

Groups of wooden 'environmental' sculptures can be seen at three of the Reserve's entrances. An impressive split oak sculpture marks an entrance from the car park of the town's former railway station off Bridge Street, opposite the Railway Inn. (This entrance is also served by a larger adjoining car park, on a lower level, reached from the one-way system: turn left at the Penuel chapel along Ffordd Glandŵr). The oak sculpture, by Nigel Talbot, contains a 'seam' of 150 copper discs. Schoolchildren have decorated the discs with a series of motifs, representing aspects of Anglesey life. The sculpture also reveals lines from the poem *Nant y Pandy* by Rowland Jones ('Rolant o Fôn', 1909-62). The poet was born close to Llangefni at Rhostrehwfa and spent his life on the island in practice as a solicitor. He was also the first secretary of Llangefni's branch of Plaid Cymru, and a master of *cynghanedd* – the intricate and ancient system of 'sound-chiming' within a line of verse.

Paying homage to Rolant of Fôn, the name 'Nant y Pandy' has been given to the Dingle in very recent times. One of its older Welsh names, *Nant y Dilyw* ('valley of the flood'), is recorded in surveys of 1816-23, though to the oldest natives of Llangefni it remains *Coed Mawr* – 'the great wood'.

A Dingle footpath leading off the main path from *Llyn Pwmp* climbs up steps through fern-covered rocks to emerge at **Penrallt**, just to the west of the town centre. Here is Llangefni's former **County School** building (1900), known locally as the 'Grammar School' and now part of Coleg Menai.

The town's main war memorial stands in front of the old Shire Hall on Lôn Glanhwfa, but a second memorial on the lawns in front of the County School commemorates former pupils who died on military service during the Great War, 1914-18. The home villages and towns inscribed next to the 38 names cover much of the island and some districts further afield: students came to Llangefni by train from northern Anglesey before a secondary school opened at Amlwch in 1951, and some boarded here. The memorial's slate base tells where the young men fell in action: *The High Seas – Mesopotamia – Salonica – Palestine – Africa – Egypt – Belgium – France – Italy.*

Behind the former Grammar School are the playing fields and the modern buildings of today's comprehensive, **Ysgol Gyfun Llangefni**. Next to this school is the **Plas Arthur Leisure Centre** (1974), with airy, light swimming pools, squash and badminton courts, and a café. Opposite is a **skate park**.

The Cattle Drovers

Llangefni was the last of the island's cattle towns. For centuries the rural areas of Wales did not just sell cattle locally. In the spring and in autumn they took their herds to the stockyards and butchers of the industrial cities of England, where the rapidly growing population needed feeding. To cross from Anglesey to the mainland they were made to swim across the Strait. Then they were herded together and taken overland by cowboys known as 'drovers', following ancient routes across the countryside. Many drovers remained in big cities such as London. The Welsh expatriate communities they joined founded some well-known businesses, including dairies, stores and banks.

> *"**T**HEY SWIM WELL and fast, usually make their way for the opposite shore; the whole troop proceeds regularly till it arrives at about 150 yards from the landing-place, where meeting with a very rapid current formed by the tide, the herd is thrown into the utmost confusion. Some of the boldest and strongest push directly across, the more timorous immediately turn round and endeavour to return, but the greater part, borne down stream, frequently float to a great distance before they are able to reach the Carnarvonshire shore."*

— WILLIAM BINGLEY, *North Wales: Scenery, Antiquities, Customs* (1804)

A man called Christmas

Christmas Evans (1766-1838) was born on Christmas Day. In his youth he joined the Baptists and decided to become a preacher. In 1791 he moved to Llangefni to take charge of the Anglesey Baptists, and there he stayed for 35 years.

His chapel – **Capel Cildwrn** (1750, and rebuilt in 1781, 1814 and 1846) – was the first Baptist chapel in North Wales. It still stands, with its adjoining house, on Ffordd Cildwrn and is used as an Evangelical Church.

Christmas Evans was a dramatic speaker, fond of vivid imagery. He travelled all over the island and presided over the great Nonconformist enthusiasm of the nineteenth century. He wrote some much loved Welsh hymns.

Built on Ffordd Glandŵr in 1897 after Christmas Evans's death, the **Penuel** chapel, Llangefni's remaining Baptist chapel, is dedicated to his memory.

*This figurine of **Christmas Evans** is in the collection of Oriel Ynys Môn. The preacher was blind in one eye.*

Turn south from Cildwrn Road towards the residential village of **Rhostre-hwfa**. The square brick structure you pass on higher ground to the left is a disused water tank, once filled by water pumped up from Llyn Cefni to feed Llangefni's mains supply. Pass the **Cana** and **Pisgah** chapels on the way to **Tafarn y Rhos**, a public house beside the A5.

Housing estates take up the eastern part of Llangefni. The town's cemetery, with its chapel and workshop, is off New Road / *Lôn Newydd*. The playing field, opposite, lies beneath an old windmill tower, **Melin y Graig** (1828), which dominates the skyline. The tower has been re-roofed and bristles with mobile telephone aerials. On the outskirts of Llangefni along the B5109 towards Talwrn is the floodlit ground of **Llangefni Town Football Club** / *Clwb Pêl Droed Tref Llangefni* – one of the island's top teams.

St Joseph's Catholic Church opened in 1971 to replace a predecessor on Bridge Street. It is set back from the B5420 Penmynydd road, just past the junction of the B5109 Talwrn road. Beyond the church lies the **Pencraig** campus of the **Coleg Menai** technical college, which also has a campus in Bangor. This offers a wide range of vocational training as well as adult education classes. Nearby is **Theatr Fach**, a barn converted into a little theatre club in 1955 by the inspirational Francis George Fisher (1909-70). The enterprise has thrived ever since, with amateur productions and an annual Welsh-language pantomime which involves many young people from the local community. Theatr Fach also rents out costumes to other theatre, film and television companies. (The theatre is closed during July and August.)

Leaving town northwards by **Lôn Las**, turn on to the B5111 for the 9-hole public **golf course** ✆ 01248 722193. Here too is the island's principal heritage centre and art gallery, **Oriel Ynys Môn**.

Oriel Ynys Môn. (All year, every day of the week ℂ 01248 724444.) The Oriel – Welsh for 'gallery' – was opened by the local authority in 1991 and, along with the Ucheldre Centre in Holyhead, is firmly established as one of the island's major centres for the arts. A permanent exhibition in its **heritage gallery**, including museum displays, covers some aspects of the history and culture of *Môn Mam Cymru*. A new compilation of this exhibition opened in 2005. It includes the Celtic stone head reproduced on this guidebook's cover.

Temporary displays are presented in a central area of the heritage gallery. The Oriel's main **art gallery** mounts seven or eight major exhibitions each year. The work of individual artists and groups of artists, together with thematic exhibitions, are all part of the programme. Pictures from the Oriel's own collection may also be featured in the art gallery's displays. They include important works by the island's pre-eminent artist, Sir Kyffin Williams OBE RA ▶13 , together with a major collection of drawings and sketchbooks by the superlative wildlife artist

The Oriel's Heritage Gallery tells the island's story

C F Tunnicliffe OBE RA ▶19 (who spent most of his working life on Anglesey) and more than 500 detailed botanical illustrations by the Massey sisters of Llangoed ▶66 (active from around 1890 to the 1940s). A smaller gallery has its own programme of exhibitions; the Oriel also has a shop and a café.

Bwthyn / Cottage is a signed print, limited to an edition of 350 – one of a series of twelve made from the Sir Kyffin Williams collection at Oriel Ynys Môn.

The sale of these prints will help fund a 'Kyffin Williams Gallery' within the Oriel, providing new exhibition space, not only for Sir Kyffin's work but for other artists too.

CENTRAL ANGLESEY

Annual events in and around Llangefni

✦ **Gŵyl Cefni** is a festival of 'Welsh popular culture', held annually since 2001 during the middle of August. Some performances take place in the streets and public houses of the town, others may be at the *Pafiliwn Môn* on the Anglesey Showground at Mona. The majority of the programme is musical, but other events, such as Welsh-language comedy, are also included.

✦ **The Christmas Crafts exhibition** at Oriel Ynys Môn, held during the weeks before Christmas, is a popular marketplace for the work of the region's craftworkers. Pottery, toys, textiles and woodwork are all part of the displays.

Llangristiolus

6C

*2½ml (4km)
SW of
Llangefni,
turn off
A55 at
junction 6*

The A55 cuts through through the eastern borders of this peaceful, rural parish near the **Nant yr Odyn** hotel. The elegant **Church of St Cristiolus** (SH450736) dates back to the eleventh century, but underwent major restoration in 1852. Its chancel window belongs to the early sixteenth century. The church's buttressed wall and bellcote top a hill which provides the best views of the flat wetlands of the Cefni river valley to the south and west, also known as the **Malltraeth marshes / *Cors Ddyga***. This section of the Cefni river is now channelled between high, straight banks and the valley floor is drained and reclaimed as sheep pasture.

The village of **Llangristiolus** lies amidst a network of small, leafy lanes on the slopes of a ridge that runs parallel to the Cefni. It is bounded to the north-west by the B4422, a long, straight road which runs from Rhostrehwfa on the A5. **Cerrigceinwen** lies just off this road. Its church of **St Ceinwen** (SH424737) has the same patron saint as Dwyran – Cain or 'Ceinwen', sister of Dwynwen – see *The Saint of Love*. ▶213 The lintel of the south doorway is formed by a twelfth-century carved gravestone. A gravestone of Morris Lloyd, a Royalist who died in 1647 during the Civil War, is set into another wall. The church (reconstructed in 1860) is set amidst farmland in a grassy hollow. A path winds down through elder and wildflowers, past the saint's sacred well.

Continue along the B4422 to **Capel Mawr**. Just to the east of this hamlet is **Henblas**, the site of a large, stone-built seventeenth-century house. In the eighteenth century Henblas was the home of Elizabeth Morgan, a cousin of William Bulkeley of Brynddu – see *The Squire from Brynddu* ▶122

Snakeroot and Snail Water

The inventories, accounts and gardening diaries kept by **Elizabeth Morgan** of **Henblas**, until her death in 1773, reveal how housekeeping was managed in her day. The medicinal recipes she recorded make for interesting reading:

For the Ague [fever]

An ounce of Bark, an ounce of Salt of Wormwood and an ounce of Snakeroot and an ounce of Salts of Steel, mix them in a quart of Brandy for Men and in a quart of red Wine for Women, take a wine glass full of it, the first thing in a morning and the last at Night.

Snail Water

*Take a peck of garden snails, shells and all, wash 'em in spring water, wipe 'em, bruse 'em in a stone mortar, steep 'em in a three gallons of best Ale, add hartshorn rapt six ounces, cloves, brus'd two ounces, Liquorice half a pound, Aniseeds an ounce, Cinammon, Nutmegs each an ounce, beat 'em grossly together.
Let 'em steep a day and night.
Distill it in a Limbach with a slow fire.*

For the Green Sickness [anaemia in young girls]

Take a pound of Hob nailes and steep 'em in a quart of white wine for 4 or 5 days, and drink a glass of the wine every morning and walk moderately after it.

For a Stitch

Take a gallon of New Ale in the working and put to it as much Horse Dung (just fresh from the horse) as will make it pretty thick, add to this a pound of treacle, an ounce of ginger sliced, six pennyworth of saffron mix these together and distill. When taken with a still take three or four spoonsfuls of this water by itself or in any proper liquor you like best.

The house of **Henblas** is not open to the public, but the land of the estate is now **Henblas Park / Parc Henblas**, clearly signed from the road. (Whit to September; and school holidays from Easter to October. Closed Saturdays except Bank Holidays © 01407 840440). This offers visitors demonstrations of sheep-shearing and falconry, a covered adventure playground and other attractions for an enjoyable family day out. It is also the venue for the annual **Anglesey Vintage & Steam Rally / Sioe Hen Gelfi Ynys Môn**, held in May during the weekend before the Whit Bank Holiday.

Within the grounds of Henblas is a structure resembling a neolithic burial chamber, though this is probably a natural feature. Note also the massive stone barn (1776), now roofless.

Paradwys lies to the southwest. The district's name, 'paradise', almost certainly referred originally to a walled garden. Wooded lanes climb northwest, from the farmland which fringes the Malltraeth marsh, to scattered residential areas.

The region was immortalised in the writings of Ifan Gruffydd (1896-1971). Welsh-speakers should read *Gŵr o Baradwys* ('A Man from Paradise', 1963) which gives a lively account of his upbringing and a way of life now vanished from Anglesey. Its sequel was *Tân yn y Siambr* ('A Fire in the Room', 1966).

Y Ffair Gyflogi gyntaf

Gosodais fy hun 'ar y farchnad' megis, o flaen y Bull Hotel, ym mhlith ugeiniau o las lanciau'r sir, yn ôl yr arfer mewn ffair gyflogi. Profiad hyfryd oedd bod yn un oedd yn cyfri yn y traddodiad amaethyddol, a theimlwn fy mod yn un o'r rhai oedd yn dal y byd. Cerddai'r amaethwyr bach a mawr yn hamddenol drwy'r rhengau, gan fesur a phwyso maint a nerth yr ymgeiswyr yn ôl y galw ...

Yr oedd cyflogi prysur yn mynd ymlaen ers oriau cyn i neb sylw fy mod i yno o gwbl, ac er i mi ymsythu a gwthio fy mrest allan gorau gallwn, mynd o'r tu arall heibio i mi yr oedd pawb rywfodd. Digon o fynd ar hwsmyn a chertmyn, ond fawr neb i'w weld eisiau gwas bach, a minnau mor awyddus.

Dechreuais ddigalonni gan ofn cael fy ngadael ar y clwt, ys dywed pobl Sir Fôn. Daeth gŵr o Langristiolus heibio, un a adwaenwn yn iawn, a'i blant wedi troi allan yn dda.

'Wyt ti wedi cyflogi?' meddai.

'Nag ydw', meddwn innau.

'Hogyn rhy ddrwg wyt ti yntê, was, pwy cymith di?'

Ni bu gennyf ormod o gariad at y gŵr hwnnw weddill ei ddyddiau, er cywilydd i mi efallai.

My first Hiring Fair

I put myself 'on the market' so to speak, in front of the Bull Hotel [in Llangefni], amongst scores of raw young lads from the county, as was the custom during a hiring fair. Being part of this agricultural tradition was a wonderful feeling and I felt as if I had the world at my feet. Farmers from all backgrounds, great and small, wandered leisurely amongst the ranks, weighing up the size and strength of those available ...

Business had been hectic for many hours before I was even noticed, and, despite my best efforts to stand tall and straight, I was totally ignored. Bailiffs and waggoners fared well, but few seemed to want a young farm lad, despite my eagerness.

I began to lose heart and worried about being left on the scrapheap. A man from Llangristiolus came by, whom I knew well. His children had been brought up properly.

'Have you been taken on?' he said.

'No', I replied.

'You're too much trouble, aren't you lad? Who would take you?'

Perhaps I should be ashamed, but I did not feel over friendly towards that man for the rest of his living days.

Ifan Gruffydd, *Gŵr o Baradwys* (1963)

Llangwyllog — *see* Llyn Cefni ▶188

Llannerch-y-medd *also known as* Llanerchymedd

5F

*7ml (11km)
north of
Llangefni
on B5111*

The landscape around this small town in Central Anglesey is dotted with pre-historic remains including standing stones and Bronze Age mounds.

Llannerch-y-medd means 'glade of the mead' – mead being the honeyed drink popular in ancient and medieval Wales. Today's residents are more likely to quench their thirst with a beer at the **Bull Inn** or the **Twr Cyhelun Arms**.

The parish **Church of St Mary** *(Santes Fair)* is right at the centre of the town. It has a massive stone tower, with medieval foundations, capped by an unusual bellcote. The large stone lychgate is dated 1755. Most of the present church dates from the 1840s. Following storm damage in 1998 the church reopened, after renovation, in 2006.

Nonconformist chapels include the square **Capel Ifan** (1870, Independent), **Jerusalem** (Welsh Presbyterian) and a **Baptist church**.

From the Middle Ages into the nineteenth century, Llannerch-y-medd was renowned for its fairs and cattle markets (established in 1657) and also for the skill of its harpists. Lewis Morris – see *The Morris Brothers'* ▶114 – established a printing press here in 1732. At the peak of the Anglesey copper boom the mineworkers were supplied with footwear by Llannerch-y-medd's 250 cobblers: boots and clogs were made until the late nineteenth century.

Llannerch-y-medd

Llannerch-y-medd was a station on the branch railway line to Amlwch which opened in 1866 but closed to passenger traffic in 1964. The present town includes housing estates and a primary school.

The **Gallt y Benddu windmill** on the junction with the Llangefni road was built in the 1737, the oldest known tower mill still standing on Anglesey. Severely damaged by a storm over a century ago it was converted in 1964 and is now holiday accommodation. **Llwydiarth Fawr**, to the east of the Amlwch road, was the site of a nobleman's dwelling as early as the twelfth century. The present building has its origins in the seventeenth century. In 1900 its owner at the time, wealthy building magnate William 'Klondyke' Jones (1840-1918), opened a brickworks on the estate. It operated until 1922.

The meeting place

There were once two sacred wells at **Clorach**, to the east of Llannerch-y-medd. Only one survives today, the course of water to the other having been damaged by road-building in the nineteenth century. The two wells were associated with Anglesey's most celebrated saints of the early Middle Ages, Seiriol of Penmon and Cybi of Holyhead. In the days before telephones, the two holy men would walk from their respective corners of

the island in order to meet up at Clorach and discuss matters of mutual interest. Coming from the east, Seiriol had his back to the sun in the morning and also on his return in the afternoon, and so his face always remained pale. Coming from the west, Cybi walked into the rising sun in the morning and towards the setting sun on his way home, so his face was always tanned brown. It was not long before the two men were given affectionate nicknames: Seiriol *Wyn* – 'the fair', and Cybi *Felyn* – 'the tanned'.

Lôn Leidr is a lane which leads northwards from **Clorach** to the hamlet of **Llandyfrydog**. The parish **Church of St Tyfrydog** (SH444853) has a nave which is about 600 years old and a fourteenth-century chancel arch. The restoration dates from 1862. The 'burial chamber' of **Maen Chŵyf** (SH433 857) may in reality be a natural feature.

Llwydiarth Esgob, in Llandyfrydog parish , was the home of Huw ap Huw (1693-1776) a famous poet known as *Y Bardd Coch o Fôn* ('the Red Bard of Anglesey'). He was a friend of Richard Morris, another of the Morris brothers.

The Botanology

Hugh Davies (1739-1821) was born in the parish of Llandyfrydog. He was educated at Beaumaris grammar school and at Jesus College, Oxford, later becoming rector of Abergwyn-gregyn, on the mainland. However he spent most of his time exploring Snowdonia and Anglesey in search of plants, which were his passion. He became an eminent botanist, elected a Fellow of the Linnaean Society in 1790, two years after its foundation. His *Welsh Botanology* of 1813, which carried on the work of William Morris *(see page 114)*, was a systematic catalogue of over 800 species, named in Latin, Welsh and English. Many were previously unknown in the British Isles and some were new to science.

Davies died in 1821 and was buried in Beaumaris. The genus *Daviesia* (Leguminosae), commemorates his services to botany.

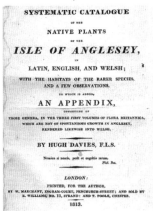

SYSTEMATIC CATALOGUE

OF THE

NATIVE PLANTS

OF THE

ISLE OF ANGLESEY,

IN

LATIN, ENGLISH, AND WELSH;

WITH THE HABITATS OF THE RARER SPECIES,
AND A FEW OBSERVATIONS.

TO WHICH IS ADDED,

AN APPENDIX,

CONSISTING OF

THOSE GENERA, IN THE THREE FIRST VOLUMES OF FLORA BRITANNICA,
WHICH ARE NOT OF SPONTANEOUS GROWTH IN ANGLESEY,
RENDERED LIKEWISE INTO WELSH.

BY HUGH DAVIES, F.L.S.

LONDON:

PRINTED, FOR THE AUTHOR,
BY W. MARCHANT, INGRAM-COURT, FENCHURCH-STREET; AND SOLD BY
E. WILLIAMS, NO. 11, STRAND: AND T. POOLE, CHESTER.

1813.

Llechgynfarwy — *see* **Carmel** ▶176

Llyn Alaw

5F

1ml (1.5km) south of Llan-babo, or 2ml (3km) north of Llannerch-y-medd

Anglesey's largest lake, of 777 acres (314 ha), is the Llyn Alaw reservoir. It was formed in 1966 by the flooding of Cors y Bol, and is mostly shallow. By the car park at **Bod Deiniol**, at the southwestern corner of the lake, is a visitors' centre with an exhibition and picnic sites. At **Gwredog**, northwest of Llannerch-y-medd, there is another car park, a picnic site and a birdwatchers' hide. Permits for fishing brown and rainbow trout (during the summer season, end of March to October) are issued by machine at Bod Deiniol. **Afon Alaw** flows from the lake southwest towards Llanfachraith.

Bedd Branwen

The river meanders past **Bedd Branwen** (SH361849), a burial site traditionally associated with Branwen, heroine of the *Mabinogion*. These ancient tales, first written down in the medieval period, tell how Branwen, daughter of Llŷr, returned to Anglesey after her disastrous marriage to Matholwch, King of Ireland, and died of a broken heart on the banks of the Alaw, where she is said to have been buried. The site is actually far older, for

CENTRAL ANGLESEY

it is a round barrow from the middle of the second millennium BC. The central stone is even more ancient than that. Excavations revealed cremated bodies, jewellery of jet and amber as well as pottery, now in the Gwynedd Museum in Bangor. The burial chamber was dismantled by farmers in 1813.

> *"THEY LANDED at Aber Alaw in Talybolion and sat down and rested, but Branwen looked at Ireland and the Island of the Mighty, at what she could see of them, and said. 'Alas, son of God, woe that I was ever born, for two good islands have been destroyed on my account.' And with that her heart broke. They made a four-sided grave and buried her on the bank of the Alaw."*

— from *THE MABINOGION* (Penguin Books, 1976, translated by Jeffrey Gantz)

Llyn Cefni

6D

Between B5109 at Bodffordd and B5111 north of Rhos-meirch

Llyn Cefni is a short drive to the northwest of Llangefni. It is a reservoir, created between 1947 and 1949 by damming Afon Cefni, which now leaves the southern shore past a pumping station, on its journey to Llangefni's Dingle / Nant y Pandy. ▶180 The lake can hold about 400 million gallons (1,820 million litres) of water. The dam helps to control flooding on the wetlands downstream. The overgrown track of the Central Anglesey Railway, no longer used, crosses a causeway over the lake. It now serves as a footpath: walkers can also take a path over the top of the dam wall. Another path and a cycle track almost encircles the lake.

Trout may be fished here, from waters surrounded by conifer plantations. Waterfowl include grebes, swans and ducks, while woodland species include goldcrests, siskins and treecreepers. Birds can be watched from a hide on the site. There is parking at the east end of the lake, off the B5111.

Around Llyn Cefni / *Bro Cefni*

Bodffordd is the village at the west end of the lake ▶176. The surrounding farmland has little settlement. **Rhos-meirch** is to the east, and is one of the larger villages, a residential satellite of Llangefni. Anglesey's first Non-conformist chapel, **Capel Ebenezer**, was built in 1749, across the fields to the east of the scattered settlement. On its site is the rebuilt chapel of 1869, a well tended building facing a neat burial ground. A polished red granite memorial was raised here on the centenary of the death of William Prichard (1702-73), 'Anglesey's first Nonconformist'. The peaceful countryside setting gives an open view to the mountains of the mainland.

The B5111 continues to **Llangwyllog**, source of Afon Cefni. The little **Church of St Cwyllog** dates back to at least the fifteenth-century, but has been restored in the nineteenth-century. It has an unusual three-stage pulpit (1769) and eighteenth-century pews. Further north along this lane, south of Llannerch-y-medd, is **Coedana**, whose **Church of St Anau** was rebuilt in the 1890s.

Capel Ebenezer, Rhos-meirch

An eastern lane from the B5111 leads to **Tregaean**, amidst farmland and stands of beech. It has a tiny church partly dating to the late fourteenth-century, dedicated to **Saint Caean**. The church stands next to long, low farm buildings that were once so typical of the Anglesey countryside. One sixteenth-century resident of Tregaian made history by living to 105, quite a feat in those days of short life expectancy. He had 36 legitimate children – seven others were said to have been born out of wedlock. When his youngest son was two years old, his oldest son was 84.

Tre-Ysgawen

The lane continues to **Capel Coch** past the mansion of **Tre-Ysgawen**. This is now a well-appointed hotel, set in undulating, wooded grounds. Patrons approach it along a drive made tunnel-like by the leaves of rhododendron and laurel. A family from Llansadwrn, the Pritchards, probably first occupied 'Trescawen' in the eighteenth-century. The present house was built in 1882 (to the plans of R C Thomas of Menai Bridge) for the sheriff of Anglesey at the time, George Pritchard-Rayner (1843-93), who had taken the additional name of Rayner on his marriage in 1871. The Tre-Yscawen estate on Anglesey once included other properties in many parishes. Trees and lawns now surround the house. Other lawns within a large walled garden are gradually becoming smaller as newly dug flower beds and vegetable plots reclaim their rightful territory. In late winter the Tre-Ysgawen woodland is carpeted by snowdrops and in spring by bluebells – walkers should wear boots along its muddy tracks. A well-tended pet cemetery is set in these woods: *Twink 1934-1939; Wickes Pheasant Jan. 7 1932; Buster 2003 age 10, 'a special soul'.*

Approaching Capel Coch note the sharply tapering, red sandstone windmill tower of **Melin Llidiart**. Dating from the middle of the eighteenth-century, this is one of the oldest of the island's surviving windmills.

Llynfaes — *see* Trefor ▶191

Mona
6D

2½ml (4km) east of Gwalchmai on A5; junction 5 or junction 6 off the A55

The hamlet of Mona lies to the southeast of Gwalchmai on the A5. When Thomas Telford's A5 was completed in 1826, the old coaching inn and stables at Gwyndy ▶191 (southwest of Trefor on the B5109) were by-passed by the more direct route to Holy Island. A new inn and stables, 'Mona', were built at Caeau Môn (SH425749). Today the Mona Inn is a private dwelling.

Telford's milestones along the Anglesey section of the A5 can still be seen. Each gives the distance from Holyhead and Bangor, and also from Mona – an eagerly anticipated refreshment point on the rough road. The milestone at the Mona Inn bears the inscription: *Holyhead 13 – Mona – Bangor 12*. The section of the A5 west of the old Mona Inn, in the direction of Holyhead,

One of the A5 'depotes'

retains many of Telford's regularly-spaced roadside 'lay-bys' – four each mile. These small rectangular insets in the road's wall were storage bays (known by Telford as 'depotes') for the sand and gravel that was needed to make repairs before the A5 was tarred in the 1890s. The bays were placed on the eastern side of the road to catch the sunlight. This thawed the gravel during the frozen months of winter, ready for the labourers to set to work.

The **RAF Mona** relief airfield stretches from the old Mona Inn eastwards to Bodffordd. During the week trainee jet pilots of the RAF practise landing manoeuvres: at weekends it is used by the light aircraft of a civilian club. The airfield dates back to the First World War: from 1915 it was a base for airship patrols, spotting U-boat (German submarine) movements in the Irish Sea and protecting trans-Atlantic convoys. Up to 150 men were stationed here. A **business park** borders the main road, which is now bypassed by the A55.

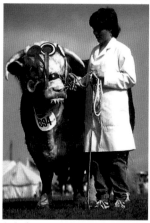

The **Anglesey Showground** lies to the east of the airfield. This is the site each August of the **Anglesey County Show / Sioe Sir Fôn**, the most important agricultural show in North Wales. Over its two days – always a Tuesday and Wednesday – between fifty and sixty thousand come to see the stands, watch international show-jumping, sheep-shearing and craft demonstrations, or simply meet up with friends for a chat. For farmers and equally for novices to the countryside, it is a treat to see magnificent bulls in their prime, immense sows, all kinds of sheep breeds, immaculately groomed ponies and shire horses. A grand parade of prizewinners takes place on the Wednesday afternoon. The County Show was first held in 1876, four years after the founding of its organising body, the Anglesey Agricultural Society,

An Anglesey Show champion

and has been at the Mona site since the 1970s. The showground has also been used for many other events and entertainments, from *eisteddfodau* to car-boot sales. Since 1992 a one-day agricultural **Winter Show** has also been held annually, at the end of November, in the showground's pavilions.

Paradwys — *see* **Llangristiolus** ▶184

Pentre-berw *also known as* **Pentre Berw**

7C

4½ml (7km) west of Britannia Bridge on A5; junction 6 or junction 7 off the A55

This small village on the A5 is adjacent to Gaerwen ▶52. Like its neighbour, it has been by-passed by the A55, which cuts through the high outcrop of Graig Fawr. The **Holland Arms** hotel is nearby, close to a popular garden centre. Another public house, **Tafarn y Gors**, is on the opposite side of the road.

The surrounding landscape is one of rocks and gorse. Pentre-berw lies at the eastern end of the ridge which forms the southern border of the Cefni valley, the **Malltraeth Marshes / Cors Ddyga** (the name Pentre-berw may mean 'village of the waterfall', or 'watercress village'). A long-term project, intitiated by the RSPB, is improving part of the wetlands. Reedbeds are being enlarged between Pentre-berw and the channelled Afon Cefni. Access is via the existing network of footpaths, and the reserve's public facilities are also being improved. The **RSPB office** is at Tai'r Gors (SH464726). A small car park nearby (SH464725), with an information board, gives access to a network of foot and cycle paths leading southwest to Malltraeth, Newborough and Llangaffo, and northwards to Llangefni.

The B4419 follows the ridge southwest to Llangaffo. **Plas Berw** (SH465718) in private ownership, lies on a lane leading eastwards from this road. The first mansion, a hall house, was built here in about 1480 by Ithel ap Hywel 'Berw'. Today's house dates from 1615 and was built by Sir Thomas Holland.

This area was once the centre of a small coalfield that served homes and small-scale industries on the island. The first records of coalmining date from about 1450. The peak of production – employing 140 coalminers – was during the first half of the nineteenth century. From the 1850s, regular flooding and difficulties with transport led to a rapid scaling down of the industry. The present-day coalyard of Cefni Fuels, across the A5 from the **Holland Arms Garden Centre** and up a private driveway, sells imported coal. During working hours, railway enthusiasts should ask the staff for permission to view the red brick building they use as an office. This is Anglesey's only remaining branch line railway station (1891), the Pentre Berw station of the Amlwch branch which was in service from 1864 to 1993. Rails still run past the platform, leading northwards underneath the dual carriageway of the A55.

Rhos-meirch — *see* **Llyn Cefni** `▶188`

Rhostrehwfa — *see* **Llangefni** `▶178`

Trefor

5E

2½ml (4km) east of Bodedern on B5109

Trefor is a hamlet built around the **Ebenezer Chapel** of the Methodists, at the crossroads of the B5109 and the B5112 between Bodedern and Llannerch-y-medd. A plaque by the crossroads commemorates the birth here of John Morris-Jones, the Welsh scholar, in 1864, see *A passion for Welsh* `▶65` Trefor is surrounded by sparsely populated farmland.

Eastwards from Trefor down the B5109 is **Llandrygarn** (or 'Llandrygan'). It takes its name from a 'large cairn', of which no trace remains. **Llandrygarn Church** (SH383796) lies amidst meadows and yellow flags to the west of the village, approached by a long, gated track from the road. It is a thirteenth-century foundation with a Victorian chancel.

The B5105 continues southwards through a landscape of rocks and fields.

During the seventeenth and eighteenth centuries, **Y Gwyndy**, a large coaching inn just to the southeast of Llandrygarn, provided refreshment, accommodation and changes of horses on the old *lôn bost* (the post road) to Holyhead. The great English painter, J M W Turner (1775-1851), lodged at Gwyndy during one of his five tours of Wales, all completed before he was twenty four. He will have found the route along the *lôn bost* from Llangefni:

… ill kept for the first five miles, being pitched with great stones but suffered to lie in great holes. The best part is between Gwyndy and Holyhead, thirteen miles. The descent to the ferry is execrably rough and dirty.
— *Topographica Britannica*, 1770s

Ruins of the coaching inn Y Gwyndy

In the nineteenth century, traffic was directed to Holyhead via the newly constructed A5 instead, a parallel route to the south, and Mona `▶189` became the site of the principal coaching inn. The abandoned inn at Gwyndy is now in ruins, thick ivy-clad walls and a chimney stack on its gable end still standing amongst the encroaching trees (SH393794).

Continuing towards Bodffordd, pass Llandrygarn's **primary school**, next to the studio of the artist Keith Andrew. The few houses of **Glanyrafon** lead on past **Capel Bethel** (1879) to **Llynfaes**, a small settlement built on the north side of the road with a tiny pebble-dashed **Neuadd Goffa** (memorial hall), dated 1920, at its centre.

Tregaean *also known as* **Tregaian** — *see* **Llyn Cefni** `▶189`

CENTRAL ANGLESEY

"*W*HAT *was the condition of Anglesey with regard to religion, godliness, and morality before the recent Methodist revival broke out is not hard to answer; the common people (except one in a thousand) had no more knowledge than the wild creatures of the Mountains; they delighted in nothing except empty sport and carnal pleasures, playing with dice and cards, dancing and singing with the harp, playing football, tennis, mock-trials, and hostages, and many other sinful sports too numerous to be mentioned. They used the Sunday like a market day to gratify every wicked whim and passion; old and young, with no one to persuade or prevent them in their ungodly course. They flocked in crowds to the parish churches on Sunday morning; not to listen to the Word of God, but to devise and relate foolish anecdotes, and to entice each other to drink at the wash-brew house of the devil's market; and to arrange places of meeting to decide upon the sports to be engaged in after the evening service.*

... No wonder the Angleseyites were once called Swine*: it is a wonder they were not called Bears, or Lions. Within the last sixty years, there has been many an entire parish in Anglesey, where not one single inhabitant could read one letter in a book; and not one in a thousand who saw the least necessity for such an accomplishment."

— SIÔN WILLIAMS *writing in 1799 to the Reverend Thomas Charles, Bala*

* A reference to the mainlanders' traditional insult to islanders: '*Moch Môn!*'

Huw Roberts plays the fiddle during Gwylmabsant Bodedern in the 1980s

SOME ANGLESEY CUSTOMS

Trefor M Owen

IT is misleading to think of Anglesey as a remote and isolated island beyond the reach of cosmopolitan influences. Even in the eighteenth-century English folk tunes were widely known, as appears from a list recorded by Richard Morris in 1717, but many centuries-old customs survived until the twentieth century.

Richard Morris's manuscripts preserve the words of numerous wassail-songs belonging to the celebration of Candlemas (2nd February) when parties of carollers wandered through the Anglesey countryside in search of warmth and good cheer by a hospitable hearth. The custom, which must have been very elaborate, involved a competition in verse at the door, followed by a solemn procession in the kitchen around a chair in which a young maiden and child were seated, representing Mary and her Child. Solemnity soon gave place to conviviality, the unbridled nature of which laid wassailing and similar customs open to attack by the straitlaced Methodists of a later period.

More innocent customs such as clapping for Easter eggs escaped this fate and some still survive in an attenuated form. It is often easy to forget their great antiquity and wide distribution. A 'clap' similar to one used in Anglesey within living memory is shown in one of the paintings of the sixteenth-century artist Pieter Brueghel in the same ritual context. Other customs may not have been so old or so widespread; for example, the race on foot from the church to the bride's home on her wedding day to be the first to bring the good news and to win the cake. All, however, seem to have been a manifestation of a neighbourliness which shaded imperceptibly into a benign charity.

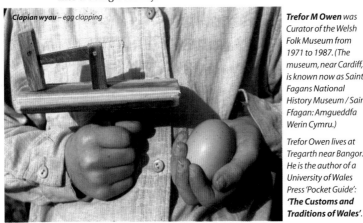

Clapian wyau – egg clapping

Trefor M Owen *was Curator of the Welsh Folk Museum from 1971 to 1987. (The museum, near Cardiff, is known now as Saint Fagans National History Museum / Sain Ffagan: Amgueddfa Werin Cymru.)*

Trefor Owen lives at Tregarth near Bangor. He is the author of a University of Wales Press 'Pocket Guide': **'The Customs and Traditions of Wales'.**

Teisennau Berffro
... *a recipe for Aberffraw cakes*

Ingredients

4oz (150g) wholemeal flour
2oz (50g) soft brown sugar
3oz (100g) salted butter (at room temperature)
Scallop shell (collected from the beach and washed)

Method

Pre-heat the oven to 150°C (gas mark 2 / 300°F).
Lightly grease a flat baking tray.
Soften the butter and beat in the sugar.
Add the flour, a little at a time, finishing the mixing by hand.
The warmth of your hands should keep the mixture soft and pliable.
Roll out to a thickness of a quarter-inch (0.5cm).
Cut out the pastry, using the rounded half of a scallop shell.
Turn the shell over and roll it on the pastry shapes, so that it leaves an imprint
Bake the shapes in the centre of the oven for
about 25 minutes, by which time they should be slightly browned.
Allow to cool for ten minutes before removing from the baking tray.

Ynys Llanddwyn – Llanddwyn Island

NEWBOROUGH
and southern Anglesey

SOUTHERN ANGLESEY is a land of dunes and saltmarsh, with long, sandy beaches to the west. The southern shore looks across the shining Menai Strait to y Felinheli and Caernarfon and the mountains of Snowdonia. More distant views to the southwest include the peaks of the Llŷn peninsula, dipping to the horizon.

This region has some of the richest natural habitats on the island, a delight for birdwatchers and botanists. Many of the island's most significant remains from the Stone Age and Bronze Age are to be found in this corner of the island, which also played a major role in Roman and medieval times.

There are no large towns in southern Anglesey. Historically, the most important are Aberffraw and Newborough. Other small centres of population are at Dwyran and Brynsiencyn. Farming and tourism offer a livelihood to some; others commute to work in Bangor, Menai Bridge or Llangefni.

The splendidly-set Plas Newydd – a National Trust property

Aberffraw (known also as 'Berffro')

4B
6ml (9.5km)
NW of
Newborough
on A4080

The parish of Aberffraw stretches to the north almost as far as Gwalchmai. It is bordered to the east by that of Trefdraeth. Both are farming districts, crossed by the mainline rail track between Bangor and Holyhead. Aberffraw means the 'mouth of the river Ffraw'.

Aberffraw itself is a small, unassuming village set between the rolling green farmland of the west and a broad sweep of coastal sand dunes. **Afon Ffraw** skirts the village, flowing southwest to enter the open sea at **Traeth Mawr**. Aberffraw Bay lies between two rocky headlands and looks southwest to the mainland. The village huddles on the west bank of the Ffraw, under grey slate roofs. Its skyline is dominated by the **Seion Methodist Church** (1887). Aberffraw is made up of a couple of stores, a Post Office and a cluster of small Victorian houses around a central square, **Sgwar Bodorgan**. The backstreets include the modest chapel of the Calvinistic Methodists (1785, 1822, 1861, restored 1905). At the higher, western end are the primary **school**, the **village hall** and some modern bungalows. There are two public houses, **Tafarn y Goron** and the **Prince Llywelyn**.

The double-aisled parish **Church of Saint Beuno** is located at the western end of the village (SH353688), looking south across the dunes to the mountains of Snowdonia. It has a late twelfth-century nave and an attractively bold stone arch in the Romanesque style, carved with chevrons and animal heads. The church was restored in 1840 and again in about 1868.

Llys Aberffraw

It is hard to believe that little Aberffraw was once the seat of royal princes. The rulers of the ancient Welsh kingdom of Gwynedd travelled between a series of courts, great halls sited in each of the various feudal districts of their domain. Llys Aberffraw served this purpose from the sixth century to the thirteenth.

When Normans attacked the eastern borders of Gwynedd, Aberffraw in the west gained strategic importance. However as Llywelyn ab Iorwerth (1173-1240) and Llywelyn ap Gruffudd (c1225-82) established firmer control, Aberffraw probably became less important than courts such as Rhosyr (near Newborough) or Abergwyngregyn (on the mainland).

Nothing of the Llys remains to be seen. It may be buried beneath the modern village. Its structure would have largely been built of timber and stone and in 1317 its beams may have been shipped to Caernarfon. Some of the court's masonry may have found

its way into St Beuno's Church (such as the carved stone arch – *below* – set into the wall to the left as you enter the church), or may have been used over the ages to build farms or walls.

When Llywelyn ap Gruffudd – 'the Last Prince' – was killed, the Anglesey poet Gruffudd ab yr Ynad Coch wrote a moving elegy in Welsh:

Oer calon dan fron o fraw, allwynin,
Am frenin, dderwin ddôr, Aberffraw.
Aur dilyfn a dalai o'i law,
Aur dalaith oedd deilwng iddaw.

Cold heart in breast with terror, grieving
For a king, oak door, of Aberffraw.
Bright gold was bestowed by his hand,
A gold chaplet befitted him.

At the northern end of the village is 'Llys' Llewelyn, an accommodation centre with a shop and displays. Welsh teas, including the local speciality, *teisennau Berffro* ▶194 are served in the café (open daily in the summer) and on

Memorial to the Welsh Princes – Y Tywysogion

fine days, outside in a pleasant leafy courtyard surrounded by beds of fennel and giant thistles. Here is a slate memorial, *Y Tywysogion*, by sculptor and author Jonah Jones (1919-2004), commemorating the princes of Aberffraw. The Llys is a starting point for coastal footpath walks and bicycle rides.

A pretty stone-arched bridge crosses the shallows by the village, the site of an ancient ford. This is **Hen Bont Aberffraw**, a village landmark and the best spot to get your bearings. It was built in 1731 by Sir Arthur Owen of Bodowen, who had also already endowed the first school in the village at Eglwys y Beili in 1729. The old bridge was not by-passed by the new road until 1932. A stone lion's head set into a wall at the village end of the bridge was the outlet for a public water supply before mains water was brought to Aberffraw.

Below the old bridge, amidst swooping black-headed gulls, Afon Ffraw runs through a long sandy channel. Small flatfish swim on the riverbed. At high tide the channel swells to fill the whole estuary. Boats are hauled up along the west bank or moored near the mouth. In the eighteenth century Aberffraw was a thriving port for fishing and for shipping grain from local farms. Walk along the east bank, bordering high dunes, to the beach of **Traeth Mawr**. Here the river meets the open sea at a broad, sandy beach with rolling waves and fine views. It is ideal for paddling and swimming and is a popular local spot for summer picnics and winter walks. Children paddling near the river mouth should beware of the depth of its waters here and the strong currents

Hen Bont Aberffraw

Tywyn Aberffraw is the wide expanse of sand bordering the eastern shore of the river, the beach and the approaches to the village. The whole area as far as Llyn Coron is open to public access: use the footpaths to explore the bleak landscape of the high, windswept dunes, held fast by marram grass. Avoid damaging or disturbing this habitat. It is still occasionally grazed by domestic livestock, but mostly by rabbits, which have created a short, flower-rich sward. The 'slacks' (valleys and hollows between the dune ridges) are particularly rich in rare plants. Look out for bee orchids, pyramidal orchids and marsh helleborine. In winter small flocks of chough feed on insects.

Walking along the west bank of the river brings one to **Trwyn Du** ('black point'), accessed by the path through the gate to the top of the headland (SH353679). About 9,000 years ago, during the Mesolithic period or Middle Stone Age, this was the site of a hunting camp. Flint arrowheads, scrapers and axes have been excavated here. The round cairn marks a burial site of the early Bronze Age, perhaps a mere 3,700 years old. Footpaths continue westwards around the headland to Porth Cwyfan.

SOUTHERN ANGLESEY

Porth Cwyfan

A mile to the west of Aberffraw is a beach of reefs and rolling waves, where flocks of clamouring gulls are buffeted by salt-laden winds. Its twin inlets are called **Porth Cwyfan** and **Porth China** (where it is said that a ship loaded with china was once wrecked). On a walled island on the sand and shingle of the lower shore is the little **Church of St Cwyfan** (SH336683), an early Christian site dedicated to the saint known in Irish as Caoimhghin ('Kevin'), who settled at Glendalough in Wicklow, directly west across the Irish Sea. The present church was built in the 1100s and extended in the fourteenth century. A north aisle was added in the sixteenth century, but this was removed in the 1800s, though the arcade can still be seen in the north wall. The attractive arch-braced collar beam roof trusses were probably inserted when the north aisle was built. The church was restored in 1893 by Harold Hughes, when a wall was built around the cemetery to prevent erosion. In recent years, plans to lime-render the external walls for protection, as has been done at Llaneilian and Llanfechell, met with local opposition. Services are occasionally conducted here. Porth Cwyfan is reached by a lane from the west end of Aberffraw or by footpath from Trwyn Du, Aberffraw.

Halfway between Aberffraw and Rhosneigr, turn off the A4080 for the **Anglesey Circuit /** *Trac Môn* ✆ 01407 840253, or 24hr information ✆ 01407 811100. It is also signposted from junction 5 of the A55. Since 1997 this has been a championship racing circuit. It is busy most weekends of the year.

The site, **Tŷ Croes**, is a former Royal Artillery camp. During the Second World War, gunners were trained here, practising their aim on airborne targets towed by aircraft from temporary base, RAF Bodorgan. As a child, the broadcaster John Peel (1939-2004) spent many of his summer holidays on Anglesey, and between 1959 and 1960 was back on the island, completing his National Service at Tŷ Croes. He went on to become an ardent supporter of innovative Welsh pop music: the idiosyncratic *Super Furry Animals*, themselves with strong Anglesey connections, have been one such band.

Bethel — *see* **Bodorgan** ▶200

Saint Beuno and the curlew

The patron saint of Aberffraw, Beuno, was born in Powys at the end of the fifth century, a member of the royal family of Glamorgan. He fled attacks by the Saxons and came to Gwynedd, where he is said to have converted King Cadfan of Gwynedd (whose memorial stone is in Llangadwaladr church) to Christianity. Beuno was based at Clynnog-fawr on the mainland. It was said that one day he was walking home along the shore of the Menai Strait when he dropped his book of sermons in the sea.

Reaching his cell at Clynnog-fawr, he found that the book had already been returned, having been carried there in the beak of a curlew.

Bodorgan

5C

7ml (11km) SW of Llangefni on B4422

This is a broad district of Anglesey, embracing several scattered villages. It extends across the western part of this guide's central and southern sections. The mouth of the Cefni river is guarded by the cliffs of **Pen y Parc**, the site of an ancient promontory fort.

Bodorgan takes its name from the Meyrick family's house and estate which lies on the wooded northwestern shore of the Cefni estuary, below Malltraeth. The present house was built between 1779-84 to designs by John Cooper, who had started his professional career as assistant to Samuel Wyatt and went on to work at Plas Newydd. Modifications were made in the 1850s by James Defferd. The Meyrick family has a history in the area dating back to the Middle Ages. Llywelyn ap Heilyn had supported Henry of Richmond (of the Tudors) and is said to have fought at the battle of Bosworth Field in 1485. During the battle, the last in the Wars of the Roses, the Yorkist king Richard III was killed and the victor was crowned Henry VII. Llywelyn's son, Meurig, gave the family its surname. Meyricks later played an important part in the emer-

gence of party politics on the island. Owen Meyrick of Bodorgan (1682-1759) was a Whig, supported by many of the island's squires, who took on the vested power of the Bulkeleys of Beaumaris ►45 who at this time were Tories. By 1873 the Meyricks owned 16,918 acres (7,613ha) on Anglesey. The Meyrick family still occupies its ancestral home, which is not open to the public.

Bodorgan offers fishing and birdwatching at **Llyn Coron**. This was once an arm of the sea which became landlocked by the advance of the sand dunes at Aberffraw.

The Bodorgan Estate and the Cefni estuary

Afon Gwna flows into its northern end and **Afon Ffraw** leaves it from the west. The name *ffraw* probably once had the meaning 'flowing' or 'flood'.

The primary school, **Ysgol Bodorgan**, is just beyond the A4080 / B4422 junction. A plaque on its wall commemorates William Williams (1738-1817), the son of a poor Trefdraeth family. He first worked as a weaver and was then apprenticed to a saddler. From 1782, now an official of the Penrhyn slate

quarry on the mainland, he devised a series of innovations that greatly boosted production. After his retirement in 1802, whilst living near Bangor at Llandygái (the Penrhyn estate's 'model village'), he achieved greater fame as a prominent antiquary and author.

The small village of **Hermon** borders woodland by the dog-leg section of the A4080. It took its Old Testament name, and indeed its original existence, from its chapel. Today there is a small housing estate here. The derelict windmill tower (Melin Hermon, 1843) on the edge of the village is typical of the island.

Melin Hermon

Llangadwaladr, an attractive little village, lies just to the west of Bodorgan. Its sandstone parish **Church of St Cadwaladr** (SH383693), one of Anglesey's *Grade 1* protected churches, is an architectural gem – turn off the A4080 down a small lane. The stone-arched gate leads to a churchyard of daisies and buttercups beneath branches of chestnut and yew. The nave may date back to the late twelfth century, the chancel to the fourteenth. The east window of the chancel was provided by Meurig ap Llywelyn in thanks for the return of his son Owain from the Battle of Bosworth in 1485. The North

Chapel was endowed by Richard Meyrick in 1640 (rebuilt in 1801) and the south transept by Anne Owen of 'Bodeon' (Bodowen) in 1661 in memory of her late husband, Colonel Hugh Owen. The church is associated with the early medieval *llys* (the court) at Aberffraw ▶196. It is probably dedicated to Cadwaladr 'the Blessed', a king of Gwynedd who died in AD664 after a peaceful reign. The Tudor dynasty claimed descent from this ruler; Henry VII maintained that his red dragon standard was the ancient flag of Cadwaladr.

A fifteenth-century stained glass window honouring King Cadfan

Cadwaladr's grandfather was named Cadfan: a stone set into the north wall of the church dates from about AD625. It records in Latin that 'Catamanus' (Cadfan) was the 'wisest and most renowned of all kings'. A 2002 publication by Charles Thomas, Director of the Institute of Cornish Studies, investigates the inscription as an early medieval detective story in *Whispering Reeds, or the Anglesey Catamanus Inscription Stript Bare*. This light-hearted but fascinating piece of Celtic scholarship arrives at some irreverent conclusions: was Cadfan really a sex-crazed provincial ass? Who knows, but there is little doubt that this gravestone is of great historical significance!

Catamanus stone

Lanes to the northeast lead to **Bodorgan Station**, a request stop on the main railway line to Holyhead. Small villages nearby include **Bethel**, gathered around its chapel and National School (rebuilt 1859) and **Trefdraeth**. Trefdraeth's small church (SH408704), like that of Aberffraw, is dedicated to **Saint Beuno**. Turn northeast off the lane to the large car park opposite the church. The church is thirteenth century, but extensively rebuilt. Continue along the lane past the **Glantraeth restaurant** to the dykes and reclaimed farmland of **Cors Ddyga**, the Malltraeth marshes.

A lane from Bodorgan station leads northwards to **Soar** and **Din Dryfol** (SH395724), which is located to the northeast of that village. Look for the 'ancient monument' sign just off the lane. This Neolithic site has a series of collapsed but impressive burial chambers belonging to the fourth and third millennia BC and lies on the lower slopes of an Iron Age hill fort.

Brynsiencyn

7B

4½ml (7km) SW of Llanfairpwll on A4080

Brynsiencyn means 'Jenkin's Hill'. A sizeable village surrounded by farmland, Brynsiencyn has views south across the Menai Strait to Mynydd Mawr and southwest to the Llŷn Peninsula. The **Groeslon** public house stands at the eastern end of this village, which consists of some stone cottages, pebble-dashed terraces and modern housing estates. The only large building is the formidable **Horeb Chapel** (1883).

The Calvinistic Methodist minister John Williams (1854-1921), who was born at Llandyfrydog on Anglesey and was called to the pastorate of Brynsiencyn in 1878, is said to have been 'the greatest master of "classical" pulpit oratory', possessing 'a fine presence, a powerful voice, clear articulation, a rich vocabulary, a lively imagination, and incomparable eloquence'. However, as honorary chaplain to the Welsh division in the First World War he dismayed many of his pacifist-inclined flock with his newly found militarism.

The present-day village owes its existence to the slate quarries of Snowdonia. In the Victorian era labourers from Anglesey would cross the Strait by ferry each week to the ports and quarries of the mainland, such as Y Felinheli. That village was linked by railway to the Dinorwig quarries near Llanberis and so became known as Port Dinorwic. The Anglesey workers would sleep at the quarry 'barracks' during the week, before returning to their homes on the island for Sunday. An early campaigner for workers' rights was W J Jones 'Brynfab', of the Half Moon Stores, who founded the *Undeb Gweithwyr Môn* (Anglesey Workers' Union) in 1909. It was officially registered as a trades union from 1911 to 1922. There is little work to be had locally today, other than farming or seasonal tourist enterprises. However the village is within easy reach of Bangor and other larger centres.

Brynsiencyn

Reaching for the Stars

A plaque in Brynsiencyn's Ffordd Barras commemorates **John Jones** (1818-98). He styled himself *Ioan Bryngwyn Bach* ('Bryngwyn Bach' being the name of his birthplace beside the ancient henge site at Castell Bryngwyn), and he was also known as *John Jones 'y Sêr'* ('the Stars').

He became a farm worker and at the age of 32 started labouring at Port Penrhyn, Bangor, where his job was to load slate on to the ships. Like many working people of his era, he studied for himself in his spare time and absorbed an astonishing range of

knowledge. He learned languages with the greatest of ease, owning 26 dictionaries and reading scriptures in Hebrew, Greek, Welsh and English. In *Men of Invention and Industry*, Samuel Smiles described how Jones led him, in 1883, 'to his tiny room upstairs, where he had his big reflecting telescope, by means of which he had seen, through the chamber window, the snowcap of Mars'.

Jones y Sêr was a Welsh-language poet and a musician, too, but is best remembered as a constructor of telescopes and first-rate astronomer.

The countryside around Brynsiencyn is dotted with important prehistoric sites. In the Neolithic and Bronze Age, this may have been the cultural centre of the island. Between Dwyran and Brynsiencyn, a sign beside the A4080 indicates **Castell Bryngwyn** (SH465670). Leave cars at the lay-by and follow the signed route for a five-minute walk to this grassy, circular mound, interrupted by farm buildings. It dates back to between 4,000 and 4,500 years ago. This was probably a ritual site or henge which was later occupied as a settlement. It was reoccupied and fortified during the Roman period and again at a later date.

Standing stones from the Bronze Age and ancient hut circles are to be found along **Afon Braint**, the river to the north of the village. Turn north off

SOUTHERN ANGLESEY

the A4080 at the junction to the west of the village. This passes **Caer Lêb** (SH473674), the 'wet' (in this case meaning moated) fort, set back from the lane, an almost rectangular settlement with double banked defences – *see the reconstruction drawing* ▶26. Finds of Roman pottery, a brooch and a coin of the third century AD show that this site was occupied during the Roman period, although it may well have been in use much earlier

Continue northwest along this lane to the **Bodowyr** burial chamber (SH463682), a Neolithic tomb of the fourth or early third millennium BC.

During the Middle Ages life centred on the **Llanidan** area to the south-east of the modern village. This today is an area of peaceful farmland, where hedgerows, stately old trees and banks of wildflowers turn the lanes into tunnels of green and white lace in summer. Saint Nidan worshipped here in the early seventh century. Dedicated to him is a large ruined church, **Llanidan Old Church**, in woods near the Menai Strait (SH489674). It dates from the fourteenth century but was closed and partially demolished in 1844, although it continued to serve as a mortuary chapel. Its 'miraculous' holy water stoup by the south door was said never to dry out. Two crudely carved stone heads on either side of this door may be medieval or perhaps of pagan Celtic origin. The churchyard is green with yews, ivy and and lily-of-the-valley. The church has been restored by the owners of Plas Llanidan and is occasionally opened to the public, as is the 1³/₄ acre (0.6ha) walled garden, including physic and herb gardens, of the Plas. The architect of the 'new' parish **Church of St Nidan** (1841) was John Welch of St Asaph, who in the same year completed the Church of St Ffinan near Talwrn. St Nidan's church overlooks the main road to the east of Brynsiencyn village and is set in a walled churchyard amidst beech, holly and windswept yews.

Anfon y Nico

Llanidan's 'new' church at Brynsiencyn has a square stone tower, rather top heavy in its design, which is a well-known local landmark.

Brynsiencyn came to the mind of the poet Albert Evans-Jones ('Cynan', 1895-1970) while serving at Salonika (Thessaloniki) in the First World War. He dreamed of the flight of a goldfinch across southern Anglesey:

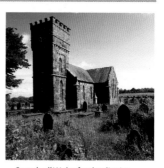

... Chwilia Gymru am yr ardal
Lle ma'r gog gynara'i thôn,
Os cei dei di yno groeso calon,
Paid ag ofni – dyna Fôn;
Hed i'r gogledd dros Frynsiencyn,
Paid ag oedi wrth y Tŵr,
Ond pan weli di Lyn Traffwll
Gna dy nyth yng ngardd Glan Dŵr.

... Search all Wales for the district
Where the first cuckoo makes its call,
Should you have a heartfelt welcome
Do not take fright – for this is Môn;
Fly due north over Brynsiencyn
Do not tarry by the Tower
But when you spy Llyn Traffwll's waters,
At Glan Dŵr's garden make your nest.

To the east of Brynsiencyn, farmland borders the A4080, with farm shops and opportunities to pick your own produce.

Ffordd Barras, opposite the Groeslon public house, leads southwards from Brynsiencyn, past the village's former primary school (recently refurbished to provide small business premises), to **Foel**. The Menai shore is of mudflat and shingle, with fine views over to Caernarfon castle and the mountains.

This is a tranquil place today, but it may well have had a violent history. The shore here is one of the possible sites for the Roman attack on Anglesey AD60, when Druids and screaming women on the shore scared the battle-hardened Roman legions. Also, during a battle fought probably near here in 1157, the men of Anglesey routed a marauding force sent by Henry II of England during the king's abortive expedition against Owain Gwynedd. The poet Gwalchmai ap Meilyr – see *The joyful poet* ▶177 – normally a cheerful enough fellow, describes a veritable tide of blood flowing into the Menai Strait. The jetty by the former Menai Hotel (subsequently called the Mermaid Inn and now a holiday complex) marks the site of the **Tal-y-foel** ferry across the Menai Strait, which was once an important route from the island to Caernarfon. The ferry service was discontinued in 1954.

Along the shore road is the **Anglesey Sea Zoo**, *Sw Môr Môn* (February to October ℂ 01248 430411) one of the island's most popular tourist attractions. Walk over pools of gliding rays, be surrounded by curved glass walls of fish and pass through a 'wreck' (salvaged from the timbers of the *Seven Sisters* at Moel y Don) complete with huge conger eels. The well stocked shop is the place to buy Anglesey Sea Salt and there is a variety of open-air attractions.

The Sea Zoo,
Sw Môr Môn

Foel Farm
Park, *Parc*
Fferm y Foel

Continue along the shore to **Foel Farm Park**, *Parc Fferm y Foel* (March to October ℂ 01248 430646) with its tractor and trailer rides and, in spring and early summer, lambs or calves to bottle-feed. Covered areas for rainy days include a play-den. Chocolate is made on the premises: its workshop, shop and tearoom opens throughout the year.

The B4419 returns you to the main A5025 road near Dwyran.

Dwyran

6B

2ml (3km)
east of
Newborough
off the A4080

Dwyran means 'two parts'. In the Middle Ages, half of the land in the village was owned by St Beuno's Church in Clynnog-fawr, while the other half belonged to the estates of the bishopric of Bangor. Today this pleasant village is accessed by three lanes leading northwards off the A4080 between **Pont Cadach** and the **Tal Ponciau** public house. It is more sheltered than the coastal villages, being set in a green, pastoral landscape on the banks of **Afon Braint**, a small river which takes its name from Brigantia, a goddess of the ancient Celts. It has a chapel, a post office and general store, a small bakery and both Victorian and modern dwellings.

The parish **Church of Llangeinwen** is by a sharp bend in the A4080 at the western end of the village. It is dedicated to Ceinwen, 'Cain the pure', sister of Dwynwen – see *The Saint of Love*. ▶213 The nave is probably twelfth-century, its buttresses set with gravestones whose carvings of crosses date back to the ninth and eleventh centuries. The font is thirteenth-century. The church was largely rebuilt from 1812, its lichen-covered tower dating from 1829.

Close to the church, at **Tŷ Croes** farm, a vineyard became productive in autumn 2005 – a sign of changes to come in British agriculture in times of climate warming. It is hoped that the soil here, a mulched sandy loam on shale sub-soil, will be suited to the vineyard's speciality: grape varieties producing a dry, white wine.

The Labourer's Friend

John Owen Jones (1861-99) was born at Trefdraeth but raised in Dwyran. Apprenticed to a draper in Caernarfon, he read and studied voraciously, until he qualified to study at the University of Wales in Aberystwyth. John Owen Jones became a successful, chiefly Welsh-language, journalist and also established a school in Dwyran. His writings, under the pen name *Ap Ffarmwr* ('Farmer's Son'), tirelessly championed the lot of the farm labourer on Anglesey, which in Victorian times was dire. John Owen Jones campaigned to improve conditions and reduce working hours. At a meeting in Llangefni on Easter Monday 1890 the farm labourers negotiated an historic reduction of two hours a day from the employers, a remarkable achievement. There followed repeated attempts to form an agricultural trade union, but it failed. Nevertheless John Owen Jones remained a hero to the workers.

He later worked as a journalist and newspaper editor in Merthyr and in Nottingham, and wrote a Welsh-language biography of Liberal prime minister William Gladstone.

He was buried in the Calvinistic Methodist burial ground in Dwyran, where a column is surmounted by a marble bust .

At **Rhuddgaer**, one mile (1½ km) south of Dwyran, three lead sides of a fifth-century coffin were discovered in 1878. **▶27** The molten metal had been cast in sand moulds. Two pieces from this Christian burial have the Latin inscriptions – 'CAMVLORIS H S I'. Inscribed lead coffins are very rarely found in Britain: the Rhuddgaer coffin may be seen, together with gravestones of the period, at the Gwynedd Museum in Bangor.

Further along Newborough road is the **Anglesey Model Village** / *Pentref Modelau Môn* (Easter to September ✆ 01248 440477) where island landmarks are recreated to one-twelfth scale. The village's railway train recharges its batteries whilst halted at the station: the train has travelled more than twelve thousand miles.

Riding at Tal-y-Foel

South of Dwyran, lanes lead through woods and fields to the Menai Strait and the **Isle of Anglesey Riding Centre** / *Canolfan Farchogaeth Ynys Môn*

at **Tal-y-foel** (all year, closed Mondays ✆ 01248 430377) offering rides along the shore of the Strait, along country lanes and through fields.

Due north of Dwyran village on a back lane is the little church of **Llanfair-yn-y-Cwmwd** (SH447668), a medieval foundation rebuilt in the eighteenth century. Further restoration in 1936 was undertaken by diocesan architects Harold Hughes and William Griffith Williams. **Saint Mary's Church** contains a rood screen, a twelfth-century font and a thirteenth-century coffin lid with rich, foliated carving.

Hermon — *see* **Bodorgan ▶199**

Llanedwen

7C

2½ml (4km) SW of Llanfair Pwllgwyngyll on A4080

The Menai Strait narrows and turns north as it approaches Y Felinheli on the mainland shore. On the island side it borders the peaceful, rural parish of Llanedwen, with its fields, woods and scattered cottages of stone or brick. Land bordering the Strait was built on during the fifteenth and sixteenth centuries, and several large houses remain.

The A4080 skirts the long stone wall of the Plas Newydd estate. ▶214 On the other side of the road is Plas Llwyn Onn (in private ownership), once the home of Colonel Henry Stapleton-Cotton (1849-1925), an uncle of the fourth Marquess of Anglesey and a veteran of the Zulu wars. His work with the Newborough Mat-Makers' Cooperative – see *The Marram Crafts* ▶209 – and the Women's Institute ▶64 is documented elsewhere. In addition to these projects, he set up various agricultural projects on the island, and a bacon factory, in order to help regenerate the island's economy.

To the west of the Plas Newydd estate, the A4080 crosses the lane from Llanddaniel-fab ▶54 to Moel y Don. This southern turning takes you past the red sandstone mansion of **Plas Coch** (c1569, with subsequent reconstruction and additions), which in modern times serves as a caravan site. Its grounds extend to the shore of the Menai Strait.

Church of St Edwen

Llanedwen takes its name from a seventh-century saint. The spired parish **Church of St Edwen** (SH517683), rebuilt in 1856 by Henry Kennedy of Bangor, is found down a narrow lane to the east. It is still lit by candles. The churchyard, with its ancient yews and cowslips, lies between fields and the Menai Strait. From his grave of 1829, John Rowlands, once a 'gardiner', reminds visitors of their mortality:

Stop a foot and cast an eye, as you are now so once was I
As I am now so must you be. Prepare yourself and follow me.

At the water's edge is **Moel y Don**, with views across to Y Felinheli. Oaks line the shore and wading birds strut along the peaceful waterline. In 1282, some 300 soldiers of the English invader, Edward I, were massacred here by a Welsh force as they built a bridge of boats across the Strait. For centuries this was one of the chief ferries across the Menai Strait, a route to the slate ports and quarries of the mainland. Local men would cross the Strait to work from Monday to Friday in the Dinorwig quarries. At Y Felinheli they took a ride up to the workings on the empty slate train that ran between

The Seven Sisters wreck at Moel y Don

quarry and dock. Reminders of the days when the Moel y Don shore bustled with activity can still be seen. No ferry route was complete without its inns: on the Anglesey shore the long building at the head of the bay was 'The Old Cutter Inn' (1717, now a private house); at Y Felinheli the 'Gardd Fôn' is still serving patrons.

The ship's timbers in the Moel y Don mud are those of the *Seven Sisters* that until the 1950s brought over to Anglesey slate for roofing and gravestones. The slate fence running along the lane leading to the jetty is typical of the fencing that divides fields close to the quarries. The house near the jetty was originally a terrace of three cottages accommodating the ferrymen and their families.

Llangadwaladr — *see* Bodorgan ▶199

SOUTHERN ANGLESEY

Llangaffo

6B

3ml (5km) SW of Pentre-berw on B4419

This small village borders the road from Pentre-berw to Newborough, sited on rising ground to the southeast of the Cefni river flatlands. The pointed spire of its church is a landmark for miles around. The B4119 forms a lane which heads south to the A4080 east of Dwyran, while a northward lane skirts the Hengae quarry to cross the railway and **Cors Ddyga**, the Malltraeth marshes. It culminates in the stone arches of **Pont Marquis**, a bridge con-

structed about 200 years ago across the newly re-aligned course of the Cefni.

The **Church of St Caffo**, designed by Sheffield architects, was built in 1847 to replace an earlier foundation. It is approached through a stone arch which once formed the churchyard door of the fifteenth-century building. The iron gate is in the 'rays of sun' style of the Telford gates of the A5. Follow the cut through the churchyard and to your left, fastened to the wall, are some inscribed stones and cross fragments dating from the seventh to the thirteenth centuries. They were perhaps gathered here from an early cemetery nearby. More examples may be seen inside the chancel and vestry, making up one of the most significant such collections in Wales and suggesting that this was an important ecclesiastical site in the early Middle Ages. The church also contains a twelfth-century font.

Inscribed stones, Llangaffo

Malltraeth

5B

2½ml (4km) north of Newborough on A4080

The name *Malltraeth* means 'rotting shore', which is a fair description of much of its marshy ground. The small village lies on the shores of the Cefni estuary. It includes a post office, a tiny church/hall now named **Christ the King**, **Crist y Brenin** (first used in 1874 as a Mission Church and schoolroom), and two public houses, the **Joiners' Arms** and **The Royal Oak / Y Derwen Frenhinol**. 'Shorelands', a private house, was the home between 1947 and 1979 of the wildlife artist C F Tunnicliffe – see *A Shorelands View* ▶19

The Cefni river valley stretches from here to Llangefni – a footpath and cycle track follows its course. This was once a navigable river, and Viking long-ships and coastal vessels sailed up the meandering waterway. However flooding caused considerable loss of life and livelihood over the centuries. Today the **Malltraeth marsh / Cors Ddyga** is drained and its flow is controlled. Only aerial views now reveal the courses of the ancient tidal creeks. The angular drainage system imposed on the lansdcape carries water from the adjacent slope in clay-lined channels to the left- and right-hand main drains which discharge to the sea at Malltraeth, through tidal flaps. The Cefni itself is channelled between high, straight banks.

An embankment was built at Malltraeth between 1790 and 1812, but it was breached by the tide in 1796. The embankment, known as the **Cob**, still stands today, for the consultant engineer for its reconstruction was the great Thomas Telford (1757-1834). His work enabled the A5 to be built across the northeastern end of the marsh. Soon it would be joined by the mainline railway to Holyhead, which crosses over a low-arched viaduct on the landward side. The construction of the Cob halved the size of the estuary, reducing the daily tidal exchange and leading to the rapid infilling of the remaining estuary by sand and mud. This has been consolidated by cord grass (spartina) which has colonised the mud flats, and is followed by sea rush, sea arrow-grass and saltmarsh grass in the succession to land.

Malltraeth Cob

The seaward side of the road to the village borders **Malltraeth Pool**, with yellow gorse and rippling reed beds. Beyond lies the shining expanse of the estuary, flanked on the northwest by the Bodorgan estate ▶199 and on the south by the dark green band of Newborough Forest. The Pool and the magnificent sweep of saltmarsh and dunes which stretch south to Llanddwyn island are all part of a National Nature Reserve, managed by the Countryside Council for Wales. Herons, redshanks, godwits, ruffs, pintail and shelduck are to be seen. 'Twitchers' may well spot vagrant birds, far from their normal homes.

Footpaths from the end of the Cob pass through the forest which fringes the saltmarsh of the southern shore. These can also be reached from a car park on the edge of Newborough Forest, just off the A4080.

Menai Strait / *Afon Menai* ▶76

Newborough / *Niwbwrch*

6B
9ml (14km)
SW of
Llanfairpwll
on A4080

This small town lies on the edge of forests and dunes at the southwest corner of the island. Its appearance is fairly typical of the district: a medieval parish church, an **Ebeneser chapel** of 1785, plain Victorian houses rising directly behind the pavements, modern housing estates, Post Office stores, the **White Lion** public house. The town may be prosaic, but its surroundings are some of the most spectacular in Wales and its history too fires the imagination.

Newborough and its district enter history as the *cantref*, or hundred, of 'Rhosyr', a domain of the Welsh princes of medieval Gwynedd. It was the site of a *llys*, one of several great halls used as a royal court. The hall and its compound occupied an area of 6,220 sq yds (5,200 sq metres). The date in which Llys Rhosyr began to be used is unknown, but we do know that Llywelyn ab Iorwerth (Llywelyn 'the Great') issued a charter from here in 1237. Sometime after the death in 1282 of his grandson Llywelyn ap Gruffudd (Llywelyn II, 'the Last'), Llys Rhosyr was abandoned. Following the English conquest, a 'New Borough' (transcribed into Welsh as *Niwbwrch*) was founded here – on a new site to the east of the earlier Llys – to house inhabitants of Llan-faes ▶60 evicted during the building of Beaumaris Castle in 1295.

This period is marked by incursions of sand, and significantly these coincided with the doubling of population as a result of the influx from Llan-faes. Shallow, infertile sandy soils were exploited by the burgeoning population, creating ideal conditions for soil erosion and a subsequent 'dustbowl' as destabilised dunes were blown inland. A final inundation probably came during a great storm in 1330, during which 211 acres (85ha) were covered with windblown sand.

SOUTHERN ANGLESEY

An artist's reconstruction of Llys Rhosyr

John Hodgson / MAGMA

The site of **Llys Rhosyr** (SH419653) lies just to the west of the parish church, beside the lane which leads to Newborough Forest and the Beach. It has recently been excavated – the only such site to survive in North Wales – revealing stone foundations of buildings and walls. (Before visiting the site, it is worth viewing the audio-visual presentation shown in Newborough's Prichard Jones Institute.) The perimeter wall is clearly visible, as is the great hall and a second building, possibly the private quarters of the prince when he visited the Llys. A third building is of uncertain use and other buildings are yet to be excavated.

In medieval times the new town achieved rapid prosperity. Dafydd ap Gwilym (fl.1340-70), perhaps the greatest of all Welsh poets, sung its praises in the middle of the fourteenth century:

Hawddamor, mireinwawr maith,	*Blessed, eternal, splendid dawn,*
Tref Niwbwrch, Tref llawn obaith,	*Newborough Town, so full of hope,*
A'i glwysdeg deml a'i glasdyr,	*Its church's fair sanctuary and its grey tower,*
A'i gwin a'i gwerin a'i gwŷr,	*And its wine and its people and its men,*
A'i chwrw a'i medd a'i chariad,	*And its ale and its mead and its love,*
A'i dynion rhwydd a'i da yn rhad.	*Its generous people and its wealth to share.*

Detail from the font in Newborough's parish church

The **church** (SH420655) referred to by Dafydd ap Gwilym still stands in the west of the village, next to the site of Llys Rhosyr. It is dedicated to **Saint Peter** *(Pedr)*. The font, and parts of the nave, date from the twelfth century. The chancel was added in the fourteenth century, when new windows were installed. Built in the 'decorated' style, likely to be appreciated by the recently settled burghers from Llan-faes, these windows have no other parallels on Anglesey other than those at the church of St Mary and St Nicholas in Beaumaris. It is likely that the same English-influenced masons were responsible for work in both churches. St Peter's Church was restored in 1850 and further work was undertaken in 1886, when the vestry was added. The long, low building stands within a large, walled churchyard amidst slate memorial stones.

Newborough fell on hard times in the later Middle Ages as disastrous storms continued to bury dwellings in shifting sands. In the reign of Elizabeth I laws were brought in to protect the marram grass, the roots of which stabilised the treacherous dunes. From the 1600s onwards, Newborough declined further. The town found itself far from the *lôn bost*, the new postal route from Beaumaris to Holyhead. In the 1800s the town was by-passed once again by the new commercial arteries of the island, the A5 and the railway. Most inhabitants lived by seafaring or farming.

The road leading northeast to Llangaffo passes a **clock tower**, **war memorial** and **almshouses** and half-timbered buildings of the **Prichard Jones Institute** (1905). These were endowed by local philanthropist Sir John Prichard Jones, a draper who went to London in 1874 and ended up as chairman of the department store Dickins & Jones of 232 Regent Street. Sir John kept a home at Dwyran near Newborough and continued to play an important part in Welsh public life. (His store became part of Harrods in 1914, and from 1959 – until its closure at the beginning of 2006 – was part of House of Fraser.) In addition to a presentation about Llys Rhosyr, the Institute houses a public **library**. The library's vintage Cotgreave Indicator, together with an impressive bust of Sir John, are presently removed from public display, but they can be seen by making viewing arrangements (through the library) with the Institute's Trustees. The Cotgreave system of keeping track of book loans is something to make the heart of any librarian flutter.

Further along the A4419 at Tyddyn Pwrpas is a transport museum, **Tacla Taid** (Easter to October ✆ 01248 440344). Its restored classic cars, motorcycles including a rare Enfield Sports, tractors and other vehicles and memorabilia are set in a recreation of a village street of the 1940s.

To the east of Newborough on the A4080 is a collection of aviary displays.

The marram crafts

The story of this craft is told in the booklet **The Marram Weavers of Newborough** by Miriam Griffiths (Magma, reprinted 2007)

The roots of marram grass were used to anchor the ever shifting dunes, but for centuries the green spiky leaves served an additional purpose. They were used to make brooms, whitewash brushes, baskets, nets or ropes. They could also be plaited into strips called 'laces' which were then joined together to make agricultural or household mats and haystack covers. The harvesting, drying and plaiting of the marram was women's work. Some were employed for a small wage by Newborough farmers, others shipped their produce across the Menai Strait to Caernarfon, where it was sold in the town's market. A Newborough Matmakers' Cooperative was founded in 1913 under the patronage of Colonel Henry Stapleton-Cotton of Llanedwen, who endeavoured to promote cottage industries in the region. However, the marram weaving industry declined in the 1930s.

Newborough Warren / *Tywyn Niwbwrch*

A National Nature Reserve today protects the sand dunes of the warren, the beach and island of Llanddwyn, the Cefni saltmarshes and Afon Braint. The reserve is managed by the Countryside Council for Wales.

Newborough Warren provided a living for the people of Newborough from the Middle Ages onwards, for as its name suggests it was a breeding ground for rabbits. In its heyday it provided many thousands of rabbits a year. However its area was much reduced by forestry plantation, and the rabbit population has declined since the first myxomatosis outbreak of 1954. To reach the 1,500 acres (600ha) of dune that remain unforested, turn off the A4080 at the roundabout immediately to the southeast of Newborough. Either turn immediately left to park at **Pen Lôn** or continue down the road to park by the small lake of **Llyn Rhos-ddu**, where you can use a hide to watch moorhens, coots, ducks and grebes. From these car parks, footpaths lead across the other-worldly landscape of high dunes, bound together by coarse marram grass that rustles in the wind. Here too there is thyme, trefoil, lady's smock and meadow saxifrage. The pools which form in the hollows are called 'slacks'. Look for creeping willow, northern marsh orchids and the round-leaved wintergreen.

Wild Thyme – drawn by the Massey sisters of Llangoed – carpets the dunes in early summer

The shifting dunes at the edge of the warren bear the brunt of the south-westerly gales. Here, plants must be hardy to survive the salt spray: they include dune pansies, sea holly and spurge. The warren is home to skylarks, meadow pipits and oystercatchers, as well as toads and lizards.

Newborough Warren

It is only from the air that this chaotic terrain of dunes and slacks attains order, for then at least four series of broken ridges and parabolic dunes are apparent, snaking across the coastal plain parallel to the shore.

Abermenai

Footpaths lead south across the dunes to **Abermenai**, a long spit of sand and shingle (severely eroded in places) which guards the entrance to the Menai Strait, shielding **Traeth Melynog** and the **Afon Braint** estuary from the open sea. It lies opposite Fort Belan on the mainland shore. Beware of incoming tides.

Abermenai Point was the site of an ancient ferry across the Strait, and this is one of several sites mooted for the Roman invasion of Anglesey. When one of the royal courts of Gwynedd was established at Rhosyr, Abermenai became an important harbour, linked to the mainland by a causeway. Gruffudd ap Cynan (c1055-1137) sailing to Anglesey from Ireland, landed here in 1075 in the first of his attempts to reclaim Anglesey and Gwynedd, his father's kingdom. On his death in 1137 as King of Gwynedd, Gruffudd bequeathed to his wife, Angharad, the income accruing from Abermenai. He was buried in the cathedral church of Bangor.

In 1144, Cadwaladr (Gruffudd's third son), fighting against his elder brother, the great Owain Gwynedd (c1100-70), crossed over from Ireland to Abermenai with a fleet of Dublin Norse mercenaries. However the two brothers made their peace at Abermenai and the Dubliners were forced to leave. By 1165 Owain had fully restored the power of rule

Abermenai Point

from Aberffraw. Cadwaladr survived his brother by two years. Until Bangor Cathedral was destroyed by the English King John in 1210, they lay there together in a double tomb, near the high altar.

The importance of Abermenai in medieval Wales is echoed in the *Mabinogion*, the collection of ancient tales first written down during this period. One of these describes a royal fleet of thirteeen ships leaving Abermenai after Branwen's marriage to Matholwch, King of Ireland ▶187

Newborough Forest / *Coedwig Niwbwrch*

On warm summer days, the glimpses of blue sea, the sandy tracks and the scented resin of the Corsican pines give Newborough Forest a feel of the Mediterranean. In winter, the forest is more severe, with its sombre ranks of timber rising from banks of fallen pine needles.

The 2,000-acre (800ha) conifer forest was planted between 1948 and 1965 as a managed, commercial plantation and it thus stabilised a large section of the dunes. In places, the undulating ground shows the original structure of the dunes. Recent conservation plans have proposed reducing the area under conifer plantation to allow the recovery of Newborough's natural dune system, which is of international significance. More mixed forest is planned too. These plans have aroused public anxiety about, amongst other issues, the forest's recently introduced red squirrel population. Some people have been unaware that the forest is itself a relatively recent intrusion: few of the trees are more than thirty years old.

The forest is reached by the westward lane from the centre of Newborough, which leads to a **toll road** (have coins ready for the machine). This winds down to a large beach-side car park, which has picnic and toilet facilities (all very 'green', with reed-bed purification of toilet waste). From here a network of footpaths leads through the forest. The two principal routes are the *'Hendai' Red Trail* (one mile/1.6km) and the *Blue Trail* (two miles/ 3.2km). The distances may be short, but allow an hour for the *Red* and one and a half for the *Blue* as there is plenty to see. The forest trails offer wildflowers in abundance including marsh and bee orchids, wintergreen and bright blue viper's bugloss. There are toadstools and all sorts of birds from goldcrests to crossbills. One can also view the foundations of the **Hendai**, medieval houses excavated from the sand that overwhelmed them.

In the north of the Forest, a second car park may be reached from the A4080 just below Malltraeth Cob. It borders the Cefni saltmarshes. ▶206 A third northern car park may be found on the other side of the A4080. Paths lead from its picnic site through the pines to **Llyn Parc Mawr**, an attractive, shallow lake of over 10 acres (4ha) created in 1987. From its hides one can watch teal, mallard, pochard and green sandpipers. Picnic tables are provided.

Newborough Beach
– *Traeth Llanddwyn, Traeth Penrhos*

The sea can be reached by footpath from the Warren or the Forest, but the most common access is from the large car park which lies at the bottom of the Toll Road from the western edge of Newborough town. Here are maps to gain your bearings, picnic tables (including a picnic area accessible to wheelchairs) and toilets, but no ice-cream kiosks.

Traeth Llanddwyn is a long ribbon of sand and some shingle, backed by forest and three miles (5km) of high dunes, which stretches between Abermenai and Ynys Llanddwyn. The mountains of the Llŷn peninsula dip into the misty horizon. The northern section of beach between Ynys Llanddwyn and the mouth of Afon Cefni is called **Traeth Penrhos**. Together they are often referred to as **Newborough Beach**. These are wide seascapes under a big sky, spectacular in any season and any weather. The beach is popular with bathers (if a bit shallow for adults) and beachcombers may search for shells, driftwood or stranded jellyfish.

Llanddwyn Island / *Ynys Llanddwyn*

The small, rocky island of Llanddwyn is reached by a long but worthwhile tramp along Newborough Beach. Except at the highest tides, it is really more of a peninsula, being attached to Newborough Beach by a narrow isthmus of sand called **Gwddw Llanddwyn**, where a map of the island and its paths is displayed. Ringed plovers scuttle at the water's edge. Geologists will recognise the pillow lava formations in the volcanic rocks that outcrop above the sands of the isthmus.

This is a world in itself, a magical place: the sort of island that any child would like to declare their personal kingdom. It is owned by the local authority and is part of the National Nature Reserve, with springy turf dotted by blue squills, pink thrift on rocky ledges and tracts of marram grass. It has its own shores and cliffs and its own beaches for swimming and shell-collecting.

Amongst the pebbles of Llanddwyn's beaches, look out for tiny, glistening cowrie shells

Cormorants stand on the small rocks offshore, such as **Ynys yr Adar** and **Ynys y Clochydd**, their black wings outstretched to dry. The island is not as lonely as it used to be, with increasing numbers of walkers, and pleasure boats and yachts mooring up in the cove on summer weekends. The island is crossed by trails: help preserve the environment by keeping to the paths. One patch is grazed by Welsh mountain ponies.

At the end of the island are the **Tai Peilot**, a low line of cottages (1826-45) which were home to the pilots who guided ships into Caernarfon harbour. Today (in summer) the buildings house the reserve's auxiliary warden, an interesting exhibition on the local environment and a cottage furnished as it would have been a century ago. A lifeboat station was located here from 1826-36, and again from 1840-1907. In an emergency, the cannon that still stands in front of the cottages was used to summon help from Newborough, and it was the difficulty of recruiting a regular crew to attend such an isolated station that led to its closure.

Llanddwyn Island

Beacons were placed at the tip of the island: **Twr Bach**, the 'little tower' (1800), was superseded by the white-washed **Twr Mawr** 'large tower' lighthouse in 1845, which although redundant today, still dominates the western end of the island. It was built in the sturdy tapering style of Anglesey's stone windmill towers.

Twr Mawr at the tip of Llanddwyn Island

The saint of love

Llanddwyn takes its name from **Dwynwen** (Dwyn 'the Pure', or 'blessed'), a saint of the Celtic church who died in AD465. She was said to be a princess, one of the 24 children of a king of Irish descent named Brychan, who ruled over Brycheiniog in the Usk valley. When Dwynwen's love affair with a youth called Maelon turned unpleasant, God gave her a potion to forget her passion, and turned him into a block of ice. Rather perversely, she was henceforth known as the patron saint of Welsh lovers and founded a hermitage on the island.

Dwynwen is still remembered in Wales every 25th January, with the sending of Saint Dwynwen's Day cards to one's sweetheart, a chance to pre-empt the better known festival of Saint Valentine on 14th February.

The ruins of the largely sixteenth-century **Church of St Dwynwen** (SH386627) are still to be seen at the centre of the island, within a circular churchyard, a sign of the site's antiquity. Only the chancel and its arched windows stand to view. Many pilgrims visited this church in the Tudor period, and the poet Dafydd Trefor, who died in about 1528, wrote of Dwynwen as *Mam pob daioni* – 'the mother of all goodness'. Love-lorn maidens would try to tell their fortune by throwing their kerchiefs into a nearby freshwa-

The ruins of Saint Dwynwen's church

ter spring dedicated to the saint and seeing how they moved. The location of this ancient well, **Ffynnon Ddwynwen**, is disputed: some locate it on nearby Traeth Penrhos rather than on the island itself.

Two large crosses on the island, one Latin and one Celtic in style, commemorate the saint and all those buried here:

> *"They lie around did living tread,*
> *This sacred ground, now silent, dead."*

Plas Newydd

8B
1½ml (2.5km) SW of Llanfair Pwllgwyngyll on A4080

The most imposing mansion surviving on Anglesey stands on the Menai Strait's shores by Llanedwen. **Plas Newydd**, administered by the National Trust and open to the public (Easter to the end of October, closed on Thursdays and Fridays ✆ 01248 715272) is the family seat of the Marquesses of Anglesey. The present Marquess, the seventh, lives in private apartments at the Plas. The old dairy, by the car park, serves as the tearoom and National Trust shop. A walk leads past the cricket field to the house itself.

The limestone ashlar walls of the house are covered with Virginia creeper: its leaves turning crimson in autumn. The building faces southwest and overlooks a bend in the Menai Strait, with views towards the Vaynol estate and Snowdon.

Plas Newydd

The estates originally belonged to the Griffiths of Penrhyn, but passed by marriage to the Bayly family, who were created Earls of Uxbridge in the eighteenth century. From 1783-85 Plas Newydd was rebuilt by John Cooper in a neo-Classic style and between 1793 and 1799 parts were re-modelled in the then fashionable neo-Gothic style by James Wyatt and Joseph Potter. Further building work took place in the early nineteenth century, when the gardens were laid out by the English designer Humphrey Repton (1752-1818), who first used the phrase 'landscape gardening'.

Tours of the house start in the entrance hall, whose paintings include the portrait of an unknown lady by Sir Anthony van Dyck (1599-1641), and proceed through a music room (occupying the site of the original Great Hall), a dining hall and domestic quarters. A coffee shop and second-hand bookshop are situated in the North Wing.

The 58ft-long maritime **mural** in the dining room was painted on canvas in 1937 by the artist Rex Whistler (1905-44), a friend of the family. The artist depicts himself as Romeo, standing beneath an arch and gazing up at his Juliet (Caroline, daughter of the sixth marquess) on a balcony. Plas Newydd's extensive Whistler collection includes paintings, drawings, illustrations and costume designs.

Part of Rex Whistler's mural

Other family mementoes include photographs of Henry Cyril Paget, fifth marquess – a moustachioed aesthete who bemused visitors and estate workers with his theatrical impressions and converted the family chapel to a private theatre. He spent a fortune on jewels and furs, and died bankrupt in Monte Carlo in 1905, at the age of 29.

A **military museum** contains weapons and uniforms of the Napoleonic Wars, in which the first marquess played a leading role.

Cool in the face of fire

Henry William Paget (1768-1854) served in the British army during the French Revolutionary War and the Peninsular War, and was also a Member of Parliament. He became Earl of Uxbridge in 1812. He was overall second-in-command at Waterloo, in charge of the cavalry. He was renowned for his stiff upper lip. As a cannonball came his way, he glanced down and observed:

"By God, sir, I've lost my leg!"

"By God, sir, so you have!" was the famously laconic reply from the Duke of Wellington.

For his bravery, he was made Marquess of Anglesey. With Frederick Gray he invented a new type of jointed wooden leg, the 'Anglesey Artificial Limb', which is on display at Plas Newydd.

The first marquess served as Lord Lieutenant of Ireland. There he supported Catholic civil rights, but lost popularity when he took action against the agitator and orator Daniel O'Connell, 'the Liberator' (1755-1847).

The marquess became a Field Marshal in 1846. 'Old One Leg's' monument is the 112ft-high (34m) Anglesey Column in nearby Llanfair Pwllgwyngyll ▶187

To the east of the house, on a private section of the Plas Newydd estate, is the **Conway Centre / *Canolfan Conway***, a large group of buildings built in 1964. After the loss of *HMS Conway*, wrecked in the Menai Strait in 1953 (whilst being towed to Birkenhead for a re-fit), this part of the Plas Newydd Estate became the site of a tented camp and blocks of huts belonging to a Merchant Navy training school. The school occupied the buildings from 1964 until 1974. Its former cadets include Clive Woodward (rugby union player and England coach) and Iain Duncan Smith (leader of the Conservative Party from 2001 to 2003). Since 1974, when funding for the school was withdrawn, the *Canolfan* has been operated by Cheshire County Council, as an educational and outdoor pursuits centre for short-term residential stays and a venue for conferences.

The **grounds** of Plas Newydd include sweeping lawns, rhododendrons and camellias, exotic plants and woodland adventure trails for children. Beautiful gardens and fountains occupy terraces above the Menai Strait: the herbaceous borders are at their best in July and August.

Planting in the **rhododendron garden** began in the 1930s, and included scented species and hybrids from the famous garden at Bodnant in the Conwy Valley. This part of the grounds closes when the flowering of the rhododendrons ends in mid-June.

Two other sections of the gardens are open throughout the season. The **Australasian arboretum**, protected by a eucalyptus shelter belt, is stocked with southern hemisphere plants, from South America as well as from Australia and New Zealand. Wild flowers from Anglesey, including some orchids, are also featured here. A **West Indies garden** (the origins of its name are obscure) lies to the south of the house. This is the property's principal shrub garden, with islands of massive plantings of flowering shrubs around an expanse of lawn.

The grounds of Plas Newydd are occasionally used for spectacular firework displays or for family 'fun' days including Punch and Judy shows and treasure hunts.

A walk gives access to views of the Menai Strait. From the stone-built **boathouse** at the water's edge, boats leave Plas Newydd for a tour as far as the Britannia Bridge **▶49** passing the Pwll Fanogl inlet, the Nelson Memorial at Llanfairpwll **▶62** and the wooded Faenol shore, which is also National Trust land. As the trees of the Faenol conifer plantations are felled for timber, they are being replaced by broadleaved species. The informative commentary given to passengers describes the history and the environment of the Strait.

Plas Newydd burial chamber

The Stone Age **Plas Newydd burial chamber**, which dates from about 5,000 years ago, may be seen on the north side of the house. A second chamber called **Bryn yr Hen Bobl** ('hill of the old people') lies on farmland at the southern edge of the estate. Excavation of the burial site revealed the remains of 30 adults, a baby, animals and fragments of pottery. The Home Farm (1804) may be viewed from the drive to the Walled Garden, which is now (though not part of The National Trust) a horticultural centre.

Trefdraeth — *see* **Bodorgan ▶199**

LOST CHORDS

Ynys Môn has a tradition of harp playing that stretches back from the present day into ancient times. Its medieval harpists were praised and highly respected. But what kind of music did they play?

Peter Greenhill, *a researcher from Llanllechid near Bangor, traces their history and explains how the discovery of an obscure seventeenth-century manuscript offered the modern world a key to this music.*

ANGLESEY occupies an extraordinary position in the history of music. Unlike elsewhere in Europe, professional musicianship in the Celtic regions survived the fall of the Roman Empire. Over many centuries the bardic tradition in Wales continued to flourish and develop, so that by the late Middle Ages its music had become extremely sophisticated and mature. But in the Tudor era (1485-1603), patronage of the traditional music declined as very different music in the mainstream European style displaced it. Very fortunately, in Anglesey detailed records of the music were preserved, otherwise we would be quite unable to know what the ancient music indigenous to the British Isles had been like.

Anglesey had long been important in this musical tradition, because of the pre-eminence of the Princes of Aberffraw. As early as around 1094, we learn that a master harpist, Gellan, was killed in the retreat from the Battle of Aberlleiniog ▶68. His lord, Gruffudd ap Cynan (c1055-1137), Prince of Aberffraw, was the central figure in the traditional history of the music. Apparently, he was a great patron of music who, having been raised in Dublin, brought about important standardisations between the closely-related Welsh and Irish traditions.

Gellan's successors, the chief musicians in Wales, had a tendency to be resident in Anglesey, it appears, even after the Conquest of Edward I. Information on particular musicians is scarce, but there are records from the fourteenth to the sixteenth century that show, across the island, a number of harpers and crowders (players of the *crwth*, a form of bowed lyre). There are references in the Alaw district, also at Newborough, Penmon and perhaps at Trefddisteiniaid and Llangadwaladr, near Aberffraw itself.

Mindful, no doubt, of the traditional importance of Anglesey, it was an Anglesey harper from the Tudur (or 'Tudor') family of Penmynydd, Robert ap Huw of Bodwigan near Llanddeusant, who collected and copied old transcripts of the ancient music, in about 1613. His manuscripts came to be kept at Bodorgan, near Aberffraw, but only one collection of music seems to have survived. It is now housed in the British Library.

The Robert ap Huw Manuscript, as it is now known, has become famous. Lewis Morris ▶114 was excited to come across it at Bodorgan and called attention to the curious tablature symbols used there to describe the archaic music that had, by this time, long been unknown. Not surprisingly, for a long time very little progress could be made in understanding it, and even by the 1930s, when the great pioneer of early music performance, Arnold Dolmetsch, put it at the very top of the agenda of early music studies, the research needed to produce accurate renditions had barely been started. But by the 1970s research in earnest was underway, and that has recently been brought to the point where the musical pieces can at last be reconstructed with a high degree of accuracy.

The glowing terms that medieval writers and poets used to describe their much-loved music seem justified. The pieces do indeed charm and delight the ear, particularly through the sweetness of their harmonies and the epic scope of their development. For this was not plain folk music but classical craftsmanship, honed in the landscapes and climate of the British Isles, and it seems probable that several of the pieces in the manuscript were composed on Anglesey.

Music from the Robert ap Huw Manuscript
Volume 1 (PDCD002; **www.**pauldooley.com) was recorded by the Irish harpist Paul Dooley in 2004. Its musical arrangements are by Peter Greenhill.

ISLAND RECORDS

THE ISLAND'S vibrant underground music scene may not be instantly apparent to the visitor. Venues in Trearddur Bay and Holyhead often quake to the exciting high energy sounds of *Entity*, *Valleum* or *Dethkit*, but the full extent of Anglesey's subculture is as likely to be found in cyberspace or on CD as on stage.

The golden age of Welsh rock saw landmark records by *Datblygu*, *Gorky's Zygotic Mynci* and *Super Furry Animals* recorded in Anglesey studios and released on local labels, inspiring an eclectic creativity in the island's cognoscenti.

Towering over Anglesey's thriving scene stand the labels Ankstmusik and R-Bennig, whose adventurous release schedules have brought numerous left-field island artists a quietly far-reaching cult acclaim.

Recently R-Bennig have introduced us to the avant-fauvism of Rhoscefnhir's Jack Sharp, the neo-pastoralism of Llanddaniel's *Wrightoid* and the vibro-abstractions of Llanfairpwll's Duncan Black, whilst Ankstmusik have given us the post tonalist refractions of *Ectogram* and unsettling sonic convulsions of Holyhead's *Wendykurk*.

Studios such as Llanfaelog's *Ofn* and Moelfre's *Gossamer Dome* appear on the credits to many a classic recording. Mavericks abound and thrive: award winning composer Dewi Evans – the musical genius behind Ankst's *Rheinallt H Rowlands* – now divides his time between touring multi-media projects around the world and playing with Menai Bridge's psychogeographers *Parking Non-Stop*, whilst nautical boffin Ben Powell manages to conjure up astonishing dreamscapes by putting Menai Straits tidal current data through sonification software in his Mank project.

A web search will yield information on all these people and more.

Alan Holmes, the contributor of this piece, is a musician, producer and one-man indie label. The Independent described him as the 'godfather' of the Welsh underground scene.

Wendykurk

10 Môn Beat greats

Modernaires. We did it again / Illuminated 1981.

The Kaseo Kid. Hey, it's the Kaseo Kid Solchromatics 1983.

Nid Madagasgar. Lledrith lliw / Ofn 1989.

Plant Bach Ofnus. Weitharmonisch / Ofn 1990.

Rheinallt H Rowlands. Hendaid Brân a straeon eraill / Central Slate 1993.

21 Chimneys. Cream of Chimneys / Chimneys 2001.

Wendykurk. Soft meat / Ankstmusik 2003.

Duncan Black. The ubiquitous guitar mercenary Judmusic 2005.

Ethania. Wedi pydru / R-Bennig 2005.

Ectogram. Electric deckchair / Ankstmusik 2005.

WWW

Buy music: www.ankst.net

General information / labels etc:

www.link2wales.co.uk

www.ankst.co.uk

www.r-bennig.com

www.angleseymusic.co.uk

Individual artist sites

www.mankymusic.co.uk

www.xms3.com   www.yamoosh.com

www.ectogram.co.uk

www.dewievansmusic.com

www.garageband.com/artist/Dethkit

www.duncan-black.co.uk

www.parkingnonstop.org

ANGLESEY DIRECTORY

New tourist attractions spring up, others close. Opening times vary and telephone numbers and websites change. Leaflets go out of print. Nothing stays the same.

To avoid disappointment it is prudent to confirm what is on offer by telephoning the places you intend to visit (or check through a Tourist Information Centre – see the telephone numbers at the top of the page) before setting out on your journey.

Môn Mam Cymru is an independent publication. This edition accepted no advertising.

Comments that reflect readers' experiences will be welcomed.
The publisher would also be pleased to receive information about errors or omissions.

Robert Williams, MAGMA, Llansadwrn, Porthaethwy, Ynys Môn LL59 5SR, Cymru/Wales. *email* magmawales@hotmail.com

Emergencies

Rescue services

TELEPHONE 999 or 112 for
Police *Heddlu*
Fire *Tân*
Ambulance *Ambiwlans*
Coastguard *Gwylwyr y Glannau*

Police. Enquiries that are not urgent:
✆ 0845 607 1002 *Cym.*✆*0845 607 1001*
Coastguard Maritime Rescue.
Enquiries that are not urgent can be
answered by the Holyhead operations
centre. ✆ 01407 762051 ✆ 01407 763911

Hospitals

The main regional hospital, with a casualty
department and a full range of general and specialist
services is **Ysbyty Gwynedd on the mainland at
Bangor**, located one mile from Menai Bridge town.
Follow the signs from either of the two bridges.
✆ 01248 384384.

On Anglesey, Penrhos Stanley Hospital at Holyhead
has a minor injury department 9am–9pm and also
deals with acute cases and post-operative care.
✆ 01407 766000

Doctors

For loss of consciousness, severe chest pain,
serious accidents or serious loss of blood call 999
or 112 or go to Ysbyty Gwynedd's Accident and
Emergency Department, signposted from the
mainland side of either of the Menai bridges.

For urgent out-of-hours medical care in the local
area, **weekdays 6.30pm–8am**, and **all day Saturday,
Sunday and public holidays**, contact the Local Health
Board service: ✆ 0845 850 1362.
For medical advice NHS Direct Wales ✆ 0845 46 47

Pharmacies

LOCATED IN THE MAIN TOWNS AND VILLAGES:
✦ Amlwch   ✦ Llanfair Pwllgwyngyll
✦ Beaumaris   ✦ Llangefni
✦ Benllech   ✦ Menai Bridge
✦ Cemaes Bay   ✦ Rhosneigr
✦ Holyhead   ✦ Valley
Most are open for part of Saturdays and some operate
a rota system for Sundays, bank holidays and
evenings. A notice in the window of each pharmacy
directs you to those offering out-of-hours opening.

Dentists

If you are experiencing dental pain, Anglesey's
emergency service operates two days a week at the
Llanfair Pwllgwyngyll Dental Clinic
in the Health Centre on Penmynydd Road.
✦ Thursday 5pm–8.30pm:
by appointment only ✆ 01286 662750.
✦ Sunday 9.30am–1pm:
first come, first served ✆ 01248 714727
or call **NHS Direct Dental Helpline** ✆ 0845 6010128

The Samaritans

**24-hour confidential emotional support helpline
for anyone in crisis.** Local number ✆ 01248 354646
or national number ✆ 08457 90 90 90

Citizens' Advice Bureaux

Advice line ✆ 0845 120 3708, Monday to Thursday:
9.30am–2pm (Recorded information at other times)

Ynys Môn Citizens Advice Bureaux
✦ **Amlwch**, Town Council Office, Lôn Goch
Tuesday and Thursday: 9.30am–2pm
✦ **Beaumaris**, Canolfan Iorwerth Rowlands, Steeple
Lane. *Thursday: 9.30am–noon*
✦ **Holyhead**, Victoria Terrace ✆ 01407 762278
Tuesday and Thursday: 9.30am–2pm
✦ **Llanfaelog**, Community Centre
Monday: 9am–noon
✦ **Llangefni**, Ffordd yr Efail ✆ 01248 722652
Monday and Wednesday: 9.30am–2pm
✦ **Bangor** (on the mainland), Deiniol Road
Monday to Friday: 10am–3pm ✆ 08707 502350

Planning your visit

Tourist Information Centres

A network of Tourist Information Centres has up-
to-date information about accommodation, offers
a bed-booking service, and can answer your
questions about the region's tourist attractions.

ON ANGLESEY
✦ **Holyhead** ✆ 01407 762622. In Terminal One of the
Stena Line port. Daily all year: 8.30am–6pm.
www.gonorthwales.co.uk *(holyhead@nwtic.com)*
✦ **Llanfair Pwllgwyngyll** ✆ 01248 713177. By the
entrance to James Pringle Weavers. Daily all year:
Monday to Saturday, 9.30am–5.30pm in summer (to
5pm in winter), Sundays: 10am–5pm. Closed 25/26
December and 1 January.
www.gonorthwales.co.uk *(llanfairpwll@nwtic.com)*

ON THE FERRY
✦ For people travelling to Anglesey from Dun
Laoghaire a tourist information point operates on
board the *HSS Stena Explorer*.

DISTRICT TOURIST INFORMATION
✦ **Amlwch**, Industrial Heritage Centre, in the *Sail Loft*
at the Port. Daily from Easter to the end of September
until 5pm. Café. ✆ 01407 832255 www.amlwch.net
✦ **Beaumaris**, Town Hall, Castle Street. Easter, and from
Whit to the school half term in October: Monday–
Saturday, 10am–4.45pm. www.beaumaris.org.uk
✦ **Cemaes**, Heritage Centre, High Street. All year.
Information, internet access, café, displays of old
photographs. Café opening hours, Summer:
10.30am–4pm (closed Sundays). Winter: 11am–3pm
(closed Sundays, and Thursday afternoons from 1pm).
✆ 01407 710004 (during weekday café hours).
www.cemaes-bay.co.uk

TOURIST INFORMATION ON THE MAINLAND
Bangor . . . . ✆ 01248 352786
Betws-y-coed . . . . ✆ 01690 710426
Caernarfon . . . . ✆ 01286 672232
Colwyn Bay . . . . ✆ 01492 530478
Conwy . . . . ✆ 01492 592248
Llanberis . . . . ✆ 01286 870765

Llandudno	✆ 01492 876413
Llangollen	✆ 01978 860828
Mold	✆ 01352 759331
Porthmadog	✆ 01766 512981
Pwllheli	✆ 01758 613000

Accommodation

A brochure, listing the majority of the Wales Tourist Board's verified accommodation available on Anglesey, is published annually by the local authority. It includes caravan and camping sites. Copies of the free brochure are available over the counter at Anglesey's Tourist Information Centres, or can be ordered on the telephone and sent to you by post. ✆ 01248 713177

ACCOMMODATION BOOKING LINES (charging a small administration fee if a booking is made):
✦ **ON ANGLESEY**, accommodation advice and booking services are provided by the Tourist Information Centres:
either Holyhead ✆ 01407 762622. Daily: 8.30am–6pm. (Closed 25/26 December and 1 January.)
or Llanfair Pwllgwyngyll ✆ 01248 713177. Monday to Saturday: 9.30am–5.30pm in summer, 9.30am–5pm in winter; Sundays: 10am–5pm. (Closed 25/26 December and 1 January)
✦ **NORTH WALES** ✆ 08705 168767
Monday to Friday 9am–6pm; Saturday 10am–5pm.
www.gonorthwales.co.uk

YHA Youth Hostels

There are plans to open a YHA Hostel in the grounds of the Holyhead Breakwater Park. The nearest mainland YHA Hostel is at Tan y Bryn, Bangor, off the A5122 on the outskirts of Bangor 2½ miles from Menai Bridge
✆ 0870 770 5686. bangor@yha.org.uk
www.yha.org.uk *(The Holyhead hostel will be administered from the Bangor hostel)*

Maps

The best maps for those intending to get to know the island: **OS Explorer 1:25 000** *(4cm:1km, 2½ in:1mile)*
262 Anglesey West / Gorllewin Ynys Môn
263 Anglesey East / Dwyrain Ynys Môn

A good single-sheet map: **OS Landranger 1:50 000**
(2cm:1km, 1¼ in:1mile) **114** Anglesey / Môn

www.ordnancesurvey.co.uk/leisure

Public transport

GENERAL INFORMATION
Tourist information centres can supply the free, annual **Bus, Rail and Tourist Map & Guide to Wales.** Local timetables are also available in print.
and on-line at www.anglesey.gov.uk
Local and national travel information for bus and rail, is also available daily (8am–10pm): ✆ 0870 608 2608
and on-line at www.traveline-cymru.org.uk

BUSES. Arriva bus enquiries ✆ 0870 120 1088
www.arrivabus.co.uk
National Express bus enquiries ✆ 0870 580 8080

TRAINS. National rail enquiries ✆ 0845 748 4950
www.nationalrail.co.uk

Trains from Chester and Crewe provide connections to the national rail network. Direct services link Cardiff and London to Holyhead.

Anglesey is served by the North Wales Coast Railway:
— Holyhead — Valley — Rhosneigr — Tŷ Croes —
— Bodorgan — Llanfair Pwllgwyngyll

The line crosses over the Britannia Bridge to the mainland stations of:
— Bangor — Llanfairfechan — Penmaenmawr —
— Llandudno Junction
and onwards along the North Wales coast to Chester.

Journey times on the fastest services

Crewe / Holyhead	1hr. 57mins.
London Euston / Holyhead	3hr. 49mins.
Cardiff / Holyhead	4hr. 42mins.
Crewe / Bangor	1hr. 30mins.
London Euston / Bangor	3hr. 22mins.
Cardiff / Bangor	4hr. 13mins.

Steam trains occasionally visit Holyhead on excursions from Crewe.

Motorists

AA Breakdown Service ✆ 0800 887766
RAC Breakdown Service ✆ 0800 828282

ALL-NIGHT PETROL/DIESEL
On Anglesey
✦ Shell Britannia, Menai Bridge ✆ 01248 718000
At Bangor, on the mainland
✦ Esso Bangor Service Station ✆ 01248 370508
(junction 11 of A55, at the A5 intersection)
✦ Texaco, Garth ✆ 01248 387910
(opposite the fire station)
✦ Tesco, Caernarfon Road ✆ 0845 6779034
(junction 10 of A55, take A4087 Bangor road)

LPG Autogas
✦ **Amlwch** Central Garage ✆ 01407 830444
Monday to Friday 7.30am–7.30pm; Saturday 8am–6pm; Sunday 9am–6pm.
✦ **Gaerwen** Camgas ✆ 01248 421502
Monday to Friday 8am–5pm; Saturday 8am–12.30pm.
✦ **Bangor** Brynllwyd Service Station, Caernarfon Road. ✆ 01248 372265 *6.30am–11pm every day.*

CAR HIRE
✦ **Hertz**, office in the Terminal Building at Holyhead Port. Monday to Friday, 8am–6.30pm; Saturday, 8am–3pm; Sunday, noon–3pm. ✆ 01407 761800.
✦ **Wheels Hire**, Victoria Road, Holyhead ✆ 01407 765397 (office hours).
✦ **Quayside Self-Drive Hire**: Newry Beach, Holyhead ✆ 01407 760912 (out of hours ✆ 07703 107078). and Gaerwen ✆ 01248 421133 (seven days a week during office hours).
✦ **Central Garage**, Amlwch ✆ 01407 830444 (closed on Saturday afternoons and all day Sunday)

Tours

✦ **Cambrian Tour Guides**
Special interest tours in industrial archaeology. Walking. History and cultural tours of North Wales. ✆ 01248 470655 www.cambriantourguides.co.uk
✦ **North Wales Tourist Guiding Association**
Provides qualified, professional, special interest guides for guided walks, coach tours, and historic itineraries. ✆ 01286 660431 www.northwalestouristguides.com
✦ **Tywys Tourism Services**
A choice of itineraries or tailor-made tours for individuals or small groups.
✆ 01248 352402 www.tywys.com
✦ **Crwydro Môn** A range of tour and guide services. ✆ 01248 713611 www.angleseywalkingholidays.com

Tidal information

Many of the island's coastal newsagents stock the annual *Liverpool & Irish Sea Tide Table*. This is a useful purchase – not only for sailors, but also for all visitors to Anglesey's coast.

Weather forecasts

✦ **Met Office Weatherline** ℃ 0870 900 0100.
✦ **Marinecall Wales** for Meteorological Office information about conditions around Anglesey ℃ 09068 500460.
✦ **Tidal information** from Holyhead Coastguards ℃ 01407 762051.
✦ **Mountaincall** for Snowdonia ℃ 09068 500449.
✦ www.bbc.co.uk/weather/ukweather/wales

A weather website for meteorological and water conditions in the Menai Strait is operated by the University of Wales, Bangor, and the Countryside Council for Wales. Although a conservation tool, this site provides a variety of information. For example, it indicates water clarity. (Edited data is made available with a month's delay.) Be aware that conditions in the Strait can change rapidly, and that attention is always necessary. www.straitsbangor.ac.uk

Ferries to and from Ireland

✦ **Stena Line**
℃ 08705 707070 www.stenaline.co.uk
(A Stena Line telephone service, *Ferrycheck*, provides 24 hour recorded information about that day's arrivals and departures, sea conditions and timetable changes ℃ 08705 755755.)
✦ **Irish Ferries**
℃ 08705 171717 www.irishferries.com

Airports

The nearest scheduled-flight airports to Anglesey:
✦ **Manchester**
℃ 0161 484 3000
✦ **Liverpool**, John Lennon Airport
℃ 0870 750 8484

There are moves to establish passenger flights to Cardiff (and eventually to Dublin and further afield) from a terminal next to RAF Valley, using the facilities of the RAF airfield.

Caernarfon Airport, Dinas Dinlle south of Caernarfon. Facilities for visiting pilots of private aircraft. (The *Airworld* aviation musem here is open from March to October).
℃ 01286 830800 www.air-world.co.uk

Bureaux de Change

Main post offices in Holyhead and Llangefni offer a foreign exchange service on weekdays and Saturday mornings, as do some banks (weekdays only)

The Stena Line desk in the Holyhead ferry terminal is open for most of the 24 hours in a day and offers an exchange service.

The larger High Street travel agents in Bangor High Street (on the mainland) offer counter services from Monday to Saturday.

County and town councils

The Isle of Anglesey County Council is the county's local authority. Its website is a useful source of general information. ℃ 01248 750057 www.anglesey.gov.uk

TOWN COUNCILS
Amlwch .... ℃ 01407 832228
Beaumaris / *Biwmares* .... ℃ 01248 810317
Holyhead / *Caergybi* .... ℃ 01407 764608
.... www.holyheadtowncouncil.com
Llanfair Pwllgwyngyll .... ℃ 01248 715101
Llangefni .... ℃ 01248 723332
Menai Bridge / *Porthaethwy* ℃ 01248 716959 / 440611

Public conveniences

Aberffraw Llys Llewelyn
Amlwch Dinorben Square + Lôn Goch
Beaumaris near the castle entrance
Benllech the Square + beach car park
Brynsiencyn car park
Bull Bay
Cemaes Bay High Street + beach car park
Church Bay
Llanddona Beach
Llaneilian
Llanfaelog Porth Ty'n Tywyn,
Llanfair Pwllgwyngyll post office car park
Llangefni library car park on Mill Street / *Lôn y Felin*
Llannerch-y-medd High Street
Marian-glas Traeth Bychan
Menai Bridge Beach Road + the pier (by St George's Road / *Ffordd Cynan*) + the library
Moelfre car park
Newborough High Street,
Red Wharf Bay next to the *Ship Inn*
Rhosneigr library car park
Valley Station Road

ON HOLY ISLAND
Holyhead Newry Beach + Swift Square + Cenotaph
Holyhead Breakwater Country Park
Penrhos / Penrhos Beach / Penrhos Coastal Park
Porthdafarch
Rhoscolyn Beach
South Stack
Trearddur Bay

Markets & early closing

Amlwch .... Friday 9am–4pm
Holyhead .... Monday 8am–4pm
Llangefni .... Thursday & Saturday 8am–4pm

FARMERS' MARKETS. A small market is held on the mainland at Bangor, in Morrison's car park, every other Sunday. Joanne Robertson ℃ 01248 421661.
Farmers markets may also take place on the island –
National Farmers' Markets Association: ℃ 0845 610 6496

Menai Bridge Fair / *Ffair y Borth*. Each year, on 24th October. (If this is a Sunday, the fair is held on the 23rd).

EARLY CLOSING. Post offices and some shops may close on the afternoons of these days:
Holyhead, Llangefni .... Tuesday
Menai Bridge, Beaumaris .... Wednesday
Amlwch .... Wednesday and Saturday
Benllech .... Thursday

CAR BOOT SALES
✦ *Mona Showground* – Sundays ℃ 01407 840179
Others have taken place during the summer season at Valley (Tuesdays) and Benllech (Saturdays).

The Media

Broadcasting

RADIO
The following stations broadcast specifically to Wales:
✦ **BBC Radio Wales**
English-language, 882 Khz medium wave
✦ **BBC Radio Cymru**
Welsh-language, 92.4–92.6 FM
✦ **Commercial radio**
Coast 96.3FM and Champion 103FM are amongst the
region's commercial stations.

WALES-BASED TELEVISION
✦ **S4C** Welsh-language during primetime, mainly
taking material from independent companies. English
Channel 4 programmes at other times. S4C's twice-
weekly Welsh-language series *Rownd a Rownd* –
following the lives of a group of youngsters working
their newspaper rounds – is filmed in Menai Bridge.
✦ **S4C Digital** Welsh-language, with optional English
subtitling.
✦ **BBC1 Wales** English-language: much the same fare
as in the rest of Britain, with local variants including
sport and news.
✦ **BBC2 Wales Digital** English-language primetime
programming for Wales.
In some parts of the island, Irish radio stations and
television channels can also be received.
Analogue television transmissions in Wales begin to
be superseded by digital from 2009.

Newspapers and magazines

ENGLISH-LANGUAGE DAILY
✦ *Daily Post*, North Wales edition. ☎ 01492 584321

ENGLISH-LANGUAGE WEEKLY
✦ *The Mail*: in two editions, *Holyhead & Anglesey*
and *Bangor & Anglesey* (Wednesdays)
☎ 01407 760250 www.icnorthwales.co.uk
✦ *North Wales Chronicle* (Thursdays)
☎ 01248 387400 www.northwaleschronicle.co.uk

WELSH-LANGUAGE WEEKLY
✦ *Y Cymro* is the national Welsh-language weekly
(Wednesdays), which first appeared in 1932 under the
editorship of Anglesey journalists. ☎ 01766 515514
✦ *Y Herald Cymraeg* is a Welsh-language supplement
to Wednesday's *Daily Post*. ☎ 01492 584321
✦ *Golwg* is the most prominent of the many Welsh-
language magazines.

WELSH-LANGUAGE MONTHLY
Papurau Bro are community-based papers in Welsh,
compiled and distributed by volunteers.
(There are, normally, no August editions)
✦ *Yr Arwydd*
East and northeast Anglesey. ☎ 01407 830144
✦ *Y Glorian*
Llangefni and central Anglesey. ☎ 01248 430507
✦ *Papur Menai*
Penmon to Llanddaniel-fab. ☎ 01248 712615
✦ *Y Rhwyd*
Northwest Anglesey and Holy Island. ☎ 01407 742040

Anglesey's Welsh-language bookshops (with some
English-language stock) include:
✦ **Llangefni**: Cwprwdd Cornel. ☎ 01248 750218
✦ **Menai Bridge**: Awen Menai. ☎ 01248 715532

What to see

Museums and attractions

Also see … *HISTORY* page 226
NATURE page 230
ARTS & CRAFTS page 239

The island's five most visited attractions
✦ **Anglesey Sea Zoo**
✦ **Beaumaris Castle**
✦ **Holyhead Breakwater Park**
✦ **Oriel Ynys Môn**
✦ **Plas Newydd**

Anglesey Sea Zoo / *Sw Môr Môn*, Brynsiencyn.
An aquarium displaying local underwater life. Sea
horse breeding, lobster hatchery. Crazy golf course.
A good toy shop. Licensed coffee shop. The place to
buy Anglesey Sea Salt. February to October: daily.
☎ 01248 430411 www.angleseyseazoo.co.uk

Beaumaris Castle / *Castell Biwmares*. Moated castle
of the English invasion, begun in 1295 by Edward I and
certainly the most impressive medieval site on
Anglesey. Remarkably sophisticated walls-within-walls
design, state of the art for the late thirteenth century.
A World Heritage Site. Summer events have included
medieval displays and open-air theatre.
Daily (closed 24, 25, 26 December and 1 January).
☎ 01248 810361 www.cadw.wales.gov.uk

Holyhead Breakwater Country Park / *Parc Gwledig*
Morglawdd Caergybi (SH225832). The park opened in
1990 on the site of the quarry which supplied stone
during the construction between 1846 and 1873 of
Britain's longest breakwater. Open all year. ☎ 01407
760530 ☎ 01248 752428 www.angleseyheritage.org
A North Wales Wildlife Trust kiosk in the Park, supplying
refreshments and items for sale, opens most afternoons
(weather permitting) from Easter to the end of October.

Oriel Ynys Môn, signposted on outskirts of Llangefni:
take the B5111 to Rhos-meirch. Free admission to
Anglesey's purpose-built heritage museum, together
with its art galleries. Some special events. Café, shop.
All year, every day (except Christmas and New Year)
10.30am–5pm. The gallery closes for rehanging
between exhibitions. ☎ 01248 724444
www.anglesey.gov.uk www.angleseyheritage.org

Plas Newydd, Llanedwen, near Llanfair Pwllgwyngyll.
The seat of the Marquesses of Anglesey, on the Menai
Strait, now owned by National Trust. Rebuilt in the late
eighteenth and early nineteenth centuries. Paintings,
family mementos. A Military Museum in the house
displays uniforms and weapons of the Napoleonic
wars. Extensive gardens. Adventure play area. Boat
trips on the Menai Strait. Shop and tea room near the
car park. Coffeeshop and secondhand bookshop
inside the house. Easter to the end of October:
Saturday to Wednesday, and Good Friday. House
noon–5pm, gardens 11am–5.30pm, shop & tea room
10.30am–5pm. Last admissions at 4.30pm. The shop
and tea room also open on Saturdays and Sundays
from November to December 11am–4pm.
Recorded information ☎ 01248 715272
Office ☎ 01248 714795 www.nationaltrust.org.uk

Beaumaris Courthouse / *Llys Biwmares*. Take an
audio guide around the old assize court (1614),
refurbished in Victorian times. Wheelchair access to
most areas. Daily, Easter to the end of September:
10.30am–5pm. ☎ 01248 811691 ☎ 01248 724444
www.angleseyheritage.co.uk

Beaumaris Gaol / *Carchar Biwmares*, Bunkers Hill. The harsh reality of Victorian Britain is revealed in this remarkable penal institution (1829), complete with a treadwheel for prisoners. Dramatic reconstructions are sometimes staged. Wheelchair access is limited. Easter to end of September, daily 10.30am–5pm or by appointment. ✆ 01248 724444
✆ 01248 810921 www.angleseyheritage.co.uk

Anglesey Bird World / *Byd Adar*, Dwyran. Easter to October. Aviary displays, shop, snacks. ✆ 01248 440849

Anglesey Model Village and Gardens / *Gerddi a Phentref Modelau Môn*, Newborough. Anglesey's landmarks built to one-twelfth scale. A working garden railway. Tearoom, play and picnic areas. Open Easter, then May bank holiday to the end of September, daily.
✆ 01248 440477 www.angleseyattractions.com

Foel Farm Park / *Parc Fferm y Foel*, Brynsiencyn. A working farm on the shores of the Menai Strait. Farm animals, adventure playgrounds, tractor trailer rides, tea room, bistro and chocolate workshop. End of March to October: daily. *The chocolate workshop additionally opens from November to March on weekdays. It closes for a fortnight at Christmas.*
✆ 01248 430646 www.foelfarm.co.uk

Haulfre Stables / *Stablau Haulfre*, Llangoed. A small equestrian and transport museum in restored stable buildings, offering a glimpse into the work of grooms, coachmen and stable boys in Victorian times. Visitors should make an appointment.
✆ 01248 724444 www.angleseyheritage.co.uk

Henblas Park / *Parc Henblas*, Llangristiolus (from the A5 south west of Llangefni take the B4422 towards Aberffraw). Tractor and train tours, sheepdog demonstrations, indoor children's playground, café. Whit to the end of September (and school holidays, Easter to October), daily. Closed on Saturdays except on bank holiday weekends. *The grounds also open for one weekend in February to view the snowdrops.*
✆ 01407 840440 www.parc-henblas-park.co.uk

Holyhead Maritime Museum / *Amgueddfa Arforol Caergybi*. In the old lifeboat house on Newry Beach. The maritime history of Holyhead: the port, its ships and its seamen. Café/bistro. Permanent collection. Temporary displays often take notable anniversaries as their themes. Main season: Easter to Autumn.
✆ 01407 769745 during opening hours.
✆ 01407 764374 (museum's secretary) at other times.

Llynnon Mill / *Melin Llynnon*, Llanddeusant. A working windmill, producing stoneground flour. Tea room, Anglesey Craftworkers' Guild shop. An 'Iron Age settlement' is being established on adjoining land. Easter to the end of September, daily 11am–5pm.
✆ 01407 730797 www.angleseyheritage.co.uk
*A three-mile (4.5km) circular walking trail leads from Llynnon Mill and past its bakery to the privately-owned watermill, Howell Mill.
Mill enthusiasts can also make private arrangements to view two other restored Anglesey watermills:*
✦ *Pandy Parc* ✆ *01248 470655, between City Dulas and Llannerch-y-medd (SH453868). Pandy Parc's owner is a tour guide: www.cambriantourguides.co.uk*
✦ *Llynon Hall Mill* ✆ *01407 730203, situated close to Llynnon windmill (SH333847).*

Moelfre Seawatch / *Gwylfan*. The village's maritime history and the starting point of 'heritage walks'. Easter to the end of September, Tuesday to Sunday 11am–5pm; closed on Mondays except bank holidays. ✆ 01248 410277 ✆ 01248 724444 www.angleseyheritage.co.uk

Museum of Childhood / *Amgueddfa Plentyndod* Beaumaris. *The future of this excellent small museum is under review. Please check current arrangements before making your visit.* ✆ 01248 712498

Pili Palas Nature World / *Byd Natur*. On Penmynydd road out of Menai Bridge. Butterflies fly freely in a garden hothouse. Reptiles and spiders. Playground, nature trail, pets' corner, café and shop. Open every day from the school half-term holiday in February to the end of December. *In recent years an RSPB 'nestcam' has broadcast live pictures of nesting bluetits (and, out of the nesting season, of feeding wild birds) into the café.*
✆ 01248 712474 www.pilipalas.co.uk

South Stack Lighthouse / *Goleudy Ynys Lawd*, near Holyhead. In a spectacular location at the tip of Holy Island. Descend 400 steps and cross the bridge to see displays about the history of the lighthouse, the island's bird life and the surrounding sea. Easter to September: open daily for guided tours, 10.30am–5pm (and in winter by appointment). Admission subject to weather conditions and minimum height of 1 metre. Tickets available from the South Stack Kitchen ✆ 01407 762181 and on the South Stack bridge.
✆ 01407 763207 ✆ 01248 724444
www.angleseyheritage.co.uk

Stone Science / *Gwyddor Carreg*, Bryn Eglwys, Llanddyfnan, on the B5109 between Pentraeth and Talwrn. Archaeological and geological exhibits and sales. Easter to the end of October and winter weekends and school holidays, daily. Closed January to mid-February. *(Stone Science is also the venue of meetings of the Talwrn Archaeology Group).*
✆ 01248 450310 www.angleseyattractions.com

Swtan, Church Bay / *Porth Swtan*. A traditional Anglesey thatched cottage (SH301891), restored and furnished to its state in around the year 1900. Next to the Church Bay car park (with public conveniences). Easter to September: Friday, Saturdays, Sunday and bank holidays: afternoons.
✆ 01407 730501 www.swtan.co.uk

Tacla Taid Transport Museum, on B4419 between Llangaffo and Newborough. Restored classic cars, motorcycles, agricultural vehicles and memorabilia. Easter to October, daily. ✆ 01248 440344

————————————————————————

Two private displays welcome visitors – by appointment only. Cemaes Maritime Collection opens occasionally throughout the year and more regularly during the month of August. ✆ 01407 710650 www.cemaesmaritimecollection.co.uk
A second small, informal museum, at Llanbedrgoch, is a vast, mixed hoard of all manner of things, from babies bottles to copper boilers. ✆ 01248 450449

Mainland attractions

North Wales's five most visited attractions are
✦ **Bodnant Garden, in the Conwy Valley**
✦ **Caernarfon Castle**
✦ **Conwy Castle**
✦ **Penrhyn Castle, near Bangor**
✦ **Portmeirion, near Porthmadog**

Bodnant Garden in the Conwy Valley, 27 miles from Menai Bridge. Signposted off the A470 (in the direction of Llanrwst from junction 19 of the A55). 80-acres of magnificent National Trust gardens, amongst Britain's finest. Rhododendrons, camellias, magnolias, azaleas, laburnum arch. Mid-March to early November, daily 10am–5pm. Licensed tearoom.
✆ 01492 650460 www.bodnant-garden.co.uk

Caernarfon Castle / *Castell Caernarfon* on the mainland 7 miles from Menai Bridge. One of Europe's great castles, begun by Edward I in 1283 and designed to impress as well as suppress. Exhibitions, summer events. The castle and walled town is a World Heritage Site. Open daily all year, except 24/25/26 December and 1 January. *(The museum of the Royal Welch Fusiliers is housed in one of the castle's towers.)*
✆ 01286 677617 **www.cadw.wales.gov.uk**

Conwy Castle / *Castell Conwy* on the mainland, 17 miles from Menai Bridge. Another castle of Edward I's invasion, built between 1283 and 1287. Fine views from the walls and turrets over the Conwy estuary and to the mountains. The castle and walled town is a World Heritage Site. Exhibitions, summer events. Open daily all year, except 24/25/26 December and 1 January. ✆ 01492 592358 **www.cadw.wales.gov.uk**

Penrhyn Castle / *Castell Penrhyn*. Llandygái, near Bangor, 4 miles from Menai Bridge. A National Trust property. Museums of dolls and of industrial locomotives, in a Victorian mansion. Daily (closed Tuesdays), April–October, noon–5pm. Last admissions 4.30pm. Gardens and tearoom from 11am. During July and August the castle opens at 11am, the gardens and tearoom at 10am.
✆ 01248 371337 **www.nationaltrust.org.uk**

Portmeirion Village & Gardens / *Pentref a Gerddi Portmeirion*, south of Porthmadog, 30 miles from Menai Bridge. An Italianate village created by architect Clough Williams-Ellis in a spectacular coastal location between Porthmadog and Penrhyndeudraeth. Restaurants. No dogs. Daily 9.30am–5.30pm. (Shops closed 25/26 December, 1 January.)
✆ 01766 772311 **www.portmeirion-village.com**

Bodelwyddan Castle / *Castell Bodelwyddan*, on A55 (junction 25), 33 miles from Menai Bridge. This Gothic crennelled house was built (1830-40) for the Williams family by the partnership of Joseph Hansom and Edmund Welch, who, in Anglesey, were also responsible for some prominent Beaumaris buildings. From 1920-82 it housed a girl's boarding school, Lowther College. The house was refurbished in the 1980s to display part of the collection of the National Portrait Gallery. Furniture came from the V&A and sculpture from the Royal Academy of Arts. Changing exhibitions are presented, with linked talks. The grounds include a maze, formal gardens, putting, a woodland walk and a large play area for children. Café. Other seasons: Easter to the end of October (daily during August, but closed on Fridays in other months) 10.30am–4.30pm. November to Easter, Thursdays, 10.30am–5pm; weekends, 10.30am–4pm.
✆ 01745 584060 **www.bodelwyddan-castle.co.uk**
(Plas Rhianfa, on the Menai Strait between Menai Bridge and Beaumaris, was built in the 1850s for the owner of Bodelwyddan, Sir John Hay Williams.)

GreenWood Forest Park / *Gelli Gyffwrdd*, off B4366 on the mainland close to the Britannia Bridge, sign-posted between Bangor and Caernarfon. People-powered roller coaster and the longest sledge-slide in Wales. Jungle boats, maze, den building, rainforest boardwalk and 'Treetop Towers'. Café and snackbars. Mid-March to the end of October, daily.
24-hour information line: ✆ 01248 670076.
✆ 01248 671493 **www.greenwoodforestpark.co.uk**

Gwynedd Museum & Art Gallery / *Amgueddfa ac Oriel Gwynedd*, Bangor, between the library and bus station). Includes exhibits from Anglesey as well as the mainland. Free. *Wheelchair access only to ground floor shop and gallery.* Tuesday to Friday, 12.30pm–4.30pm;

Saturday 10.30am–4.30pm. Closed on Sundays, Mondays, public holidays and at Christmas.
✆ 01248 353368 **www.gwynedd.gov.uk/museums**

Llanberis Lake Railway, Llanberis. 9 miles from Menai Bridge. The line, following Llyn Padarn's shore, formerly carried slate to Felinheli. A one-hour trip offers fine views of lake and mountains. Café. Easter to October, daily. ✆ 01286 870549 **www.lake-railway.co.uk**

Segontium Fort & Roman Museum, Caernarfon, 7½ miles from Menai Bridge. Find out about the Romans who invaded Anglesey (the island they called 'Mona') in the informative exhibition at the entrance to the excavated fort, then wander around its remaining walls. This was the main Roman base in north Wales, an auxiliary to the legionary fortress of Deva (Chester). The site is unlocked between 9.30am–4.30pm. The museum opens 12.30–4.30pm (closed Mondays except bank holidays, and reduced opening in the winter). ✆ 01286 675625 **www.cadw.wales.gov.uk**

Snowdon Mountain Railway / *Rheilffordd yr Wyddfa*, Llanberis. 9 miles from Menai Bridge. Steam or diesel rack-and-pinion locomotives haul carriages to the highest point in Wales and England. Especially worthwhile in clear weather. Cafés at base and summit. Operates daily, weather permitting, from mid-March to October. (In March and October trains do not reach the summit). The round trip, with a half hour stay at the summit, takes 2½ hours. Closed in winter.
✆ 0870 458 0033 **www.snowdonrailway.co.uk**

Weish Highland Railway / *Rheilffordd Eryri* *(Caernarfon section)*. Runs from April to the end of October. The track presently extends from Caernarfon to Rhyd Ddu. By 2009 it will reach Porthmadog, to link to Blaenau Ffestiniog along the Ffestiniog Railway.
✆ 01286 677018 ✆ 01766 516000 **www.festrail.co.uk**

Welsh Slate Museum / *Amgueddfa Lechi Cymru* Padarn Country Park, Llanberis, 9 miles from Menai Bridge. Branch of National Museums & Galleries. Dressing sheds and foundry of the former Dinorwig quarry, workplace for many Anglesey men. Immense working waterwheel. Easter to October, daily 10am–5pm. November to Easter (closed Saturday) 10am–4pm. ✆ 01286 870630 **www.museumwales.ac.uk**

FURTHER AFIELD

Centre for Alternative Technology / *Canolfan y Dechnoleg Amgen* on the A487 north of Machynlleth in mid-Wales. Founded in 1973, one of the world's leading eco-centres, exploring new ideas to find practical solutions to environmental problems. The Visitor Centre has seven acres of interactive displays, a well-stocked bookshop and a vegetarian restaurant. Courses. Open all year (except Christmas and mid-January). ✆ 01654 705950 **www.cat.org.uk**

National Museum & Gallery of Wales, Cardiff / *Amgueddfa ac Oriel Cenedlaethol Cymru*. If you are in South Wales, do visit. Many of Anglesey's antiquities are here, including the Llyn Cerrig Bach treasure hoard and the stone carving from Bryn Celli Ddu. All year (but closed on Mondays except bank holidays) 10am–5pm.
✆ 029 2039 7951 **www.museumwales.ac.uk**

St Fagans National History Museum, near Cardiff. *Sain Ffagan: Amgueddfa Werin Cymru ger Caerdydd.* A 5-hour drive from Anglesey, but if you are in the south visit this excellent site. It offers a comprehensive survey of Welsh rural life in the past, from costume to architecture to farm equipment. Daily 10am–5pm, closed 24th–26th December and New Year's Day
✆ 0292 057 3500 **www.museumwales.ac.uk**

History

Anglesey Antiquarian Society & Field Club
Cymdeithas Hynafiaethwyr a Naturiaethwyr Môn.
Publishes an annual journal (*Transactions / Trafodion*)
on topics of Anglesey history, and a series of books.
Regular programme of lectures and field excursions.
Further information: Siôn Caffell ✆ 01248 600083
(home) ✆ 01248 752116 (work)
www.hanesmon.btinternet.co.uk

Talwrn Archaeology Group / *Grŵp Archaeoleg
Talwrn* (founded in 1996). Talks, events and excursions
explore topics of the island's archaeology and history.
Meetings from September to Easter (usually Mondays
at 7.30pm) are held at Stone Science on the B5109
between Pentraeth and Talwrn. Visitors to single
sessions are welcomed. Ann Benwell ✆ 01248 712967

Isle of Anglesey County Council / *Cyngor Sir Ynys
Môn*. Various departments keep records, documents
and photographs, manage sites (such as Oriel Ynys
Môn's heritage gallery, Beaumaris Courthouse & Gaol
and the Holyhead Breakwater Park), administer the
county's ten libraries (listed on page 248), and
organise exhibitions, events and educational projects.
✆ 01248 750057 **www**.anglesey.gov.uk
Archives / *Archifdy*, Shire Hall, Llangefni, is the county
record office, with a search room, reference library and
publications for sale. Help with tracing the history of
families and Anglesey houses. ✆ 01248 752080
Monday to Friday: 9am–1pm & 2pm–5pm.

Cadw. The body responsible for historic sites in Wales.
On Anglesey these include Beaumaris Castle as well as
smaller open locations such as Din Lligwy and Bryn
Celli Ddu. *Although Beaumaris Castle is the only Cadw
site on Anglesey that charges admission, if you intend to
visit other sites on the mainland (such as Caernarfon and
Conwy castles) a **Heritage in Wales Pass** may offer
better value than the purchase of individual tickets.*
✆ 01443 336000 **www**.cadw.wales.gov.uk

Amlwch Industrial Heritage Trust. The Trust is a
leading partner in an interpretation project that is
intended to link Amlwch and Parys Mountain as the
'Copper Kingdom'. A small but interesting exhibition,
presently in the *Sail Loft* at the Port, opens daily from
Easter to the end of September. More ambitious visitor
facilities are likely to emerge as the project develops.
✆ 01407 832255 **www**.copperkingdom.co.uk

Prosiect Menai (Community Heritage Trust) has a
particular interest in the two Menai bridges. It is hoped
to establish a exhibition centre at the Prince's Pier on
the Menai Bridge town waterfront. A temporary
exhibition has been on view during the summer in the
old schoolroom of St Mary's Church (opposite the
supermarket) on Ffordd Mona in Menai Bridge.
✆ 01248 715046 **www**.prosiectmenai.co.uk

Gwynedd Archaeological Trust / *Ymddiriedolaeth
Archaeolegol Gwynedd*, Bangor.
Undertakes excavations on Anglesey and the
mainland. ✆ 01248 352535 **www**.heneb.co.uk

Ynys Môn Young Archaeologists' Club is the local
branch of a national group administered by the
Council for British Archaeology. Events are organised
during National Archaeology Week in July.
Pat West ✆ 01248 751289 **www**.britarch.ac.uk/yac

Gwynedd Archives Service / *Gwasanaeth Archifau
Gwynedd*, Victoria Dock, Caernarfon. A section of
Gwynedd County Council. Search room Tuesday to
Friday, 9.30am–12.30pm and 1.30pm–5pm (to 6.25pm
on Wednesdays). ✆ 01286 679095

Gwynedd Family History Society
Cymdeithas Hanes Teleuoedd, Caernarfon.
Genealogical research facilities, regular meetings and
a journal, *Gwynedd Roots / Gwreiddiau Gwynedd*.
✆ 01492 515558 **www**.gwynedd.fsbusiness.co.uk

CAPEL: The Chapels Heritage Society / *Cymdeithas
Treftadaeth y Capeli*. **www**.rcahmw.org.uk/capel

───────────────────────────────

*The following listings suggest some of the places
that are worth visting. Many more sites are included in
the Gazetter sections of this guidebook.*

Prehistoric sites

Barclodiad y Gawres (SH329707), Cable Bay.
Important Neolithic burial chambers beneath a
'restored' mound on a beautiful rocky headland.
Unusual decorated stones.
Key to chambers from *The Wayside Stores*, Llanfaelog
✆ 01407 810153 (daily 7am–7pm)

Bodowyr (SH463682) near Brynsiencyn. Neolithic
burial chamber. Three uprights and capstone; once
covered by a stone cairn. c3000BC. Open site.

Bryn Celli Ddu (SH507702), Llanddaniel-fab.
Impressive Neolithic remains. Site of a henge
(c2500BC) replaced by a passage grave. Remarkable
decorated stone (a replica is on view, the original
having been taken to the National Museum of Wales
in Cardiff). Mound partially restored. Open site.

Castell Bryn Gwyn (SH465670), Brynsiencyn. Circular
earthwork, possibly a former henge. Occupied in the
Stone Age, Bronze Age and Iron Age. Open site.

Din Dryfol (SH395724) near Soar.
Neolithic chambered tomb with a massive portal
stone. Open site.

Lligwy burial chamber (SH501860), Lligwy.
Its capstone, one of the heaviest in the British Isles, is
supported by three short uprights. c3500–2000BC.
Open site.

Presaddfed (SH347809) near Bodedern. The site of
two adjacent Neolithic burial chambers, as yet
unexcavated. Pre-3500BC. Open site.

Trefignath (SH259805), Holyhead. An impressive
jumble of stones, the remains of three ancient burial
chambers (adjacent to the Anglesey Aluminium site).
Dates from c37450–2250BC. Open site.

Tŷ Newydd (SH344738) near Rhosneigr.
Neolithic burial chamber, pre-3500BC. Open site.

Ancient Celts and Romans

Caer Gybi Roman fortress, Holyhead.
Original Roman walls partially surround the Parish
Church at the centre of town. The site was a Roman
naval base at the end of the third century. Open site.

Caer Lêb (SH473674) near Brynsiencyn.
Banks and ditches reveal the outline of a 1,700 year-
old farmstead. Open site.

Caer y Twr (SH218830), Holyhead Mountain.
Extensive hillfort on summit; also the site of a Roman
watchtower. Open site.

Din Lligwy (SH497861), Lligwy.
A Celtic farmstead during the Roman occupation of
Anglesey. Impressive remains of huts and outer walls,
with views over Lligwy Bay. Not to be missed.
Open site. (*A reconstruction of a small Iron Age
settlement is being developed on land next to Llynnon
windmill, Llanddeusant.*)

Din Sylwy (SH586814), Bwrdd Arthur, near Llanddona. Hillfort of ancient Celts, occupied from c300BC onwards, through the Roman occupation. Lonely plateau looking out to sea. Open site.

***

ON THE MAINLAND

Great Orme Mines at Llandudno offers an underground tour into the only Bronze Age copper mine accessible to the public. Surface attractions include the smelting site and an audio-visual introduction. Open from March to October.
✆ 01492 870447 **www**.greatormemines.info

Segontium Fort & Roman Museum, Caernarfon. 7 miles from Menai Bridge. Site on a Roman road (A4085) near the town centre. A fortress of Rome's northwest frontier, controlling Anglesey AD80-395. Tidy foundations on clipped turf brought to life by a museum. All year, but closed Mondays except bank holidays. ✆ 01443 336000 **www**.cadw.wales.gov.uk

Saints and holy places

Church Island / Ynys Tysilio (SH552716), Menai Bridge. The seventh-century religious foundation of Saint Tysilio, reached by a causeway. Open site.

Llanbadrig Church (SH375946), Llanbadrig. This medieval church (keys available as posted by gate) marks one of earliest Christian sites in Wales, traditionally associated with Saint Patrick (cAD385-461). Sparkling stained glass.

Llanddwyn Island (SH387627). Beautiful rocky promontory associated with Saint Dwynwen, the fifth-century patron saint of Welsh lovers. Open site.

Penmon Priory / Priordy Penmon (SH630807). Medieval buildings endowed by the princes of Gwynedd 1120-70. The adjoining church, still in use, is of great interest (though with difficult access for less mobile people, up stone steps). Ancient stone crosses. Fee for car parking. Open site; church open until dusk.
Ffynnon Seiriol: Saint Seiriol's holy well. Foundations of a stone hut (cAD540) next to the well. Open site.

Also visit parish churches at Llangadwaladr, Llaneilian and Holyhead, and Bangor Cathedral.

Princes and castles

Llys Rhosyr (SH419653), Newborough, next to the parish church on the road to Llanddwyn. *Walk from a car park close to the village crossroads.* The foundations of a court of the Welsh princes before the English king Edward I invaded Wales at the end of the thirteenth century. Open access. A display at the Prichard Jones Institute near the village centre is open most days of the summer: check at the library in the Institute:
✆ 01248 440770 **www**.angleseyheritage.com

Beaumaris Castle / Castell Biwmares. Moated castle of the English invasion, begun in 1295 by Edward I and said by many to be the finest of his Welsh castles – certainly the most impressive medieval building on Anglesey. Remarkably sophisticated walls-within-walls design, state of the art for the late thirteenth century. A World Heritage Site. Summer events have included medieval displays and open-air theatre. Daily (closed 24, 25, 26 December and 1 January). ✆ 01248 810361 **www**.cadw.wales.gov.uk

Church of St Mary and St Nicholas, Beaumaris. Thirteenth-century, partly rebuilt 1500. Coffin of *Siwan* (Joan), the wife of Llywelyn Fawr and daughter of King John of England.

ON THE MAINLAND

Caernarfon Castle / Castell Caernarfon on the mainland 7 miles from Menai Bridge. One of Europe's great castles, begun by Edward I in 1283 and designed to impress as well as suppress. Exhibitions, summer events. The castle and walled town is a World Heritage Site. Open daily all year, except 24/25/26 December and 1 January. *(The museum of the Royal Welch Fusiliers is housed in one of the castle's towers.)*
✆ 01286 677617 **www**.cadw.wales.gov.uk

Conwy Castle / Castell Conwy on the mainland, 17 miles from Menai Bridge. Another castle of Edward I's invasion, built between 1283 and 1287. Fine views from the walls and turrets over the Conwy estuary and to the mountains. The castle and walled town is a World Heritage Site. Exhibitions, summer events. Open daily all year, except 24/25/26 December and 1 January. ✆ 01492 592358 **www**.cadw.wales.gov.uk

Dolbadarn Castle / Castell Dolbadarn. Between lakes Padarn and Peris, on the mainland at Llanberis, 9 miles from Menai Bridge. Picturesquely set ruined castle of Welsh princes, its circular tower built by Llywelyn ab Iorwerth in about 1225. Open site from 10am–4pm. ✆ 01443 336000 **www**.cadw.wales.gov.uk

Dolwyddelan Castle / Castell Dolwyddelan The remains of a medieval castle built by Llywelyn ab Iorwerth in the thirteenth century. The castle keep contains an exhibition about the castles of the Welsh princes. ✆ 01443 336000 **www**.cadw.wales.gov.uk

Aberconwy House, Conwy. 17 miles from Menai Bridge. A fifteenth-century town house in the care of the National Trust. Daily (except Tuesdays) mid-March to October, 11am–5pm. Last admission 4.30pm. ✆ 01492 592246 **www**.nationaltrust.org.uk

Squires and scholars

Beaumaris Courthouse / Llys Biwmares. The local authority offers audio guides to the assize court of 1614, later refurbished in Victorian times. Wheelchair access to most areas. Daily, Easter to the end of September : 10.30am–5pm. ✆ 01248 811691 ✆ 01248 724444 **www**.anglesey.gov.uk

Llynnon Mill / Melin Llynnon (SH341853), near Llanddeusant. See Lloyd Jones, the miller, at work and buy his stoneground flour. An adjoining building has a small display about the history of milling, a tea room and the Anglesey Craftworkers' Guild shop. Daily, Easter to September, 11am–5pm. ✆ 01407 730797 ✆ 01248 724444 *A group of reconstructed Iron Age circular huts is being built on adjoining land. From the mill, a three-mile walking trail takes you to **Melin Howell**, a privately owned watermill.*

Ye Olde Bull's Head Inn, Beaumaris. An old posting inn, rebuilt in 1617 and retaining its atmosphere. Billeted by Parliamentary forces during the Civil War. Courtyard. Record-breaking yard doors. *A hotel and public house with a brasserie and restaurant.*

Parys Mountain Copper Mines, Amlwch. During the eighteenth century these were the most productive copper mines in the world. A platform gives views to the chasm of the 'Great Opencast'. See precipitation pits, visit one of the oldest Cornish enginehouses in Britain and learn about Thomas Williams the Copper King, a leading figure of the Industrial Revolution. A signposted walking tour (leaflets from the car park dispenser: SH438906) guides visitors to main points of interest. A conservation and interpretation project is

presently linking Amlwch and Parys Mountain as the
'Copper Kingdom'. Amlwch Industrial Heritage Trust:
✆ 01407 832255 www.copperkingdom.co.uk
(Underground Group: www.parysmountain.co.uk)

Penmon Dovecote / Colomendy Penmon
(SH630807). A stone building designed to house a
thousand pigeon nests, built for Sir Richard Bulkeley
c1600. Unlocked during the daytime in summer.

The Tudor Rose in Beaumaris is a fifteenth-century
building that was restored during the 1940s and '50s
by Hendrik Lek. A carved Tudor rose was discovered on
one of the barrel-braced beams in the Hall at the back
of the building and this, together with the Anglesey
associations of the Tudor monarchs, gave the building
its name. The front of the half timbered building can
be viewed from Castle Street.

_____

ON THE MAINLAND

Plas Mawr, Conwy. 17 miles from Menai Bridge.
Built 1577-80 for a powerful local squire, Robert
Wynne. Elizabethan town house with fine plasterwork.
Easter to October, Tuesday to Saturday from 9.30am.
(Closed on Mondays except bank holidays).
✆ 01492 580167 www.cadw.wales.gov.uk

The nineteenth century

Anglesey Column / Colofn Môn, Llanfair Pwllgwyngyll
A 112ft (34m) memorial to the first Marquess of
Anglesey erected in 1816-17 after Waterloo; its statue
dates from 1860. 115 steps lead to a viewing platform
high above the Menai Strait. Open every day from
9am. Refreshments, toilet. ✆ 01248 714393

Beaumaris Gaol / Carchar Biwmares, Bunkers Hill.
The harsh reality of Victorian Britain is revealed in this
remarkable penal institution (1829), complete with a
treadwheel for prisoners. Dramatic reconstructions are
sometimes staged. Wheelchair access is limited.
Easter to end of September, daily 10.30am–5pm or by
appointment. ✆ 01248 724444
✆ 01248 810921   www.angleseyheritage.co.uk

Britannia Bridge / Pont Britannia. William Fairbairn's
and Robert Stephenson's engineering masterpiece
first opened to rail traffic in 1850. (Its adaptation to a
road and rail bridge after the 1970 fire spoiled the
lines of the original). *Information about the North
Wales coast railway from www.page27.co.uk/nwales*

**Holyhead Breakwater Country Park / Parc Gwledig
Morglawdd Caergybi** (SH225832). The park opened in
1990 on the site of the quarry which supplied stone
for Britain's longest breakwater, constructed 1846-73.
Information centre. Open all year. ✆ 01407 760530
✆ 01248 752428 www.angleseyheritage.org
*A North Wales Wildlife Trust kiosk in the Park, supplying
refreshments and items for sale, opens most afternoons
(weather permitting) from Easter to the end of October.*
The Holyhead 'land train' (an articulated road vehicle),
operated by the Holyhead Breakwater Railway
Company, carries passengers between the Maritime
Museum on Newry Beach and the Breakwater Country
Park, with other trips along the length of the breakwater to its lighthouse. (The train has one wheelchair
lift.) Its operating season has been Easter to the end of
the summer, running subject to demand.
✆ 01407 760357 www.holyheadbreakwater.com

Lighthouses of Anglesey / Goleudai Môn
Anglesey has several fine Victorian lighthouses.
South Stack lighthouse offers public access (though
restricted to visitors of at least one metre tall).
Others have no public access but are well worth viewing:

Llanddwyn (footpath access to two disused beacons)
Penmon (view from Black Point)
Point Lynas (view from Porth Eilian)
Skerries (view from Carmel Head)
www.lighthouse-visits.co.uk

Menai Suspension Bridge / Pont Grog Menai
The world's first large iron suspension bridge, built to a
design by Thomas Telford. Opened in 1826. Make sure
you leave or enter the island at least once by this
route, and stop off to view it from the waterfront.

Plas Newydd, Llanedwen, near Llanfair Pwllgwyngyll.
The seat of the Marquesses of Anglesey, on the Menai
Strait, now owned by National Trust. Rebuilt in the late
eighteenth and early nineteenth centuries. Paintings, a
museum of the Napoleonic wars, family mementoes.
Extensive gardens. Boat trips on the Menai Strait.
Easter to the end of October: Saturday to Wednesday,
and Good Friday, (house noon–5pm, gardens
11am–5.30pm, shop and tea room 10.30am–5pm).
The shop and tea room also open on Saturdays and
Sundays from November to December 11am–4pm.
Recorded information ✆ 01248 715272
Property office ✆ 01248 714795
www.nationaltrust.org.uk

Swtan (SH301891), Church Bay / Porth Swtan
A traditional Anglesey thatched cottage, restored and
furnished to its appearance around the year 1900.
Easter to September: Friday, Saturday, Sunday and
bank holidays: noon–4.30pm. ✆ 01407 730501

_____

ON THE MAINLAND

Bangor Pier at Garth, Bangor. A restored Victorian pier
offering views of Anglesey across the Menai Strait.
Open daily until dusk. *Closed Christmas Day, Boxing
Day and New Year's Day.* ✆ 01248 352421

Penrhyn Castle / Castell Penrhyn. Llandygái near
Bangor, 4 miles from Menai Bridge. A mansion built
c1820-45 in the supposed style of a Norman castle.
Home of the Pennant family, then owners of Penrhyn
Quarry and breakers of a long, bitter quarrymen's
strike at the turn of century. A National Trust property,
including exhibitions of dolls and locomotives.
Easter to the end of October: daily (except Tuesdays),
noon–5pm (last admissions 4.30pm); gardens and
tearoom 11am– 5pm. During July and August the
gardens open at 10am, the castle at 11am. ✆ 01248
371337 www.nationaltrust.org.uk

Tracing ancestors

www.homecomingwales.com

_____

Anglesey Archives / Archifdy Môn, Shire Hall,
Llangefni. Access to census records for Anglesey,
parish records, old maps. Monday to Friday 9am–1pm
and 2pm–5pm. ✆ 01248 752083 ✆ 01248 752080.

Gwynedd Archives Service / Archifdy Gwynedd
Victoria Dock, Caernarfon. These archives hold local
information, national census information and registers
of births, marriages and deaths. Tuesday-Friday
9.30am–12.30pm; 1.30pm–5pm (until 6.25pm on
Wednesdays). ✆ 01286 679095

**Gwynedd Family History Society / Cymdeithas
Hanes Teleuoedd Gwynedd,** Canolfan yr Aelwyd,
Church Street, Caernarfon LL55 1SW.
Membership provides research facilities, regular
meetings and a journal, *Gwynedd Roots / Gwreiddiau
Gwynedd*. Local groups in Anglesey, Bangor,
Caernarfon, Dolgellau, Llandudno and Pwllheli.
✆ 01492 515558 www.gwyneddfhs.org

Memorial plaques

The following eminent people – *Enwogion o Fri* – are amongst those commemorated by memorials on the island.

Hywel ab Owain Gwynedd (c1120-70), prince of Gwynedd and poet, killed in battle at Pentraeth. *At the bridge over Afon Nodwydd, Red Wharf Bay*. See page 93.

Llywelyn ab Iorwerth (c1173-1240), 'Llywelyn the Great', prince of Gwynedd. *The memorial is a slate sculpture at Llys Llewelyn, Aberffraw by the sculptor, calligrapher and author from the Llŷn, Jonah Jones (1919-2004)*. See page 197.

Gruffudd ab yr Ynad Goch (fl.1280), poet. *By the war memorial at the Talwrn crossroads* See page 96.

Siôn Dafydd Rhys (1534-1620), humanist and grammarian. *Griffith Reade Coffee House, Llanfaethlu*. See page 161.

Robert ap Huw (c1580-1665), harpist and compiler of manuscripts. *Melin Llynnon / Llynnon Mill, Llanddeusant*. See page 217.

Lewes ('Lewis') Roberts (1596-1641), merchant and author of 'The Merchants Mappe of Commerce', 1638. *In the arched entrance of the Town Hall, Beaumaris*. See page 40.

William Jones (c1675-1749), mathematician and Vice-President of the Royal Society. Two memorials, each bearing the 'π' symbol, one at *Ysgol Tŷ Mawr (Capel Coch)*, the other at *Ysgol Gymuned Llanfechell*. See page 84.

William Bulkeley (1691-1760), diarist. *The parish churchyard by the Square, Llanfechell*. See page 122.

Morrisiaid Môn / The Morris Brothers
The lives of these four brothers are described on page 114. *A monument (SH478873) overlooks the Traeth Dulas estuary*, near the *Pilot Boat Inn* on the A5025 just northwest of Brynrefail.

✦ **Lewis Morris** 1701-65
✦ **Richard Morris** 1703-79
✦ **William Morris** 1705-63
✦ **John Morris** 1706-40

Richard Evans (1772-1851), bonesetter, third son of Evan Thomas of Llanfair-yng-Nghornwy. *Cilmaenan, Llanfaethlu*. See page 108.

Thomas Williams (1737-1802) developer of the Parys Mountain copper mines. *The Old School, Llansadwrn*. See page 124.

William Williams of Trefdraeth and Llandygái (1738-1817), antiquary, author and a reformer of slate quarry administration. *Ysgol Bodorgan*. See page 199.

Christmas Evans (1766-1838), Baptist minister and hymnist, the greatest preacher of his day. *Capel Cildwrn, Llangefni*. See page 182.

Owen Williams (1774-1859), musician. *Ysgol Llannerch-y-medd*

Robert Roberts (1778-1836), almanacist and printer. *Holyhead Public Library*

John Jones (1816-98), astronomer. *Brynsiencyn*. See page 201.

Lewis William Lewis, 'Llew Llwyfo' (1831-1901), poet and journalist. *Village Hall, Pen-y-sarn*. See page 126.

Samuel Jonathan Griffith, 'Morswyn' (1850-93), hymnist. *Porthdafarch beach*. See page 169.

John Owen Jones, 'ap Ffarmwr' (1861-99), campaigner for the Agricultural Union in Anglesey *Ysgol Dwyran*. See page 204.

Edward Greenly (1861-1951), author of 'The Geology of Anglesey', 1919. *The plaque is mounted on a glacial erratic block west of Porth Eilian*. See page 119.

Sir John Morris-Jones (1864-1929), Welsh scholar and poet. *Tŷ Coch, Llanfair Pwllgwyngyll*. See page 65.

Thomas Jesse Jones (1873-1950), sociologist and educator. *Pont yr Arw Chapel, Llanfachraith*. See page 161.

William David Owen (1874-1925), author of 'Madam Wen'. *Ysgol Bryngwran*. See page 140.

William Ellis Williams (1881-1962), mathematician and engineer. *Picnic Area, Llanddona Beach*. See page 111.

Sir Ifor Williams (1881-1965), linguist. *Wenllys, Porthaethwy / Menai Bridge*

Ifor Thomas (1892-1956), opera singer and photographer. *The Square, Pentraeth*

William Bradwen Jones (1892-1970), music teacher, accompanist, organist, composer and conductor. *Plaque at the base of the modern Celtic cross in Market Square, Holyhead*

W Mitford Davies (1895-1966), illustrator, cartoonist and artist. *Memorial Hall, Llanfair Pwllgwyngyll.*

Ifan Gruffydd (1896-1971), lay-preacher, playwright and author of autobiographical tales of life in his home district, Paradwys. *Llangristiolus*. See page 185.

Richard Huws (1902-80), cartoonist, sculptor, designer and engineer. *Bryn Chwilog, Talwrn*

John Tudor Jones, 'John Eilian' (1904-85), journalist and poet. *Penlan, Pen-y-sarn, on the B5025*. See page 118.

Tom Parri Jones (1905-80), poet and author of short stories of Anglesey life. *'Malltraeth', Bodorgan*.

Richard 'Dic' Evans (1905-2001), lifeboat coxswain. *Statue outside Seawatch/Gwylfan, Moelfre* (This memorial commemorates the gallantry of *all* lifeboat crews – but it is in the image of Dic Evans who twice won the Gold Medal of the RNLI). See page 81.

Rowland Jones, 'Rolant o Fôn' (1909-62), poet. *Llangefni*. See page 180.

John Roberts (1910-84), hymnist. *Ysgol Ffrwd Win, Llanfaethlu*. See page 162.

Hugh Griffith (1912-80), Oscar-winning actor (for his supporting role in *Ben-Hur*). *Hen Ysgol, Marian-glas*. See page 97.

R S Thomas (1913-2000), poet and Church in Wales clergyman. *Holyhead High School*. See page 152.

William Charles Williams, 'Charles Penffordd' (1915-90), entertainer. *Ysgol Bodffordd*. See page 176.

Bedwyr Lewis Jones (1933-92), linguist. *Ysgol Pen-y-sarn*. See page 101.

Dennis Wood (1934-2001), geologist. *Coastguard lookout, Rhoscolyn Head*. See page 165.

All those recognised by the local authority's advisory panel so far have been men.

Do readers have proposals for any women? Elen Roger Jones? Anglesey's women harpists? Princess Siwan? … *Your suggestions to the County Council !*

Nature

Anglesey has many areas that are officially
protected (there are scores of SSSIs for example).
*A number of organisations are concerned with the
conservation and management of Anglesey's
ecology and its nature reserves …*

COUNTRYSIDE COUNCIL FOR WALES
CYNGOR CEFN GWLAD
**CCW is the government body responsible for the
National Nature Reserves and Sites of Special
Scientific Interest (SSSIs) in Wales.** Some important
reserves on Anglesey are under its management.
Area office ℂ 01248 672500
Enquiry line ℂ 0845 130 6229 **www**.ccw.gov.uk

✦ **Newborough Warren** / *Tywyn Niwbwrch*, a
magnificent 1500-acre (607ha) National Nature
Reserve with dunes, beach, saltmarsh and a rocky
island in southwest corner of Anglesey. Good for
walkers, with numerous footpaths. Bird hide, car park;
spectacular views. Open site.

✦ **Cors Bodeilio** (SH507773), near Pentraeth. Fenland,
accessed by footpath and boardwalk.

✦ **Cors Erddreiniog** (SH477805), Benllech. This is a
sensitive site, the habitat of rare plants such as orchids.
Visitors should keep to the paths and boardwalks. Two
small car parks, along a track with a cattle grid, give
access. Warden: ℂ 01248 853427 ℂ 0774 8180551

NORTH WALES WILDLIFE TRUST
YMDDIRIEDOLAETH NATUR GOGLEDD CYMRU
**The NWWT manages some important nature
reserves on Anglesey such as Cemlyn and Cors
Goch.** Those interested in natural history should
consider membership.

The Trust's Bangor office is soon to be relocated.
Until then its telephone number is ℂ 01248 351541.
The North East Wales office – ℂ *01352 810469 – can
also provide up to date information, as can the website
(which also offers useful pdf downloads of site guides).*
www.wildlifetrust.org.uk/northwales

✦ **Cors Goch** (park at SH505817). Large calcareous
fenland reserve near Llanbedr-goch. Information
boards. Open access. Walk onwards to the Craig Wen
acid heath reserve, habitat of the marsh gentian.

✦ **Cemlyn** (SH337932). A pebble bar with some
specialised maritime plants on Anglesey's north coast
protects a brackish lagoon, with an important tern
colony in summer; ducks and waders in winter. Open
access, but avoid the bar in the nesting season from
April to July.

✦ **Caeau Pen y Clip**, Menai Bridge (SH555728).
A half mile from the town centre at the end of Penlon.
Wet grassland with good hedgerows.

✦ **Mariandyrys** (SH603811). Former quarry site at
Glanrafon, Llangoed; open site. A limestone outcrop
with herb-rich grassland, heathland and scrub – an
ideal habitat for butterflies, moths and snails.

✦ **Porth Diana** (SH256781), Ravenspoint Road, south
of Trearddur Bay. Coastal heathland, with dry heath
and damp grassland. A habitat of Anglesey's emblem,
the Spotted Rock Rose.

✦ Access to the limestone woodland of **Coed
Porthamel** (SH508678) is restricted to visitors with
permits; enquire at the NWWT office ℂ 01248 351541.

FORESTRY COMMISSION WALES
COMISIWN COEDWIGAETH
**The Welsh Assembly Government's Department
of Forestry.** Welsh headquarters ℂ 0845 604 0845
Regional office ℂ 01492 640578
www.forestry.gov.uk/wales

✦ **Newborough Forest** / *Coedwig Niwbwrch* is a
large coniferous forest bordering the dunes, created in
1948. Two waymarked nature trails and many paths
with numbered posts to aid orientation. The northern
section of the forest includes Llyn Parc Mawr, a lake
with birdwatching hides, and picnic areas. Proposals to
clear part of the forest – in order to restore the natural
ecology of the dunes – are under consideration.

✦ **Pentraeth Forest** / *Coedwig Pentraeth*
Conifer plantations cover the ridge of Mynydd Llywyd-
iarth. This has been the site of efforts to re-establish
the red squirrel. There is a small lake, Llyn Llwydiarth.
Access is on foot through the gate off the Beaumaris
road to the east of the village (SH534784), but this is
not a site for which public facilities are provided, and
sections of the forest and its tracks are in private
ownership. Opportunities to park cars are limited.

THE NATIONAL TRUST WALES
YR YMDDIRIEDOLAETH GENEDLAETHOL CYMRU
**As well as owning the house and estate of *Plas
Newydd*, the Trust protects and maintains several
stretches of the Anglesey coastline.**
The National Trust Wales, Trinity Sqare, Llandudno.
ℂ 01492 860123 **www**.nationaltrust.org.uk

The Trust's Anglesey property includes land at

✦ **Cemlyn**: the Cemlyn Reserve is owned by the Trust
and managed by the North Wales Wildlife Trust.
✦ **Swtan**: the thatched cottage of Swtan is owned by
the Trust and managed by The Friends of Swtan.
✦ **Llanbadrig**   ✦ **Pen y Graig**
✦ **Porthdafarch**   ✦ **Cemaes**
✦ **Carreg-lwyd**   ✦ **Bryn Offa**
✦ **Mynachdy**   ✦ **Fedw Fawr**
✦ **Clegir Mawr**   ✦ **Cae Glan y Môr**

ROYAL SOCIETY FOR THE PROTECTION OF BIRDS
*The RSPB establishes and manages reserves,
protects rare species and encourages public
interest in ornithology.*
North Wales Regional Office ℂ 01248 363800
www.rspb.org.uk/reserves/wales

✦ **South Stack Cliffs** / *Ynys Lawd*
and **Ellin's Tower RSPB Information Centre**
An RSPB reserve – open at all times – with vertiginous
cliffs above the South Stack lighthouse. More than
4,000 seabirds breed here each year. See guillemots,
razorbills, puffins, fulmars in breeding season; choughs
and ravens. Ellin's Tower visitor centre (daily Easter to
September) houses RSPB staff, exhibitions, viewing
windows with telescopes. Watch live television
pictures of the breeding seabirds at Ellins Tower and
also at the lighthouse (which is not RSPB
owned). Reserve office ℂ 01407 764973

✦ **Valley Wetlands**, an RSPB nature reserve
(SH311769), open at all times, two miles south of
Caergeiliog, including the reed-fringed lakes around
RAF Valley. This is one of the best places in Wales to see
wildfowl all year round. Tufted ducks, pochards,
shovelers, gadwalls and grebes all breed here, their
numbers swelled in the winter with the arrival of
wigeons and goldeneyes. (Wear waterproof boots in
the winter.) In spring and early summer, reed and
sedge warblers populate the reedbeds: water rails,

marsh harriers and Cetti's warblers may also be seen. Two mile nature trail.   Reserve office ✆ 01407 764973

✦ **Malltraeth Marshes** have a number of footpaths open to the public. They link with the Newborough to Llangefni cycle track. The RSPB is presently improving the nature reserve's public facilities. The marshes can be approached from many directions; there is a small car park (SH464725). The RSPB reserve's office is nearby, at Tai'r Gors. (SH464726)   ✆ 01248 421100 (The wildlife artist Charles Tunnicliffe spent his working life at 'Shorelands' on the Malltraeth estuary).

✦ **Boat trips** as part of the *Aren't Welsh Birds Brilliant!* scheme, are organised by the RSPB. On two or three days in previous summers, several trips have been run from Beaumaris around Puffin Island, accompanied by volunteers giving bird and wildlife commentaries. For information, RSPB Office: ✆ 01248 363800

Birdline Wales ✆ 0906 870 0248 (not part of the RSPB) provides information about unusual birds in the region – such as the Sooty Tern at Cemlyn, and the Green Heron at Red Wharf Bay, both spotted in 2005. Other visitors in recent years have included a Siberian Black Lark and Terek Sandpiper, and a Greenland Falcon. *Rare sightings should be reported to ✆ 01492 544588.* Some of of the less 'exotic' species to be seen on the island may nevertheless be endangered. For example, *Yellowhammers* are birds under threat – 'red' on the conservation list. They can be seen on farmland in the northeast corner of the island, from Parys mountain to Mynydd Bodafon, Amlwch to Benllech.

OTHER CONSERVATION BODIES

BTCV Cymru – **Conservation Volunteers** undertake practical fieldwork on Anglesey such as conserving dunes and repairing walls. Their work also includes small-scale environmental projects (for example, improvements to a small wetland area at Lôn Goch park, Amlwch). Contact the Bangor office of the BTCV: ✆ 01248 354050 **www.btcvcymru.org**

Marine Awareness North Wales is a group of Bangor-based volunteers with an interest in marine conservation. They undertake beach cleaning tasks at Aberffraw and elsewhere, arrange talks and other events, and have conducted porpoise surveys from vantage points such as Point Lynas. For more information: info@saveourseas.co.uk – or through the Wildlife Trust: ✆ 01248 351541 **www.wildlifetrust.org.uk/northwales**

Friends of the Anglesey Red Squirrel Efforts have been made in recent years – with some success – to eradicate the island's grey squirrels, and thereby stimulate repopulation by red squirrels. **www.redsquirrels.info**

LOCAL NATURE RESERVES LNRs are places for people and wildlife, enabling community access along with nature conservation.

Managed by the County Council's Countryside Service ✆ 01248 752428 **www.angleseyheritage.org**

✦ **Nant y Pandy** / *The Dingle*, Llangefni. A wooded river valley with boardwalks allowing wheelchair access. Car parks. Sculptures, footbridges, benches and picnic tables. The waters of a dammed pool run over a weir with fish ladders. Dippers and kingfishers along the river, treecreepers and woodpeckers in the woodland, bats and dragonflies. A carpet of bluebells and wood anemones in the spring. *Fungus Forays* have taken place here in the autumn.   ✆ 01248 752428

Managed by Menter Môn in association with local community and town councils. A series of leaflets describe the routes of public access and what to look out for at each reserve: ✆ 01248 725700 **www.mentermon.com** *The Ordnance Survey map references provided locate car parking sites that give the most convenient access.*

✦ **Llanddona Common**: a series of mixed, open areas connected by paths and roads. The common is being managed to restore the heathland habitat. *and* **Llaniestyn Common**: lowland heath with uncommon species such as pale heath violet and lesser butterfly orchid. *These two LNRs can be reached from SH576797 – by the village bus stop in Llanddona .*

✦ **Llangoed Common**. A ribbon of woodland, scrub and damp meadow, with a footpath extending from the car park (SH611796) along Afon Lleiniog.

✦ **Wylfa Head** near Cemaes (car park at SH356938). Grass/heathland under conservation management. *(A nature trail, managed by the operators of the nuclear power station, leads from the Wylfa visitor centre:* ✆01407 711400)

✦ **Coed Cyrnol** (SH554719, the Ffordd Mona car park), Menai Bridge. The woodland above the island church of St Tysilio includes Scots pines, oak and other diverse species. Woodland birds include nuthatch, coal tit, tree creeper and tawny owl; wading birds along the shore may include little egret, a recent arrival in the area. *In addition to Coed Cyrnol, Coed Marquis (between the library and Ffordd Mona) and Coed yr Orsedd (close to the suspension bridge at the start of the Belgian promenade) are both part of this 18-acre (7.5ha) reserve.*

✦ **Cytir Mawr**, Llandegfan. 16 acres (6.5ha) of common land – birch woodland and heathland – off the road to Beaumaris from *Hen Bentref Llandegfan /* Llandegfan old village. Take the path into the woods following the footpath sign (SH578750) immediately after the 'Llyn y Gors' entrance.

Other wildlife sites

Other places on the island that are not designated reserves can offer equal interest to those who appreciate the natural world. Amongst such places, the following two areas offer good public facilities.

✦ **Penrhos Coastal Park**, near Holyhead. *The park is owned by Anglesey Aluminium.* Woodland bordering mudflats with waders and waterfowl. A network of signposted walks. Picnic areas, public conveniences.   ✆ 01407 762634. *(The area southwest of the Stanley Embankment remains a bird reserve, with restricted access. For a permit:* ✆ 01407 762634*).* *The Toll House Tearooms* at the entrance to the Coastal Park are housed in one of Thomas Telford's octagonal tollhouses. Open all year – every day of the summer, and Monday to Friday (and bank holiday weekends) during the winter.   ✆ 01407 760247

✦ **Llyn Alaw**, near Llantrisant. A small visitor centre (SH373855) at the south-western end of Anglesey's largest body of fresh water – a reservoir newly created in 1966 – gives access to two lakeside footpaths. (These do not completely circle the lake.) Two bird hides (with posters to identify ducks, geese and other birds) are available for public use. Bring binoculars! The abundance of smaller birds also attracts raptors. Four nature trails can be followed. Pond. Picnic garden.   ✆ 01407 730762

Many of Anglesey's smaller lakes, and the Llyn Cefni reservoir, are also good birdwatching sites.

Outdoors

Beaches

When using Anglesey's beaches, warnings or signals should be carefully observed.
Be aware of the dangers that may be present.
✦ Do not swim where currents are dangerous or tides are fierce.
✦ Beware of becoming cut off by incoming tides.
✦ Do not attempt to climb cliffs unless you are an experienced rock-climber, properly equipped and on a recognised site.
✦ Beware of using inflatables and small craft off beaches; they can easily be swept out to sea.
✦ If you see small craft in distress, telephone 999 or 112 and ask for the Coastguards.
✦ Do not disturb beaches where birds are nesting; keep vehicles and motorbikes off the beach.

BEACH AWARDS

European Blue Flags have been awarded annually since 1987 to beaches that satisfy the strictest environmental criteria and have the highest standards of public access and facilities. Anglesey beaches flying the coveted flag in recent years include:

✦ **Benllech**   ✦ **Llanddwyn**
✦ **Traeth Mawr**, Cemaes   ✦ **Porth Dafarch**
✦ **Llanddona**   ✦ **Trearddur Bay**

In recent years other beaches have also been graded, winning *Seaside Awards* and *Green Coast Awards*:

✦ **Beaumaris**   ✦ **Borth Wen**, Rhoscolyn
✦ **Broad Beach** / *Traeth Llydan*, Rhosneigr
✦ **Cable Bay** / *Porth Trecastell*
✦ **Cemlyn**   ✦ **Llanfaethlu**
✦ **Moelfre**   ✦ **Penmon**
✦ **Porth Eilian**, Llaneilian ✦ **Porth Nobla**, Llanfaelog
✦ **Porth Trwyn**, Llanfaethlu
✦ **Porth Ty'n Tywyn**, Llanfaelog
✦ **Red Wharf Bay** / *Traeth Coch*
✦ **Church Bay** / *Porth Swtan*
✦ **Saint David's**, Red Wharf Bay – Benllech
✦ **Sandy Beach** / *Porth Tywyn Mawr*, Llanfwrog
✦ **Silver Bay**, Rhoscolyn   ✦ **Traeth Bach**, Cemaes
✦ **Traeth Crigyll**, Rhosneigr
✦ **Traeth Lligwy**, Dulas   ✦ **Traeth Mawr**, Aberffraw

Beach Wardens have been stationed in recent years at Llanddona, Benllech, Traeth Bychan, Cemaes, Trearddur, Porth Dafarch, Rhoscolyn, Rhosneigr and Newborough. A roving patrol covers some other beaches.

DOGS ON BEACHES. Between 1st May and 30th September dogs are excluded from designated areas at a number of Anglesey's beaches. Porth Dafarch, north of Trearddur Bay, a small beach, is presently the only beach with a complete dog ban. Dogs must be kept on their leads on the promenades of Benllech, Cemaes Bay and Trearddur Bay.

Anglesey has a long and varied coastline, with many secret places.
The following is a selection of popular beaches.

Aberffraw. Sandy estuary, fine views. Public conveniences at Llys Llewelyn in village. Beach 1½ miles walk across dunes or along the bank of the Cefni from a car park.

Benllech. A beach for family holidays, in popular resort: sand. Beach shop, cafés. Public conveniences at beach car park and village square.

Cable Bay. Pleasant sandy cove with rockpools and walks to headland. Swimming, canoeing, surfing. Car park.

Cemaes Bay. Sandy beach, with other coves nearby. Bathing, walking, cafés. Public conveniences at beach car park and in the High Street.

Church Bay. Attractive sandy beach between low rocks and cliffs. Bathing, car park, café. Public conveniences.

Holyhead, Newry Beach. Shingle, protected by giant breakwater. Sailing, boating, fishing. Car park, public conveniences.

Llanddona Beach. Eastern end of Red Wharf Bay. Steep lane down. Shallow sea; bathing and paddling; long, fast tide. Walking, beachcombing. Sands backed by green hills stretch all the way across to the *Ship Inn*; walkers beware of being cut off by tidal channels. Parking; beach café/shop. Public conveniences .

Ty'n Tywyn, Llanfaelog

Lligwy Beach / *Traeth Lligwy*. Sandy beach, swimming, walking. Car park, beach shop.

Moelfre. Attractive shingle cove forms harbour for small village. Sailing, fishing, boating, picnics, walks. Cafés in village. Public conveniences at car park.

Llanddwyn, Newborough. Long, sandy beaches with views across to the Llŷn Peninsula, backed by dunes and forest. Swimming. Canoeing. Car park, public conveniences.

Porth Dafarch. Public conveniences. No dogs.

Porth Cwyfan. Shingle and sand, offshore island with old church.

Porth Eilian. Attractive shingle beach sheltered by cliffs and headland. Bathing, walking. Car park.

Porth Nobla. Sandy beach, swimming. Car park.

Porth Tywyn Mawr. Sandy beach, dunes. Bathing.

Red Wharf Bay. Five miles of shining sands. Fast tide (goes out almost to horizon), shallow water. Boating, cafés. At the northwest end of the bay is a car park, *The Ship Inn*, a restaurant and public conveniences. Access also (to a muddier section) from Pentraeth.

Rhoscolyn. Public conveniences

Rhosneigr. Sandy beach for resort, backed by dunes. Windsurfing, kite-surfing and wave surfing. Water-skiing. Nearby cafés. Car parks, public conveniences at library car park.

Traeth Bychan. Sand and shingle backed by rocks; swimming near shore; boating, walking. Car park, public conveniences, beach shop.

Trearddur Bay. Series of sandy inlets amongst rocks; beach has protected bathing area marked by yellow buoys. Outside this, windsurfing, canoeing, waterskiing etc. Cafés, car parks, public conveniences.

Trwyn Du, Penmon. White pebble beach by lighthouse, backed by open country. Fishing, walking, beachcombing. Strong currents, no bathing. Parking, café in summer.

Boat trips

BEAUMARIS PIER

✦*MV Island Princess*. Pleasure trips during summer to Puffin Island *(Ynys Seiriol)* and along the Menai Strait, with commentaries. Evening cruises.
✆ 01248 810251   Pier kiosk ✆ 01248 810379
www.starida.co.uk

✦*MV Cerismar*. Puffin Island cruises and fishing trips.
✆ 01248 810746 ✆ 07860 811988
www.puffin-island.co.uk

CEMAES PIER
✦MV Stingray.The Skerries and coastal excursions.
© 01407 710510 www.seafishingtrips.co.uk

PLAS NEWYDD PIER, near Llanfair Pwllgwyngyll.
Historic Cruises. Boat trips along the Menai Strait
from the pier, weather/tide permitting, between Easter
and the end of October during normal opening hours
of Plas Newydd, the National Trust property. For sailing
information on the day, contact the reception desk
after 11am © 01248 715218. Recorded
information © 01248 715272 www.plascruises.co.uk

RIB TRIPS – *Rigid Inflatable Boats*
✦From Moelfre: Ynys Ribs Moelfre. Trips aboard
Seaeagle to explore Anglesey's east coast and its bird
life. Ask at the kiosk on Moelfre's seafront.
© 07891 507992 www.ynysribs.fsnet.co.uk
✦From Trearddur Bay: SBS Rib Charter. Available for
trips and dives. (Also RYA powerboat training).
© 01407 740083 www.angleseydivecharter.co.uk
**✦From Caernarfon: Menai Rib Ventures / Menter
Rib Menai**. Trips along the coast of Anglesey and the
Strait, from Victoria Dock, Caernarfon.
© 01286 674540 © 07914 040001 www.ribride.co.uk

Gardens & gardening

Up-to-date information about gardens open to the
public are available from Tourist Information
Centres, libraries and the Holland Arms Garden
Centre at Pentre Berw.

Plas Newydd Gardens. These National Trust grounds
near Llanfair Pwllgwyngyll set aside a 'Scheme Day'
early in the season to benefit charities. Plas Newydd's
extensive gardens can also be visited from April to the
end of October (closed Thursdays and Fridays),
between 11am and 5.30pm. The 5-acre *Rhododendron
Garden* is reached along a wooded walk following the
bank of the Menai Strait. (It closes in early June.) The
Australasian Arboretum displays southern hemisphere
trees. The *West Indies Garden* is the principal shrub
garden. There are woodland walks and a marine walk
along the Menai Strait. Children can use a play area
with climbing frames near the car park, and an
adventure trail in the woods.
Recorded information © 01248 715272. (Property
office © 01248 714795) www.nationaltrust.org.uk

The National Gardens Scheme administers the
occasional public opening of private gardens. These
gardens are listed in an annual 'Yellow Book' – available
from some bookshops and from NGS headquarters:
© 01483 211535 www.ngs.org.uk (Secretary of the
North Gwynedd branch– © 01286 831195).
A regional extract from the *Yellow Book* which includes
Anglesey's NGS gardens is distributed at some
libraries. In 2006, nine Anglesey locations were listed
(but not all will necessarily participate in subsequent
years). New gardens join the scheme each year. Apart
from Plas Newydd, most open for only one or two days
a year. Some welcome private visits by appointment.
✦ Cae Newydd, Rhosgoch © 01407 831354
✦ Glanrafon Isaf, Pen-y-sarn © 01407 831642
✦ Gwydryn Bach, Llanedwen © 01248 430244
✦ Plas Llanidan, near Brynsiencyn © 07759 305085
*(During Plas Llanidan's open days, the adjoining
Llanidan Old Church can also be viewed).*
✦ Rhyd, Trefor © 01407 720320
✦ Tan Dinas, Llanfair Pwllgwygyll © 01248 714373
✦ Treffos, Llansadwrn *(no private visits)*
✦ Ty Cae Isaf, Llangefan *(no private visits)*

Cestyll Garden (SH345933), overlooking Porth y Felin
between Cemaes and Cemlyn. This rock garden is

usually opened to the public on the late Spring and
August bank holidays. At other times it is occasionally
opened by arrangement. As there is no car parking at
Cestyll, on open days buses run from the Wylfa Visitor
Centre to the gardens, where there are stalls and
refreshments. From 1922 until the early 1950s the Hon.
Violet Vivian (a maid of honour to Queen Alexandra)
developed the valley of Afon Cafnan with informal
plantings of shrubs, lush waterside plants and
ornamental trees. Later a conifer windbreak was
created. There are many azaleas and rhododendrons.
Miss Vivian died in 1962, and the derelict house was
demolished in 1991, but her custom of opening the
garden to the public was revived in the 1980s by the
new owners, the operators of the nuclear power
station. The grounds include a water mill (c1840),
owned by the National Trust. © 01407 711400

Carreg-lwyd (SH309878), Llanfaethlu. A walled
garden, wooded gardens and a lawn with specimen
trees in the seventeenth-century mansion's grounds.
Footpaths offer circular woodland and lakeside walks.
Open for 25 days every May, 1pm–5pm. © 01407
730208 © 0770 864 5000. Carreg-lwyd's website gives
up-to-date information: www.carreglwyd.co.uk

A National Plant Collection, the only such collection
on Anglesey, of *Rhapis* palms (a Japanese miniature
palm) is maintained by the artist Keith Andrew. His
collection can be viewed, by appointment, at **Gwyndy
Bach**, **Landrygarn** © 01248 470903 © 01407 720651
www.kannonchiku.co.uk – this website links to the
*National Collections site, administered by the National
Council for the Conservation of Plants & Gardens.*
Other National Collections nearby are those of
Polygonatum, Paris and *Corriaria* at **Crûg Farm
Gardens / Gerddi Fferm Crûg**, on the mainland
between Y Felinheli and Caernarfon.
© 01248 670232 www.crug-farm.co.uk

ON THE MAINLAND

Treborth Botanic Garden. A university site at the
mainland end of the Menai Suspension Bridge.
Programme of events. Plant sales three times a year.
© 01248 353398 www.treborthbotanicgarden.org

Bodnant Garden in the Conwy Valley, 27 miles from
Menai Bridge. Signposted off the A470 (in the
direction of Llanrwst from junction 19 of the A55).
80-acres of magnificent National Trust gardens,
amongst Britain's finest. Rhododendrons, camellias,
magnolias, azaleas, laburnum arch. Mid-March to early
November, daily 10am–5pm. Licensed tearoom.
© 01492 650460 www.bodnant-garden.co.uk

Penrhyn Castle Gardens, Llandygái, near Bangor,
4 miles from Menai Bridge. A National Trust property
with large gardens, walled garden with ponds,
wetlands, and woodland play area for children. Daily
(except Tuesdays), April to October. Gardens and
tearoom from 11am; during July and August from
10am. © 01248 371337 www.nationaltrust.org.uk

**Portmeirion Village & Gardens / Pentref a Gerddi
Portmeirion**. South of Porthmadog 30 miles from
Menai Bridge. An Italianate village created from 1926
by the architect Clough Williams-Ellis in a spectacular
coastal location between Porthmadog and Penrhyndeudraeth. Woodlands with rare and exotic plants,
sandy beaches, and gardens between the houses.
Some paths have steep steps. (The grounds are a
designated Conservation Area: dogs are not
permitted.) Shops, cafés and restaurants.
9.30am–5.30pm, every day except Christmas Day.
Shops closed 25, 26 December and 1 January.
© 01766 772311 www.portmeirion-village.com

GARDEN CENTRES & NURSERIES

✦ **Holland Arms Garden Centre**, Pentre-berw between junctions 6 and 7 of the A55. Events include a bulb festival in mid-August, and a Christmastime theme from the autumn. Café. Open daily all year. The Centre's programme is published in print and on its website. ✆ 01248 421655 **www**.hollandarms.co.uk
✦ **Cae Gwyn Herb Nursery**, Carmel, Llannerch-y-medd. Culinary and medicinal herbs.
✆ 01407 470231 **www**.herbsfromwales.co.uk
✦ **Mary's Acre**, Garreg Lwyd, Dwyran. Perennials and alpines. Bedding plants from May. ✆ 01248 430536
✦ **Penrhos Garden Centre**, Bryn Refail, Dulas
✆ 01248 410843
✦ **Pentraeth Nurseries**, with café. ✆ 01248 450269
✦ **Plas Newydd Nursery** & **Menai Water Gardens** (not National Trust) in the walled garden of the old home farm next to Plas Newydd. ✆ 01248 716386

Medwyn's of Anglesey. A talent for growing prize-winning vegetables gained Medwyn Williams ten gold medals for displays at the Chelsea Flower Show. The website for his island seeds business includes growing advice. **www**.medwynsofanglesey.co.uk

Sport & recreation

For many visitors, Anglesey is synonymous with **outdoor pursuits**: wind, wave and kite surfing, kayaking, waterskiing, sub-aqua and even sand-yachting are all popular. There are stables for pony-trekking and horse-riding, crown greens for bowls, and several golf-courses. Fine summer days bring people to the beaches, many of which are perfect for bathing. On the mainland, Snowdonia offers canoeing, climbing, mountain walking, and dry-slope skiing.

Leisure centres

✦ **Amlwch** ✆ 01407 830060
Sports hall, squash courts, fitness room, swimming pool, outdoor tennis courts, café.

✦ **Canolfan Beaumaris** ✆ 01248 811200
Sports hall, fitness rooms, exhibition gallery, full theatre facilities with evening events. Arts and dance classes as well as sports.

✦ **Holyhead** ✆ 01407 764111. Swimming pools, sports hall, fitness room, squash courts, and café.

✦ **Llangefni** Plas Arthur Leisure Centre ✆ 01248 722966. Swimming pools, sports hall, squash courts, fitness room, climbing wall and café. Outside is an all-weather football pitch and a skate park.

✦**The Play House**, presently on B5109 at Parc Cefni near Llangefni, though with plans to relocate, soon, to Gaerwen. (Until the move, the telephone number is ✆ 01248 751444). Activities for children up to 12 years old. Daily 10am–6pm. Slides, rope swings, mirror maze, climbing, ball pool. Toddler mornings and children's parties. Café. **www**.theplayhouseparccefni.co.uk

ON THE MAINLAND

✦ **BANGOR**. **Maes Glas Sports Centre**, off Ffriddoedd Road ✆ 01248 382571. No swimming pool, but a full range of other facilities in a modern centre, including four squash courts, tennis and a climbing wall.
✦ **CAERNARFON**. 7½ miles from Menai Bridge.
Two separate buildings on the same site –
The Leisure Centre ✆ 01286 676451 has a swimming pool, sports hall, squash courts, fitness room and café.
The Tennis Centre ✆ 01286 676945 has eight indoor and outdoor tennis courts, an outdoor practice wall, fitness room and café.

Indoor swimming pools

✦ **AMLWCH Leisure Centre**
✆ 01407 830060 ✆ 01407 830232
✦ **HOLYHEAD Leisure Centre** ✆ 01407 764111
✦ **LLANGEFNI, Plas Arthur Leisure Centre**
✆ 01248 722966

ON THE MAINLAND
✦ **Bangor Swimming Pool**, Garth Road
2½ miles from Menai Bridge. ✆ 01248 370600
✦ **Plas Menai**, near Y Felinheli, 5 miles from Menai Bridge. ✆ 01248 670964 **www**.plasmenai.co.uk
✦ **Arfon Leisure Centre**, Caernarfon
7½ miles from Menai Bridge. ✆ 01286 676451

Outdoor pursuits courses

See also the entry for Plas Menai **under 'watersports'.**

✦ **Anglesey Adventures**, Porthdafarch Road, Holyhead. Adventure days, mountaineering and climbing courses. ✆ 01407 761777 ✆ 07906 006360
www.angleseyadventures.co.uk

✦ **Rock & Sea Adventures**, Llanallgo, near Moelfre. A variety of pursuits, including a two-day sea-kayak voyage around the coast of Anglesey, mountaineering and rock climbing, all with qualified instructors.
✆ 01248 410877 **www**.rockandseadventures.co.uk

✦ **Plas y Brenin**, at Capel Curig on the mainland, 20 miles from Menai Bridge.
A UK National Centre for Mountain Activities. Day taster courses, canoeing, climbing. Dry ski-slope.
✆ 01690 720214 **www**.pyb.co.uk

Walking

Anglesey has a vast network of coastal and inland footpaths. In recent years many have been restored and clearly signposted.

A network of paths now rings much of the coast, a 125-mile long-distance route around the Heritage Coast. Most of the walking is easy. Set aside twelve days for the circular walk right around Anglesey – or choose one of the path's sections for a walk of just an hour or two. The official start/finish point is St Cybi's Church, Holyhead.

When you are in the countryside, observe the country code, control dogs and do not disturb crops or livestock. An extension to the rights of countryside access came into force in 2005. On Anglesey, a further 3,700 acres (1,500ha) have been designated, including land around Newborough Forest, Holyhead Mountain, Bwrdd Arthur (at Llanddona), and Tywyn Trewan Common (near Rhosneigr). Cultivated farmland and gardens, and sensitive conservation areas, are excluded from the 'right to roam'. Detailed information about access, with ideas for routes, together with maps, weather information and links to other useful sites, is provided by the Countryside Council for Wales: **www**.ccw.gov.uk/countrysideaccesswales **www**.countrysideaccess.gov.uk

BODIES CONCERNED WITH PATHS AND WALKING

Isle of Anglesey County Council Rights of Way Unit
✆ 01248 752300 **www**.anglesey. gov.uk

The Anglesey Coastal Path Project, a section of the Rights of Way Unit, can provide general advice about walking the coastal path © 01248 752300. The Project publishes a series of durable guide sheets, dividing the coastal path into a dozen sections and containing route descriptions and maps.
A folder of guides can be purchased from the tourist information Centres, or can be downloaded from:
www.angleseycoastalpath.com
Tourist Information Centres can also supply coastal path accommodation lists and bus timetables.
Friends of the Coastal Path / Cyfeillion Llwybr Arfordirol. An independent group with a programme of guided walks and talks.
c/o Menter Môn © 01248 725700

Ramblers' Association / Y Cerddwyr
The Ynys Môn Group (within the Ramblers' North Wales Area), organises walks of all grades. Programme booklets may be available from libraries or from the Welsh HQ of the Association © 02920 644308.
The Ynys Môn Group also organises 'Stepping Stones' walks. These take less than half a day, and are relatively easy. The Group also publishes detailed routes for a number of Anglesey walks, such as the long distance *Two Lighthouses Walk* across the island from Penmon to Holyhead, which is described in a pamphlet compiled by a local member.
© 01248 722764 www.ramblers.org.uk

Anglesey Step Out / Camu Allan organises short walks as part of the national *Walking the Way to Health* programme. A series of graded walks of varying lengths in the countryside around Amlwch, Benllech, Gaerwen, Llangefni, Llangoed, Holyhead and other districts, are led by volunteers and take place in all weathers. © 01248 723247 © 01248 752034

Two groups extend a welcome to visitors to the island. For information about their occasional walks:
Cefni Walking Club, *Llangefni* (Ted Thomas © 01248 422362) and **Gaerwen Community Walking & Leisure Society** (Meirion Thomas © 01248 421200)

WALKING GUIDEBOOKS & LEAFLETS

A great number of walking guides to Anglesey are available. They can be purchased over the counter (or sent to you by post) from the Tourist Information Centres. Some may also be available from newsagents and tourist shops. Tourist Information Centres can supply bus timetables to assist in the planning of walks that are not circular.

Route descriptions and maps for the Anglesey Coastal Path (including high and low tide alternatives) are also stocked by the Tourist Information Centres and can be downloaded from: www.angleseycoastalpath.com
This website also lists other walking guides to the island, such as the bilingual *Isle of Anglesey Coastal Path*, by Carl Rogers (Mara Books, 2005). The route description is divided into twelve day-walk chapters.

The Church in Wales (Bangor Diocese) publishes a pack of illustrated information cards: *A Guide to Churches on or near the Isle of Anglesey Coastal Path*. It is available from Tourist Information Centres.

CIRCULAR WALKS: The Saints' Walks
Eight signposted circular walks on Anglesey are named after Celtic saints. Leaflets are available from the Tourist Information Centres.
✦ **HOLY ISLAND:** *Cybi* –2 or 6 hours
✦ **AMLWCH:** *Elaeth* –2hrs / *Eilian* –1hr
✦ **LLYN ALAW:** *Ceidio* –5¹⁄₂hrs / *Sannan* –4¹⁄₂hrs
✦ **MOELFRE:** *Cadog* –3¹⁄₂hrs / *Gallgo* –2 hrs

✦ **PENTRAETH:** *Dona* –5hrs / *Cawrdaf* –1hrs / and *Iestyn* –3hrs / *Seiriol* –3hrs
✦ **BRYNSIENCYN:** *Nidan* – 3hrs
✦ **ABERFFRAW:** *Beuno* –1hr / *Cwyfan* – 2¹⁄₂hrs

Many other leaflets and booklets – often free – describe footpaths and 'heritage' trails through Anglesey's towns, villages and countryside. They include maps and illustrations, and often include historical information. *Some become out of print, and new leaflets replace them: the Tourist Information Centres can provide up-to-date details.*
✦ **AMLWCH**
Mountain Walk: The Copper Trail. Dispensers at the mountain car park (SH438906) provide a leaflet giving a description of a self-guided tour of the mountain. (for tours underground, enquire about the visits organised by the Parys Underground Group, in which the old workings of the mine are accessed via a series of stone steps leading from the nineteenth-century 'Parys Footway'. www.parysmountain.co.uk)
Port Walk. A leaflet describes a self-guided port tour.
Enquire about the 'Copper Kingdom Heritage Walks' that are scheduled during the summer
Information about them from the Amlwch Industrial Heritage Trust in the *Sail Loft* at the Port.
© 01407 832255 www.copperkingdom.co.uk.
A professional guide service also offers tours of the Copper Kingdom, all year. © 01248 470655
✦ **BEAUMARIS**
A pull-out guide to the town, describing a half-hour walking tour taking in its main sights, is included in the book *Beaumaris: the town's story*, on sale in Beaumaris at the Bull's Head, Beaumaris Newscentre and at Henllys Hall (or £10, including postage, details from © 01248 810833 or magmawales@hotmail.com).
The walking guide pamphlet is also available from the Beaumaris Newscentre .
✦ **CEMAES & CEMLYN**
The essential guide to Cemaes contains a number of descriptions and sketchmaps of walks in the locality. The booklet is available from the Cemaes Heritage Centre. © 01407 710004
Two National Trust booklets, *Walks on Anglesey*, provide information for walkers around Cemlyn and Cemaes. They include Ordnance Survey mapping, and are on sale at shops along the north coast, or from the National Trust's North Wales headquarters.
© 01492 860123 www.nationaltrust.org.uk
✦ **GAERWEN**
Four trails around the centre of Anglesey include part of a drovers' way, the quarrymens' way and a path past a windmill. The 'Heritage Trails & Footpaths' leaflet is available from Tourist Information Centres. A car park at Pentre Berw (SH464725) affords signposted access to the Malltraeth marshes and beyond.
To join the *Gaerwen Community Walking Society* on their excursions: Meirion Thomas © 01248 421200
✦ **HOLYHEAD**
A leaflet (and a website download) describes the town's Heritage Trail. The principal sites of interest and a series of informative display panels are on its route.
www.holyheadtowncouncil.com
✦ **MOELFRE**
A series of themed walks are organised from **Seawatch / Gwylfan** throughout the summer holidays. They have included *Charles Dickens & the Royal Charter, Moelfre's Wild Coast* and *Seven Splendid Beaches*. The Seawatch Centre publishes a programme leaflet. © 01248 410277 © 01248 724444

✦ NEWBOROUGH FOREST
A Forestry Commission Wales / *Menter Coedwigaeth* leaflet outlines two signposted walks in the forest behind Llanddwyn Bay and Newborough Warren Beach. *The Blue Trail*, is an easy walk in the woodlands. *The Hendai Trail* passes over the reputed site of the medieval village of Rhosyr, which lies buried under the sand: there are remains of old cottages along the way.
✆ 0845 604 0845 www.forestry.gov.uk/wales

Cycling

The island provides ideal terrain for touring. There are many peaceful lanes with little motor traffic.

The National Cycle Network links Anglesey to mainland Wales. *Two routes, 5 and 8, lead across the island from Menai Bridge to Holyhead.*
Information from ✆ 0845 1130065 (weekdays).
To view interactive maps of the Anglesey routes:
www.nationalcyclenetwork.org.uk
Maps and guides can be ordered on-line from:
www.sustransshop.co.uk

Four signposted bicycle tours, mostly on country lanes, have been established on the island to link with the National Cycle Network routes. Full routes may be available to download from the internet: enter the names of the routes, **nico giach hebog telor**, in your search engine. *(The names are of birds: Welsh for goldfinch, snipe, falcon and warbler.)*
1. NICO. The north-west of the island from Llyn Alaw visitor centre (SH373855 ✆ 01407 730762). *Generally easy.* Main tour, including Llynnon & Howell mills, 20 miles; short tour circling Llyn Alaw, 12 miles.
2. GIACH. The south-west of the island fromLlys Llewelyn visitor centre Aberffraw (SH355691). *Easy.* Main tour, extending to Llangristiolus, 18 miles; short tour in the vicinity of Aberffraw, 11 miles.
3. HEBOG. The east of the island from Benllech. Includes Lligwy and Bodafon Mountain. *Relatively easy, but with some short, steep sections.* Main tour, extending to the Cefni reservoir, 22 miles; short tour, 12 miles.
4. TELOR. The eastern point of the island from Beaumaris. Elevated views of sea and mountains. *Mostly easy. Some short, steep sections and one long uphill climb (but not steep) from Llan-faes to Llanddona.*
Two routes: 13 miles or, including Penmon, 17 miles.

A 15-mile cycleway and footpath, **LÔN LAS CEFNI** links Llangefni and the Newborough forest. Additional trackway is being developed to extend this route, from Nant y Pandy in Llangefni to the Cefni Reservoir.

Within a five-acre section of the Newborough Forest is a mountain biking track: the *Coed Mawr Dirt Track*.

Many cyclists (and walkers) hope that the track of the disused Anglesey Central Railway, from Gaerwen to Amlwch, may one day be adapted as a pathway. Railway enthusiasts have other ideas!

Annual bicycle ride, on the first Sunday in July, from Plas Arthur Leisure Centre in Llangefni. Three signed and marshalled routes: 14 miles, 26 miles and 50 miles. *An event organised by the Rotary Clubs of Holyhead and Llangefni to raise funds for charity.* ✆ 01407 840907

✦ Cefni Bike Club / *Clwb Beicio Cefni*, Llangefni.
For all ages and abilities and new members – together with visitors to the island – are welcome. Saturday rides from Capel Cildwrn. Routes are both long and short, either on the island or further afield. Rides are also advertised in the *Chronicle* newspaper. Hywel Meredydd ✆ 01248 750323

✦ Holyhead Cycling Club
✆ 01407 860010 www.holyheadcc.8m.com
✦ Clwb Rasio Mona. A cycling club for all abilities and interests, not only speed cycling. ✆ 01248 715490
✦ Energy Cycles
A Llanberis-based club, with excursions to the island. ✆ 07733 121585 www.energycycles.com

BICYCLE HIRE

✦ Beics Menai, 1 Slate Quay, Caernarfon. Cycle the Anglesey lanes, or alternatively, cycle from Caernarfon along *Lôn Eifion*, a 12½ mile cycle path running south to Bryncir or east to Y Felinheli. ✆ 01286 676804 ✆ 07770 951007 www.beicsmenai.co.uk
(Bicycles may also be hired from the Beics Menai sites in Anglesey, such as Llys Llewelyn, Aberffraw ✆ 01407 840940, and Canolfan Iorwerth Rowlands, Beaumaris ✆ 01248 811508. *In case of difficulty at these locations, please contact the Caernarfon office; bicycles can be delivered from there to your location on Anglesey.*)
✦ Lian Cycle Hire, Gwynfa, Llannerch-y-medd. Hire of bicycles and repairs. Enquire about the delivery and collection of bicycles. ✆ 01248 470336
✦ Snowdonia Surf & Mountain
75 High Street, Bangor. ✆ 01248 354321

Bowls

CROWN GREEN BOWLING
✦ Beaumaris ✆ 01248 810084.
✦ Benllech ✆ 01248 852389.
✦ Holyhead, Stanley Park ✆ 01407 764621 *and* Clwb Peibio, Môr Awelon (where there is also an indoor green) ✆ 07742 759089.
✦ Llanfair Pwllgwyngyll ✆ 01248 714364.
✦ Llangefni ✆ 01248 723313.
✦ Llannerch-y-medd (artificial crown green), ✆ 01248 722087 after 6pm.
✦ Menai Bridge Bowls Club ✆ 01248 714867.

Other Anglesey bowling locations with artificial greens are **Rhosneigr** and **Trearddur Bay**.

Competitive leagues include Anglesey & Bangor, Gwynedd Senior Citizens, North Wales Coast, Welsh Counties and Inter-County bowls leagues.

Cricket

Four Anglesey teams play in the **North Wales League**. *Menai Bridge* was promoted to the Premier Division at the end of the 2005 season: their well-equipped Tyn-y-caeau field on a spectacular site overlooking Snowdonia is reached along a lane immediately to the left of the entrance to David Hughes School.
Teams from **Amlwch**, **Anglesey Aluminium** and **Bodedern** play in lower North Wales League divisions. Other island teams, and juniors, play in a series of minor leagues. *Check the local press for fixture details.* (Amongst the more informal matches played is the August bank holiday Sunday match at Rhoscolyn, in which holidaymakers take on a team of locals.)

Fishing

Anglesey's many lakes offer fishing in season, and there is onshore and offshore sea fishing.

SEA FISHING
Be aware of the Sea Angling Code
Abiding by it will help to preserve the coastal ecosystem. Boats can be chartered from Amlwch, Beaumaris, Cemaes and Holyhead.
Tuition in sea fishing from the island's shores is given

by a company based in Bodedern. ✆ 01407 740030
✆ 07738 635372 **www**.fishing4u.co.uk

FRESHWATER FISHING
The season, in general, runs from March to the end of
October. Rod licences are compulsory. They can be
bought at a post office. Some lakes that offer club
fishing or syndicate fishing also issue day tickets: the
Tourist Information Centres will provide the details.
(Also see: **www**.environment-agency.gov.uk/fish
and the fishing section at: **www**.visitwales.com)

✦ **Llyn Alaw**, Llantrisant. Permits from a machine in
the car park (SH373855); licences from one of the lake
rangers. Rainbow and brown trout. Motor boat hire.
Bird hides, nature trails and picnics. ✆ 01407 730762

✦ **Cwm Reservoir**, Llaingoch, Holyhead
Carp, bream, perch, roach, tench ✆ 01407 765479
✦ **Llyn Edna**, Parc Newydd, Llannerch-y-medd. Fly-
fishing. ✆ 01248 470838 **www**.angleseyfishing.co.uk
✦ **Llyn Bryntirion**, Dwyran. Carp and perch.
✆ 01248 430232
✦ **Llyn Cefni**, north of Llangefni. Fly-fishing for rainbow
& brown trout. ✆ 01248 421238 **www**.llyncefni.co.uk
✦ **Llyn Coron**, Llanfaelog, Aberffraw. Brown trout and
sea trout. ✆ 01407 810801
✦ **Llyn y Gors**, Llandegfan. Coarse-fishing.
✆ 01248 713410 **www**.llynygors.co.uk
✦ **Llyn Llwydiarth**, Llannerch-y-medd. Coarse and
game-fishing, fly-fishing all year. ✆ 01248 470540
✦ **Tyddyn Sargent**, Benllech. Carp, rudd, roach, bream,
perch. ✆ 01248 853024 **www**.lakehouseholidays.com
✦ **Tŷ Hen**, Rhosneigr. Carp and tench.
✆ 01407 810331 **www**.tyhen.com

Flying

✦ **Mona Flying Club** / *Clwb Hedfan Mona*
Operates during weekends from Mona Aerodrome
(which is used during the week by RAF Valley).
Full training and trial flights.
✆ 01407 720581 during evenings and weekends,
or ✆ 07778 268510 **www**.flymona.com

✦ **Caernarfon Airworld**, Dinas Dinlle. On the
mainland, 6 miles south of Caernarfon off the A499.
(This was the wartime Air Observers' School where, in
1943, the RAF Mountain Rescue Service was officially
recognised.) Aviation museum, March to October
daily. Café. Pleasure flights – for example a 25 minute
flight over Caernarfon and Beaumaris castles. Pilot
training and trial lessons. Facilities for visiting pilots.
✆ 01286 830800 **www**.air-world.co.uk

The Mountain Paragliding Centre
Snowdon Gliders, Llandygái, Bangor ✆ 01248 600330
www.snowdongliders.co.uk

Golf

For general information about golfing on Anglesey:
www.golfanglesey.com **www**.islandofchoice.com

The *Island Golf Pass* (✆ 01248 752434) offers one
round at each of Anglesey's four 18-hole golf courses,
and gives discount at the five 9-hole courses.

BEAUMARIS
✦ **Baron Hill Golf Club**. 9-hole heathland course
overlooking Snowdonia. ✆ 01248 810231
www.baronhill.co.uk
✦ **Henllys Golf Course**, Llan-faes, near Beaumaris.
18-hole parkland course. ✆ 01248 811717

BRYNTEG, near Benllech
✦ **Storws Wen**. 9-hole (with a second set of tees)

✆ 01248 852673 **www**.storwswengolfclub.co.uk

BULL BAY, near Amlwch
✦ **Bull Bay Golf Club**. 18-hole coastal heathland
course. ✆ 01407 830960 **www**.bullbaygc.co.uk

TREARDDUR BAY
✦ **Holyhead Golf Club**. 18-hole heathland course.
✆ 01407 763279 **www**.holyheadgolfclub.co.uk
✦ **Beach Golf Course**. 9-hole course amongst low
gorse-covered hillocks. ✆ 01407 861935

LLANDDANIEL-FAB
✦ **Penrhyn Golf Complex**. 9-hole, with an all-weather
floodlit driving range. ✆ 01248 421150

LLANGEFNI
✦ **Public Golf Course**. 9-hole ✆ 01248 722193
Môn Mini-masters Golf Competition, for 5 to 12 year-
olds, is held at the Llangefni Golf Course on the first week
of the summer school holidays. To enter ✆ 01248 722193

RHOSNEIGR
✦ **Anglesey Golf Club**. 18 hole links course amongst
dunes and heathland.
✆ 01407 811202 **www**.angleseygolfclub.com

Horse riding

Not all those listed are open throughout the year.

✦ **DWYRAN: Isle of Anglesey Riding Centre**
Tal-y-Foel. Open all year (but closed on Mondays).
✆ 01248 430377 **www**.tal-y-foel.co.uk
✦ **LLANDDONA Riding School**
✆ 01248 810183
✦ **RHOSNEIGR: Ty'n Morfa Riding Centre**
✆ 01407 810072
✦ **TREARDDUR BAY: Porth-y-Post Riding School**
North of Trearddur at Porth y Post. ✆ 01407 861358
✦ **TYNYGONGL: Cromlech Manor Farm**
✆ 01248 853489

Haulfre Stables / *Stablau Haulfre*, Llangoed.
A small equestrian and transport museum in restored
stable buildings, offering a glimpse into the work of
grooms, coachmen and stable boys in Victorian times.
Visitors should make an appointment.
✆ 01248 724444 **www**.angleseyheritage.co.uk

Working Horse Trust, Plas y Gwynt, Llanfaethlu, near
Church Bay / *Porth Swtan*. A centre devoted to raising
awareness about working horses. How to train a horse
to drive, harrow, or pull logs – and the rehabilitation of
rescued horses and finding new homes for them.
Visits by arrangement. ✆ 01407 730067

Motor sports

Anglesey Circuit / *Trac Môn*, between Rhosneigr and
Aberffraw (junction 5 of the A55, then off the A4080).
Car and motor cycle races on a one mile tarmac major
race circuit. Rallycross, Super Moto and Sprint events.
Events are held throughout the year: a fixture list is
available. A *Performance Driving Centre* offers a range
of courses. They include half-day training sessions for
novices, at first under instruction in a saloon car and
afterwards in a single seat racing car. A number of
'Track Days' allow drivers and riders the chance to
improve skills. During office hours: ✆ 01407 840253.
24hr info: ✆ 01407 811100 **www**.angleseycircuit.com

Go-karting. The Cartio Môn track is at Bryn Golau, off
the A5 north of Bryngwran and south of junction 4 of
the A55. Take an individual ride, or organise a group to
compete in a mini grand prix. ✆ 01407 741144

Rock climbing

Rock climbers may practise on the climbing wall at the Plas Arthur Leisure Centre in Llangefni; experienced climbers tackle the cliffs at South Stack or take a short trip southwards to the mountains of Snowdonia.

The cliffs from South to North Stack, known as *Craig Gogarth*, offer some of Europe's best sea cliff climbs. The routes are only suitable for climbers who are competent at grades of VS and above – there is little scope for climbers of limited ability. Good ropework and route-finding are essential. Many of the climbs are affected by the tide and involve access by abseil. The climbing is steep and strenuous on good quality rock in dramatic situations. Routes vary from the classic *A Dream of White Horses* (HVS, 5a), to the infamous *The Bells, the Bells* (E7, 6b).

Rugby

Although soccer is the island's dominant team game, rugby is also played. **Llangefni**, for example, plays in the Welsh Rugby Union League, Division 3 West. The sport's annual events on the island include **Llangoed Rugby Sevens** each June, contested by teams from all over north Wales and some from further afield.

Running & athletics

✦ **Ynys Môn Athletics and Sports Club**, Mill Bank Fields, Holyhead. Thursdays after school, all ages welcome. Sports Development Unit: ✆ 01248 752037
✦ **Menai Track & Field Athletics Club**, at the Treborth athletics track on the mainland, approached from the end of the suspension bridge. All ages are welcome but there is a particular focus on 7 to 13 year-olds. Contact for information of meetings ✆ 01407 840396
✦ **Anglesey Marathon & Fun Day** takes place late September. As well as the full 26.2 mile event, 10km and 5km runs are held on the same day. The marathon starts and finishes at the Anglesey Showground at Mona, passing through the south-west of the island ✆ 01248 725700 **www**.angleseymarathon.com
✦ **Menai Bridge 10km mini-marathon**, from Ysgol David Hughes, is organised by the Anglesey Central Lions ✆ 01407 710766 and takes place on the last Sunday in January. The route to and from Ysbyty Gwynedd on the mainland crosses the suspension bridge – winning times are around 35 minutes for the men, 45 minutes for the women.

Breakwater Country Park at Holyhead has a one-mile running trail, starting and finishing near the warden's office and following footpaths around a rocky coastal section. Signs indicate the distance covered, allowing runners to monitor their progress.

Skateboarding

Skateboard parks with open access at all times:
✦ **Stanley Park, Holyhead**, by the tennis courts.
✦ **Plas Arthur, Llangefni**, outside the Leisure Centre.

Snooker

TREARDDUR BAY. The Beach Snooker Club, Lôn St Ffraid. Ten snooker tables, two pool tables, licensed bar. All year: weekdays from 2pm, weekends from noon. ✆ 01407 860199

Soccer

All towns and most villages have senior and junior football teams. Fixtures are publicised in the local newspapers. Five Anglesey teams – Bodedern, Glantraeth, Holyhead Hotspur, Llanfair Pwyllgwyngyll and Llangefni Town – play in the top regional league, the *Cymru Alliance*. **Llangefni Town Football Club**'s new floodlit ground on the Talwrn road, ✆ 01248 724999, is well equipped and the team has its sights on a place in the Welsh Premier League. Their rivals, **Glantraeth**, have achieved greater success with much more modest facilities. In 2006 they won the 'double': becoming champions of the Cymru Alliance League and winners of the Cup final. In recent years, other Anglesey teams have played in the *Welsh Alliance, Gwynedd League*, and there is an *Anglesey League*. The Holyhead Hotspur youth team, **Peibio**, won the North Wales Coast FA Youth Cup Final in 2006. There are three junior local leagues.

Squash

Amlwch, **Holyhead**, **Llangefni** all have courts. *See under Leisure Centres.*

Tennis

Clubs around the island are struggling to retain their members, to maintain their courts and to protect their premises from vandalism. Many courts have closed.
✦ **Amlwch**   ✆ 01407 830060   ✆ 01407 830232.
✦ **Holyhead**   ✆ 01407 762416

On the mainland:
✦ **Arfon Tennis Centre**, Bethel Road, Caernarfon. Eight indoor and outdoor courts, outdoor practice wall and café.   ✆ 01286 676945

Watersports

Plas Menai, a UK National Watersports Centre, is set on the Menai Strait opposite Anglesey's Llanidan shore, between Y Felinheli and Caernarfon. Its residential and non-residential courses for children and adults are excellent – sailing, windsurfing, kayaking, canoeing, navigation, etc. Taster days are also available in sailing, canoeing, windsurfing and mountain biking. Plas Menai also has an indoor swimming pool. ✆ 01248 670964 **www**.plasmenai.co.uk

Surfing

Surfing conditions in North Wales are posted daily – **www**.westcoastsurf.co.uk – with a regular webcam image of the sea at Hell's Mouth / *Porth Neigwl*, near Abersoch, and a daily report on sea conditions.

The best beaches for surfing on Anglesey are Cable Bay *(Porth Trecastell)* on the west side of the island, and the beaches northwards: Porth Nobla and Rhosneigr's 'Broad Beach' *(Traeth Llydan)*. A Rhosneigr webcam is at **www**.camserv.co.uk/rhos

───────────────────

✦ **Funsport**, Beach Terrace, Rhosneigr. Windsurfing, wakeboarding and kitesurfing tuition from April to October. Sales of equipment and surfwear.   ✆ 01407 810899 **www**.buckys.co.uk

✦ **FKS Kite Surfing School**, run at Rhosneigr by Alex Tritten, a British Kite Surfing Association champion. ✆ 01407 810598   ✆ 0787 633 8952 **www**.fks.me.uk

Diving

✦ **Anglesey Divers**, Church Terrace, Holyhead. This is a five-star PADI Dive Centre, offering certified courses for all levels. Sea snorkelling. Equipment servicing and sales. Powerboat training.
ℂ 01407 764545 www.diveanglesey.co.uk
✦ **Diving Services Anglesey** and **Menai Scuba**, Ravenspoint Road, Trearddur Bay. Air supply, equipment and clothing. Also operates PADI diving courses from Plas Menai, Caernarfon. ℂ 01407 860318
✦ **SBS Rib Charter** (Trearddur Bay).
Also RYA power boat training.
ℂ 01407 740083 www.angleseydivecharter.co.uk

Kayaks

✦ **Sea Kayaking UK**, Porthdafarch Road, Holyhead. Run by Nigel Dennis, the first person to circum-navigate Britain by kayak. Courses at all levels, expedition organisation and the sale of sea kayaks.
ℂ 01407 762425 www.seakayakinguk.com
✦ **Chris Wright**, kayak coach. Guiding, training and assessment. Sea and inland – Anglesey and Snowdonia. ℂ 01248 713763 ℂ 07775 697886

Sailing

Menai Strait Regattas are held during the last week in July and the first week in August. *Week 1* is based at a different venue each day: Bangor, Caernarfon, Y Felinheli, and includes the Beaumaris to Caernarfon race that sails under the bridges. *Week 2* is based at Beaumaris, with the *Round Puffin Island Race* on Tuesday. www.menaistraitregattas.org.uk

MARINAS

✦ **Holyhead marina** lies within the new harbour: work began in 2005 to double its two hundred berth capacity and to build waterfront apartments.
ℂ 01407 764242 www.holyheadmarina.co.uk
✦ **Beaumaris**. Dredging of the Menai Strait for a new marina at Gallows Point near Beaumaris began in 2006 – the first stage of a development that may eventually create more than 400 berths.

Marinas on the mainland include those at
✦ **Y Felinheli** ℂ 01248 671500 (during office hours: Monday to Friday, 9am–5pm) www.portdinorwic.com
✦ **Conwy**
ℂ 01492 593000 www.crestnicholsonmarinas.co.uk
✦ **Pwllheli**
ℂ 01758 701219 www.hafanpwllheli.co.uk

SAILING CLUBS

✦ **Holyhead Sailing Club** / *Clwb Hwylio Caergybi* Newry Beach Road. Easter to the end of October. A private club with a limited number of visitors' moorings. ℂ 01407 762526 ℂ 01407 762496 www.holyheadsailingclub.org.uk
✦ **Red Wharf Bay Sailing Club**, Traeth Bychan. Junior sail training through the summer holidays, Tuesday and Thursday, visitors welcome.
ℂ 01248 853754 (membership ℂ 01248 713188)
✦ **Royal Anglesey Yacht Club**, Green Edge, Beaumaris. ℂ 01248 810295
✦ **Trearddur Bay Sailing Club**. The Club only operates during the month of August. ℂ 01407 861293

SAILING CLUBS ON THE MAINLAND
✦ **Plas Menai**. On mainland, 5 miles from Menai Bridge. National Watersports Centre. Courses for

children and adults, sailing, kyaking, windsurfing, navigation etc. Swimming pool. *(Plas Menai is also the base of the Welsh Yachting Association* ℂ 01248 670738)
ℂ 01248 670964 www.plasmenai.co.uk
✦ **Port Dinorwig Sailing Club** / *Clwb Hwylio'r Felinheli*, on the mainland at y Felinheli, 4 miles from Menai Bridge. Racing between March and December, with club evenings on Wednesdays and Fridays from May to September.
ℂ 01248 670446 www.pdsc.org.uk
✦ **Royal Welsh Yacht Club**, on the mainland at Porth yr Aur, Caernarfon. www.royalwelshyachtclub.org.uk

Slipways and powerboats

Marine safety patrols are operated throughout the summer by the **Maritime Department** of the local authority. ℂ 01248 752331 www.anglesey.gov.uk
The Maritime Department is also responsible for the *public slipways* at:
✦ **Menai Bridge**	✦ **Porth Eilian**
✦ **Beaumaris**	✦ **Trearddur Bay**
	✦ **Traeth Bychan**

(A public slipway at Porth Amlwch, within the harbour, has less easy access and cannot be used at low tide.)

All personal water craft and powerboats above 10hp can use Council launching facilities on payment of a registration fee and launch fees. To enquire about registration, ask one of the slipway attendants, or contact the Maritime Department's officer:
ℂ 01248 752320 ℂ 07990 531594
To register, boat owners will be asked to produce their insurance certificates. Certain recognised powerboating qualifications may entitle owners to a discount – to take advantage of the discount, proof must be shown.

A number of other slipways around Anglesey's coast are managed by bodies other than the local authority, for example, yacht clubs and camp sites.

The arts & crafts
The following groups are active in the arts in Anglesey and North Wales.

Anglesey Arts Forum / *Fforwm Gelf Ynys Môn*
Membership of the forum is open to all involved in the arts. It organises the Easter *Arts Weeks*, giving the opportunity to visit artists and makers in their studios, to attend workshops in art and creative writing, and to see drama and music performances at venues around the island. A leaflet is available from Tourist Information Centres, libraries and attractions.
ℂ 01407 763361 www.angleseyartistsforum.org

The Association of Anglesey Art Groups, Secretary ℂ 01407 840413, organises a biennial exhibition (2007, 2009, etc) at Oriel Ynys Môn, Llangefni.
The following groups belong to the Association:
✦ **Anglesey Art Group** *Monica Morris* ℂ 01407 840439
✦ **Anglesey Outdoor Landscape Art Group**
Richard Watson ℂ 07771 624127
✦ **Beaumaris Art Workshop** exhibits at Canolfan Beaumaris in October. *Gill Schaffer* ℂ 01248 715453
✦ **Holyhead Art Club** *Gwyneth Ryder* ℂ 01407 763048
✦ **Island Art Group** *Bridget Wright* ℂ 01407 840413
✦ **Moelfre Art Group** Exhibition at the Community Centre each Whitsun bank holiday weekend.
Marjory Hughes ℂ 01248 470462
✦ **Straits Arts Soc.** *Eira Lloyd Jones* ℂ 01248 811403
✦ **Wylfa Art Group** *Norma Ede* ℂ 01407 831071

Anglesey Craftworkers' Guild / *Cymdeithas Crefftwyr Môn*. The Guild, formed in 1988, is responsible for the craft shop at Llynnon Mill, Llanddeusant, and also organises craft fairs. Regular venues include – **February**: Ucheldre Centre, Holyhead – **Spring bank holiday week**: Beaumaris Festival – **August**: County Show, Mona. Members also exhibit individually, for example as part of Oriel Ynys Môn's *Christmas* exhibition. They include the woodturner Jules Tattersall (Trearddur Bay), maker in wood Hugh Roberts (Bodorgan) and ceramic potter & sculptor Fiona Clai Brown (Tregele, near Cemaes). *For information about the Guild and its members:* Helen Sproston ✆ 01407 730155 **www.angleseycrafts.co.uk**

Art & Craft galleries

Oriel Ynys Môn Llangefni. Anglesey's main centre for the visual arts. A separate heritage gallery for the island's history and culture, and two art galleries with a full programme of temporary exhibitions. A new *Kyffin Williams Gallery* is under development at the Oriel. Craftwork, textiles, art materials, books, toys and prints on sale in the Oriel's shop. The Oriel's annual *Christmas Crafts* exhibition is one of its most popular events. Café. Daily throughout the year, 10.30am–5pm. ✆ 01248 724444 **www.angleseyheritage.org**

Ucheldre Centre / *Canolfan Ucheldre*, Holyhead. Exhibitions of fine art, photography and craftwork, together with an evening programme of theatre, concerts and cinema. Bookshop and licensed restaurant. All year: Monday to Saturday 10am–5pm; Sunday 2pm–5pm. ✆ 01407 763361 **www.ucheldre.org**

Keith Andrew Studio, Unit 5, Craft Workshops, Farmer Street, Llannerch-y-medd. A private gallery selling prints and original works by this established and popular Anglesey artist. **www.keithandrew-art.com** By appointment: ✆ 01407 720651 or ✆ 01248 470903

Oriel Tegfryn, Cadnant Road, Menai Bridge. A private gallery with regular exhibitions of the work of leading local artists, including Kyffin Williams, Ishbel McWhirter, Donald MacIntyre, William Selwyn, Karel Lek and wildlife artist Philip Snow. All year, daily. ✆ 01248 715128 **www.orieltegfryn.com**

Elizabeth Bradley, Plas Bodfa, Llangoed. Victorian needlework kits, made-up work. Two formal gardens. Tea garden and tea room serving traditional teas. Chickens, ducks, guinea fowl, rabbits, ponies to feed. Nature trails. All year, noon to 4pm. ✆ 01248 490100 **www.elizabethbradley.com**

Tan Lan Crafts Centre, Bethel, Bodorgan. Just off the A5 on B4422 to Aberffraw. A needlecraft centre in eighteenth-century farm buildings. Patchwork and quilting fabrics and equipment, needlework accessories and books. Courses. Local crafts. Tearoom. Tuesday to Saturday. ✆ 01407 840237

James Pringle Weavers, The Station, Llanfair Pwllgwyngyll. A vast retail outlet for woollens, designer wear and accessories. Souvenirs, books, and some crafts. The building includes a café and a Tourist Information Centre. All year. Monday to Saturday 9am–5.45pm; Sunday 11am–5pm; closed Easter Sunday and Christmas Day. ✆ 01248 717171

Oriel Tŷ Gorsaf, in the railway station building at Llanfair Pwllgwyngyll. Exhibitions of glassware by artists from Wales and further afield, together with a studio. Sale of equipment and materials for glass workers. Closed Tuesdays. ✆ 01248 717876

Canolfan Beaumaris. A small gallery with regular exhibitions by local artists, photographers and craftspeople. All year 10am–5pm. ✆ 01248 811200.

Also in Beaumaris, exhibitions in the **Community Centre** and the **Town Hall** during the Festival (Spring bank holiday week) and occasionally at other times. Enquire at the library ✆ 01248 810659

Holyhead Library / *Llyfrgell Caergybi* A small gallery with regular exhibitions. Monday 10am–5pm, Tuesday 10am–7pm, Wednesday 10am–1pm, Thursday & Friday 10am–7pm, Saturday 9.30am–12.30pm. ✆ 01407 762917

Oriel Gwyngyll, next to the Post Office, Llanfair Pwllgwyngyll. The work of local artists. Picture framing. Craftwork. Monday–Saturday (half day on Wednesday). Closed Sundays and bank holidays. ✆ 01248 713963 **www.artcymruwales.com**

Oriel Glyn Davies Gallery, Waverley House, Bridge Street / *Stryd y Bont*, Menai Bridge. Fine art photographs. ✆ 01248 715511 **www.glyndavies.com**

Oriel Cemaes, Cemaes Bay. Original work and prints by local artists. Picture framing. Daily (afternoons only on Sundays). ✆ 01407 711300

Anglesey has other craft shops and galleries – for example **Brynrefail Crafts** *(at Dulas) and* **Llys Llewelyn** *(Aberffraw). There are many more.*

ON THE MAINLAND

Gwynedd County Council's listing of arts events on the mainland is posted on the arts pages of its website **www.gwynedd.gov.uk**

Gwynedd Museum and Art Gallery, Bangor / *Amgueddfa ac Oriel Gwynedd* (between the library and bus station). A changing programme of arts and crafts. Wheelchair access to the shop and gallery only: no wheelchair access to the museum displays. Tuesday to Friday afternoons; Saturday 10.30am–4.30pm. ✆ 01248 353368 **www.gwynedd.gov.uk/museums**

Oriel Mostyn, Heol Vaughan, Llandudno. 24 miles from Menai Bridge. The region's major gallery for the fine and applied arts, with local and national touring exhibitions. Monday–Saturday 10am–5pm. ✆ 01492 879201 **www.mostyn.org**

The Potters' Gallery / *Oriel y Crochenwyr* on the mainland at 1 High Street, Conwy, is the showroom of the North Wales Potters group. ✆ 01492 593590 **www.northwalespotters.co.uk**

Bodelwyddan Castle / *Castell Bodelwyddan*, on A55 (junction 25), 33 miles from Menai Bridge. Exhibits part of the collection of the National Portrait Gallery. Major temporary exhibitions. School summer holidays: 10.30am–5pm. Other seasons: Easter to the end of October (closed Fridays), 10.30am–5pm; November to Easter, weekends only, 10.30am–4pm. ✆ 01745 584060 **www.bodelwyddan-castle.co.uk**

Oriel Plas Glyn y Weddw, Llanbedrog on the Llŷn Peninsula 32 miles from Menai Bridge. Monthly exhibitions in the gallery. Sculpture gardens. Tea-rooms, serving good food. Craftwork, books and cards. Easter to the end of September: daily 10am–5pm. Winter: Wednesday to Monday, 11am–4pm. ✆ 01758 740763 **www.oriel.org.uk**

Royal Cambrian Academy / *Academi Frenhinol Gymreig* , Conwy. (Behind Plas Mawr). The Academy, founded in 1882, is devoted to the Welsh visual arts. Tuesday–Saturday 11am–5pm. Sunday 1pm–4.30pm. Closed Mondays, except bank holidays. *The gallery is closed for one week before each exhibition.* ✆ 01492 593413 **www.rcaconwy.org**

Entertainment

Theatres and halls

Halls and schools all over Anglesey are used by touring **Welsh-language** theatre companies such as **Theatr Bara Caws**. **Theatr Ieuenctid Môn** is a theatre group for young Welsh-speakers, rehearsing and performing in on and off the island. ✆ 01248 725730 English-language amateur groups giving performances include the *Castle Players*, *Beaumaris*. In *Benllech*, groups such as *Melody Makers* and a barbershop quartet, together with touring companies, stage regular performances throughout the year at the Community & Ex-Servicemen's Hall. *Loose Cannons* of *Holyhead* is an amateur company formed to take part in festivals around the country.
✆ 01407 760511 www.loosecannons.freeuk.com

✦ **Theatr Fach** Llangefni. Tiny theatre converted from old farm buildings. Productions in Welsh and in English. Local youth theatre projects. Productions run from September until July**.**
✆ 01248 750348 ✆ 01248 723377

✦ **Boston Centre Stage**, The Old Church House, Boston Street, Holyhead. The venue for a variety of visiting theatrical groups and performers. ✆ 01407 763962
✦ **The Ucheldre Repertory Company**, at the Ucheldre Centre, Holyhead ✆ 01407763361
✦ **Amlwch Memorial Hall** – an occasional venue for entertainment. ✆ 0772 281 8968 www.amlwch.net
✦ **Beaumaris Castle** and **Plas Newydd** stage theatrical productions in their grounds during the summer.

ON THE MAINLAND
Theatr Clwyd, Mold, 55 miles from Menai Bridge: about an hour by car. The main theatre for northeast Wales, with an excellent programme. Drama, dance, music, film, art displays. Its productions enjoy regular critical acclaim. Café/restaurant and bar.
✆ 0845 330 3565 www.clwyd-theatr-cymru.co.uk (Tourist Information Centres at Holyhead and Bangor can issue tickets.)

Theatr Gwynedd, Bangor, 1½ miles from Menai Bridge. The main theatre for northwest Wales. Drama, dance, music, film, art displays. Bar.
✆ 01248 351708

Galeri, Victoria Dock, Caernarfon.
A new development on the water's edge for art and the creative industries in North Wales. Drama, dance, music, film, art displays. Café/restaurant and bar.
✆ 01286 685222 www.galericaernarfon.com

North Wales Theatre, Llandudno. Shows, pantomime, ballet, opera, touring musicals, drama, comedy (and rather too many tribute bands). Bar.
✆ 01492 872000 www.nwtheatre.co.uk

Cinema

AT HOLYHEAD ON ANGLESEY
✦ **Empire Cinema**, Stanley Street. A twin-screen cinema showing current films.
✆ 01407 761128 www.holyhead.com/empirecinema
✦ **Ucheldre Centre** programmes occasional film screenings. ✆ 01407 763361 www.ucheldre.org

ON THE MAINLAND
BANGOR
✦ *Plaza Cinema*, High Street, near the railway station. Two screens showing current films. Tickets, noon–8pm

✆ 0871 223 3440. 24-hr information ✆ 0871 223 3441 www.plazabangor.co.uk
✦ *Theatr Gwynedd*, Deiniol Road, opposite the Post Office. Occasional film screenings are part of the programme. Closed in August. ✆ 01248 351708
LLANDUDNO JUNCTION 18 miles from Menai Bridge along the A55 (junction 19).
✦ *Cineworld*. Nine-screens.
✆ 0871 220 8000 www.cineworld.com

Choral music

Wales has a long choral tradition, encouraged by local and national competition in eisteddfodau. Check the local press for concerts on the island. Most choirs welcome an audience at their rehearsals.

MALE VOICE CHOIRS
✦ **Côr Meibion y Traeth**. Rehearses on Mondays at 7.30pm, Goronwy Owen School, Benllech. This is Anglesey's premier male-voice choir, winners of the chief choral competition of the National Eisteddfod.
✆ 01248 600848
✦ **Côr Meibion Caergybi**. Tuesdays 7.15pm, Llanfawr School, Holyhead. Gwyn Jones ✆ 01407 769771
✦ **Lleisiau'r Frogwy**
Wednesdays 8pm, Bodffordd Community Hall.
✆ 01248 723506 www.lleisiaur-frogwy.org
✦ **Hogiau'r Ddwylan**. Thursdays 7.30pm, Capel Mawr Vestry, Menai Bridge. Arfon Thomas ✆ 01248 355364

MIXED CHOIRS
✦ **Cantorion Menai**. Tuesdays 7.30pm, Capel Mawr Schoolhouse, Menai Bridge. ✆ 01248 717204
✦ **Côr Bro Ddyfnan**. Thursdays 7.30pm, Pentraeth Primary School. ✆ 01248 712726
✦ **Cantorion Bro Cefni**. Tuesdays 7.30pm, Ysgol Corn Hir, Llangefni. ✆ 01248 712916

*Other male voice choirs include **Hogiau'r Bodwrog** and **Côr Meibion y Foel**. Other mixed choirs include **Adlais**, **Côr Aelwyd yr Ynys** and **Lobsgows**. **Lleisiau'r Lannerch** is an Anglesey women's choir.*

Classical music

Concerts are held during the **Beaumaris Festival** (Spring bank holiday week) and the **Holyhead Arts Festival** (durin g the second part of October). See the festival programmes for details.

The University of Wales at Bangor on the mainland stages classical recitals and, occasionally, concerts of traditional Welsh music, with performances during term-time by professional artists and students. Venues include Bangor Cathedral, and the University's Powis Hall and Prichard Jones Hall. The programme includes details of other University events, such as public lectures in the Arts and Sciences, poetry readings and exhibitions. Dr Hazel Robbins ✆ 01248 388142 www.bangor.ac.uk/musicatbangor

Ensemble Cymru stages recitals across the island. Live music is brought to public venues, as well as schools, hospitals and homes for the elderly. ✆ 01248 383257

Folk music and dance

The island's Welsh folk dance traditions are upheld by two groups of dancers and musicians, *Dawnswyr Môn* and *Ffidl Ffadl*. A feature of their performances is a faithful use of the traditional dress of northwest Wales country folk – far more subtle and pleasing than 'Welsh' picture-postcards might suggest.

Folk music, in all its varieties (traditional and less so, Welsh-language and English) may be seen at many of the island's hotels and pubs. Check the local press.

On the mainland, folk concerts by British and overseas performers are sometimes on the programmes of
✦ **Theatr Gwynedd** in Bangor ✆ 01248 351708
✦ **Galeri** in Caernarfon ✆ 01286 685222.

Brass bands

Menai Bridge Band was formed in the 1890s, and has been meeting in its former chapel in Mount Street for more than 100 years. Many of its current members are at school or are university students. The Senior Band, which in recent years has qualified for National Finals, rehearses from 7pm–9pm in the Bandroom on Mondays and Fridays; its conductor is Chris Williams. The Band has two other sections, Intermediates and *Band Bach* (the juniors).
✆ 01248 355547 **www**.menaibridgeband.org.uk

Beaumaris Band / *Seindorf Beaumaris*
Beaumaris has had a band since the early part of the nineteenth century, but it became all brass in the 1920s. The band has won first prizes in their sections at National Brass Band Championships of Great Britain and National Eisteddfodau of Wales, and have represented Wales abroad. The two current ceremonial trumpeters of the National Eisteddfod of Wales – Paul Hughes and Dewi Griffiths – are band members. Paul Hughes (the principal cornet player) played the flugelhorn solo for the part played by the actress Tara Fitzgerald in the 1996 film *Brassed Off*, about a colliery band during the time of pit closures. In 2006, nine members qualified to join the National Youth Band of Wales. Few bands in the UK have had such consistent success. Its four sections are: Senior, 'B' Band, Youth and Junior. Musical directors include Gwyn M Evans, his father Fred Evans MBE, and Paul Hughes. Performances are announced on the website.
✆ 01248 811281 **www**.beaumarisband.org.uk

Jazz

Check the local press for performances at hotels throughout the island or on the mainland.
✦ **Ucheldre Jazz Club**, Ucheldre Centre, Holyhead: ✆ 01407 763361
✦ **Victoria Hotel**, Menai Bridge. Monthly jazz evenings. ✆ 01248 712309.
✦ **Beaumaris Festival** (Spring bank holiday week) has included jazz concerts.

Venues for popular music

All genres are to be heard. The region has a thriving music scene with Welsh- and English-language bands, local recording studios and independent labels.

✦ **Bwyty Glantraeth Restaurant**, Bodorgan. *Noson Lawen*. Convivial evenings of song and music each Saturday. Meals from 7pm, entertainment from around 9.30pm. Bookings: ✆ 01407 840401

A number of public houses and hotels also present regular evening entertainment … for example, music at the Victoria Hotel and the Bulkeley Arms (both Menai Bridge) and the Seacroft Hotel (Trearddur Bay), and quiz nights at the Benllech Hotel.
Check the press for details.

VENUES ON THE MAINLAND
The best mainland gigs are at Bangor, Caernarfon, Llandudno and Rhyl.

✦ **Amser Time**, the public entertainment venue of Bangor University Students' Union, often with major touring bands during term time. ✆ 01248 388031
✦ **Hendre Hall**, Talybont, A55 junction 12. The venue for a variety of popular music events. ✆ 01248 371116

Nightclubs offering occasional bands, mostly disco and theme nights: **Octagon**, Bangor ✆ 01248 354977
Cofi Roc & **K2**, Caernarfon ✆ 01286 673100

Discography

The Welsh record label **Sain** (based on the mainland near Caernarfon) has a full catalogue of contemporary, traditional and classical CDs, including *Branwen* by Tudur Morgan, Catatonia's first recordings, Bryn Fôn, Moniars, Elin Fflur, choirs, and a series of compilations.
✆ 01286 831111 **www**.sainwales.com

Another leading label, **Fflach**, is based in west Wales. **www**.fflach.co.uk

For an overview of the national folk and dance music scene, also try the compilation **The Rough Guide to the music of Wales** (RGNET1052CD). It includes harp music from **Llio Rhydderch** of Marian-glas.

Four CDs provide a good introduction to the island's musical heartbeat …

◆ *Traditional Welsh folk dance from Anglesey, played by the musicians of the folk dance group* **Ffidl Ffadl** *of Llangefni:* **Dawns a chan a chroeso cynnes**. Dances and other tunes associated with the island and north Wales, played on fiddles, Welsh triple harps and the pibgorn (hornpipe). Including *Y Ddafad Gorniog, Meillionen, Three Sheepskins, Clog dance, Y Gelynnen, Mae'r ddaear yn glasu, Titrwm Tatrwm, Had Maip Môn.*
✆ 01248 750561 **www**.welshfolkdance.org.uk
◆ *Welsh traditional fiddle music:* **Ffidil** (Fflach CD182H). Players from all over Wales, including Huw Roberts of the Llangefni group Ffidl Ffadl. Some Anglesey tunes, such as those from the manuscripts of Morris Edwards, an eighteenth-century Anglesey fiddler.
◆ *Welsh triple harp music, performed by* **Llio Rhydderch** *of Marian-glas, Anglesey:* **Telyn** (Fflach CD196H). Traditional music from Anglesey, including *Biwmares March, O Langefni, Malltraeth* and tunes from the manuscripts of Morris Edwards.
www.llio.rhydderch.freeuk.com
◆ *Ancient Welsh harp music, performed by* **Bill Taylor** *on the Bray harp:* **Two worlds of the Welsh harp** (Dorian DOR-90260). Contains many tunes from the Robert ap Huw manuscript, played in the traditional manner on the harp of the period.

Music from the Robert ap Huw Manuscript
Volume 1 (PDCD002) recorded by the Irish harpist Paul Dooley in 2004. **www**.pauldooley.com

To buy CDs of Welsh music on the island, try …
Awen Menai, Menai Bridge ✆ 01248 715532
Cwpwrdd Cornel, Llangefni ✆ 01248 750218
Oriel Ynys Môn, near Llangefni ✆ 01248 724444

Five hectic years brought international fame to singer **Aled Jones** from Llandegfan in Anglesey. A recent recording is *New Horizons* (Universal Classics & Jazz, 2005). **www**.aledjones.co.uk

For indie and experimental popular music, see the article *Island Records* by Alan Holmes on page 218.

A diary of events

Very many more events take place on the island than those listed here. To find out 'what's on', ask the locals or ask at one of the Tourist Information Centres:
✦ Llanfair Pwllgwyngyll ☎ 01248 713177
✦ Holyhead ☎ 01407 762622.
Keep an eye, too, on the island's newspapers, and look out for posters in libraries and shop windows.
Pick up the booklet *Anglesey What's On* or visit the local authority's website **www.anglesey.gov.uk**

Annual events

■■■ **SUMMER** – June to August

Isle of Anglesey Walking Festival. Two weeks during the middle of June, with a full programme of walks, varying from easy to moderate and from short to long. A pamphlet provides all the details.
☎ 01248 725700 **www.angleseywalkingfestival.com**

Llan-faes Carnival, often held in late-May/June, with a parade to Beaumaris and back. Carnival queens and fancy dress floats followed by an afternoon of fun on the playing field with stalls, food, live music and dancers. ☎ 01248 811659

Celtic Longboat Race at the end of the May school holiday week. 12 miles, from Caernarfon to Beaumaris.

Benllech Carnival, third Saturday in June. A Sea Cadet band leads a parade, with fancy dress floats and carnival queens. Entertainment and stalls. A sports event for children is held on the evening before the carnival. ☎ 01248 853682

Wales Biodiversity Week in June promotes the appreciation of wildlife and works to maintain, enhance and monitor biodiversity in Wales. Anglesey's events include visits to natural sites. A greater number of activities take place on the mainland, in Gwynedd. **www.**biodiversitywales.org.uk

Sheepdog Trials. Anglesey trials are less frequent than in former times. Dwyran and Valley have held events on the first Saturday in July. Tourist Information Centres can provide the details.

Annual bicycle ride, on the first Sunday in July, from Plas Arthur Leisure Centre in Llangefni. Three routes: 14 miles, 26 miles and 50 miles. *An event organised by the Rotary Clubs of Holyhead & Llangefni to raise funds for local charities.* ☎ 01407 840907

Three Castles Classic Welsh Trial, on the first full weekend in July. One of the largest annual rally events of its type, bringing classic car enthusiasts to towns with castles in North Wales – including Beaumaris.
☎ 0208 255 4860 **www.**three-castles.co.uk

Amlwch Viking Festival / *Gŵyl Llychlynwyr*, every two years at the end of July (2006, 2008 etc), with a re-enactment of a Viking raid on the island. Recreations of Viking village life. Ceremonial burning of a Viking longboat at Porth Amlwch. Archery displays, competitions and stalls. In previous years two recreated longboats have rowed here across the Irish Sea from Ireland. ☎ 0772 281 8968 ☎ 01407 831076 **www.**amlwchvikingfestival.co.uk

Amlwch Carnival, a Saturday 'community festival', usually held in mid-July. Sports competition, a parade from Amlwch Port to the primary school with visiting carnival queens, fancy dress, stalls. ☎ 07900 462237

Cemaes Strawberry Tea, mid-July. Brass band, raffles, cake stalls, tombola, and strawberries and cream. Proceeds to the RNLI. ☎ 01407 710893

Plas Newydd *Summer fair*, on the fourth Tuesday in July. Previous attractions have included stalls, tombola, games, children's races and sheepdog displays.
☎ 01248 714795

Holyhead Leisure Festival is held on Newry Beach during the last full weekend in July each year. It has included carnival fun and sports, drum majorette competitions, cabaret nights, live music, funfairs and craft fairs. ☎ 01407 764020

Dog Flyball Tournament, **Bryngwran**, at Tai Lawr, Tyn Towyn. Last week in July. Teams from all over the UK compete in these four-dog relay races. (Flyball races are also held here at other times of the year.)
☎ 01407 810610 **www.**pods-flyball.co.uk

Llanfechell: *Ffair Mechell*, end of July. Entertainment, stalls and games. A procession includes carnival queens, fancy dress and floats. Dance displays, school prizes. The fair is held in conjunction with the village's horticultural show. Mary Hughes ☎ 01407 710938

Country Fair at Rhos Farm, Pentraeth on the first Sunday of August. Shire horses, pony rides, dog shows, children's activities, classic cars and tractors, stalls, crafts, refreshments. Organised by the Rotary Club of Bangor and first held in 1987. ☎ 01248 810272

Llanddona/Beaumaris Horse & Pony Show Bryn Glas farm, on the Beaumaris to Llanddona road. The first Saturday in August. A one-day event first held in the 1970s, with mounted sections, show jumping, breed sections and a gymkhana for young riders.
☎ 01248 810487 ☎ 01248 811370

Cemaes Lifeboat Day, the first or second Sunday in August. The Holyhead lifeboat ties up at the quay for inspection. Stalls and barbecue around the car park.
☎ 01407 710893. *(An RNLI gift shop, opposite the Stag Inn, opens during the summer.)*

Beaumaris Lifeboat Day, a Saturday in mid-August, depending on the tides. Lifeboat demonstration with capsize drill, sometimes with rescue helicopter. Onshore activities include a band, funfair, stalls, refreshments and an RNLI shop.
☎ 01248 810577 **www.**beaumarislifeboat.com

The Anglesey County Show / *Sioe Sir Fôn* at the Mona Showground on the Tuesday and Wednesday of the second full week in August is the main agricultural event in North Wales. Prizewinning bulls and rams, shire horses and international showjumping. Sheepdog trials and gun dog trials, poultry, pigeon and rabbit marquee, parades, displays and shows, stalls, food hall, pavilions and demonstrations.
☎ 01407 720072 **www.**angleseyshow.org.uk

Holyhead Maritime Festival. At Newry Beach over a weekend in August, the exact date depending on the tides. The event is centred around safety at sea and maritime history, featuring lifeboats, coastguards, the RAF, the Navy, sea cadets, diving, trips around the bay. Live music. Activities and entertainment for children.
☎ 01407 763911 **www.**holyheadmaritimefestival.com
Holyhead Lifeboat Weekend coincides with the festival. A lifeboat display, with divers demonstrating a rescue, is often presented on the Sunday afternoon.
☎ 01407 762583 **www.**holyhead-lifeboat.co.uk

Menai Strait Swimming Races. During August (dates depending on the states of the tide) and open to any capable swimmer belonging to a FINA-affiliated club. *Each swimmer must be accompanied by a kayak.*
✦ Pier-to-Pier. Two miles, from the Beaumaris pier beach to the Bangor pier slipway. The piers provide spectators with excellent vantage points. For safety reasons, the number of competitors is limited to 20.

✦ **Across the Strait** from the Mermaid Inn at Foel (Brynsiencyn) to Porth yr Aur (a slipway by a tower in the medieval town walls of Caernarfon). This one mile course was first swum in 1955. Winning times can be around 25 minutes. Claire Wilson of Bethesda has been victorious six years in succession: 1999 to 2005. *Organised by the Arfon Masters Swimming Club:* ✆ 01248 430811 **www**.arfonmasters.org.uk

Cemaes Flower Show, Saturday in late August. A horticultural show with garden produce, arts and crafts, flowers and photography. Proceeds to the RNLI. ✆ 01407 710893

Bryn Terfel's Faenol Festival / Gŵyl y Faenol. At the end of August in the Faenol estate, immediately south of the mainland end of the Britannia Bridge. The first festival was held in 2000: it now extends over several days. Performers have included Aled Jones, Katherine Jenkins and Catrin Finch as well as the founder. Dafydd Iwan, Van Morrison, Westlife and Shirley Bassey have been on the bill, as well as international stars, such as Andrea Bocelli and Joseph Calleja. A magnificent firework display concludes the festival. ✆ 01492 872000 ✆ 01248 351708 **www**.brynfest.com

Moelfre Lifeboat Day, usually the Saturday of August bank holiday weekend. **www**.moelfrelifeboat.org.uk

Trearddur Bay Lifeboat Day, usually the Sunday of August bank holiday weekend.

Cemaes Carnival on August bank holiday Saturday with a parade through town to the beach road. Visiting queens and stalls. ✆ 01407 710435

Cemaes Duck Race on August bank holiday Sunday. Rubber ducks and miniature boats are raced along the Wygyr river to the finishing line. Proceeds benefit the RNLI. ✆ 01407 710983

Gŵyl Cefni has been held annually in August or early September, around Llangefni, since 2001. Some events have also been staged at the Anglesey Showground's Pavilion Môn, served by a shuttle bus service to and from the town centre on Saturday night. Lively performances of Welsh folk, rock, pop and country music. Comedy and celebrity football has also been featured in previous programmes. ✆ 01248 725732

■ ■ ■ AUTUMN – September to November

Amlwch & District Threshing Day, on one of the early Saturdays in September at Penrallt farm outside Amlwch. Vintage vehicles and farm machinery with a steam-driven threshing machine in action. Refreshments. Previous years' demonstrations have included butter churning and the making of straw ropes and baskets. ✆ 01407 710007

Anglesey Beer Festival. The second weekend in September, in the pavilions of the Anglesey Showground at Mona. A wide selection of real ales to sample. Popular music on the Friday evening and on Saturday afternoon and evening. Free camping. Organised by the Anglesey Central Lions. ✆ 01407 710766 **www**.angleseybeerfestival.com

✦ **Anglesey Marathon & Fun Day** takes place late September. As well as the full 26.2 mile event, 10km and 5km runs are held on the same day. The marathon starts and finishes at the Anglesey Showground at Mona, passing through the south-west of the island ✆ 01248 725700 **www**.angleseymarathon.com

Anglesey Oyster & Welsh Produce Festival is held in a marquee at Trearddur Bay Hotel during the second weekend in October. Demonstration kitchens, food fair, competitions. Evening events & entertainment. ✆ 01248 725700 **www**.angleseyoysterfestival.com

Holyhead Arts Festival is usually held over seven or eight days during the second part of October. Wide-ranging events take place at various sites in Holyhead, most of them at Canolfan Ucheldre. Previous events have included music and theatre, exhibitions and talks. The BBC Welsh Symphony Orchestra and the Welsh National Opera have performed at the Festival. Details from Canolfan Ucheldre ✆ 01407 763361 Festival Director, Gladys Pritchard ✆ 01407 762090

Menai Bridge Fair / Ffair y Borth, engulfs the town for a few days. The main fair day is 24 October (if it is a Sunday, the fair is held on 23rd.) Roaring funfair rides are set up in car parks and along the main street. Strings of lights, fortune tellers' caravans, stalls and the smell of chestnuts roasting on a chilly autumn evening mark this 300 year-old tradition.

Hallowe'en. A family fun day, including 'spooky' activities for children and quiz trails, is part of Plas Newydd's annual programme. *nb: This event is not necessarily held on All Saints Day, 31 October.*

Fireworks. Community bonfires and firework displays take place all over the island in the days around 5th November. **Beaumaris** has a bonfire on the beach with fireworks set off from the pier. This is usually on a Saturday night, with the Beaumaris Band playing, hot food served and funds raised for local charities. *(Car parking may be difficult for this very popular event.)* The **Holyhead** and District Round Table hold a bonfire and firework display on Penrhos Beach, with all proceeds going to charity. The bonfire is lit at 6.45pm and the fireworks go off soon after. ✆ 01407 762495

Remembrance Day. The Sunday nearest to November 11th. Memorial services and parades take place in towns and villages across Anglesey. In previous years, two minutes of silence have been observed at the war memorials in Amlwch, Benllech, Beaumaris, Holyhead, Llangefni, Moelfre and Rhosneigr.

The Anglesey Winter Show, held in the pavilions of the Mona Showground on the last Saturday in November. Displays of livestock and produce by the farming community. Competitions, cookery, floral art, crafts and Father Christmas. ✆ 01407 720072

■ ■ ■ WINTER – December to February

Beaumaris Victorian Evening from about 6.30pm, usually the first Wednesday in December. Carol singing, bellringing and brass band music. Stalls. Mince pies, hot chestnuts, mulled wine and baked potatoes. Late night shopping. Victorian costume parade in Castle Square. Free car parking on the Green.

Christmas Crafts Exhibitions
Oriel Ynys Môn, Llangefni ✆ 01248 724444
Ucheldre Centre, Holyhead ✆ 01407 763361

Rhoscolyn Boxing Day Walk, following a circular route from the *White Eagle Inn*, with funds raised for charities. ✆ 01407 861069

New Year's Eve fireworks at midnight from the walls of Beaumaris Castle. Viewing from Castle Square.

New Year's Day. Volunteers brave the cold water of Newry Beach, Holyhead (next to the Maritime Museum) in this charity event. Some swim; most take a hasty dip before recovering with a mug of hot soup.

Mini Marathon around Menai Bridge, a 10km run on the last Sunday of January, organised by the Anglesey Central Lions. ✆ 01407 710766

Ploughing Match (depending on the weather, usually held in February, with half a dozen or more teams of shire horses. Organised by the Anglesey Vintage Ploughing Society / *Cymdeithas Aredig Ynys Môn*. ✆ 01407 710007 **www**.angleseyploughing.co.uk

■■■ **SPRING** – March to May

Anglesey Drama Festival, Boston Centre Stage, Holyhead. In the spring, during a three day period, one act dramas are performed by many of the island's amateur dramatic groups. Winners compete for the chance to perform in the Drama Association of Wales national finals in June. ✆ 01407 760511

Easter egg trails and children's entertainments are organised at tourist attractions including Plas Newydd and the Holyhead Breakwater Country Park. The local press and Tourist Information Centres provide details.

Anglesey Arts Weeks take place during the Easter period. Many studios are open to the public. Exhibitions and events at the island's tourist attractions and arts centres, including art and creative writing workshops, drama and music performances. The *Arts Weeks Guide* provides the full programme. ✆ 01407 763361 **www**.angleseyartsforum.org

Country & Western Festival, the first or second weekend in May at Wylfa Sports & Social Club, organised by Anglesey Central Lions. ✆ 01407 710766 ✆ 01248 853059

Gŵyl Llynnon / **Llynnon Festival**, part of the 'National Mills Weekend' programme, during the second weekend of May. This celebration of rural life is centred on Llynnon Mill, Llanddeusant. Evening entertainment may include music, dance and Welsh-language poetry. Daytime activities have included basketmaking, cider pressing, shepherding and crook-making, folk dancing, archery, a craft fair, pony rides and a farmers' market. ✆ 01407 730797 ✆ 01248 724444

Anglesey Vintage Rally / *Sioe Hen Gelfi*, Henblas, Llangristiolus. The weekend before the Whit bank holiday. The programme in previous years, arranged by the Anglesey Vintage Equipment Society, has included parades of vehicles, a vintage steam fair, axemanship displays and craft tents. ✆ 01407 840440

Eisteddfod Môn is held every May. This Eisteddfod is the island's premier Welsh festival. First meeting at Holyhead in 1907, its programme includes music, dance and literary competitions and visual arts exhibitions. Organised by a different community each year, the forthcoming eisteddfod is 'proclaimed' one year and one day before its start. A series of fundraising events are held during the months before the eisteddfod. Three important ceremonies are conducted during the eisteddfod by the Bards of the Gorsedd: presentations of the Chair, the Crown and the Prose Medal. *Ynys Môn's Centenary Eisteddfod* of 2007, held in the Mona Showground pavilion, is the responsibility of Bodffordd.

Anglesey also holds an **Urdd Eisteddfod** for young people, and **local eisteddfodau** such as those at Llanddeusant and Llandegfan, which present competitive performances of music and drama in village halls and chapels.

The all-Wales *Eisteddfod Genedlaethol Cymru*, the **National Eisteddfod of Wales** is held annually at the beginning of August. It last came to Anglesey in 1999. **www**.eisteddfod.org.uk
An annual **International Eisteddfod** with music and dance from Wales and all over the world is held each July on the mainland at Llangollen. ✆ 01978 862001 **www**.international-eisteddfod.co.uk

Carreg-lwyd (SH309878), Llanfaethlu. A walled garden, wooded gardens and a lawn with specimen trees in the seventeenth-century mansion's grounds. Footpaths offer circular woodland and lakeside walks. Open for 25 days every May, 1pm–5pm. ✆ 01407 730208 ✆ 0770 864 5000. Carreg-lwyd's website gives up-to-date information: **www**.carreglwyd.co.uk

Beaumaris Festival, during the Spring bank holiday week, was first held in 1986. Most of the performances are of classical music. The programme also includes art and craft exhibitions and talks. Details are published in April (copies from Llanfair Pwllgwyngyll Tourist Office ✆ 01248 713177). Tickets: Bulkeley Hotel, Beaumaris ✆ 01248 810415 **www**.beaumarisfestival.co.uk

The Great Strait Raft Run. Subject to the tides, held on bank holiday at the end of May, though it can be a week earlier. From near the *Garddfôn Inn* on the mainland waterfront at Y Felinheli, and under the two bridges to Menai Bridge pier. Thirty or forty rafts are propelled by enthusiastic teams. Depending on the weather, the fastest rafts take just over 30 minutes to complete the course – other crews enter just for the fun of it. This is a Round Table event, with proceeds to local causes. Presentations at the *Mostyn Arms*, behind Menai Bridge pier. Entries ✆ 01248 713915

Rhoscolyn Rowing Race, May bank holiday. Sponsored by the *White Eagle Inn*. ✆ 01407 860267

Frequent events

■■■ **SUMMER**

Summer activities for children are held around the island during the school holidays. Open to all young people and organised by trained staff of the local authority's Sports Development Unit. The island's leisure centres have the details. ✆ 01248 752034

Beaumaris Castle Square. Free entertainment every Sunday during the summer, including brass bands, folk dancers and Punch & Judy. **www**.beaumaris.org

Plas Newydd. *Musical recitals* have occasionally been held in the Music Room of Plas Newydd on Sunday afternoons during June, July and August. *Open air theatre* has been performed during the summer, including Shakespeare and shows for young people. ✆ 01248 714795

■■■ **THROUGHOUT THE YEAR**

Anglesey Craftworker's Guild organises regular displays at venues around the island, including the Beaumaris Festival (Spring bank holiday week) and the Anglesey County Show at Mona (August). From Easter to September the Guild also runs a shop at Llynnon Mill, Llanddeusant. ✆ 01248 410632

RSPB guided walks & events. Programme of activities at Ellin's Tower, South Stack. Take guided walks, learn about birds, flowers and other wildlife. Fun and games for children. Dave Bateson ✆ 01407 764973 **www**.rspb.org.uk/cymru

Windsurfing & kitesurfing. European and national championships are held at Rhosneigr in the spring and autumn. ✆ 01407 810899 **www**.buckys.co.uk

District Horticultural Shows held throughout the island in the summer and autumn often present magnificent displays of produce and crafts. The local press publishes details.

Gaerwen Auction Centre. Livestock markets weekly. Other auctions are held twice monthly: often the first Thursday in the month for household goods and the last Thursday for antiques, but check the Morgan

Evans advertisement – announcing forthcoming sales – in each week's *Holyhead & Anglesey Mail*, or telephone the Auction Centre: ✆ 01248 421582

Canolfan Beaumaris Antiques Fairs are held on the third Sunday of the month, with up to forty stalls. ✆ 01248 810624 ✆ 01248 713722

Oriel Ynys Môn, **Llangefni**. A full programme of exhibitions, events and workshops in Anglesey's centre for the arts. 10.30am–5pm daily. Shop. Café. ✆ 01248 724444 www.angleseyheritage.org

Ucheldre Centre, **Holyhead**. A full programme of exhibitions and events. Evening entertainment, including films, is presented all year round. Shop. Café. ✆ 01248 724444 www.ucheldre.org

Canolfan Beaumaris. As well as offering sporting facilities, this is a year-round venue for the performing arts, though with a limited programme. The Centre also has a programme of temporary art exhibitions and organises holiday activities for children. ✆ 01248 811200

Library exhibitions. Art and craft exhibitions are held occasionally in Holyhead library. ✆ 01407 762917

Food & drink

Anglesey's major culinary event is the *Anglesey Oyster & Welsh Produce Festival*, held in a marquee at Trearddur Bay Hotel around the middle of October. Food fair and cookery demonstration kitchens. Evening events and entertainment. ✆ 01248 725700 www.angleseyoysterfestival.com

www.walesthetruetaste.com – offers information about food and drink, recipes, farmers' markets and farm shops throughout Wales.

A Directory of Anglesey Food Producers may be available from Tourist Information Centres. ✆ 01248 725700 www.mentermon.com

Fresh produce

Hooton's Homegrown, Brynsiencyn, on the A4080. Farm shop and pick-your-own. Daily 10am–5.30pm. Meat, eggs, soft fruit, vegetables, cakes and preserves. Coffee shop, and meals: 10am–5pm. ✆ 01248 430322 www.hootonshomegrown.com

Tyddyn Môn Farm Shop, Bryn Refail, Dulas. Midway between Moelfre and Amlwch on the A5025. Eggs, vegetables, plants and shrubs. Monday to Friday. ✆ 01248 410648

Anglesey new potatoes. During the season for new potatoes, from May until July, a stall – *Tatws Newydd Sir Fôn* ('Anglesey new potatoes') – is set up by a local farm at the Llanbedr-goch layby, between Pentraeth and Benllech on the A5025.

E T Jones, Sons & Daughter, Church Street, Bodedern, is the only butcher remaining on the island with its own abattoir. Produce can also be sent by post. ✆ 01407 740257

A small **farmers market** is held on the mainland at Bangor, in Morrison's car park, every other Sunday. Joanne Robertson ✆ 01248 421661.

Eating out

Premises open and close; reputations rise and fall. People who know the island well can suggest their own favourite cafés and restaurants to you.

One established Anglesey restaurant consistently gains recommendations from respected guides, such as *The Good Food Guide* and *Dining Out in Wales*:
✦ **Ye Olde Bull's Head Inn**, on Castle Street in Beaumaris, offers a choice, daily, all year: *The Brasserie* – informal (no bookings are taken), and *The Loft Restaurant* – 'fine dining'. ✆ 01248 810329 www.bullsheadinn.co.uk
✦ **Courtyard**, also in Beaumaris, at 17 Church Street, opened its doors in 2005 and may well consolidate a reputation for quality that matches that of the *Bull's Head*. ✆ 01248 810565

Other well-appointed Anglesey hotels also run good restaurants.
For example:
✦ **Trearddur Bay Hotel**
✆ 01407 860301 www.trearddurbayhotel.co.uk
✦ **Tre-Ysgawen Hall**, on the Capel Coch lane, off the B5111 north of Llangefni. ✆ 01248 750750 www.treysgawen-hall.co.uk
✦ **Nant yr Odyn**, Turnpike Nant, west of Llangefni. ✆ 01248 723354 www.nantyrodyn.co.uk

VEGETARIAN
Simple vegetarian fare is served at the island's cafés. The better known restaurants may offer more imaginative dishes.

In **Bangor**, on the mainland, wider vegetarian choices may be found on the menus of:
✦ **Java** 236 High Street ✆ 01248 361652
✦ **Herbs** 162 High Street ✆ 01248 351249

Island wines and ales

Gwinllan Padrig Vinyard, Llanbadrig, near Cemaes. Red, white and sparkling wines. Tours by appointment. ✆ 01407 710416

Tŷ Croes Vineyard, Dwyran. Specialising in dry white wine, and also making red wine. Tours by appointment. ✆ 01248 440358

Further reading

Out-of-print books listed might be found in the island's libraries. Llangefni library in particular has an excellent Anglesey reference collection.
Welsh Books Council / Cyngor Llyfrau sells a good selection of current books: **www.gwales.com**

Anglesey, Marquess of: *One-Leg, The Life and Letters of Henry William Paget;* Leo Cooper, London 1961 (reprinted1996)

Aris, Mary: *Gwynedd & Anglesey: Photographic Memories;* Francis Frith, 2004

Bates, D E B & Davies, J R: *Geologists' Association Guide: No.40, Anglesey;* The Geologists' Association, London 1981, reprinted 2004

Borrow, George: *Wild Wales (1862);* reprinted by Bridge Books, 2002

Brooks, John: *Anglesey: museums and mysteries* (also published as a Welsh edition, *Ynys Môn: chwedlau a chreiriau*); Anglesey Museums in association with Jarrold, Norwich 2005

Carr, A D: *Medieval Anglesey;* Anglesey Antiquarian Society, Llangefni 1982

Conran, Tony (translator): *Welsh Verse;* Seren, Bridgend 1967, reprinted 2003

Cowell, John: *Edwardian Anglesey;* two volumes in a pictorial history series published by the author, Menai Bridge, 1991 and 1992
– by the same author: *Beaumaris: a pictorial history;* John Cowell, Menai Bridge 2005

Davies, J C & Hughes, Margaret: *Môn yr Ynys Hardd : Beautiful Island;* Gwasg Carreg Gwalch, Llanrwst 2006. *(This publisher's list contains many other local-interest titles.* **www.carreg-gwalch.co.uk***)*

Davies, Janet: *The Welsh Language (A Pocket Guide);* University of Wales Press, Cardiff, reprinted 2005.

Davies, John: *A History of Wales;* Allen Lane/Penguin Books, London 1990/1993. (Also published in a Welsh edition: *Hanes Cymru*)

Davies, R R: *The Revolt of Owain Glyn Dŵr;* Oxford University Press, Oxford & New York 1997

Dickens, Charles: *Shipwreck! Charles Dickens and the Royal Charter;* Magma, Llansadwrn 1997 (reprinted 2007)

Eames, Aled: *Ships and Seamen of Anglesey;* Anglesey Antiquarian Society, Llangefni 1973 (paperback reprint: National Maritime Museum, London 1981)

Eames, Aled: *Y Fordaith Bell;* Gwasg Gwynedd, Caernarfon 1993

Esgobaeth Bangor / Bangor Diocese: *Directory of Open Churches* / *Cyfarwyddiadur Eglwysi Agored* (bilingual text); Bangor 2003

Gantz, Jeffrey (transl.): *The Mabinogion;* Penguin Classics, London 1976 (reprinted 2003) – *see also Jones, Gwyn & Jones, Thomas, 'The Mabinogion'.*

Griffith, W P: *Power, Politics & County Government in Wales, Anglesey 1780-1914;* Anglesey Antiquarian Society, Llangefni 2006

Griffiths, Miriam: *Chester to Holyhead: Travelling the Old Post Road* / *O Gaer i Gaergybi: Teithio ar hyd yr Hen Lôn Bost* (bilingual text)
– by the same author: *The Marram Weavers of Newborough* / *Plethwyr Moresg Niwbwrch* (bilingual text); both published by Magma, Llansadwrn 1997 (reprinted 2007)

Guise, Barry & Lees, George: *Windmills of Anglesey;* Attic Books, Builth Wells 1992

Gwyn, David. *A book to be published at the end of 2006* (Phillimore, Chichester) comprehensively covers the **industrial archaeology** of northwest Wales. Its author is a Gwynedd-based archaeologist of industrialisation.

Hope, Bryan D: *A Curious Place: the industrial history of Amlwch 1550-1950;* Bridge Books, Wrexham 1994. – by the same author: *A Commodious Yard: the story of William Thomas & Sons* [of Amlwch]; Gwasg Carreg Gwalch, Llanrwst 2005.

Hughes, D Lloyd & Williams, Dorothy M; *Holyhead: the story of a port*, published by the authors, Holyhead 1981

Humphries, P H: *Castles of Edward I in Wales;* Cadw, Cardiff 1983

Huws, Gwyn Parri a Beggs, Terry: *The Menai Strait (also published in a Welsh edition, Y Fenai),* Gwasg Gomer, Llandysul 2002

Jones, Bedwyr Lewis: *Iaith Sir Fôn;* Llygad yr Haul, Bangor 1983

Jones, Dewi & Thomas, Glyndŵr (gol): *Nabod Môn;* Gwasg Carreg Gwalch, Llanrwst 2003

Jones, Gwilym T: *The Rivers of Anglesey* / *Afonydd Môn* (bilingual text) 1990; *The Fords of Anglesey* / *Rhydau Môn* (bilingual text) 1992; both published by Research Centre Wales / Canolfan Ymchwil Cymru, Bangor

Jones, Gwilym T & Roberts, Tomos: *The Place-names of Anglesey* / *Enwau Lleoedd Môn* (bilingual text); Cyngor Sir Ynys Môn, Llangefni / Canolfan Ymchwil Cymru, Bangor, 1996

Jones, Gwyn & Jones, Thomas: *The Mabinogion;* Random House, 2001 – *see also Gantz, Jeffrey: 'The Mabinogion'.*

Jones, P H & Whalley, P: *Birds of Anglesey* / *Adar Môn* (bilingual text); Menter Môn, Llangefni 2004

Jones, Rhiannon Davies: *Llys Aberffraw* (ffuglen); Gwasg Gomer, Llandysul 1977

Jones, W Eifion (ed): *A New Natural History of Anglesey;* Anglesey Antiquarian Society, Llangefni 1990

Large, Frank: *Faster than the Wind: the Liverpool to Holyhead Telegraph;* Avid Publications, Wirral 1998

Lazarus, Maureen & Smith, John: *'It was the Most Beautiful Day': The Work of the Massey Sisters* / *Gwaith y Chwiorydd Massey* (bilingual text); Oriel Ynys Môn, Llangefni 2004

Lilly, Gweneth: *Y Drudwy Dewr* (ffuglen); Gwasg Gomer, Llandysul 1980

Lord, Peter: *The Visual Culture of Wales: Industrial Society* (1998, reprinted 2004) and *Medieval Vision* (2003); both published by University of Wales Press, Cardiff.

Lynch, Frances: *Prehistoric Anglesey;* Anglesey Antiquarian Society, Llangefni 1970 (revised 1991)
– by the same author: *A Guide to Ancient and Historic Wales: Gwynedd;* Cadw, Cardiff 1995

McKee, Alexander: *The Golden Wreck: the tragedy of the Royal Charter;* Souvenir Press 1961 & 1986

Morgan, D Densil: *Christmas Evans a'r Ymneilltuaeth Newydd;* Gwasg Gomer, Llandysul 1991

Morris, Jan: *The Matter of Wales;* Oxford University Press 1984 (paperback edition Penguin Books 1986)

Owen, Trefor M: *The Customs and Traditions of Wales (A Pocket Guide);* University of Wales Press, Cardif

Pretty, David A: *Anglesey, the concise history;* University of Wales Press, Cardiff 2005

Ramage, Helen: *Portraits of an Island: eighteenth century Anglesey;* Anglesey Antiquarian Society, Llangefni 1987 (paperback edition 2001)

Roberts, R H: *The flowering plants and ferns of Anglesey;* National Museum of Wales, Cardoff 1982

Redknap, Mark: *Vikings in Wales: an Archaeological Quest;* National Museums & Galleries of Wales, Cardiff 2000. (Chosen as Archaeological Book of the Year.)

Richards, Emlyn: *Potsiars Môn* 2001; *Bywyd Gŵr* 2002; *Rolant o Fôn* 1999 – all Gwasg Gwynedd, Caernarfon

Richards, Melville (editor): *An Atlas of Anglesey;* Anglesey Community Council, Llangefni 1972 (Also published in a Welsh edition: *Atlas Môn*)

Roberts, Dewi: *An Anglesey Anthology;* Gwasg Carreg Gwalch, Llanrwst 1999

Roberts, Huw & Rhydderch, Llio: *The harpers of Llannerch-y-medd / Telynorion Llannerch-y-medd. (A book and CD set)* Isle of Anglesey County Council, Llangefni 2000.

Rogers, Carl: *The Isle of Anglesey Coastal Path;* Mara Books, 2005

Ross, Anne: *The Pagan Celts;* Batsford, London 1970; reprinted by John Jones, Ruthin 1998.

Ross, Anne & Robins, Don: *The Life and Death of a Druid Prince;* Century Hutchinson / Rider, London 1989

Rowlands, John: *Copper Mountain;* Anglesey Antiquarian Society, Llangefni 1966 & 1981; paperback edition by Stone Science, Talwrn 2002.

Royal Commission on Ancient & Historical Monuments in Wales & Monmouthshire: *Anglesey: a Survey and Inventory;* HMSO, London 1937, reprinted 1968.

Skidmore, Ian: *Lifeboat VC;* David & Charles, Newton Abbot 1979

Steele, Philip: *Beaumaris, The Town's Story / Biwmares, Hanes y Dref* (bilingual text); Magma, Llansadwrn 1996

Stephens, Meic (editor): *Oxford Companion to the Literature of Wales;* Oxford University Press, Oxford & New York 1986; also published in a Welsh-language edition: *Cydymaith i Lenyddiaeth Cymru;* Gwasg Prifysgol Cymru, Caerdydd 1986

Taylor, Arnold: *Beaumaris Castle;* Cadw, Cardiff, new edition 2004

Thomas, Charles: *Whispering Reeds,* or the Anglesey *Catamanus Inscription Strip Bare;* Oxbow Books, Oxford 2002.

Thomas, R S: *Autobiographies,* translated and with an introduction by Jason Walford Davies; Dent, London 1997 (an English-language edition of the poet's prose autobiographies, including *Neb* [No-one], first published in Welsh by Gwasg Gwynedd, Caernarfon 1985). – by the same author: *Collected Poems, 1945-1990;* Dent, London 1993, *and Collected Later Poems, 1988-2000;* Bloodaxe Books 2004

Tunnicliffe, C F: *Shorelands Summer Diary;* William Collins 1952, reprinted by Clive Holloway Books 1984, and by Orbis, London 1985 – by the same author: *Shorelands Winter Diary;* Constable & Robinson 1992

Williams, Kyffin: autobiographies – *Across the Straits;* Duckworth, London 1973; reprinted by Gwasg Gomer, Llandysul 2004, *and A Wider Sky;* Gwasg Gomer, 1991 (reprinted 2001) – by the same author: *Drawings;* Gwasg Gomer, 2001

Yates, M J & Longley, David: *Anglesey: a guide to ancient monuments;* Cadw, Cardiff, third edition 2001

The novel *Mr Vogel* by Lloyd Jones (Seren, Bridgend 2004) includes many references to Anglesey.

Libraries and internet

Anglesey has a good library service. Please make use of it! Visitors from outside Anglesey may borrow books with temporary tickets (using their home tickets as identification), although most of the local interest books are on the reference shelves and may not be borrowed. *You can also access the internet at all Anglesey libraries.* The largest libraries are at Llangefni and Holyhead. For general information about services: ✆ 01248 752095.

Amlwch *Ffordd Parys* ✆ 01407 830145
Tuesday 9.30am–12.30pm & 2pm–5pm
Wednesday 9.30am–12.30pm.
Thursday 2pm–7pm
Friday and Saturday 9.30am–12.30pm

Beaumaris *Hen Ysgol David Hughes* ✆ 01248 810659
Monday 4pm–7pm
Wednesday 10am–1pm
Thursday 10am–1pm
Friday 10am–1pm & 2pm–5pm
Saturday 10am–noon

Benllech *Glanrafon* ✆ 01248 852348
Monday 5pm–7pm
Tuesday 2pm–5pm
Wednesday 10am–noon & 2pm–4pm
Friday 2pm–7pm. Saturday 10am–12.30pm

Cemaes *Lôn Glasgoed* ✆ 01407 711025
Monday 2pm–6pm
Wednesday 9.30am–12.30pm
Friday 3pm–7pm

Holyhead *Newry Fields* ✆ 01407 762917
Monday 10am–5pm
Tuesday 10am–7pm
Wednesday 10am–1pm
Thursday & Friday 10am–7pm
Saturday 9.30am–12.30pm
Holyhead library also has a small exhibition gallery.

Llangefni *Lôn y Felin* ✆ 01248 752095
This is Anglesey's main branch, with an excellent local reference section.
Monday 10am–5pm
Tuesday 10am–5pm
Wednesday 9am–1pm
Thursday 10am–6pm
Friday 10am–7pm
Saturday 9.30am–12.30pm

Menai Bridge *Ffordd y Ffair* ✆ 01248 712706
Tuesday 12.30pm–6pm
Wednesday 10am–12.30pm
Thursday 2pm–7pm. Friday 1pm–5pm
Saturday 9.30am–12.30pm

Moelfre *Community Centre* ✆ 01248 410331
Monday 1.30pm–5.30pm. Wednesday 10am–1pm
Friday 1.30pm–5.30pm

Newborough, *Prichard Jones Memorial Hall*
✆ 01248 440770. Monday 10am–noon.
Wednesday 4pm–7pm. Friday 2pm–4pm

Rhosneigr *off the High Street* ✆ 01407 811293
Monday 4pm–7pm. Wednesday 2pm–4.30pm
Thursday 10am–12.30pm. Saturday 9.30am–12.30pm

An internet café in Holyhead offers good facilities
✦ **The Internet Café**, 75 Market Street, Holyhead.
Daily in the summer, closed on Sundays in the winter.
✆ 01407 760044
Amongst other internet access locations are
✦ **Aberffraw**, Llys Llewelyn. ✆ 01407 840940
✦ **Beaumaris**, The Post Office. ✆ 01248 810320
✦ **Cemaes** Heritage Centre. ✆ 01407 710004

Yr Iaith Gymraeg
The Welsh language

The 2001 Census revealed about forty thousand Welsh speakers on Anglesey, about sixty per cent of the population.

✦ **Welsh Language Board / Bwrdd yr Iaith**
Encourages the use of the Welsh language in all walks of life. **www**.welsh-language-board.org.uk
The Board supports language initiatives undertaken on Anglesey by **Menter Iaith Môn** ✆ 01248 725700

✦ **Cyngor y Dysgwyr (Cyd)**. Facilitates social contact between Welsh-learners and Welsh-speakers. Local groups hold lively monthly meetings in Benllech, Holyhead, Menai Bridge and Red Wharf Bay.
✆ 01286 831715 **www**.cyd.org.uk

Learning the language

THE WELSH FOR ADULTS INFORMATION LINE
LLINELL WYBODAETH CYMRAEG I OEDOLION
The best source of information about language courses throughout Wales, and elsewhere too.
✆ 0871 230 0017 (weekdays, 9am–8pm)
or *email* iaith@galw.org

The following organisations organise local courses:

✦ **Lifelong Learning Unit, Coleg Menai**
Classes in Welsh, at the college and in the community.
✆ 01248 383333 **www**.menai.ac.uk

✦ **Department of Lifelong Learning, University of Wale Bangor**, coordinates and organises classes throughout North Wales. Holds an annual summer school.
✆ 01248 382752 **www**.bangor.ac.uk/ced

✦ **Worker's Educational Association**
Informal courses for adults.
✆ 01248 353254 **www**.harlech.ac.uk

✦ **Welsh Language & Heritage Centre**
On the mainland at *Nant Gwrtheyrn*, Llŷn Peninsula. Residential courses all year in this former quarry village in a beautiful, remote landscape. Courses for all abilities and for all groups, including families.
✆ 01758 750334 **www**.nantgwrtheyrn.org

INTERNET

✦ **Learn Welsh** at the BBC Wales website:
www.bbc.co.uk/wales/learnwelsh

✦ **Wales Digital College**. On-line lessons, magazine, bookshop, Welsh radio. **www**.acen.co.uk

✦ **Cadwyn** is an on-line (as well as printed) learners' magazine. **www**.cyd.org.uk

Welsh-language bookshops

These shops also stock music CDs and some English-language books. Their notice boards are a useful source of information about local events and activities.

✦ **Llangefni** Cwpwrdd Cornel ✆ 01248 750218

✦ **Menai Bridge / Porthaethwy** Awen Menai
✆ 01248 715532

The **Welsh Books Council / Cyngor Llyfrau** website is a good source of books on-line: **www**.gwales.com

Eryri – Snowdonia

Viewed from the Marquess of Anglesey's column near Llanfair Pwllgwngyll, a jagged spine of mountains rears up beyond the Menai Strait.

The mountains loom large through a July heat haze or rise steep and craggy beneath autumnal clouds, and they can be seen snow-covered on the horizon when the green fields of Anglesey are already enjoying spring sunshine. Sheltered in the mountain valleys are dense forests, closely cropped sheep pastures, shining lakes and stone-built villages. Rivers tumble over waterfalls and broaden into sparking estuaries.

Anglesey makes a wonderful holiday base and excursions from the island to Snowdonia are easy and quick. From either of the bridges across the Menai Strait you can reach *Llanberis*, at the foot of Snowdon, in fewer than twenty minutes. A slate museum set in a country park tells the story of the hardy men who once worked the region's most valuable natural resource. Enjoy a trip along the lakeshore here, or up the mountain, on one of the famous narrow gauge railways of north Wales.

Other mainland attractions within striking distance of Anglesey include the pretty village of *Beddgelert* nestling in a mountain valley, and a pleasant country-side walk from the village of *Abergwyngregyn* to a beautiful waterfall. *Bangor* (a bustling university city with a cathedral and a splendidly restored Victorian pier) and *Caernarfon* (with its Roman fort and a thirteenth century castle) are close too.

Eastwards, along the fast dual-carriageway of the A55, is the walled town of *Conwy* with a turreted castle, and the sedate Victorian resort of *Llandudno*.

A day trip to Ireland

Over Anglesey's western horizon, across the Irish Sea, are the shores of another country.

The crossing from Holyhead, less than two hours on a well-equipped modern vessel, is fun in its own right, and a visit to Ireland makes a memorable day trip. Take a look at the exquisitely illustrated *Book of Kells* at the library of Trinity College in Dublin, and then enjoy a glass of Guinness in a mirrored and wood-panelled pub to the accompaniment of jigs and reels!

Ferries sail between Anglesey's port of Holyhead and the twin ports of Dublin and Dun Laoghaire.

✦ **Irish Ferries** ✆ 08705 171717
(from Ireland: ✆ 01 661 0511) **www**.irishferries.com
✦ **Stena Line**
✆ 08705 707070 (from Ireland: ✆ 01 204 7799)
Another Stena telephone service, Ferrycheck, provides 24 hour recorded information about that day's arrivals and departures, sea conditions and timetable changes:
✆ 08705 755 755.   **www**.stenaline.co.uk

IRELAND TOURIST INFORMATION
✦ **Irish Tourist Board**
from UK ✆ 0800 039 7000 **www**.discoverireland.com
✦ **Dublin & Dun Laoghaire**
from UK ✆ 003531 605 7700 **www**.visitdublin.com

Dun Laoghaire Maritime Museum, in the Mariners' Church, Haigh Terrace, near the shopping centre. A good Irish Sea collection, and links with the Holyhead Maritime Museum. May to September: Saturday, Sunday and bank holidays, 1pm–5pm. (From Ireland: ✆ 01 280 0969)

The rest of the world

BC
- c8500 Cultivated crops, Fertile Crescent
- c6000 Copper working, southwest Asia
- c5000 Maize being grown in Mexico
- 3500 Sumerian civilisation, Mesopotamia
- 2530 Great Pyramid, Giza, Egypt
- c2500 Indus valley civilisations
- c2300 Akkadian empire, Mesopotamia
- c2050 Middle Kingdom, Egypt
- c1900 Rise of Minoan civilisation, Crete
- 1550 New Kingdom, Egypt
- c1500 Shang rule in China
- c1400 Mycenean civilisation, Greece
- c1000 Hindu Rig Veda
- c900 Rise of Etruscan civilisation, Italy
- c900 Rise of Chavin civilisation, Peru
- c800 Zapotecs, first writing in Americas
- c776 First record of Olympic Games
- c700 Celtic civilisation in Central Europe and Austria ('Hallstatt')
- c563 Birth of Gautama Buddha
- 550 Cyrus the Great, Persian empire
- 509 Rome becomes a republic
- 508 Democracy at Athens
- c500 Second phase of Celtic culture in Europe ('La Tène')
- c450 Nok civilisation, Nigeria
- 432 Parthenon temple, Athens
- 336-323 Alexander the Great defeats Persia
- 221 China becomes a united empire
- 200 Nazca lines, southern Peru
- 52 Romans conquer Gauls (Celts in France)
- 44 Assassination of Julius Caesar
- 27 Rome becomes an empire

AD
- c1 Moche civilisation, northern Peru
- 9 Germanic tribes defeat Romans
- c30 Crucifixion of Jesus Christ
- 285 Division of Roman empire
- 313 Christians gain right of worship in Roman empire
- 320-525 Gupta empire, India
- 330 Founding of Constantinople
- 400 Polynesians reach Hawaii
- 410 Alaric the Goth sacks Rome

England, Scotland & Ireland

BC
- c10,000 Ice begins to retreat
- c7600 Star Carr camp, Yorkshire
- c6500 Rising seas isolate Great Britain
- 4000 Spread of farming
- 3700 Long barrows
- c3200 Skara Brae settlement, Orkney
- Newgrange passage grave, Boyne valley
- 2700 Silbury Hill, Wiltshire
- c2500 Copper worked in British Isles
- 2200 Beaker folk; round barrows
- c2000 Bronze working in British Isles
- c1700 Main phase of building, Stonehenge
- 700 Royal fort of Emain Macha, Ireland
- c600 Iron-using Celts from Europe
- 450 First phase, Maiden Castle hillfort
- c150 Invasions of Belgic Celts
- c90 First British coins
- 55-54 Roman invasions, Julius Caesar

AD
- 9 Cunobelinus is king of Catuvellauni
- 43 Start of the final Roman conquest
- 44 Maiden Castle hillfort captured
- 50 London becomes the Roman capital
- 60-61 Revolt of Boudicca (Buddug)
- 75 Fishbourne palace, near Chichester
- 78 Aquae Sulis (Bath)
- 84 Caledonian defeat at Mons Graupius
- 122-128 Hadrian's Wall
- 142 Antonine Wall, Scotland
- 280 Saxon raids; Roman coastal forts
- 287-297 Carausius rules Britain independently of Rome
- c300 Martyrdom of St Alban
- 306 Constantine declared emperor, York
- 360 Mildenhall treasure hoard, Suffolk
- 390 St Ninian founds Scottish church
- 400 British monk Pelagius in Rome
- 401-410 Roman legions withdraw
- 433 St Patrick in Ireland
- 448 First Anglo-Saxon invasions
- 500 Gaels found kingdom of Dál Riada (N Ireland and W Scotland)
- c516 Battle of Mt Badon, victory of legendary Arthur

Anglesey

BC
- c10,000 Climate cold and dry, Birch and pine
- c8-7000 Rising sea levels isolate Anglesey
- c7000 Hunting camp, Aberffraw
- 6000 Climate warming: hazel, alder
- c5000 Sea levels at maximum
- c4000-2000 Burial chambers constructed
- c3500 Crops being grown
- c2700 Barclodiad y Gawres passage grave
- c2200 Beaker burials, eg Porth Dafarch
- c2100 Bryn Celli Ddu passage grave
- c1900 Standing stones raised
- c1700 Round barrow at Aberffraw
- c1500 Castell Bryn Gwyn
- c1500 Mining, Parys Mountain
- c1500 Round barrow: 'Bedd Branwen'
- c750 Bronze axes and gold bracelets in Irish style
- c500 Ty Mawr hut group, Holyhead Mountain
- c300 Din Silwy hillfort, Bwrdd Arthur
- c200 Caer Lêb, near Brynsiencyn
- Bryn Eryr, near Llansadwrn
- c100-60 Llyn Cerrig Bach treasure hoard

AD
- 60 Roman general Suetonius Paulinus invades Anglesey, destroys sacred groves of Druids
- 78 Agricola reconquers Anglesey for the Romans
- Mona insula is governed from Segontium
- c100 Din Lligwy settlement
- c290-390 Roman naval base, Holyhead
- Beacon, Caer y Twr
- c400 Gaels raid Anglesey from Ireland
- Votadini govern North Wales
- c440 Early Christian sites, eg Llanbadrig, Llanbabo, Treardur, Llanelian
- c450 Irish settlers defeated and expelled from Anglesey by Cadwallon Lawhir
- 465 Death of St Dwynwen
- 500s Increased Christian activity, eg Beuno, Cybi, Pabo
- Ercagnus stone, Bodedern
- Probable origins of Llys Aberffraw
- 520s Inscribed memorial stones, eg Catamanus (Cadfan)
- c525 Maccudecceti stone, Penrhos Lligwy
- c540 Saint Seiriol at Penmon
- c547 Death of Maelgwn Gwynedd

Wales

BC
- c10,000 Ice in retreat
- c8300 Melting of last glaciers
- c5000 Spread of oak forest
- c4000-2000 Burial chambers, South Wales
- c3500 Henge, Llandygái near Bangor
- c2250 Stones transported from South Wales to Stonehenge
- c1000 Beginning of the age of hillforts
- c600 Start of the Celtic Iron Age
- c200 Fortified mountain settlements, eg Tre'r Ceiri, Llŷn peninsula

AD
- 47-51 Caratacus (Caradog) flees to Wales, resists Romans
- c55-60 Roman conquest of South Wales
- 70 Roman gold mining in Wales
- 75 Roman fort at Caerleon (Isca Silurum)
- 75-78 Roman forts, eg Segontium (Caernarfon)
- c77 Roman town at Caerwent
- 78 Agricola defeats Ordivices
- 80 Baths at Caerleon
- 90 Amphitheatre at Caerleon
- c120 Roman road to Segontium
- 314/359 Britons attend Christian councils in Gaul and Italy
- 383 Magnus Maximus (Macsen Wledig) marches on Rome
- 401-410 Roman legions leave Britain
- 400s Dinas Emrys, Beddgelert
- 430 Battle of Maes Garmon against Picts
- 445 First entry in medieval Annales Cambriae (Annals of Wales)
- 450-460 Early kingdoms founded: Gwynedd, Powys, Dyfed, Glywysing
- 517 Deganwy castle, Maelgwn Gwynedd
- c550 Welsh language evolves from Brythonic
- First flowering of Welsh poetry
- 577 Battle of Dyrham: Saxons divide Welsh from other West Britons
- c584 Bangor cathedral, St Deiniol
- c589 Death of Dewi Sant (St David)
- c615 Battle of Chester; defeat of Welsh
- 615 Monastic settlement on Bardsey
- c635 Welsh first described as Cymry
- 654 Welsh cut off from the Old North

768 Welsh accept Roman date for Easter
c784 Offa's Dyke
844-76 Reign of Rhodri Mawr
c850 First Viking attacks on Wales
855 End of royal house of Powys
881 Anarawd defeats Mercia at Conwy
904 End of royal house of Dyfed
c915-950 Reign of Hywel Dda ('the Good')
c945 Welsh law codified by Hywel Dda
1039 Reign of Gruffudd ap Llywelyn
1067 Normans invade Gwent
1071-94 Norman advance into North Wales
1081 Gruffudd ap Cynan rules Gwynedd
1092 Normans control Pembroke
1094 The Marcher Lordships established
1115 Castle building by Welsh princes
1131 Tintern Abbey
1137-70 Reign of Owain Gwynedd
c1147-97 Rhys ap Gruffudd restores kingdom of Deheubarth
1164 Ystrad Fflur abbey (Strata Florida)
1165 Owain Gwynedd defeats Henry II
1170-97 The Lord Rhys rules South Wales
1170 Dafydd ap Owain Gwynedd reigns
1174 Dafydd m. Emma of Anjou
1176 Cardigan eisteddfod
1180 St David's Cathedral rebuilt
c1186 Aberconwy Abbey
1195-1240 Reign of Llywelyn ab Iorwerth
1198-99 Cymer Abbey, Dolgellau
1201 Valle Crucis abbey, Llangollen
1218-40 Llywelyn I overlord of all Wales
1240 Reign of Dafydd ap Llywelyn
1246 Llywelyn II ap Gruffudd on throne
1256 Llywelyn II seizes power in Gwynedd
1267 Treaty of Montgomery
1276-77 First War of Welsh Independence
1277 Edward I castles at Flint, Rhuddlan
1282-83 Second War of Welsh Independence
1282 Death of Llywelyn II ap Gruffudd, Cilmeri

c600 Farmstead remains, Llanbedr-goch
625 Cadfan (Catamanus) stone, Llangadwaladr
630 Saint Tysilio founds island church in the Menai Strait
664 Death of Cadwaladr Fendigaid
800s Earliest parts of ruined Llanfihangel Esceifiog church, Gaerwen
856 Rhodri Mawr defeats Vikings on Anglesey
872 Vikings defeated at Parciau
878 Rhodri Mawr killed in battle on Anglesey
c890 Viking settlement, Llanbedr-goch
960-70s Further Viking attacks
961 Viking attack on Holyhead
968 Viking attack on Aberffraw
971 Dublin Vikings sack Llan-faes and Penmon
987 Vikings kill 1,000, and enslave 2,000 from the island
c1088 Norman motte and bailey, Aberlleiniog
1094 Gruffudd ap Cynan burns Aberlleiniog castle
1098 Battle of Aberlleiniog
1100s Stone churches across the island
1120-70 Penmon priory rebuilt
1130 fl. Gwalchmai ap Meilyr, poet
1137 Death of Gruffudd ap Cynan
1157 English sack Llanbedr-goch
1170 Battle of Pentraeth
1188 Gerald of Wales visits Anglesey. Archbishop Baldwin preaches the Crusade, Porthaethwy
1200s Great phase of church building, eg St Cybi's, Holyhead
1203 fl. the poet Einion ap Gwalchmai
1205 Llywelyn the Great marries Siwan (Joan)
1230 Llywelyn styles himself 'Prince of Aberffraw and Lord of Eryri'
1237 Llywelyn's charter, Llys Rhosyr Death (at Abergwyngregin) of Princess Siwan (Joan)
1240 Consecration of Llan-faes friary
1245 Anglesey invaded by forces of Henry III
1282 English force slaughtered crossing the Menai Strait The bard Gruffudd ab y'Nad Goch writes his lament for Llywelyn ap Gruffudd

c539 Battle of Camlan, d Arthur
c550 Rise of the Irish monasteries
563 Colmcille (St Columba) on Iona
597 St Augustine lands in Kent
600 Rise of O'Neill dynasty in Ireland
625 Sutton Hoo burial, East Anglia
635 Lindisfarne monastery founded
664 Synod of Whitby attempts to unite Celtic and Roman Christianity
698 Lindisfarne Gospels, Northumbria
700 Beowulf, poetry in Old English
731 History of the English church, Bede
757 Mercia principal Anglo-Saxon kingdom
789 First Viking raids
800 Book of Kells, Ireland
829 Wessex chief Anglo-Saxon kingdom
841 Viking settlement, Dublin
843 Kenneth MacAlpin unites Scots and Picts
850 Viking settlement, England and Man
926 Cornwall under Saxon rule
1014 Dublin Vikings defeated by Irish High King Brian Boru at Clontarf
1016 England part of Danish empire
1034 Duncan I unites British Strathclyde with Scotland
1040 Macbeth rules Scotland
1042 Edward the Confessor rules England
1057 Malcolm Ceann Mor kills Macbeth
1066 Norman conquest of England, under William I
1086 The Domesday Book
1097 Normans defeat Donald III, Scotland
1100-35 Henry I, King of England
1136 Melrose Abbey, Scotland
1152 Eleanor of Aquitaine marries English heir
1154-89 Henry II rules England and much of France
1170 Norman-Welsh Earl of Pembroke invades Ireland Murder of Thomas à Becket, Canterbury
1172 Christchurch Cathedral, Dublin
1189-99 Richard I rules England
1199-1216 King John rules England
1215 Magna Carta limits royal power in England
1250 Westminster Abbey rebuilt
1265 First English parliament

433-453 Attila rules the Huns
476 Fall of the West Roman empire
c500 Slavic migrations in Europe
500 Tiwanaku city, South America
529 Justinian codifies Roman law
535 End of Gupta empire, India
570 Birth of Muhammad, Mecca
600 Rise of Ghana kingdom, Africa
618 Tang dynasty, China
641 Arab invasion of North Africa
c700 Mississippi temple mounds
Anasazi, Hohokam & Mogollon cultures, N America
711 Moslem Moors capture Spain
750 Trade across the Sahara desert
786 Haroun al-Rashid rules Baghdad
800 Charlemagne, Holy Roman Emperor
802 Angkor Kingdom, Cambodia
c850 Maoris settle New Zealand
900 Chimu empire, South America
c900 Rise of Swahili culture, East Africa
912 Viking warlord Rollo becomes Duke of Normandy
950 Toltec city of Tula, Mexico
962 Otto I of Germany becomes Emperor
969 Cairo founded, Egypt
1000 Vikings reach North America
c1000 Easter Island statues, Pacific Great Zimbabwe, citadel
1096 The First Crusade
1100 First Inca emperor, Peru
1148 The Second Crusade
1189 The Third Crusade
1190 Rise of Mongol warlord Genghis Khan
1192 The Shogunate in Japan
1200 Mali empire, West Africa Hausa city states, West Africa
1202 Crusaders attack Constantinople
1206 The Delhi Sultanate, India
1220 Frederick II Holy Roman Emperor
1226 Louis IX (St Louis) rules France
1250 Benin empire, West Africa
1271 Kublai Khan is emperor of China

The rest of the world

- 1300 Maya revival, Central America
- Founding of the Kongo kingdom, Central Africa
- 1344 The Hanseatic League
- 1345 Rise of the Aztecs, Mexico
- 1346 English defeat French at Crécy
- 1348-50 The Black Death, Asia and Europe
- 1350 Classic Maori age, New Zealand
- 1368 Chinese Ming dynasty
- 1378 Split in papacy, Rome v Avignon
- 1405 Death of Timur (Tamerlane) ruler of vast Asian empire
- 1415 English defeat French at Agincourt
- 1428 Aztec expansion, Mexico
- 1431 English burn Joan of Arc at Rouen
- 1450 Songhai empire, West Africa
- 1453 End of the Hundred Years' War
- Turks capture Constantinople
- 1462 Lorenzo de Medici rules Florence
- 1470 Incas conquer Chimú empire, Peru
- 1469 Castile and Aragon unite to form kingdom of Spain
- 1492 Final defeat of Moors in Spain
- Colombus lands in the New World
- 1497 John Cabot discovers Newfoundland
- 1498 Vasco da Gama in India
- Inca empire at its peak, Peru
- 1500 Portugal claims Brazil
- 1503 Mona Lisa by Leonardo da Vinci
- 1512 Michelangelo paints the Sistine Chapel, Rome
- 1517 Turks conquer Egypt
- German monk Martin Luther starts the Protestant movement
- 1519 Cortés starts conquest of Mexico
- 1522 Magellan's fleet circumnavigates the globe
- 1526 Babar founds the Moghul empire
- 1532 Spanish start conquest of the Incas
- 1547 Ivan the Terrible crowned Tsar of Russia
- 1562 Start of the English slave trade
- 1566 Ottoman (Turkish) empire at its greatest extent
- 1568 Dutch rise against Spanish rule
- 1570 The Iroquois Confederacy of Native Americans
- 1575 Portuguese colonise Angola
- 1587 Abbasid empire in Persia

England, Scotland & Ireland

- 1296 Edward I defeats Scots at Dunbar
- 1297 Scots under William Wallace defeat English at Stirling Bridge
- 1314 Scots under Robert Bruce defeat English at Bannockburn
- 1320 University founded at Dublin
- 1366 Statutes of Kilkenny, Ireland
- 1371 Stewart dynasty, Scotland
- 1381 Peasants' Revolt, England
- 1337-1453 'Hundred Years' War, England against France
- 1348-49 The Black Death
- 1387-1400 Canterbury Tales, Chaucer
- 1415 English defeat French, Agincourt
- 1413-22 Henry V rules England
- 1455-85 Wars of the Roses
- 1471 Caxton's printing press, London
- 1485 Tudor victory at Bosworth Field
- Henry Tudor becomes Henry VII
- 1504 James V of Scotland marries Margaret Tudor
- 1509-47 Reign of Henry VIII
- 1512 England at war with France
- 1513 Flodden: death of James IV of Scotland
- 1534 Henry VIII breaks with Rome
- Offaly rebellion, Ireland
- 1535 First complete Bible in English
- 1536-39 Dissolution of the Monasteries
- 1542 Reign of Mary, Queen of Scots
- 1547 Scottish Reformation, John Knox
- Reign of Protestant Edward VI
- 1549 Book of Common Prayer in English
- Rebellion in Cornwall
- 1553 Reign of Catholic Mary I in England
- 1555 Persecution of Protestants
- 1558-1603 Reign of Elizabeth I
- 1568 Mary, Queen of Scots, flees to England
- 1587 Shakespeare arrives in London
- Mary, Queen of Scots executed
- 1588 Persecution of Catholics
- 1588 Spanish Armada sails for England
- 1593 O'Neill rebellion, Ulster
- 1599 Globe Theatre, London
- 1560 The Church of Scotland

Anglesey

- 1284 Anglesey becomes a shire
- 1294 Sheriff of Anglesey is hanged
- 1295 Inhabitants of Llan-faes evicted to Newborough and work starts on Beaumaris castle
- 1296 Beaumaris chartered as borough
- 1298 Beaumaris is one of four official ports of Wales
- 1298 End of first phase of building, Beaumaris castle
- 1300s Hafoty, Llansadwrn
- 1300s Howell Mill, Llanddeusant
- Carved stone relief of St Iestyn, Llaniestyn
- 1302 Llan-faes ferry transferred to Beaumaris
- 1303 Newborough chartered as town
- c1314 Church at Beaumaris
- 1317 Demolition of Llys Aberffraw
- 1330 Great storm at Newborough: sand buries houses
- 1352 Oldest list of medical doctors in Wales, Newborough
- c1385 Tomb of Gronw Fychan, Penmynydd
- 1396 Lollards (followers of Jon Wycliffe) imprisoned at Beaumaris castle
- c1400 'Tudor Rose', Beaumaris
- 1403-05 Owain Glyn Dŵr's troops hold Beaumaris castle
- 1405 English troops recapture Beaumaris
- 1406 Anglesey submits to English forces
- 1414 Town walls, Beaumaris
- 1430 Fulling mill, Llanfechell
- 1440 Black Affray of Beaumaris
- William Bulkeley constable of Beaumaris castle
- 1450 Coalmining, Cefni valley
- 1472 Bull's Head Inn, Beaumaris (rebuilt 1617)
- 1480 Plas Berw built by Ithel ap Hywel
- c1500 Chancel of Beaumaris church rebuilt
- 1507 Newborough becomes county town
- c1537 Dissolution, Penmon Priory
- 1534 Birth of Siôn Dafydd Rhys, scholar, at Llanfaethlu
- 1538 Llan-faes friary dissolved
- 1549 Beaumaris becomes county town again
- 1569 Plas Coch, Llanedwen
- 1576 Plas Penmynydd
- 1573 Town Hall, Beaumaris (rebuilt 1808)
- 1588 Beaumaris fits out ship to fight Spanish Armada
- 1593 Martyrdom of Catholic William Davies, Beaumaris
- 1599 Holyhead declared official posting station for Ireland

Wales

- 1283-94 Caernarfon, Harlech, Conwy castles
- 1284 Statute of Rhuddlan
- 1287 Rebellion of Rhys ap Maredudd
- 1294 Rebellion of Madog ap Llywelyn
- 1295 First mention of the Welsh longbow
- 1301 Edward I declares his son Prince of Wales at Caernarfon
- 1316 Rebellion of Llywelyn Bren
- 1320-70 fl. Dafydd ap Gwilym, poet
- 1349 Black Death appears in Wales
- 1369 Rebel Owain Lawgoch (Yvain de Galles) seeks support in France
- 1400 Rising of Owain Glyn Dŵr
- 1402 Glyn Dŵr captures Carmarthen
- 1403 Battle of Shrewsbury
- 1404 Glyn Dŵr captures Harlech, Aberystwyth, Cardiff
- Glyn Dŵr, at height of power, holds parliament at Machynlleth
- 1405 French sail to support Glyn Dŵr, defeated by English
- 1408 English reassert control
- c1415 Owain Glyn Dŵr disappears
- 1420 Last outbreak of Black Death
- 1431 Catherine de Valois m. Owain Tudor
- 1451 Codification of Welsh poetic metres, Dafydd ab Edmwnd
- 1485 Henry Tudor lands at Milford Haven, Pembrokeshire
- c1485 Cochwillan house, Tal y Bont
- 1523 The first Caerwys eisteddfod
- 1536 First Act of Union (Anglo-Welsh)
- 1536-40 47 religious communities in Wales dissolved by Henry VIII
- 1542 Second Act of Union (Anglo-Welsh)
- Wales sends MPs to Westminster
- 1546 First printed book in Welsh (Yny Lhyvyr Hwnn)
- 1547 Welsh-English dictionary
- 1557 Friars grammar school, Bangor
- 1568 The second Caerwys eisteddfod
- 1571 Jesus College, Oxford, founded for Welsh students by Hugh Price
- 1573 Map of Wales, Humphrey Llwyd
- 1577 Plas Mawr town house, Conwy
- 1584 Catholic Richard Gwyn is hanged
- 1588 Welsh translation of the Bible, William Morgan

1600 First full-length play in Welsh, *Troelys a Chresyd*
1607 Great Flood in South Wales, also on the north coast at Abergele
1617 Cambriol, Welsh colony in Newfoundland (abandoned c1637)
1621 Welsh Grammar of John Davies
1630 *Y Beibl Bach*
1632 Welsh-Latin dictionary
1636-37 Outbreaks of plague
1639 First Nonconformist chapel in Wales
1646 Parliament captures Denbigh castle
1648 Battle of St Fagans, Gower
1649 First Baptist chapel in Wales, Gower
1652 Last outbreak of the plague in Wales
1653 First Quaker meeting in Wales, Clwyd
1600s Increase in cattle droving
1661 First Welsh lighthouse, St Anne's Head
1668 Henry Morgan leads buccaneer army in Caribbean
1682 Welsh Quakers settle Pennsylvania
1694 Siôn Dafydd Las dies, last known household bard
1697 Industrial tramway at Neath
1707 *Archaeologia Britannica*
1715 First London Welsh society: the 'Ancient Britons'
1719 Welsh pirates Howell Davis and Bart Roberts active in West Africa
1731 First Circulating School, Griffith Jones of Llanddowror
1743 Calvinistic Methodism in Wales
1744 First hymns of William Williams, Pantycelyn
1755 Dyfi blast furnace, Aberystwyth
1757 Iron works, South Wales
1771 Gwyneddigion Society, London
1773 243 Circulating Schools now exist
1776 Richard Price: *Obervations on the Nature of Civil Liberties*
1782 Start of North Wales slate industry
1789 First 'modern' eisteddfod, Corwen. Blaenafon iron works, South Wales
1792 First meeting of the Gorsedd under Iolo Morganwg (Edward Williams)
1794 Glamorgan Canal Co. links Merthyr and Cardiff
1797 French invasion, Fishguard

c1600 Penmon dovecote
1600s Economic decline of Newborough
1603 Beaumaris Grammar Schoool
1614 Court-house, Beaumaris
1615 Plas Berw rebuilt
1618 Baron Hill, Beaumaris
1633 Piracy common in Irish Sea
1634 Carreg-lwyd, Llanfaethlu
1638 *Merchants Mappe of Commerce* by Lewes Roberts
1642 First phase of Civil War: Beaumaris castle garrisoned
1646 Beaumaris captured by Parliament
1648 Battle at Red Hill, Beaumaris
1660 Horseback postal service to Holyhead
1675 Royal yacht *Mary* wrecked on the Skerries
1689 Charity school, Amlwch
1691 'Fairy Borth (Menai Bridge Fair)
1700s Widespread smuggling
1705 Beaumaris castle falls to ruin
1706 Mathematician William Jones first to use π (*pi*)
1715 Wreckers active on the Crigyll estuary (to 1740s)
1716 First lighthouse on the Skerries
1718 Glyn Garth ferry
1730s Diaries of William Bulkeley
1732 *Mona Antiqua Restaurata* published
1737 Lewis Morris charts the Welsh coast
1737 Gallt y Benddu windmill
1747 John Welsey and William Williams Pantycelyn preach in Llandaniel-fab
1748 Anglesey's first Nonconformist chapel, Rhos-meirch
1751 Richard Morris founds the Honourable Society of Cymmrodorion in London
1750s Turnpikes on the road to Holyhead
1763 Verse of Goronwy Owen published
1766 Pilot station, Point Lynas
1768 Copper boom, Parys Mountain
1776 Llynnon Mill, Llanddeusant
1779 First Point Lynas lighthouse
1783-85 Plas Newydd rebuilt
1785 London to Holyhead Mail Coach
1787-93 Preacher Christmas Evans moves to Llangefni
1793 Porth Amlwch enlarged

1603 James VI of Scotland / I of England Union of thrones under Stuarts
1605 The Gunpowder Plot, London
1607 Flight of the Earls, Ireland
1609 Protestant 'plantation', Ulster
1611 'Authorised version' of the Bible
1619 Harvey discovers blood circulation
1629 Charles I suspends parliament
1638 The Covenant, Scotland
1642 Start of the Civil War
1646 The Society of Friends ('Quakers')
1649 Execution of Charles I. Commonwealth:republican rule. Oliver Cromwell sacks Drogheda
1653 Oliver Cromwell is Lord Protector
1660 Restoration of monarchy
1665 The Great Plague
1666 The Great Fire of London
1675-1710 St Paul's, London, is rebuilt
1684 Newton's theories of gravity
1685 Monmouth Rebellion
1688 The 'Glorious Revolution'.
1690 Battle of the Boyne
1702 Reign of Anne, last Stuart monarch
1707 Act of Union, England/Scotland
1709 Start of the Industrial Revolution.
1714 Hanoverian dynasty: George I
1715 First Jacobite rebellion
1720 Financial crash: 'South Sea Bubble'
1721 Walpole, first Prime Minister
1728 Irish Catholics denied vote
1738 Charles Wesley founds the Methodists
1745 Second Jacobite rebellion
1753 British Museum
1759 Birth of Robert Burns, Scottish poet
1760s Great age of canal building
1769 Wedgwood's pottery
1773 London Stock Exchange
1775 Steam engine, James Watts
1785 *The Times* newspaper, London
1791 United Irishmen, Wolf Tone
1796 Edward Jenner: vaccination
1798 Rising in Ireland, French invasion

1606-42 Dutch explorers reach Australia
1607 English colony at Jamestown, Virginia
1608 French found Quebec, Canada
1609 Telescope invented, Holland
1610 Galileo's astronomical observations
1618-48 Thirty Years' War
1619 The Dutch East Indies
1620 'Pilgrim Fathers' in Massachusets
1626 Dutch found New Amsterdam (New York)
1628 Taj Mahal, India
1642 French found Montreal
1643 Reign of Louis XIV, the 'Sun King'
1644 Manchurians take China
1648 Fronde rebellion in Paris
1652 Dutch found Capetown, South Africa
1662 Académie Française founded
1670 Hudson Bay Company, Canada
1680 Extinction of the dodo
1684 French claim Louisiana
1690 Founding of Calcutta
1700 Rise of the Ashanti, West Africa
1700-21 Great Northern War
1701 Frederick I rules Prussia
1701-13 War of Spanish Succession
1703 St Petersburg is built, Russia
1707 Decline of the Moghul empire
1740-48 War of Austrian Succession
1740 Frederick II 'the Great', Prussia
1742 Celsius temperature scale
1756 Seven Years' War in Europe
1757 Britain fights France in India
1759 British capture Quebec
1768 James Cook lands in Australia
1772 First partition of Poland
1773 Boston Tea Party
1775-83 American War of Independence
1783 First balloon ascent, Paris
1788 Australia, First Fleet
1789 Washington is first US President. French Revolution. Mutiny of *HMS Bounty*
1791 French Revolutionary Wars
1793 Reign of Terror, France

The rest of the world

1804 Napoleon crowned French emperor
1805 British naval victory, Trafalgar
1806 Britain rules Cape Colony, Africa
1808 Peninsular War, Iberia
1810 Argentina independent
1814 Britain burn down US White House
1815 Battle of Waterloo
Congress of Vienna
1818 Zulu empire, South Africa
Chilean independence
1821 Greeks rise up against Turks
1822 Brazil independent from Portugal
1823 Mexico independent from Spain
1833 Slavery abolished, British empire
1840 Treaty of Waitangi, New Zealand
1842 Britain gains Hong Kong
1845 Texas joins the USA
1848 Revolutions across Europe
The Communist Manifesto
1848 Gold rush, California, USA
1851 Gold rush, Australia
1853 Livingstone explores Africa
1854-56 Crimean War
1857 The 'Indian Mutiny'
1861 Most of Italy united as one kingdom
Burke & Wills cross Australia
1861-65 US Civil War
1865 US President Abraham Lincoln asassinated
1867 Meiji Restoration: Japan
Dominion of Canada
1869 Suez Canal opens
1871 Franco-Prussian War
Germany unites as single empire
1876 First telephone message
1881 First South African 'Boer' War
1885 First petrol car, Karl Benz
1893 Women's suffrage (New Zealand)
1895 Marconi invents wireless radio
X-rays discovered, W Röntgen
1896 Gold rush in the Klondike, Canada
1898 Battle of Omdurman, Sudan
1899-1902 Second South African 'Boer' War
1901 Commonwealth of Australia

England, Scotland & Ireland

1801 Union, Britain-Ireland
1811 Luddite riots, northern England
1811-20 The Regency
1815 Miner's lamp, Humphrey Davy
1819 Peterloo Massacre, Manchester
Political riots in Scotland
1823 Catholic Association, Ireland
1825 Stockton–Darlington railway
1829 Uniformed police force, London
1832 First Reform Act
1834 Tolpuddle Martyrs: arrested for joining a trade union
1837 Reign of Queen Victoria
1839 Chartists: first national convention
1840 Penny post
The pedal bicycle
1841 Rugby football invented
1842 Young Ireland movement
1843 Disruption: Free Church, Scotland
1844 Cooperative movement, Rochdale
1845-48 Irish potato famine, emigration
1851 The Great Exhibition, London
1856 Bessemer steel production
Florence Nightingale trains nurses
1858 Brunel's *Great Eastern*
The Irish Republican Brotherhood
1859 Charles Darwin, *Origin of Species*
1863 Underground railway, London
The Football Association
1865 Lister's antiseptic treatments
1882 Phoenix Park murders, Dublin
1884 Highland Land League, Scotland
1886 Irish Home Rule Bill defeated
1900 Foundation of the Labour Party
1901 Death of Queen Victoria
1903 The 'Suffragettes' (WSPU)
1904 Rolls Royce motor company
1905 Sinn Féin founded, Ireland
1906 Militant campaign for women's suffrage launched
1912 Sinking of the *Titanic*
1914-18 First World War
1917 Easter Rising, Dublin
1918 Votes for women over 30

Anglesey

1800-1900 Chapel building and church restorations
1809 Lighthouse, South Stack
1812 Unrest between Nonconformists and Anglicans
1812-61 Coalmining at Pentre-berw
1817 The Anglesey Column
Food riots in Amlwch
1818 Malltraeth Cob
1821-26 Telford's Holyhead to London road (A5)
1821 Admiralty Arch, Holyhead
1822 Steamers between Liverpool and Anglesey
The start of tourism
1826 Menai Suspension Bridge opens
1828 Assoc. for the Preservation of Life from Shipwreck
1829 Beaumaris gaol
1830s-40s Semaphore telegraph stations
1830 First regatta in Beaumaris
1831 Wreck of the *Rothsay Castle*
1832 Princess Victoria attends *eisteddfod*, Beaumaris
Temperance society in Holyhead, first in Wales
1836 Twyn Du lighthouse, Penmon
1845-73 Holyhead breakwater
1846 Beaumaris pier, first in Wales
1850 Britannia Tubular Railway Bridge
1859 Wreck of the *Royal Charter*
1864-65 Railway branch line, Gaerwen to Llangefni
1866-67 Railway branch line, Llangefni to Amlwch
1876 Bulkeley Memorial
The first Anglesey County Show
1880 New dock and station at Holyhead
1880s Mammoth bones found in Holyhead harbour mud
1883 Tea clipper *Norman Court* wrecked in Cymyran Bay
1885 Royal Anglesey Yacht Club
1889 Anglesey County Council
Porth Wen brickworks
1901 Anglesey's population is 50,606
1909 Anglesey Workers' Union
Railway branch line to Red Wharf Bay
Suffragette meeting at Newborough
1912 Flight from Holyhead to Dublin
1913 Newborough Matmakers' Cooperative
1915 First British Women's Institute at Llanfair Pwllgwyngyll
Airship patrols, Mona. SS *Cambank* torpedoed, Pt Lynas

Wales

1804 World's first steam locomotive, Penydarren/Abercynon
1807 North Wales Chronicle, Bangor
1813 William Crawshay II manager of Cyfartha iron works South Wales
1831 Merthyr rising, South Wales
1839-44 The Rebecca riots
1839 Chartist insurrection, Newport
1840 Penrhyn Castle, near Bangor
1847 'Treachery of the Blue Books' education report on Wales
1851 75% of Welsh population is non-conformist
1855 First coal pit in Cwm Rhondda
1856 *Hen Wlad fy Nhadau* / Land of my Fathers (national anthem)
1858 *Eisteddfod*, Llangollen: becomes yearly national festival
1859 Religious 'revival'
1862 Normal College, Bangor
1865 Welsh colony founded in Patagonia
1872 University of Wales, Aberystwyth
1874 North Wales Quarrymen's Union
1875 Castell Coch, Cardiff
1881 Royal Cambrian Academy, Conwy
1883 University of Wales, Aberystwyth
1884 University of Wales, Bangor
1886 The 'Tithe War'
Cymru Fydd/Young Wales
1890 David Lloyd George Liberal MP for Caernarfon
1896 Snowdon Mountain Railway
1898 South Wales Miners' Federation
Peak of slate industry, North Wales
1900 Keir Hardie first Labour MP (for Merthyr Tydfil)
1900-03 Penrhyn quarry lock-out, Bethesda
1904 Last of the religious 'revivals'
1905 The hymn *Cwm Rhondda* is written
1907 National Museum of Wales, Cardiff
1910 Tonypandy riots
1913 Peak of coal production in Wales
Senghenydd mining disaster
1916 Lloyd George is Prime Minister
1920 Disestablishment of Anglican Church in Wales
1920 University of Wales, Swansea

1922 Urdd Gobaith Cymru (Welsh League of Youth)
1923 First Welsh-language radio
1925 Welsh Nationalist Party, Plaid Genedlaethol Cymru
1934 Gresford mining disaster
1935 First Welsh-language sound film
1936 Nationalists burn 'bombing school' on Llŷn peninsula
1946 Welsh National Opera
1947 International Eisteddfod, Llangollen
1954 Myxomatosis decimates Welsh rabbit population
1955 Cardiff recognised as Welsh capital
Farmers' Union of Wales
1958 The Welsh Academy
1961 Welsh Books Council
1962 Llanwern steelworks
Saunders Lewis broadcast ignites language debate
Welsh Language Society, Cymdeithas yr Iaith Gymraeg
1964 Establishment of the Welsh Office
BBC Wales begins broadcasting
1964-67 Clywedog dam
1965 Drowning of Tryweryn valley
1966 Gwynfor Evans first Plaid Cymru MP (Camarthen)
1966 Aberfan disaster; 116 children are among 144 dead
First Severn Bridge
M4 motorway section, South Wales
1967 Welsh Language Act
Merched y Wawr (Welsh-speaking WI) first meets at Bala
1969 Investiture of Prince of Wales at Caernarfon
Political protests
1973 Wales Trades Union Congress
1976 Welsh office of European Community opens, Cardiff
1979 Arson campaign against tai haf, second homes
Referendum rejects proposal for limited home rule
1982 S4C Welsh TV Channel
1984 Miners' strike
1985 Closure of the Big Pit, Blaenavon
1991 Halt in decline of Welsh speakers
Conwy road tunnel opened
1993 Second Welsh Language Act
1996 Second Severn Bridge
1997 Referendum approved devolution
1999 National Assembly for Wales convenes in Cardiff

1916 Belgian promenade, Menai Bridge
1920 Rhoscolyn lifeboat tragedy
1922 Beaumaris Town Band
1927 National Eisteddfod, Holyhead
1929 Megan Lloyd George (Liberal) becomes the first Welsh woman MP
1933 The rate of unemployment in Anglesey is 42%
1935 Electrification reaches Beaumaris
1939 HMS Thetis salvage, Traeth Bychan
1939-45 Naval base at Holyhead
1940 Saunders-Roe factory, Llan-faes
Holyhead is bombed
1941 RAF Valley established
1943 Llyn Cerrig Bach treasure find
1948-65 Plantation of Newborough Forest
1949 First comprehensive school, Holyhead
1951 Llyn Cefni reservoir created
1957 National Eisteddfod, Llangefni
1959/66 RNLI gold medals to Richard Evans
1962 Ysgol David Hughes moves to Menai Bridge
1966 Llyn Alaw created
1967 Trearddur lifeboat station
1970 Britannia Bridge fire
1971 Final assize court, Beaumaris
Anglesey Aluminium smelter
Wylfa power station opens
1972 Britannia rail link restored
1973-83 Oil terminal off Amlwch
1974 Anglesey becomes part of Gwynedd
1976 Inshore lifeboat station, Beaumaris
1980 Road deck on Britannia bridge
1983 National Eisteddfod, Llangefni
1986 Beaumaris Festival founded
1987 Plaid Cymru's General Election victory in Anglesey makes the constituency the only one in modern times to return an MP from all four main parties
1990s Wind farms, northern Anglesey
1991 Oriel Ynys Môn, Llangefni
1996 Anglesey becomes a unitary authority
1999 National Eisteddfod held at Llanbedrgoch
2001 Opening of the A55 across Anglesey
2005 Suspension Bridge repainting lasts ten months

1921 Civil war in Ireland
1922 The Irish Free State
The BBC is founded
1925 Television, John Logie Baird
1926 General Strike in Britain
1928 Penicillin discovered by Fleming
1929 Votes for women over 21
1932 Economic depression in Britain
1936 Edward VIII abdicates; George V
Hunger marches; Jarrow 'Crusade'
1937 New Irish constitution: Eire
1939-45 Second World War
1940 Winston Churchill is Prime Minister
1946 Nationalisation and welfare state
National Health Service, Britain
The Edinburgh Festival
1948 Computer, Manchester University
1949 The Republic of Ireland
1951 Festival of Britain
1952 Elizabeth II succeeds George VI
British Top 10 pop music charts
1953 DNA discovery, Cambridge
1957 Jodrell Bank radio telescope
1958 First motorway in UK, M1
1959 Mini Minor car
1962 First Beatles single
1964 Harold Wilson is Prime Minister
1967 First SNP MP, Scotland
1968 Decimal coinage
1969 The Concorde aircraft
British troops sent to Northern Ireland
1972 Bloody Sunday in Derry, 13 dead
1973 Britain and Ireland join EEC
1975 North Sea oil boom
1979 Margaret Thatcher is Britain's first woman PM
1984-85 Miners' strike
1989-90 The Poll Tax introduced, UK
1994 The Channel Tunnel
1997 The Scottish Parliament
1998 Good Friday Agreement, Northern Ireland
1999 Irish Republic adopts Euro
2000 Millennium celebrations
2001 Foot-and-mouth epidemic

1903 First flight by Wright brothers, USA
1904 War between Russia and Japan
1912 Collapse of the Chinese empire
1914-18 First World War
1917 Revolutions in Russia
1919 League of Nations
1922 Rise of fascism, Italy and Germany
1929 US stock market crash, Depression
1934 Nazi dictatorship in Germany
1936 Spanish Civil War
1938 Persecution of Jews, Germany
1939-45 Second World War
1945 Atomic bombs dropped on Japan
United Nations Organisation
1945-90 The Cold War
1946 First electronic computer
1949 The People's Republic of China
1950-53 Korean War
1957 Treaty of Rome establishes the EEC
The Suez Crisis
1961 The Berlin Wall; Russian Yuri Gagarin first in space
1961 USA becomes involved in Vietnam
1962 Cuban Missile Crisis stand-off
1963 US President Kennedy is shot dead
1964 Nelson Mandela jailed, South Africa
1966 Cultural Revolution, China
1967 Wars in Israel and Nigeria
1968 Martin Luther King assassinated
1969 The first Moon landing
1973 US withdrawal from Vietnam
1975 Communist victory in Vietnam War
1979 Elections to European Parliament
Islamist revolution in Iran
1981 First US space shuttle, Columbia
1982 The Falklands War
1986 Chernobyl nuclear disaster
1990 Collapse of the Soviet Union
1991-2000 Wars in Persian Gulf, Balkans
1992 First Earth Summit, Brazil
1994 Mandela becomes president of South Africa
2001 9-11 terrorist attacks, USA
2003 The Iraq War
2005 Earthquake in Pakistan; tsunami in South East Asia

Anglesey Glossary

An A to Z explanation of some of the terms used in this guide, which may not be familiar to visitors or to non-specialists ...

almshouses Dwellings endowed to provide the poor or elderly with cheap or free accommodation. Welsh: *elusendai*

ap Welsh for 'son of'. Until the eighteenth century it was a common element of Welsh personal names, eg Llywelyn ap Gruffudd. In an index, the first name is the one listed, rather than the father's. Female version: *ferch*.

awdl A long poem in traditional Welsh metre.

bailey The wooden tower at the centre of an early castle, as at Aberlleiniog; later, the outer court of a stone castle. Welsh: *beili*

bard A poet and musician in the Celtic tradition. Welsh: *bardd*

barrow A prehistoric burial mound
Welsh: *crug*

beaker A finely made pottery vessel, often decorated, found in burials of the Bronze Age and typifying a particular European culture. Welsh: *bicer, diodlestr*

bellcote The housing of bells: often a simple, exposed structure of stone on the roof of Anglesey churches. Welsh: *cwt clychau*

bonesetter A maker of splints, a healer of broken bones. Welsh: *meddyg esgyrn*

Bronze Age The period in which bronze (an alloy of tin and copper) was the chief metal used for tools and weapons. Bronze was being made in the Middle East in about 3000BC. In the British Isles the Bronze Age begins in about 1700BC. Welsh: *Oes Efydd*

burial chamber A ritual site for burying the dead. In the Neolithic period these were communal mounds or long barrows, often built over massive stones. In the Bronze Age communal burials gave way to single burials within round barrows. Generally the original stones, once buried by the mound, now stand exposed. Welsh: *siambr gladdu*

buttress A structure built to support a wall. Welsh: *bwtres*

cantref One of the administrative divisions in medieval Wales. English: a 'hundred'.

capstone The upper stone platform of a burial chamber, supporting the full weight of the mound. The normal Welsh term is *maen capan*, but the place-name *Benllech* is believed to suggest that same meaning.

causeway A raised road or footpath over wet ground, such as a marsh or a beach. Welsh: *sarn*.

Celtic [pronounced with a hard **c**] The word *Keltoi* was first used by the ancient Greeks, to describe the peoples of Central Europe who invaded their lands. Historians apply the term 'Celtic' to certain peoples of Central and Western Europe, who rose to prominence in the first millennium BC. The Celtic culture spread across a vast area of Europe and many other peoples adopted the Celtic way of life and languages. In the Classical era, Celtic peoples lived in the Iberian peninsula, in France and northern Italy (the Gauls), in Ireland (the Gaels), in Britain (the Britons) and in Turkey (the Galatians). Many Celtic tribes were attacked by Rome and displaced from their homelands by Germanic and Slavic invaders. The term 'Celtic' also refers to the branch of early Christianity which grew up in the Celtic lands after the fall of Rome. Modern peoples who describe themselves as 'Celtic' include the Scots, the Irish, the Manx, the Welsh, the Cornish, the Bretons and the Galicians of the Iberian peninsula. Welsh: *Celtaidd*

chancel The space around the altar in a church. Welsh: *cangell*

Churches in Anglesey
Many of Anglesey's parish churches – such as at Llaneilian and the island church of St Tysilio – are built to a simple rectangular plan:

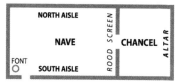

Some churches (such as Llanfechell parish church) have transepts projecting from the north and south aisles that give a more 'English' cross-shaped (cruciform) plan.

A number of Anglesey's churches lost their rood screens during Victorian 'restoration'; Bangor diocesan architect Henry Edward Kennedy, active during the second half of the nineteenth century, was a particularly assiduous rebuilder.

cob A barrier built across an estuary to prevent flooding, as at Malltraeth on Anglesey or Porthmadog on the mainland. Welsh: *cob*

comprehensive school A school which accepts all children within a single catchment area, whatever their abilities. Anglesey was the first local authority in the British Isles to introduce 100 percent comprehensive education, in 1952. Welsh: *ysgol gyfun*

concentric A term used to describe a castle consisting of a series of ring defences, offering complete fields of fire. Beaumaris is a classic example. Welsh: *consentrig*

conglomerate A rock made up of pebbles or gravel (gritstone) cemented together by another material. Welsh: *amryfaen*

corbelled Supported by a stone projection. Welsh: *corbelog*

coxswain Helmsman or head of a lifeboat crew. Welsh: *llwyiwr cwch/bad achub, cocswn*

crenellate(d) Indented, like a battlement. Welsh: *crenelog*

cruck timbers large structural end beams supporting both roof and walls. Welsh: *nenfforch*

cupola A small roof structure like a dome or a tower. Welsh: *cromen, crymdo*

cywydd A metrical form in Welsh poetry. One popular version today consists of a rhyming couplet with seven syllables per line, making use of *cynghanedd* (repetition of consonants and internal rhyme).

disestablished Of a religion, separated from the state. There has been no single established church in Wales since 1920. Welsh: *datgysylltiedig*

dovecote A building designed to house doves or pigeons. Several large seventeenth- and eighteenth-century dovecotes survive on Anglesey, where birds were raised for their eggs and meat. Welsh: *colomendy*

dune A high bank of windblown sand. Welsh: *tywyn*

druid *(a)* an aristocratic rank amongst the ancient Celts. Druids acted as priests, lawmakers, counsellors and envoys. *(b)* a member of the council or *gorsedd* in a modern *eisteddfod*. Welsh: *derwydd*.

Edwardian Dating to the reign of Edward VII, 1901-10. The term is also sometimes used in a thirteenth century context, to describe the castles of Edward I, such as Beaumaris. Welsh: *o oes Edward, Edwardaidd*

egg-clapping A folk custom formerly common on Anglesey: before Easter, village children would go from door to door, asking for eggs. They would have wooden rattles or knock pebbles together, and chant: *Clap, clap, gofyn ŵy, i hogia' bach ar y plwy'* ('Clap, clap, asking for eggs, for little lads on the parish'). Welsh: *clepian wyau*

eisteddfod Traditionally, a gathering of medieval bards. The custom was revived in the late eighteenth century with many invented rituals, but soon became rooted in Welsh popular culture as a festival in which musicians, singers and poets compete. Today an *eisteddfod* may take in all kinds of dance, recitation, popular music, theatre, visual arts and crafts, and also act as a social, political and commercial forum. It may be competed in at local, regional, national or international level, with youth participating too under the auspices of the Welsh youth movement, the *Urdd Gobaith Cymru*. Plural: *eisteddfodau*

fen Damp or inundated low-lying land, common in many parts of Anglesey. Welsh: *cors*

font A basin of stone, set up in a church for baptism of infants. Welsh: *bedyddfaen*

fulling mill A place for the cleansing, treatment and thickening of woven cloth. Welsh: *pandy*

Georgian Belonging to the Hanoverian period, when the four Georges were on the British throne, 1714-1830. Welsh: *Sioraidd*

granite A hard, granular, igneous rock common on Anglesey. Welsh: *gwenithfaen*

hamlet A cluster of houses, smaller than a village. Welsh: *pentrefan, pentref bach*

henge A circular, ditched ritual site (c3500BC–1500BC), sometimes with configurations of great stones (megaliths) or timbers. Castell Bryn Gwyn is a henge site on Anglesey. Welsh: *hengor*

hillfort A fortified settlement on high ground, typical of the Celtic Iron Age, often occupied over many centuries, through the first millennium BC to the period of Roman withdrawal. Examples on Anglesey are on Holyhead Mountain or at Din Silwy, near Llanddona. Welsh: *bryngaer*

hiring fair A market at which labourers are hired to do farm work. Welsh: *ffair gyflogi, ffair bentymor*

hut circle A group of domestic dwellings from the Celtic Iron Age. On Anglesey these were mostly large, circular buildings with walls of stone or wattle and thatched roofs. Traces of original walls remain at many sites on Anglesey, such as Holyhead Mountain. They are often referred to incorrectly as *cytiau'r gwyddelod* ('huts of the Irish'). A recreation of an Iron Age village is being established near Llynnon windmill. Welsh: *cylch cwt*

inner ward The massive inner walls of a medieval castle, as Beaumaris. Welsh: *gward mewnol*

Iron Age The period in which iron was the chief metal used for tools and weapons. Iron was being worked in the Middle East by about 1500BC and in the British Isles by about 600BC. The Celts were masters of ironworking in Europe. Welsh: *Oes Haearn*

llan A religious enclosure of the early Christian church in Wales. The name appears in villages, towns and parishes all over Anglesey.

llys *(a)* One of the regional royal courts of medieval Gwynedd, as at Llys Rhosyr, Newborough.
(b) A court of law, as the old courtroom opposite Beaumaris castle.

limekiln A kiln or furnace in which limestone is processed into powdered lime, for use in agriculture or building. Welsh: *odyn galch*

lychgate A roofed gate at the entrance to a churchyard (traditionally, where a bier could be set down). Welsh: *llidiart y cyrff*

Mabinogion A collection of ancient oral tales and episodes, first written down in about 1300 (in *The White Book of Rhydderch*) and about 1400 (in *The Red Book of Hergest*). Pagan Celtic traditions are mixed with Christian symbolism and here too is mention of the legendary Arthur. The tale most associated with Anglesey is that of Branwen, Daughter of Llŷr. Welsh: *Pedair Cainc y Mabinogi.*

mabsant This Welsh word means 'patron saint', or the saint to which a church is dedicated. The saint's day of a parish (*gwyl mabsant*) was often celebrated with merrymaking and dancing, a custom revived in recent times at Bodedern on Anglesey.

marram A coarse dune grass, *Ammophila arenaria*, formerly used in the Newborough district of Anglesey for plaiting into mats, ropes and other useful items for the household or farm. Welsh: *moresg*

Mesolithic Belonging to the Middle Stone Age, a period which in the British Isles lasted from about 8000BC to 4000BC. It was characterised by a warming climate, rising sea levels, the spread of broad-leaved woodland, and the manufacture of fine, precise flint tools and weapons. Remains of this period have been found on Anglesey on the banks of Afon Ffraw. Welsh: *Mesolithig*

misericord A wooden support for someone standing in a medieval choir stall, often decorated with carvings, as in Beaumaris church. Welsh: *misericord*

motte A palisaded earthen mound, raised to support the bailey or wooden tower of an early castle. Aberlleiniog, near Llangoed, was a Norman motte-and-bailey castle of the late eleventh century. Welsh: *mwnt*

nave The main body or length of a church building (deriving from the Latin word for 'ship'). Welsh: *corff, canol eglwys*

Neolithic Belonging to the New Stone Age, a period which in the British Isles lasted from about 4000BC to 1700BC. It was marked by the development of agriculture and domestication of livestock, and by the erection of the burial chambers which still dot the Anglesey landscape. Welsh: *Neolithig*

Nonconformist Not conforming to the (then) established Anglican church. The movement began with seventeenth-century Puritanism. It expanded during the religious revivals of the late eighteenth, nineteenth and early twentieth centuries, when chapels and churches were built for Methodists, Calvinists, Baptists, Presbyterians and Congregationalists all over Anglesey. The Nonconformist movement championed Welsh-language education and remains the dominant religious tradition on the island. Welsh: *anghydffurfiol*

obelisk A tapering, four-sided column of stone in the ancient Egyptian style, used for monuments and memorials. Examples on Anglesey include the Bulkeley memorial (near Beaumaris) and the Skinner monument (Holyhead). Welsh: *obelisg*

ore The unprocessed rock from which valuable metals are extracted by melting. Welsh: *mwyn*

Palaeolithic Belonging to the Old Stone Age, the period of human development before about 8000BC. It is characterised by the use of tools and weapons made of stone, bone and wood, and by periods of severe cold, known as Ice Ages or glaciations. Welsh: *Paleolithig*

papur bro means 'neighbourhood paper' in Welsh. These small local Welsh-language newspapers – such as *Papur Menai, Yr Arwydd, Y Glorian* and *Y Rhwyd* – appear monthly and are produced, folded and distributed by volunteers. Some villages also produce bi-lingual newsletters.

passage grave A communal burial chamber of the Neolithic period, accessed by a subterranean corridor. An example is Barclodiad y Gawres, on Anglesey's west coast. Welsh: *bedd cyntedd*

pier *(a)* A jetty or boardwalk extending over the sea, as at Beaumaris. Welsh: *pier, glanfa*
(b) The supporting tower of a bridge, as on the Menai Suspension Bridge. Welsh: *piler*

pilot A navigator with knowledge of local waters, taken on to guide a ship into port. Pilots were formerly stationed at Llanddwyn Island and Point Lynas. Welsh: *peilot*

post road An official route for carrying mail, originally by horseback or coach. Welsh: *lôn bost*

pre-Cambrian The oldest geological period (comprising rocks ranging from 590 million to almost four billion years old) such as those at Llanddwyn Island, named after rocks found in Wales. Welsh: *cyn-Gambriaidd*

promontory fort A fortified settlement on a headland, chosen for its defensive advantages: common on Anglesey through the first millennium BC to the period of Roman withdrawal. An example is Dinas Gynfor, on the north coast. Welsh: *caer bentir*

quartzite A rock made up of granules of the mineral quartz, common on Anglesey. Welsh: *cwartsit*

Romanesque An architectural style of medieval Europe, a form of which was brought to the British Isles by the Normans. Welsh: *Romanésg*

rood screen A partition found in some old churches, separating the nave from the chancel, eg the rood screen at the Church of St Eilian, Llaneilian. Welsh: *croglen*

saltmarsh A natural marine or estuarine habitat, colonised by plants and animals, where lands are flooded twice daily by the tide. Welsh: *morfa*

schist A crystalline rock whose minerals have been squeezed and pressed. Welsh: *sgist*

serpentine A decorative rock, often spotted and green in colour, once quarried on Anglesey. Welsh: *sarff-faen, serpentin*

slack The hollow or valley between high sand dunes, often collecting rainwater. Welsh: *pantle*

slate A rock formed by the compression of mudstone, quarried in Snowdonia and used as a common building and roofing material on Anglesey. Welsh: *llechfaen*

smelt To extract a mineral from its ore by melting. Welsh: *toddi, mwyndoddi*

squire (a) In the Middle Ages, an assistant to a knight, a knight-in-training, eg Owain Tudor in his youth. Welsh: *yswain* (b) The chief landowner in a district, eg William Bulkeley of Brynddu. Welsh: *sgweiar*

stack An offshore island or rock created by the erosion of a cliff, eg South Stack. Welsh: *craig, stac, ynys*

standing stone An upright pillar of stone, sometimes erected in a group, serving as a ritual monument during the Bronze Age. Example on Anglesey: Penrhos-feilw. Welsh: *maen hir*

Stone Age The period of human history before the development of metal working, characterised by tools and weapons of stone, bone and wood. It is sub-divided into the Old Stone Age (Palaeolithic), Middle Stone Age (Mesolithic) and New Stone Age (Neolithic). Welsh: *Oes y Cerrig*

stone circle A ring of stone pillars, erected probably at ritual sites in the Bronze Age. Welsh: *cylch cerrig*

stoup A deeply hollowed stone set in a niche to hold holy water. Welsh: *cawg dŵr swyn*

telegraph Any system for the rapid transmission of messages. Before electrification in the 1860s, the nineteenth-century Anglesey to Liverpool telegraph system used a chain of semaphore towers, whose pivoted arms presented coded signals, which were passed down the line at high speed by observers. The system was used to advise of movements of shipping. Welsh: *telegraff*

TIME
The traditional Christian calendar is used for dates in this book:
BC = Before Christ. The Welsh equivalent is **CC** (Cyn Crist).
AD = *Anno Domini*, Latin for 'in the year of our Lord'. The Welsh equivalent is **OC** (Oed Crist).

International visitors may be more familiar with the corresponding secular version which is increasingly applied: **BCE** (Before Common Era) and **CE** (Common Era).

To keep things simple, we have not used the common archaeologists' abbreviation for prehistoric finds, namely **BP** (Before Present).

tithe Literally, a tenth part of one's income or produce (originally stored in a 'tithe barn'). Following Biblical precedence, this became a religious tax payable even by those who supported chapel rather than church. The tithe caused widespread social unrest in Wales in the 1880s. Welsh: *degwm*

tollhouse A booth for collected payments or tolls on certain roads. The nineteenth-century octagonal tollhouses built by Thomas Telford may still be seen along the route of the A5. Welsh: *tolldy*

transept The transverse section of certain churches, at right angles to the nave. Nave and transept together make up the shape of a cross. Welsh: *transept, ale groes*

tumulus an ancient burial mound. Welsh: *gwyddfa*

Victorian Belonging to the reign of Queen Victoria, 1837-1901. Welsh: *o Oes Fictoria*

Viking A Scandinavian seafarer. Vikings from Norway controlled the Irish Sea in the ninth century, settling in Ireland and the Isle of Man. They also raided and settled parts of Anglesey, itself a Viking name. Welsh: *Llychlynnwr*

well On Anglesey, a freshwater spring used as a sacred site (from early to more recent Christian times, and often also having a pre-Christian history). An example is Gwenfaen's well on the cliffs at Rhoscolyn. Welsh: *ffynnon*

wind farm An array of wind turbines, as used to generate electricity across northern Anglesey. Welsh: *fferm gwynt*

Place-names

Some of Anglesey's geographical features are described in this guide-book using the Welsh term only.

For example, the **River Alaw** *is called* **Afon Alaw**. *The following list contains most of these place-name elements.*

aber estuary, river mouth, eg *Aberlleiniog*

allt hill, eg *Pen yr Allt*

afon river, eg *Afon Braint*

bach / fach small, little, lesser, eg *Bryngwyn Bach*

bedd grave, eg *Bedd Branwen*

bedw / fedw birch, eg *Fedw Fawr*

betws oratory, eg *Bettws*

bod a dwelling, eg *Bodedern*

bol literally 'belly', but also referring to the undulating landscape of north/central, Anglesey, eg *Rhosybol, Talybolion*

bonc bank, eg *Bonc Fadog*

bro / fro district, neighbourhood, eg *Bro Dawel*

bron hillside, eg *Fron Heulog*

bryn hill, eg *Brynddu*

bwlch gap, pass, eg *Bwlch y Daran, Tan y Bwlch*

cae field, enclosure, eg *Cae Mawr*

caer fort, stronghold, eg *Caergybi*

capel chapel, eg *Capel Coch*

carn / garn rock, cairn, outcrop eg *Mynydd y Garn*

carreg / cerrig stone, rock, eg *Cerrigceinwen*

castell castle, eg *Castell Mawr*

cefn back of, eg *Rhoscefnhir*

celli / gelli grove, eg *Bryn Celli Ddu*

celyn holly, eg *Bryn Celyn*

coch / goch red, eg *Traeth Coch*

coed wood, eg *Coedana, Llangoed*

coedwig forest, eg *Coedwig Niwbwrch*

comin common land, eg *Comin Llaniestyn*

cors marsh, bog, fen, eg *Cors Bodeilio*

craig / graig rock, eg *Melin y Graig*

croes cross, eg *Tŷ-croes*

din stronghold, hillfort, eg *Din Silwy*

dôl meadow, eg *Dolmeinir*

du / ddu black, eg *Trwyn Du*

efail / 'r efail forge, smithy, eg *Brynrefail*

eglwys church, eg *Heneglwys*

fferm / fferam farm, eg *Fferam Uchaf*

ffordd road, way, eg *Ffordd Deg, Bodffordd*

ffynnon well, spring, eg *Ffynnon Seiriol*

glan shore, bank, eg *Glanrafon*

glas / las green, blue, eg *Marian-glas*

gwern / wern wetland, bog, eg *Wern y Wylan*

gwyn white, eg *Plas Gwyn*

hafod, hafoty summer dwelling, eg *Hafoty*

hendre winter dwelling, literally 'old settlement', eg *Hendre Hywel*

hir long, eg *Rhoscefnhir*

isaf lower, eg *Tŷ Isaf*

llan early Christian enclosure, eg *Llansadwrn*

llwyn grove, eg *Llwyn Onn*

llyn lake, eg *Llyn Alaw*

llys court, eg *Henllys*

lôn lane, eg *Pen-lôn*

maen stone, rock, eg *Maen Piscar*

maes open area, field, square, eg *Maes Hyfryd*

marian stony ground, eg *Mariandyrys*

mawr / fawr big, eg *Capel Mawr*

melin / felin mill, eg *Pentrefelin*

mynydd mountain, large hill, upland, eg *Mynydd Mechell*

mynwent / fynwent graveyard, eg *Tan y Fynwent*

nant stream, or valley, eg *Tŷ Nant*

newydd new, eg *Plas Newydd*

onnen / onn ash, eg *Llwyn Onn*

pandy fulling mill, eg *Nant y Pandy*

parc park, eg *Parc yr Ynys*

pen end, head, eg *Pentraeth, Penmon*

pentre (f) / bentre (f) village, eg *Pentre-berw*

plas mansion, big house, eg *Plas Gwyn*

pont / bont bridge, eg *Pont Britannia*

porth / borth port, gate, eg *Porthaethwy*

pwll pool, eg *Llanfair Pwllgwyngyll*

rhos heath, moor, eg *Rhos-goch*, and sometimes a headland, eg *Rhosmor.*

rhyd ford, eg *Rhydybont*

sant (m) / santes (f) saint, eg *Llantrisant*

sarn causeway, roadway, eg *Pen-y-sarn*

sgwar square, eg *y Sgwar*

stryd street, eg *Stryd Fawr*

tafarn inn, eg *Tafarn y Rhos*

tal end, eg *Taldrwst*

tan under, eg *Tan y Coed*

traeth beach, eg *Traeth Lligwy*

tref / dref town, homestead, settlement eg *Trefeilir, Trefdraeth*

tros over, eg *Tros-yr-Afon*

trwyn headland, point, eg *Trwyn Eilian*

twr cairn, eg *Mynydd Twr*

tŵr tower, eg *Tŵr Bach*

tŷ house, eg *Tŷ Newydd*

tyddyn, ty'n smallholding eg *Tyddyn Bach, Tynygongl*

tywyn / towyn sand dunes, eg *Tywyn Aberffraw*

uchaf upper, higher, eg *Gwalchmai Uchaf*

wen white, eg *Gaerwen*

y the, of the, eg *Ynys y Fydlyn*

yn / yng in, eg *Llanfair-yn-Neubwll*

ynys island, isle, stack, eg *Ynys Lawd*

ysgubor barn, eg *Ysgubor Wen*

Acknowledgements

Many contributors and consultants have assisted in the preparation of this guidebook. Their advice is sincerely appreciated.

For their valuable comments on early drafts

Jill Anker *Porthaethwy*
Richard Arnold *Y Felinheli*
John Cowell *Porthaethwy*
Andrew Davidson *Bryngwran*
Alun Gruffydd *Rhostrehwfa*
Neil Johnstone *Caernarfon*
Gwilym Trefor Jones *Llangefni*
Peter Hope Jones *Porthaethwy*
John Ratcliffe *Glanyrafon*
Tomos Roberts *Llangefni*

For their assistance in general

Roy Ashworth *Porth Llechog*
Ian Cuthbertson *Bangor*
Peter Greenhill *Llanllechid, Gwynedd*
William Griffith *Llanfair Pwllgwyngyll*
Andy Harding *Y Felinheli*
Alan Holmes *Porthaethwy*
John R Hughes *Porthaethwy*
Ian Jones *Llangaffo*
George E Lees *Trearddur*
Trefor M Owen *Tregarth, Gwynedd*
Delyth Prys *Rachub*
John Smith *Coedana*
Richard B White *Kernow (Cornwall)*
David Wilson *Llanddyfnan*
Freya Williams *Llansadwrn*
Ceri Williams *Llansadwrn*
Margaret Wood *Llansadwrn*

The staff of Tourist Information Centres at Holyhead and Llanfair Pwllgwyngyll.

Officers of a number of Departments of the Isle of Anglesey County Council have been generous with their help: Education & Leisure Department (Museums & Culture; Libraries; Record Office); Environment & Technical Services (Coastal Path Project, and the Countryside and Maritime Sections).

Other helpful organisations included: The Countryside Council for Wales. Gwynedd Archaeological Trust. Gwynedd Museum & Gallery, Bangor. Menter Môn, Llangefni. The National Trust Wales. The North Wales Wildlife Trust.

✦ R S Thomas's poem on page 152, *The Bush*, is from *Later Poems* (Macmillan, 1983) and is reproduced by courtesy of the family and Estate of R S Thomas © Kunjana Thomas 2001. The photograph of R S Thomas is by Peter Hope Jones, Porthaethwy.
✦ The paragraph about Holyhead Mountain on page 154 is from *The Matter of Wales* by Jan Morris, Oxford University Press, 1984. (Revised edition: *Wales, Epic Views of a Small Country*, published by Penguin Books, 2000). It is reproduced by kind permission of the author © Jan Morris 1984.
✦ We are grateful to the families of the late Aled Eames and the late Bedwyr Lewis Jones for permission to reproduce their essays, which were written for the first edition of this

Guidebook in 1976: Bedwyr Lewis Jones's *Môn, Môn i Mi* (99) and portrait photograph © Eleri Wynne Jones 2006. Aled Eames's *The Seafarers* (131) © Estate of Aled Eames 2006.
✦ The executors of the Estate of Vernon Hughes kindly gave permission to reproduce *The Spike on the Chapel Gate* (171), written in 1976 for the first edition of this Guidebook. © Estate of Vernon Hughes 2006.
✦ C F Tunnicliffe's South Stack cliffs illustration and text (156) is from *Shoreland's Summer Diary*, William Collins 1952; reprinted Clive Holloway Books 1984 and Orbis, London 1985.
✦ The following contributions remain the copyrights of their authors: W P Griffith, *Council Talk* (9); Richard B White, *The Druids* (25); Trefor M Owen, *Some Anglesey Customs* (193); Peter Greenhill, *Lost Chords* (217); Alan Holmes, *Island Records* (218).

Picture acknowledgements

Reconstruction drawings are reproduced by permission of the copyright holders Cadw and Menter Môn, funded by *Leader+*. The printed illustrations include credits to the individual artists. *Lligwy* (21); *Bryn Celli Ddu* (22); *Din Lligwy* (23); *Caer Lêb* (26); *Bryn Celli Ddu* (55); *Din Lligwy* (71); *Penmon Priory* (87); *Roman fort* (147); *Tŷ Mawr huts* (153).
The drawing in the reconstruction of *Llys Rhosyr* (208) is by John Hodgson.

Beaumaris Town Council: *Barque Lord Stanley* (131)

The British Library, London: *harrowing, from the Luttrell Psalter* (28).

Bwrdd Croeso Cymru: *Trwyn y Gadair* (107); *tern* (111); *Twr Mawr, Llanddwyn* (213).

C Flight 22 Squadron, Royal Air Force Valley: *Sea King helicopter* (170). Photograph by Steve Upton, Holyhead.

Tom Carpenter: *Carreg-lwyd* (162)

Countryside Council for Wales / J B Ratcliffe: *rock-rose* (7); *cormorants* (16); *curlew* (198); *Tywyn Niwbwrch* (210)

Llanfair Pwllgwyngyll Women's Institute: *group photograph* (64)

Countryside Section, Department of the Environment & Technical Services, Isle of Anglesey County Council: aerial photographs – *Traeth yr Ora* (70); *Traeth Coch* (94); *Ynys y Fydlyn* (108); *Cemaes* (109); *Cemlyn* (110); *Dulas* (113); *Llanbadrig* (115); *Trwyn Eilian* (119); *Mynydd Twr* (154); *Borthwen* (164); *Trearddur* (168); *Llanedwen* (205). © 2006 Cyngor Sir Ynys Môn.

John Cowell: *La Marguerite* (43); *haymaking* (48); *RMS Leinster* (145).

William Evans, Llangefni: *Ifan Gruffydd* (100)

Douglas Gowan, Bangor: *photograph of Aled Jones* (59)

Gwynedd Museum & Art Gallery, Bangor: *Bronze Age pottery* (22); *Rhuddgaer coffin* (27); *Robert Stephenson and his engineers* (49); *woven textile* (139)

Holyhead Maritime Museum and Richard Burnell: *Celtic stone head* (23) photographed by Ian Jones / Oriel Ynys Môn.

Isle of Anglesey Coastal Path Project: *Saint Gwenfaen's well* (165).

Isle of Anglesey Riding Centre: *riding at Tal-y-Foel* (204).

Ian Jones, Beaumaris: *passengers on the Paddle Steamer La Marguerite* (134).

Dr J Glyn Jones: *Plas Newydd* (214).

Geraint Jones, Bangor: *photograph of Percy Ogwen Jones & John Eilian* (118).

Elizabeth Maddocks, Llandudno: *portrait of Elizabeth Morgan* (184)

Merseyside Maritime Museum: *sailing bill of the Royal Charter* (82).

National Museums & Galleries of Wales, Cardiff: *Lewis Morris* (114); *Llyn Cerrig Bach bronze plaque* (163)

Oriel Ynys Môn, Rhosmeirch: paintings by Gwenddolen & Edith Massey – *Sundew* (54); *Bramble* (66); *South Stack Fleawort* (153).
Also from the Oriel's collections: *Melin Seler* photographed by John Smith (158); *Christmas Evans* (182); *Urn* (183); *Botanology* (187); *Wild Thyme* (210).

Maldwyn Peris: *cartoon strip* (34).

Pili Palas: *butterfly* (52).

Linda Rogers, Llangoed: *Queen Corrie* (151).

June Show: *Wendykurk* (218)

Sothebys, Chester: *oil painting of Royal Charter wreckage, by J J Dodd* (83).

Lord Stanley of Alderley: *Margaret Owen* (150).

Stena Line Ports Limited, Holyhead: *aerial view of port* (31); *HSS ferry* (142).

Stone Science, Talwrn: *brachiopod* (95); *coral* (97).

Roger & Debbie Tebbut, Llanbedr-goch: *Celtic bronze ox head* (26).

Tre-Ysgawen Country House Hotel & Spa: *Tre-Ysgawen* (189).

Work by Charles F Tunnicliffe: *The Cattle Ring at Gaerwen* (175) is reproduced by courtesy of Mr Morgan Evans of Morgan Evans & Co, Llangefni. The scraperboard illustration of a *Stonechat* (19) was engraved for the first edition of this guidebook and is reproduced by courtesy of Richard Arnold.

Bethan Williams: *Catalina launch* (60).

Ieuan Williams, Porthaethwy: *windmill* (160)

Unless otherwise acknowledged, illustrations are in the collection of the publisher. The principal photographer is Robert Williams.

No part of the content of this guidebook (texts, illustrations and their arrangement) may be reproduced in any form without the written permission of the publisher. Contact MAGMA ✆ 01248 810833 magmawales@hotmail.com

The copyrights of all texts and illustrations are asserted by the publisher and the contributors

© MAGMA and the contributors, 2006

Index

✦ *See also the index to the Anglesey Directory, page 219.*

For multiple entries, numbers in **bold** indicate main references.